UNIVERSITY LIBRARY
UW-STEVENS POINT

MONEY AND THE REAL WORLD

D1114132

UNIVERSITY LIBRARY
UW-STEVENS POINT

By the same author

Theories of Aggregate Income Distribution
Aggregate Supply and Demand Analysis
The Demand and Supply of Outdoor Recreation

UNIVERSITY LIBRARY
UW-STEVENS POINT

MONEY AND THE REAL WORLD

PAUL DAVIDSON

Second Edition

A HALSTED PRESS BOOK

JOHN WILEY & SONS
New York — Toronto

© Paul Davidson 1972, 1978

All rights reserved. No part of this publication may be reproduced or transmitted, in any form or by any means, without permission.

First edition 1972
Second edition 1978

Published in the United Kingdom by
THE MACMILLAN PRESS LTD
London and Basingstoke

Published in the U.S.A. and Canada by Halsted Press, a Division of John Wiley & Sons, Inc. New York

Printed and bound in Great Britain

Library of Congress Cataloging in Publication Data

Davidson, Paul.
  Money and the real world.
  "A Halsted Press book."
  Includes bibliographical references and index.
  1. Money. 2. Finance. 3. Economics.
  I. Title.
  HG221.D27 1977   332.4   77–16113
  ISBN 0–470–99217–4

The paperback edition of this book is sold subject to the condition that it shall not, by way of trade or otherwise, be lent, resold, hired out, or otherwise circulated without the publisher's prior consent, in any form of binding or cover other than that in which it is published and without a similar condition including this condition being imposed on the subsequent purchaser.

HG
221
.D27
1978

To Louise, Robert, Diane, and Greg

292039

529033

Contents

List of Tables

Preface to the First Edition

IN some respects this is a very controversial book. There are many passages in which I attack with vehemence the views of others, and it is unlikely that I shall escape reprisals. . . .

It is notorious that controversy in economics is peculiarly provocative of irritation. . . . It is, I think, of the essential nature of economic exposition that it gives, not a complete statement, which, even if it were possible would be prolix and complicated to the point of obscurity but a sample statement, so to speak, out of all the things which could be said, intended to suggest to the reader the whole bundle of associated ideas, so that, if he catches the bundle, he will not in the least be confused or impeded by the technical incompleteness of the mere words which the author has written down, taken by themselves.

This means, on the one hand, that an economic writer requires from his reader much good will and intelligence and a large measure of co-operation; and, on the other hand, that there are a thousand futile, yet verbally legitimate, objections which an objector can raise. In economics you cannot *convict* your opponent of error – you can only *convince* him of it. And, even if you are right, you cannot convince him, if there is a defect in your own powers of persuasion and exposition or if his head is already so filled with contrary notions that he cannot catch the clues to your thought which you are trying to throw to him.

The result is that much criticism, which has verbal justification in what the author has written, is nevertheless altogether futile and maddeningly irritating; for it merely indicates that the minds of author and reader have failed to meet. . . . But, of course, this does not mean that all criticism is futile, and it is dangerous, I think, to be too wary of it. Moreover a candid author surely enjoys criticism which comes from a thorough understanding of his thesis. There is no greater satisfaction than in the exchanging of ideas between minds which have truly met, leading to further discoveries and a shift of view in response to difficulties and objections.

I ask forgiveness, therefore, if I have failed in the necessary goodwill and intellectual sympathy when I criticise; and to those minds to which, for whatever reason, my ideas do not find easy entry, I offer assurance in advance that they will not find it difficult, where the country to be traversed is so extensive and complicated, to discover reasons which will seem to them adequate for refusing to follow. Time rather than controversy . . . will sort out the true from the false.

These words were written by John Maynard Keynes as an early draft of the introduction to his *General Theory*.[1] Although these paragraphs did not find their way into the published preface of the English language edition,[2] I have quoted them here for, I believe, they are a fitting prelude to the work I am herein presenting. A brief statement as to what I believe was revolutionary about Keynes's work and how I view the development of Keynesian economics since 1936 will indicate why I think there is a need for this book and why I consider these unpublished lines of Keynes relevant for this volume.

Harrod, with typical lucidity, highlighted the essential nature of the Keynesian Revolution when he wrote 'classification, in economics, as in biology, is crucial to the scientific structure,'[3] and

> The real defect in the classical system was that it deflected attention from what most needed attention. It was Keynes' extraordinarily powerful intuitive sense of what was important that convinced him that the old classification was inadequate. It was his highly developed logical capacity that enabled him to construct a new classification of his own.[4]

[1] J. M. Keynes, *The General Theory of Employment, Interest, and Money* (London: Macmillan; New York: Harcourt, Brace, 1936).

[2] This introduction was quoted in its entirety by Austin Robinson in his inaugural Keynes lecture before the British Academy on 22 April 1971. (The theme of this draft is used in the preface of the French edition of *The General Theory*.) ·

[3] R. F. Harrod, *The Life of John Maynard Keynes* (London: Macmillan, 1951) p. 464.

[4] ibid., p. 463.

New definitions (e.g. savings, investment, effective demand) and new conceptual arrangements of economic phenomena (e.g. associating time preference with the propensity to consume independent of liquidity preference; identifying the precautionary and speculative demand as distinct from the transactions demand for money; using expectations in a world of non-quantifiable uncertainty as the basis of investment and liquidity decisions) were the missiles that Keynes used to breach the neoclassical fortress.

As early as 1937, however, while Keynes was still attempting to refine these new concepts (e.g. adding the finance motive to the demand for money) as a result of an exchange of ideas between Ohlin and Keynes, Hicks was publishing a 'potted version'[1] of what he believed to be Keynes's central argument. Hicks's truncated view of the Keynesian system, however, started a retrograde movement of modification and alteration of the new concepts forged by Keynes. In the forties, other writers – e.g. Dillard, Hansen, Klein, Modigliani, and Samuelson – while attempting to clarify 'The Simple Mathematics of Income Determination' which underlay Keynes's *General Theory*, accelerated this metastatic process which ultimately transformed Keynes's framework into a 'neoclassical synthesis'. By the fifties the mutant 'Keynesian' concepts were sufficiently entrenched in the orthodox macroeconomic literature for some economists to begin to warn that what had been propagated as *the* Keynesian theory of output and employment was a perversion of Keynes's own views about the real sector.[2] (Surprisingly, even today, much less attention has been focused on the fact that 'Keynesian' monetary theory is a caricature of Keynes's views on money.) These warnings went practically unnoticed

[1] The term 'a potted version' is used by Hicks to describe his famous 'Mr. Keynes and the "Classics"' article. See J. R. Hicks, *Critical Essays in Monetary Theory* (Oxford: Oxford University Press, 1967) p. vii.

[2] Weintraub was one of the first to call attention to this fact, e.g. see his 'Micro-Foundations of Aggregate Demand and Supply', *Economic Journal* (1957), and 'The Keynesian Theory of Inflation: The Two Faces of Janus?', *International Economic Review* (1960). More than a decade later, Axel Leijonhufvud was successful in drawing attention to the fact that modern macroeconomics deviated from the analysis of Keynes; see his *On Keynesian Economics and the Economics of Keynes* (New York: Oxford University Press, 1968).

and unheeded – at least till Leijonhufvud's volume in 1968 – so that currently the analytical concepts used in most macroeconomic writings are in conflict with Keynes's own grand design.

Accordingly I felt that it was necessary to go back to Keynes's own writings, especially his *Treatise on Money*[1] and his *General Theory*, and to extract, integrate, and update the original conceptual framework. Starting from Keynes's fundamental axioms that in the real world (1) the future is uncertain (in the sense that Knight and Keynes used the term), (2) production takes time and hence if production is to occur in a specialisation, monetary economy, someone must undertake contractual commitments involving performance and payment in the future, and (3) economic decisions are made in the light of an unalterable past while moving towards a perfidious future, Keynes's theoretical model is developed in this book in order to provide a rich harvest of insights into such current economic problems as accumulation, inflation, income distribution, and the growth of the stock of money. The resulting monetary analysis and conclusions of Keynes are then compared and contrasted with the framework and conclusions of the other major schools of macroeconomic thought: The Monetarists, The American Keynesian-neoclassical School, and the English Neo-keynesians. Since most professional economists tend to use the theoretical framework of one of these latter three schools, the formidable task of this book is to convince them (1) that there are significant conceptual differences between their framework and the analysis developed by Keynes, and (2) that the latter's ideas are more relevant and useful as a basis for further investigations into the problems of the real world.

At this point, the reader may be wondering as to how this volume differs from Leijonhufvud's book, since the latter also claims to draw a sharp distinction between Keynesian economics and the economics of Keynes. The differences between Leijonhufvud's volume and this one are not only significant, but they are crucial if comparisons of all major alternative macroeconomic theories and/or relevance to real world problems are used as criteria. For example, Leijonhufvud indicates that his neglect of the English Neo-keynesian school 'reflects

[1] J. M. Keynes, *A Treatise on Money* (London: Macmillan, 1930).

not a judgement of its relevance or importance, but a conscious parochial concern with the development of the "American" Keynesian tradition.'[1] This disregard for the Neo-keynesian analytical scheme prevents Leijonhufvud from making any connection between Keynesian economics and the important real world economic questions of income distribution and economic growth.

Leijonhufvud's single preoccupation with the American Keynesian-neoclassical synthesis as the alternative to Keynes unfortunately leads him to adopt the underlying framework of the former, namely Walrasian general equilibrium concepts, as the analytical device for comparing the American Keynesian school with his view of Keynes's analysis. As early as 1933, however, Keynes had warned that the concepts underlying a *Monetary Economy* were in contradistinction to the structure of a Real Exchange Economy (i.e. a neoclassical system) and consequently there were 'far-reaching' and 'fundamental differences between the conclusions of a Monetary Economy and those of the more simplified Real-Exchange Economy'.[2] Moreover, according to Keynes, it is impossible to adopt the conclusions of a neoclassical model to the real world of monetary economics, unless a pre-existing theory of a monetary economy can be used to make the transformation,[3] i.e. the analytical concepts which Keynes forged for his monetary theory of production can be used to translate neoclassical results to real world situations, but not *vice versa*. Consequently, Leijonhufvud, trapped by his desire to use a Walrasian framework as the Rosetta stone for comparing Keynesian economics with the economics of Keynes, is unable to deal with monetary phenomena in his analysis of either school.

---

[1] Leijonhufvud, op. cit., p. 116 n. In light of the recent victory of the Neo-keynesian view of Capital Theory over the American Keynesian-neoclassical view, it is obvious that, at least for purposes of analysing accumulation and growth, Leijonhufvud focused on the wrong Keynesian school.

[2] J. M. Keynes, 'On the Theory of a Monetary Economy', originally published in the *Festschrift fur Arthur Spiethoff* (Munich: Duncker and Humblot, 1933), reprinted in *Nebraska Journal of Economics and Business* (1963) p. 8. Recently Frank Hahn has reiterated the point that 'the Walrasian economy . . . is essentially one of barter', F. H. Hahn, 'Some Adjustment Problems', *Econometrica* (1970) p. 3.

[3] Keynes, 'Monetary Economy', *Nebraska Journal* (1963) pp. 8–9.

Although Leijonhufvud mentions Keynes's definition of money in seven different places in his book, he never deals with Chapter 17 of *The General Theory* – a chapter entitled 'The Essential Properties of Interest and Money'. How can one analyse Keynes's conception of money without a thorough discussion of what Keynes believed to be the *essential* properties of money? Since Leijonhufvud has ignored these essential properties, his attempt to introduce money into what is essentially a nonmonetary or barter system are, for reasons discussed in the following chapters, futile. In my own work, Keynes's essential properties are made the keystone of the monetary analysis. Leijonhufvud, working within the confines of a nonmonetary general equilibrium framework, is unable to develop any connections between money supply, contracts, and the money–wage rate – relationships which were fundamental to Keynes and which are developed in detail in this book.[1]

Without elaborating further, it is possible to indicate that because of the differences in conceptual framework, this book is quite different from Leijonhufvud's not only in its conclusions but also in how it deals directly and specifically with such topics as income distribution, inflation, the relation of incomes policy to monetary and fiscal policy, monetary institutions that 'make' spot markets, external *v.* internal finance, the Neokeynesian and Monetarist schools, the essential properties of money, Keynes's finance motive, contracts and uncertainty, and the relation of spot and forward markets to economic growth. Leijonhufvud has little or nothing to say on all of these topics. What he has done so successfully is to draw attention to the fact that there are essential differences between Keynesian economics and Keynes's analyses. He deserves kudos for highlighting this aspect (even though others had said it long before him). Nevertheless he provides little or nothing in the way of

[1] After several years of concentrated effort, Hahn admits that in an economy described by the traditional general equilibrium theory 'money can play no essential role'. See F. H. Hahn, 'Equilibrium with Transaction Costs', *Econometrica* (1971) p. 417. Hahn has stumbled on the point that uncertainty and contracts are the essence of a monetary economy.

On the first page of the text of his *Treatise*, Keynes points out that contracts and money are intimately related. Contracts in the face of uncertainty are a vital fact of economic life and are the essence of Keynes's analytical structure.

guidance to either Keynes's basic structure or to real world solutions to the major macroeconomic problems of our times – inflation, accumulation, and growth. That is where I hope this book will fit in.

In conclusion I would like to acknowledge my indebtedness to a few of the many people who aided me in this venture. Because of a grant from the Rutgers University Research Council I was able to write most of this book while visiting Cambridge University during the 1970–1 academic year. At Cambridge I was indebted to Joan Robinson for her initiation of the invitation to visit Cambridge and for her many efforts to clarify the Neo-keynesian theory for me; to Nicholas Kaldor and Luigi Pasinetti for explaining their respective positions; to Austin Robinson and Don Moggridge for providing insights into Keynes's writings; to Richard Kahn and Michael Posner for sharing their office facilities at Cambridge with me; to Ken Galbraith for reading and commenting on drafts of several chapters, and to Basil Moore for the many splendid discussions and comments on various aspects of money and portfolio theory. I would also like to thank Miles Fleming and Jan Kregel of the University of Bristol for their many useful comments on written portions of the manuscript. Last but not least I must thank my mentor, Sidney Weintraub, who has an unextinguishable faith in the ultimate victory of ideas over vested intellectual interests. His extensive critical comments, not only on the current manuscript but over the years, have saved me from many errors. His advice and friendship will always be cherished.

Princeton, New Jersey   PAUL DAVIDSON
October 1971

Preface to the Second Edition

EXACTLY six years ago this month I completed the final draft of *Money and the Real World*. At that time the majority of economists felt that the microfoundations of macroeconomics had been firmly resolved in favour of general equilibrium (axiomatic value) theory. Indeed many leaders of the economics profession believed that the only remaining task for professional economists was the empirical estimation of the stable structural parameters of the economic system. For example, it was believed that the difference between neoclassical Keynesians and Monetarists could be reduced to the empirical question of the magnitude of the slope of the LM function in a truncated general equilibrium model. In sum, by 1970, most economists believed that the end of economic theory innovation and development had been proclaimed and the age of Economist qua Engineer had begun. In the light of such a dismal prognosis, *Money and the Real World* was written as a protest.

The need for such dissent was clear. Leijonhufvud had already gained prominence for his distinction between Keynesian Economics and the Economics of Keynes, but his book accepted the view that Keynes's economics could be comprehended via a Walrasian general equilibrium framework. In fact, he argued that the 'revolutionary elements of *The General Theory*' could be reduced to the fact that Keynes merely reversed the usual neoclassical assumption about the relative speeds of adjustment of prices and quantities in response to a change in demand.[1] Thus, Leijonhufvud implied that Keynes utilised the same basic model as modern neoclassical theory; only the magnitude of some speed of adjustment parameters differed in Keynes's analytical framework.

[1] A. Leijonhufvud. *Keynesian Economics and the Economics of Keynes* (London: Oxford University Press, 1968) p. 52.

This faulty view of Keynes's analysis was unhesitatingly accepted and elaborated on by Friedman[1] and others.

Since the appearance of *Money and the Real World*, however, Leijonhufvud has admitted his misinterpretation of Keynes. He now states that 'most of the recent writings on Keynes's theory, including my own, insist on evaluating it in a Walrasian perspective . . . But Keynes was, of course, a price theoretical Marshallian, and . . . ignoring this fact simply will not do.'[2] Even more importantly Leijonhufvud recognises that ' . . . it is *not* correct to attribute to Keynes a general reversal of the Marshallian ranking of relative price and quantity adjustment velocities.'[3] Hence, one of the profession's most highly regarded neo-Walrasian-Keynesian Scholars has disclaimed his former position and has affirmed one of the basic themes of the original edition of this book.

Moreover, this is not an isolated incident of an acceptance of the validity of my arguments which when I originally proposed them were superciliously treated by Friedman[4] and others. In the past six years, pillars of the neoclassical community (including two Nobel Prize winners) have admitted the logical deficiencies of their analytical system and have indicated that general equilibrium theory is not (and cannot be) coextensive with the microfoundations of macroeconomics (see Chapter 16.)

It would be pleasing to believe that the sheer power of the logical arguments put forth by members of the Keynes and post-Keynesian Schools are solely responsible for these recent admissions from neoclassical economists. Economic events of the 70s, however, have had a dramatic impact, for they demonstrated the failure of mainstream economic theory to deal with real world phenomena. Worldwide experience with stagflation, for example, led to the collapse of the belief in the stability of downward sloping Phillips curves which Keynesians had used to buttress their rickety neoclassical synthesis. (Neoclassical analysis *per se* could never explain the absolute

[1] M. Friedman, 'A Theoretical Framework of Monetary Analysis,' *Jour. Pol. Econ.* (1970) pp. 207–10.

[2] A. Leijonhufvud, 'Keynes' Employment Function', *History of Pol. Econ.*, **6** (1974) pp. 164–5.

[3] ibid., p. 169.

[4] M. Friedman, 'Comments on Critics,' *Jour. Pol. Econ.*, **80** (1972) pp. 923–31.

price level.) Stagflation ended all hope of a predictable trade-off between inflation and unemployment; and Monetarists with their unerring sense of the deficiencies of this Keynesian-Phillips Curve approach easily ravaged the flimsy framework of Messrs Tobin, Heller, Okun, Samuelson, Solow, etc.

Monetarists, however, were also soon overwhelmed by real world occurences such as OPEC oil price increases, droughts in food producing areas, frosts in Brazil, the disappearance of anchovies off the coast of Peru, and other episodic events which seemed to induce permanent fillips to domestic price levels in all industrial capitalist systems; these price movements could not be readily explained solely by changes in the domestic money supply in each country. Further erosion of confidence in the Monetarist approach followed the 1971 adoption of floating exchange rates by the major industrial nations. The Monetarists had decreed that such an arrangement would insulate the domestic economy from the international transmission of inflation; events since 1971, however, have shown that flexible exchange rates are not the panacea Monetarists had claimed.

While events were undoing the Monetarists' position from a practical point of view, further theoretical analysis of their expectational formation models (which they had grafted onto their general equilibrium framework in order to explain inflation and unemployment) has demonstrated the inability of this approach to model real world macrophenomena (see Chapter 16).

As a result of these practical and analytical failures of both Monetarism and neoclassical Keynesianism, the corpus of orthodox theory now lies in shambles. The neoclassical (general equilibrium or axiomatic value) system has been unable to produce a well-formed macroeconomic theory which can deal with production, money and expectations. Accordingly, the time is ripe for this new edition of *Money and the Real World*.

For some time now I have felt the need not only to update *Money and the Real World* to focus attention on these matters, but also to expand the analysis into areas which had, of necessity, only been lightly touched on in the original edition. With the onset of the 'energy crisis' due to the OPEC cartel actions in

1973, however, my research activities and efforts were diverted. The recent exhaustion of the publisher's stock of *Money and the Real World*, and the resulting existence of unfilled orders has created a situation which required an immediate resolution. The most efficient way of dealing with this exigency is to publish the first 15 chapters of this book virtually unchanged (except for correcting misprints) and to add at the very end an entirely new, extensive chapter (16) on 'Why Money Matters'.

This new chapter begins by utilising the recent writings of pre-eminent neoclassical scholars and expositors (two are Nobel Prize winners) to indicate the degree to which these leaders of the Neoclassical Schools have conceded the inanities of the basic assumptions of general equilibrium (axiomatic value) theory. Had such devastating comments come from economists of the Keynes and post-Keynesian Schools, dogmatic neoclassical writers might have dismissed these as the rantings of economists qua prosecuting attorneys who do not comprehend the complex subtleties of neoclassical analysis but who have a vested interest in proving guilt. These most subversive and devastating writings have, however, emerged from some of the most respected members of the neoclassical community and hence cannot be dismissed. These indictments of the general equilibrium approach validate, beyond any reasonable doubt, the criticism presented in the first 15 chapters of this book.

After establishing the current state of disarray of neoclassical theory, Chapter 16 indicates how Keynes's use of expectations is significantly different from the various expectational formation models currently being employed by neoclassical theorists to rehabilitate their tottering theoretical structures. Utilising newly available material from volumes XIII and XIV of *The Collected Works of John Maynard Keynes* (which contain early drafts of *The General Theory*), Chapter 16 presents four different expectational models (two static and two dynamic) which are the foundation of Keynes's monetary framework. This is followed by a synthesis of Hicks's elasticity of expectations with Keynes's expectational approach. Conditions for dynamic stability in the context of an uncertain world are then developed, for, as Keynes warned Joan Robinson, 'You must not confuse *instability* with uncertainty.'[1] Keynes believed that stability over a period of calendar time was possible even in a dynamic setting because men created institutions which promoted 'sticky' expectations and behaviour; such institutions included contracts, money and organised markets.

As a basis for developing this theme of the importance of such institutions, Chapter 16 analyses how an ideal system of 'indexing' of all contracts in a market economy will be perched on a knife-edge where any movement away from equilibrium position will create economic forces which will exacerbate such movement rather than restore equilibrium. An analysis of perfect and instantaneous indexing of contracts in a Keynes model demonstrates that any movement away from equilibrium could ultimately lead to a destruction of the existing monetary system and the complete breakdown of production flows. The great German inflation is used as an historical example of such a process.

As a result of this analysis of expectational phenomena in Chapter 16 the role of buffer stocks in spot markets and an incomes policy in forward markets in maintaining price stability over time is clarified.

The middle section of Chapter 16 involves the tidying up of two concepts which have been discussed in the neoclassical macroeconomic literature since 1970—the crowding out effect and the existence of 'auction' versus 'customer' markets in the inflation process. The first concept has already created needless confusion and debate because its logical base has been in-adequately defined, while the latter threatens to create similar fruitless diversions in the future because of its inherent logical inadequacies. Both concepts, however, have logically correct counterparts (developed from Keynes's finance motive analysis) which have been discussed under different nomenclature in Chapters 4, 6, 11, 12 and 13 *infra*. Thus, in Chapter 16, these Keynes's finance notion counterparts are used to clarify:

(1) the debate over the crowding out effect and the potency of fiscal policy;
(2) the dispute between Friedman and Tobin on the

---

[1] *The Collected Works of John Maynard Keynes*, xiv (London: Macmillan, 1973) p. 137.

magnitude of shifting of the LM curve over calendar time relative to a once-for-all increase in the IS function resulting from an increase in government deficit financed expenditures;[1] and

(3) the relation of auction versus customer markets (or Hicks flexprice versus fixprice markets) to the Keynes' spot and forward market analysis of Chapter 4.

In the final section of Chapter 16, some new macroeconomic territory is explored in an attempt to develop a taxonomic structure for analysing macrofinancial flows. These financial flow considerations are basic to the ability of economic agents to undertake contractual commitments for the hiring of factors of production and the holding of asset positions. It is only within a context of calendar time, uncertainty, contracts, liquidity and the financing of the holding of positions in all types of real and financial assets that the meaning of the motto 'Money Matters' can be fully comprehended. Thus Chapter 16 ends at the point where monetary theory is finally and completely brought into direct contact with the real world.

Princeton, New Jersey   PAUL DAVIDSON
May 1977

---

[1] Friedman, *op. cit.*, pp. 915–17.

CHAPTER I

The Political Economy of Modern Theory – Keynes, Keynesians, and the Neoclassicists

'WE are all Keynesians now' has become a popular cliché used by economists, politicians, and even by Presidents of the United States. Superficially it would appear that in less than half a century, the writing of John Maynard Keynes has swept the economic thinking of modern capitalist economies.

Despite this apparent victory of Keynes's ideas and philosophy, a small but growing group of economists[1] have continued to warn that what passes for 'Keynesian' economics is nothing but pre-keynesian simplicities camouflaged with some Keynesian cosmetic terminology. For those who were unaware of this small but important literature, the appearance of Leijonhufvud's book emphasising the dichotomy between the economics of J. M. Keynes and the accepted Keynesian economics must have been a shocking experience.[2]

The naive student of economics, diligently delving into the monetary and growth literature of recent years would be led

[1] This group includes R. W. Clower, R. F. Harrod, N. Kaldor, H. Minsky, J. Robinson, G. L. S. Shackle, and S. Weintraub. In 1964 Eugene Smolensky and I attempted to bring the economics of Keynes (and not the Keynesians) to the textbook level in our *Aggregate Supply and Demand Analysis* (New York: Harper and Row, 1964).

[2] A. Leijonhufvud, *On Keynesian Economics*. Despite Leijonhufvud's emphasis on the schism between the economics of the Keynesian majority of the profession and the monetary theory of Keynes, Leijonhufvud's book does little to explain Keynes's views on the role of money and its relation to real world economic problems. For example, topics such as inflation, economic growth, income distribution, income policies, the essential properties of money and contracts are not listed in the index of Leijonhufvud's book.

to believe that, thirty years after *The General Theory*, the lead-ing scholars of economics had progressed far beyond the now-conventional wisdom of Keynes, and had provided a more comprehensive and logically coherent long-run macroeconomic analysis to replace Keynes's misleading short-run and short-sighted analysis. Thus, for example, Friedman has presented a 'Theoretical Framework for Monetary Analysis' which he claims 'almost all economists would accept',[1] in which he summarily dismisses Keynes's analysis as demonstrably 'false' because of errors in Keynes's system.[2] Simultaneously the mathematically-oriented economists at M.I.T. were influential in getting a sophisticated 'neoclassical synthesis' adopted into the average economist's tool box. This neoclassical-Keynesian syncretic view has been represented as amalgamating Keynes's macroeconomics with neoclassical microeconomic principles. In reality, it is simply a reversion to pre-Keynes sophistry larded over with some 'Bastard Keynesian' (to use Mrs Robinson's splendiferous term) concepts. Finally, in a similar manner, the long-run growth theory developed at Cambridge, England in recent years, although labelled as Neo-keynesian, tends to be based more on the writings of Ricardo, Marx, and Kalecki than on the analytical framework of Keynes.

In reality, therefore, modern macroeconomic, monetary, and growth theory – far from being unified under Keynes's aegis – has developed along at least four (or perhaps five) different analytical, philosophical, and political slants. Table 1.1 attempts to classify the various shades of analytical views into five relatively homogeneous schools of thought. Going from the extreme right to the extreme left (on Table 1.1), these are

(1) *The Monetarist-Neoclassical School.* A narrow, almost mono-lithic view of the economic system whose major base is the University of Chicago, and whose writings almost always bear the Imprimatur of Professor Friedman.

(2) *The Neoclassical-Bastard Keynesian School.* A much broader spectrum of views are in this school than in the previous one. Models range from the neoclassical capital theories of Samuel-son and Solow to the portfolio and general equilibrium views

---

[1] M. Friedman, 'A Theoretical Framework for Monetary Analysis', *Journal of Pol. Econ.* (1970), p. 234.   [2] ibid., pp. 206–10.

of Patinkin, Hicks, and Tobin. A majority of the Economics Establishment dominate this school, and therefore, not surprising a majority of the economics profession believe that the view of this school is 'Economics'.

(3) *Keynes's School.* An exceedingly small group who have attempted to develop Keynes's original views on employment, growth, and money, e.g. Harrod, Lerner, and Weintraub.

(4) *The Neo-keynesian School.* A small but important group centred in Cambridge, England, who have attempted to graft aspects of Keynes's real sector analysis onto the growth and distribution theories of Ricardo, Marx, and Kalecki. The leaders of this school are Mrs Robinson, Kaldor, and Pasinetti.

(5) *The Socialist-Radical School.* The members of this residual category span a vast spectrum of views from left of centre liberals such as Galbraith through Marxists and the new 'radical' economists. Despite the vast diversity in this category, the members share two common characteristics, namely (1) their ideas are typically dismissed as 'non-scientific' by the majority (groups to the right of centre) of the Economics Establishment and therefore unworthy of significant serious discussion in the learned professional literature[1] and (2) the members of this school advocate socialisation of those productive sectors of the economy whose faults are perceived as non-correctable by either normal market processes or over-all macroeconomic policies.

The members of the Radical-Socialist School do not claim any legitimate descent from Keynes. Furthermore, they usually have little of significance to say about monetary theory. Nevertheless, they have raised fundamental questions about the objectives and the path of economic growth in capitalist economies – embarrassing inquiries which are studiously avoided by those schools to the right of centre in Table 1.1.

Table 1.1 can be termed a *Table of Political Economy*, for it attempts to associate the various schools with different positions in the political spectrum from extreme right to extreme left. As the entries in the various cells of the Table suggest, the

[1] For example, see R. M. Solow, 'Discussion', *American Econ. Rev. Pap. Proc.* (1971) p. 67.

Table 1.1

A TABLE OF POLITICAL ECONOMY SCHOOLS OF THOUGHT

	Socialist-Radical	*Neo-keynesian*	*Keynes*	*Neoclassical-Bastard Keynesian*	*Monetarist-Neoclassical*
Politics	Extreme left	Left of centre	Centre	Right of centre	Extreme right
Money	Real forces emphasised – money merely a tool for existing power structure	Real forces emphasised, money assumed to accommodate	Money and real forces intimately related	Money matters along with everything else	Only money matters
Wage rate and income distribution	Wage rate basis of value. Income distribution the most important economic question	Money wage is the linchpin of the price level. Income distribution very important	Money wage rate fundamental; income distribution question of less importance	Wage rate one of many prices. Income distribution is the resultant of all the demand and supply equations in a general equilibrium system. Income distribution a matter of equity, not of 'scientific' inquiry.	
Capital Theory	Surplus generated by reserve army	Surplus needed over wages	Scarcity theory (quasi-rents)	Marginal productivity theory and well-behaved production functions	
Employment Theory	Any level of employment possible. Assumes growth in employment overtime. Full employment creates crisis for capitalism	Growth with any level of employment possible, although growth at full employment emphasised	Any level of employment possible; full employment desirable	Full employment assumed; unemployment is a disequilibrium situation	Full employment assumed in long run; no explicit short-run theory of employment
Inflation	Primarily due to money wage changes, but can also be due to profit margin changes	Due to money wage or profit margin changes	Due to changes in money wages, productivity and/or profit margins	In long-run primarily a monetary phenomenon being related to money supply via portfolio decisions. In short run may be related to Phillips curve	Primarily a monetary phenomenon in the sense of being related to the supply of money via portfolio decisions
Government role	Socialise the capitalist sector	Laissez-faire except for macroeconomic controls over incomes	Laissez-faire except for macroeconomic controls over money, investment decisions, and the	Laissez-faire except for externalities and some ad hoc macro-controls	Laissez-faire

position taken on various key economic issues by the different schools of thought will tend to vary monotonically with their position in the political spectrum.[1] Obviously the five columns are not watertight; views of individuals in any one school tend to be very close, and may, on certain issues, overlap with the views of those in schools of close proximity. Thus, for example, Galbraith may find easy compatibility with the Neo-keynesians on some issues, little to conflict with in Keynes, but very little common ground with those schools to the right of the centre.

This monograph will concentrate primarily on questions involving accumulation, growth, money, money-wages, and income distribution. As Table 1.1 indicates, the various schools of thought have conflicting views on these aspects and, in the recent past, these differences have led to acrimonious debates in the economic literature. For example, there has been a continuous dialogue between the Monetarists and the Bastard Keynesians as to how much 'money matters' – a discussion which most of the participants seem to have believed could be resolved by answering the empirical question of whether velocity or the multiplier provided a better statistical 'explanation' of changes in GNP. At approximately the same time there was a much more esoteric disputation about capital accumulation and income distribution between the neoclassical-Bastard Keynesians and the Neo-keynesians. The resolution of this acid debate was thought to depend on the results of the reswitching controversy.[2] It is not the purpose of this monograph to review the intricate flailing and wailing that comprised these episodes;

[1] For his own amusement the reader may wish to extend the list of economic issues to see how well this view of the spectrum of theories of political economics is maintained.

[2] The controversy between the extreme left and the right of centre groups regarding resource allocation has not yet had a head-on confrontation in the economic literature primarily because these right of centre schools find their 'tools of analysis' unacceptable to those who refuse to play by the rules of conventional economics and who instead insist on asking pertinent, practical questions. Keynes and the Neo-keynesians, on the other hand, although never taking their eyes off of the real world, attempt to dress their analysis in the fashions of conventional economic tools. It is surprising, therefore, to find that the neoclassical schools have never attempted to resolve the differences between them and Keynes. Instead they have ignored the Keynes school and engaged in squabbles between themselves and on occasion with the Neo-keynesians.

others have already presented some aspects of the historical development of these battles.[1] Instead, the focus will be on placing in a modern context Keynes's own analysis of the questions of money and accumulation which has been until now virtually ignored.

If Keynes, the monetary theorist, could provide such powerful insights into the major economic questions of the thirties so that, in a few years, governmental policy has been able to eliminate unemployment as a *major* problem in almost all capitalist economies, then it stands to reason that a development of his fundamental monetary analysis should provide a similarly rich harvest of insights for the current economic problems of accumulation, inflation, and the role of money. Moreover, since Keynes's views are solidly based in the centre of the political spectrum, his analysis and conclusions will be compatible with elements of both the right- and left-of-centre approaches. Only the extreme schools may be grievously unhappy with some of Keynes's solutions but even the extreme groups should find the Keynes's solutions more compatible than those offered by schools further away in the spectrum. Consequently, I anticipate that the policies suggested by a clear exposition and development of Keynes's original analysis should find extensive support among open-minded economists of all shades of persuasion.

Of course by developing the centralist position, this monograph will be open to attack by both the left (for being an apologetic for the status quo) and the right (for being antagonistic to the belief that a market system automatically produces an optimum allocation). Consequently, it is essential to state explicitly at the outset that it is my belief that economic theory should neither exculpate the existing economic power structure, nor should it provide a rationalisation for those who desire change for change's sake in any existing institution which currently does not function ideally. Instead, the following analysis is firmly based on a mixture of conservative and radical elements. The conservative aspect is concerned with assuring

[1] See G. C. Harcourt, 'Some Cambridge Controversies in the Theory of Capital', *Journal of Economic Literature* (1969) pp. 369–405. Also see J. A. Kregel, *Rate of Profit, Distribution and Growth – Two Views* (London: Macmillan, 1971).

that proposed changes in the existing social and economic structures do not permit backsliding from the degree of progress which the evolving human institutions have already attained; while the radical element requires the promotion of progress in those areas where obvious faults occur *and* where progress is possible without wantonly destroying institutions which at least preserve a modicum of decent behaviour.[1]

A BRIEF OUTLINE OF THIS MONOGRAPH

Keynes's criticisms of accepted economic theory (i.e. schools on the right side of the Table of Political Economy) 'consisted not so much in finding logical flaws in its analysis, as in pointing out that its tacit assumptions are seldom or never satisfied, with the result that it cannot solve the economic problems of the actual world'.[2] The organisation of this monograph is similarly oriented – not as an investigation of the intricate logical flaws in the structure of the neoclassical or neo-keynesian models. There is no desire to score debating points about the logic of these alternative views and hence the reader will find little mention of the subtle problems of obtaining an aggregate measure of capital, or of reswitching and the choice of techniques, etc. for these are theoretical conundrums which are often debated with great joy and zest by economists who essentially 'are to make their living by providing pure entertainment'[3] for other economists. Instead, the analysis will be developed on the basic assumptions that in the real world (1) the future is uncertain (in the sense that Knight and Keynes used the term), (2) production takes time and therefore, if production is to occur in a specialisation economy, someone must make a contractual commitment in the present involving performance and payment in the uncertain future, and (3) economic decisions are made in the light of an unalterable past, while moving towards a perfidious future.

It is only under these three basic assumptions that the role

[1] Cf. Keynes, *Treatise on Money*, II 300.
[2] J. M. Keynes, *The General Theory*, p. 378.
[3] Cf. F. H. Knight, *Risk, Uncertainty and Profit* (London: London School of Economics, 1937) p. xxv.

of money in the real world can be analysed. As Keynes has stated

> *For the importance of money essentially flows from its being a link between the present and the future.* We can consider what distribution of resources between different uses will be consistent with equilibrium in which our views concerning the future are fixed and reliable in all respects; with a further division, perhaps between an economy which is unchanging and one subject to change, but where all things are foreseen from the beginning. Or we can pass from this simplified propaedeutic to the problems of the real world in which our previous expectations are liable to disappointment and expectations concerning the future affect what we do to-day. It is when we have made this transition that the peculiar properties of money as a link between the present and the future must enter into our calculations.[1]

In the real world, booms and slumps are not merely erratic episodes which can be readily superimposed onto the long-run steady-state growth path of an economy. The actual historical path of economic activity for real world monetary economies is not one which can be decomposed into separate and logically independent secular trend and short-run trade cycle aspects. (Such a dichotomous construction is merely the handiwork of the economist's imagination, and if accompanied by empirical analysis of the historical record, it is likely to be the artistic creation of the economist misemploying the statistician's basic tools.)[2] Any theoretical model which is logically applicable only to an economy which is in long-run equilibrium or steady-state growth may be a useful 'warming up' exercise for the muscles of scientific inquiring minds, but it should never be taken as a serious description of a real world alternative, and no reliance as either a predictor or as a basis of policy can be given to such callisthenics where money is concerned. It is because the monetary and growth models of the alternative

[1] Keynes, *The General Theory*, pp. 293–4.

[2] For example, the naive mind might boggle at the basic assumption that each observation in an economic time series is independent in the sense of drawing chips from an infinitely large urn *with replacement*. The 'trained mind', on the other hand, never worries about the applicability of such an assumption.

schools of political economy are either explicitly or implicitly based on some variant of the axiom that in a growing economy, all changes can be foreseen from the beginning *and expectations are never disappointed*, that they represent retrograde rather than progressive developments in monetary theory as compared to Keynes's views.

It was in his *Treatise on Money* that Keynes hoped to take 'the critical leap forward which will bring it [Monetary Theory] into effective contact with the real world'.[1] It is therefore particularly apropos in view of the current interest in the Monetarism school and economic growth that Keynes's views be developed in a modern setting. If this monograph succeeds in achieving this limited objective, it will represent one small step for monetary theory, but one great leap for mankind.

In Chapters 2 to 5 the relevance of the aforementioned assumptions regarding uncertainty, time, and commitments will be developed in analysing pricing, production, and accumulation decisions in a decentralised economy, and the analytical results compared with the views on decision-making propounded by the other schools. In Chapters 6 to 11 the implications of these fundamental assumptions for the financial sector of a market economy will be developed and compared with the views of the neoclassical and neo-keynesian schools. Finally in Chapters 12 to 14, the implications and policy proposals for growth, inflation, and income distribution which logically follow from Keynes's expanded model will be developed.

[1] Keynes, *Treatise on Money*, II, p. 406.

CHAPTER 2

Uncertainty and the
Historical Model Approach

A PARABLE: THE FABLE OF THE P'S, OR WHAT
MORTALS THESE P'S FOOL!

MANY years ago in the never-never land of Chicago where
the busy P's of economic theory often flourish, there dwelt a
wise and famous Knight (Frank H.) who recognised the sterility
of the use of 'classical' economics in providing guidance for
social policy. Hence this Knight attempted to redirect the
economics profession towards the study of relevant economic
problems[1] by forging meaningful and realistic concepts. Risk,
this Knight maintained, is measurable and hence is distinct-
ively different from uncertainty which is incapable of measurement. Hence the term uncertainty must be restricted to 'non-
quantitative' views about the future and it is this 'true' uncertainty, and not risk, the Knight insisted, which forms the basis
of economic decision-making.[2]

At about the same time, in a distant land across the seas,
the brave and intelligent warrior, Keynes, who had also
laboured in the field of probability and non-measurable uncertainty, took up the cudgel and started a revolution in economic thinking. In summarising the foundation of his attack on
the Establishment, Keynes proclaimed that the mischief was
done when the neoclassicists insisted on analysing models where

> at any given time facts and expectations were assumed to be
> given in a definite and calculable form. . . . The calculus of
> probability . . . was supposed to be capable of reducing
> uncertainty to the same calculable status as that of certainty

---

[1] F. H. Knight, *Risk, Uncertainty and Profits*, 1937 ed., p. xxiv.
[2] ibid., pp. 19–20.

itself. . . . I accuse the classical economic theory of being itself one of these pretty, polite techniques which tries to deal with the present by abstracting from the fact that we know very little about the future.

I daresay a classical economist would readily admit this. But even so, I think he has overlooked the precise nature of the difference which his abstraction makes between theory and practice, *and the character of the fallacies into which he is likely to be led.*

This is particularly the case in his treatment of money. . . . Our desire to hold money as a store of wealth is a barometer of the degree of our distrust of our own calculations and conventions concerning the future.[1]

Now it came to pass that the power and realism of the Keynesian view, removed the classical cataracts from the eyes of economists throughout the free world and for several decades there was continuing progress and growth of understanding of the workings of the economic system. But after a time, in the land of Chicago, new leaders appeared who desired to resurrect the neoclassical structure; and one, who was the most exalted neoclassical savant of all, mounted a balcony and said to his followers:

Oh Students, Scholars, wherefore art thou Scientists? Deny thy forefather (F. H. Knight) and refuse his conceptual distinctions between risk and uncertainty. If thou wilt but do this we can reconquer the free world with the elegance of mathematics and the scientific laws of probability.

What's in a name? That which we call Uncertainty by any other name can be handled more easily. So Uncertainty were it but called Risk, would obtain that dear perfection without which scientific quantification and probability analysis is inapplicable.

J. M. K. is dead and his friends have become old and their voices weak. His younger disciples have become fat in body and mind with the prosperity of success of the last few decades. If you, the next generation of neoclassicists have but the will

[1] J. M. Keynes, 'The General Theory of Employment', *Quarterly Journal of Economics*, 1937, reprinted in *The New Economics*, ed. S. E. Harris (New York: Knopf, 1952) pp. 184–7 [italics mine]. All references are to the reprint.

to do, and the soul to dare, then we will win out. Today Chicago, Tomorrow the free world!!

And this modern generation of students were taken by these words and they said of their new scientific leader:

> He speaks the kindest words, and looks such things, Vows with so much passion, swears with so much grace. That 'tis a kind of heaven to be deluded by him.[1]

And thus it was that the modern neoclassicists recaptured the heavens and the earth and the dark ages descended once more upon the economic community. Moral: Those who insist on quantifying non-quantifiable concepts can only provide a regressive form of analysis.

UNCERTAINTY AND THE REAL WORLD

Economists often construct models that assume away uncertainty. These models are often justified on the grounds that (1) they eliminate subjective factors, (2) they ease the mathematical and verbal exposition, and (3) a world of disappointed expectations results in a level of turbulence beyond the skill of model builders to analyse. Uncertainty, it is often implied merely 'muddies the waters' without altering the essential conclusions. A world of perfect certainty, it is averred, provides a manageable model for drawing conclusions about the real world.

In the real world, however, uncertainty is significant in its effects on all economic activity. Many of the institutions of our modern economy would have no function in a world of certainty. There would be no need for stock market speculation, for forward commodity and foreign exchange markets, for pecuniary contracts. In a certain world, there would be no reason for holding money, nor would there be any involuntary unemployment. Uncertainty plays a vital role in the determination of employment, investment, growth, pricing, and income distribution only in a world – our world – where the future is enigmatic and full of potential surprise.

Time is said to be a device to prevent everything from

---

[1] N. Lee, *The Rival Queens* (London: Gain & Bently, 1684) Act I.

happening at once. The existence of durable goods, money, financial assets, and contracts link the economic future to the present. The inherited stocks of durables, contractual obligations, and the existing stock of money provide a continuity between irrevocable past economic behaviour and the current environment, while the existence of durable goods, contracts and money provide the essential links between an uncertain perfidious future and present economic activity.[1] A monetary–production economy operating with complete certainty is a contradiction in terms.

For some economic activities, the future consequences of present activity may be relatively unimportant, e.g. the current consumption of an apple which was recently produced. Nevertheless, the future plays an important role in most human activities – and a predominant role in one important aspect – the accumulation of wealth. The whole purpose of the accumulation of wealth is to produce results and provide for contingencies at a relatively distant and often unspecified date in an uncertain future. Thus any economic model which alleges to explain the accumulation of capital and economic growth in the real world must be firmly based on explicit relationships between the uncertain future and present economic behaviour.

The existence of unpredictable uncertainty is also important for all production decisions. Since production takes time, in a decentralised market-orientated economy, the entrepreneur must recognise that he will have to undertake contractual commitments in order to secure the services of the factors of production over a period of time to produce a flow of goods whose value can never be known in advance. (If the producers produce only 'to contract', then the buyers will be contractually committed to purchase goods in the future at a specified price, while they will not be certain of the value of the goods to them at the time of delivery.) Accordingly, pricing, production, and purchasing decisions are, in the real world, always made under conditions of uncertainty.

In most growth and production models, however, the analysis of time involvement and ignorance about the future is eliminated by assumptions of either 'perfect and complete knowledge' about past, present, and future, or all changes in

[1] Keynes, *The General Theory*, pp. 293–4.

the future are 'fully anticipated', or even all past expectations have been completely realised, and consequently all individuals act as if their expectations about the future will always be, and always are, realised. All three of these assumptions alter the status of an uncertain future into one of complete certainty and as such must create an unbridgeable gulf between theory and practice. Models based on assumptions suggesting that present decisions are either (a) based on complete data about future events or (b) no member of the economy ever expects to be surprised by future events as they come to pass, emasculate the very concepts of time and uncertainty in economics. Such constructions reach their pinnacle of intellectual achievements in neoclassical general equilibrium steady-state growth models – models which permit a 'groping' towards equilibrium via the mechanism of a Walrasian auctioneer to exist side-by-side with the assumption of perfect and complete knowledge about all future markets!

The Keynesian revolution in economics, however, is based on an analysis which is the polar opposite of the neoclassical timeless equilibrium view of the world. Keynes recognised that time normally elapses between the point when decisions are made and the ultimate outcome of these decisions. Specifically, Keynes recognised the importance of expectations and uncertainty about the future in his analysis of (1) production and employment decisions, (2) investment in physical capital decisions, and (3) liquidity preference decisions. The expectations underlying these behavioural relationships are the basic foundations upon which Keynes built the independent variables of his *General Theory*.

To adopt the Keynes view of accumulation in the real world is, in simple terms, to conceive of the economic decision-maker as a chooser among courses of action whose full outcomes he does not and cannot know despite any amount of mathematical calculation.

In discussing accumulation decisions, Keynes noted:

. . . our decisions to do something positive, the full consequences of which will be drawn out over many days to come, can only be taken as a result of animal spirits – of a spontaneous urge to action rather than inaction, and *not as the outcome of a weighted average of quantitative benefits multiplied by quantitative probabilities.*[1]

This view implies that neither past evidence in the form of frequency distributions nor the assumptions of a set of subjective probabilities summing to unity for all expected events (in the absence of frequency distributions) can be used to make probability statements about future events, when uncertainty is present. Probability statements based on frequency distributions have nothing to say about uncertainties. It may, perhaps, be argued, that for certain aspects of economic behaviour when the individual can be sure that there will be many repetitions of the identical circumstances (which must therefore occur in the near future), the use of probability statements based on past evidence may not do violence to an analysis of the current choices.[2]

If, on the other hand, what Shackle calls a *crucial experiment* is concerned, then such probability statements are not applicable to evaluating the possible outcomes of any action. In a crucial experiment, the decision-maker believes in the possibility that the very choice of a course of action may alter the existing circumstances in a manner which makes quick restoration of the situation if the results turn out to be undesirable, exceedingly costly if not impossible.[3]

Investment, liquidity preference, and even production and many purchasing decisions, involve commitments which are likely to be significantly large, to require a considerable period of time before the outcomes of our actions are realised, and, if from hindsight an imprudent decision has been made, it may

[1] Keynes, *The General Theory*, p. 161 [italics mine].

[2] To use the mathematical laws of probability, the concept of probability *must* be defined as the limit the frequency of any particular event will approach as the number of observations increases. Shackle has always argued that probability cannot be used as a proxy for uncertainty. See G. L. S. Shackle, *Expectations in Economics* (Cambridge: Cambridge University Press, 1949).

[3] G. L. S. Shackle, *Uncertainty in Economics* (Cambridge: Cambridge University Press, 1955) pp. 6, 7, 25. For example:

> Napoleon could not repeat the battle of Waterloo a hundred times in the hope that, in a certain proportion of cases, the Prussians would arrive too late. His decision to fight . . . was what I call a crucial experiment, using the word crucial in the sense of a parting of the ways. Had he won, repetition would for a long time have been unnecessary; when he lost, repetition was impossible. [Ibid., p. 25.]

be costly if not impossible to restore the pre-existing circumstances. Consequently, decisions to take action in these areas are crucial experiments, where probability statements based on the frequency of past events are not useful. Uncertainty becomes of utmost importance and those actions which are the least costly to reverse may often become the most preferred as the degree of uncertainty increases. In a world of uncertainty, he who hesitates is saved to make a decision another day.

In sum, all discussions of macroeconomic problems involving investment, accumulation, economic growth, employment, and production and money must involve an analysis of decisionmaking under conditions of uncertainty if these discussions are to be relevant to social policy. To assert that 'money matters' in a world of complete predictability, is to be logically inconsistent, for money's special properties as a store of wealth, is due to its ability to postpone the undertaking of rigid and far reaching resource commitments. *Money only matters in a world of uncertainty*!

To analyse the accumulation of capital under assumptions of tranquility – or what Shackle refers as the economics 'of Confident Foresight, the economics of a world where changes of circumstance are believed to proceed no faster than the physical decay of equipment, so that we have the equivalent of a handto-mouth connection between act and results,'[1] is to surreptitiously introduce the deluding and fatal assumption that individuals accumulate wealth with perfect confidence in their knowledge of future events. Economic models based on tranquillity assumptions must, by their very nature, be applicable only to non-monetary or barter economies.

> . . . in a barter system, or one where money serves only as a *numeraire*, knowledge is *effectively* bound to be perfect. For

[1] G. L. Shackle, *The Years of High Theory* (Cambridge: Cambridge University Press, 1967) p. 290. Interestingly enough, the English Neokeynesian school is currently utilising the Economics of Tranquillity in their Analysis of Golden Ages, while simultaneously attacking modern neoclassicists for utilising the 'capital malleability assumption', which in essence, is equivalent to assuming changes never exceed the physical decay of equipment, so that there is never redundant capacity. For example, see L. L. Pasinetti, 'Switches of Technique and the "Rate of Return" in Capital Theory', *Economic Journal*, 79 (September 1969). Of course, Joan Robinson has continually insisted that Golden Age economies are myths which have no relevance to the historical path of real world economies.

nothing can be sold except by the concomitant purchase of some other resource-embodying thing. Without money [as a store of wealth], we cannot put off deciding what to buy with the thing we are in the act of selling. If we do not know precisely what use a thing will be to us, we are compelled nevertheless, by an absence of money, to override and ignore this ignorance. It is *money* which enables decisions to be deferred.[1]

In the real world – our world – uncertainty, growth, and money are inextricably related.

The problems of the real world . . . [occur because] our previous expectations are liable to disappointment and expectations concerning the future affect what we do today. It is when we have made this transition that the peculiar properties of money as a link between the present and the future must enter into our calculations.[2]

It is this fundamental proposition which is the basis of all the analysis which follows. Nevertheless, habits developed in one's formative stages become difficult to slough off, and since the overwhelming body of economic analysis involves analysis in which assumptions eliminate uncertainty, it is difficult to avoid such patterns of expression. Consequently, even in the following chapters there is a tendency to slur the differences between the uncertainties of the real world and the surety of the traditional 'rational economic man'. If the reader notices occasional expositional backsliding in the following pages, then he can be confident that he has become more aware of the significance of uncertainty in understanding behaviour and that he will be less tolerant of others presenting *certainty* models as useful guides to policy.

UNCERTAINTY AND DECISION-MAKING UNITS

Having recognised that uncertainty is basic to decisions which have macroeconomic repercussions, it is essential to decide on

[1] ibid., p. 290. And Shackle concludes 'it is not by accident that the Economics of Employment, that is, the Economics of Uncertainty, were approached by way of the theory of money'.

[2] Keynes, *The General Theory*, pp. 293–4.

a methodology to handle the analysis of this phenomenon.

In a Keynesian model, entrepreneurs (firms) and households play key causal roles in the system. The formidable task facing the entrepreneur is to determine what will be produced, the quantities he will produce, the technique he will employ, and the inputs that will be the least costly. These actions involve making production and investment decisions which, in a market economy, always requires the commitment of resources to a particular line of production in advance of output and actual sales. Production and investment decisions because they involve the passage of time involve uncertainty as to costs, the market value of the final end-product, and the actual future dates, when the end product will be marketed. Although institutional arrangements can be made to shift the burden of some of the uncertainties from entrepreneurs to others via contractual arrangements, someone must bear the uncertainty which is inevitable in the fact that the commitment to action and the resulting consequences do not take place simultaneously. The types of production and investment actions ultimately chosen by entrepreneurs will depend on (1) their views of the perfidious future, (2) their subjective feelings about the degree of confidence in their view of the future, or the degree of potential surprise if events were to prove expectations wrong, (3) their desire or 'tastes' to bearing uncertainties, and (4) the institutional arrangements available for shifting the burden of some of the uncertainties.[1]

Households can be visualised as being involved in important decision-making activities, namely (1) the decision of how much to consume out of income receipts (or current claim on resources) and (2) the form in which to store potential command over resources arising from that portion of current income which is not currently being consumed. The first decision, the propensity to consume (or time preference), is usually analysed as if it occurred with complete information. Although conceptual

[1] In *The New Industrial State* Galbraith suggests that the increasing span of time which separates the beginning of economic tasks from their completion, the increased requirements for specialised resource commitments, and the inflexibility of such commitments due to the growth of technology, induce the development of government institutions to remove some of the burdens of uncertainty from the entrepreneur. See J. K. Galbraith, *The New Industrial State* (Boston: Houghton Mifflin, 1967).

models which base consumption decisions on 'permanent in-come' should involve an analysis of uncertainty since future 'permanent' income can never be known with certainty, these aspects are typically ignored by assuming that past trends in measured income are reliable predictors of future permanent income. Although the omission of the analysis of the effect of uncertainty on consumption behaviour tends to ignore certain interesting aspects of consumer behaviour, for simplicity in most of the analysis of consumer behaviour in this volume, uncertainty will be played down by assuming that consump-tion is a function of received income and consumers expect stability in consumption goods prices.[1]

Hence, at least at the early stages of our analysis, uncertainty plays a crucial role for households only in their decisions on how to store wealth. If wealth is stored in any asset except as money, then there must exist a continuous spot market for that asset so that the household can, at any time in the future, ob-tain the medium of exchange. Moreover, there will be transac-tions costs incurred at the time money income receipts are converted to another form for storing wealth *and* again when it will become necessary to reconvert the store of wealth back to the medium of exchange at that point of time in the future when the wealth holder desires to exercise command of re-sources. These transactions costs lower the effective yield of all other assets which might be used as a store of wealth. More-over, since the future date of reconverting the asset back to money is uncertain, there may be additional costs involved, if the spot market price at realisation date differs from the current price. Accordingly as long as the individual is free to store wealth in the form of money or securities which are traded on well-organised developed spot markets, it is unlikely that the purchasing of physical capital goods can be made sufficiently attractive (especially to the individual who does not manage

---

[1] In Chapter 9, expectations of future price changes will be permitted to influence consumer behaviour. Until then we are assuming that the consumer, at the moment of purchase, can make a judgement on the basis of past experience as to how worthwhile the goods he buys will be to him. Since much of consumption activity involves repetitive acts in similar circumstances each day, this assumption does not do much violence to the facts surrounding most consumer purchases.

these capital goods and is ignorant about their technical attributes) except if continuous spot markets could be organised for second-hand capital which made the costs of converting capital goods to money negligible.[1] Thus, as will be discussed in detail in Chapters 4, 6, and 8, the existence of money and spot security markets, in an uncertain world, permits decision-makers to store wealth without making simultaneous commitments for resource-embodying goods: uncertainty, therefore, is basic to households' and firms' liquidity preference decisions.

Table 2.1 presents a summary of the discussion of the basic types of economic decisions in which uncertainty plays a determining role.

Table 2.1

DECISION AND UNCERTAINTY

Decision	*Decision unit*	*Impact on*
Production	Firm (Entrepreneur)	Output, employment, prices, income distribution
Investment	Firm (Entrepreneur)	Capital accumulation, economic growth
Liquidity Preference	Households Firms	Interest rate, Financial conditions

The objective of this monograph is to provide an understanding of the behavioural interrelationships of firms and households as they make these decisions while confronted with sets of circumstances in an uncertain world.

SHORT RUN *v.* LONG RUN EXPECTATIONS

In the analysis that follows, Keynes's distinction between *short-term and long-term* expectations will be adopted.[2] The importance of uncertainty will be explicitly introduced into the production decision of firms deciding their 'daily' outputs via the *short-term expectations* of entrepreneurs about the point of effective demand. Given their inherited plant and equipment at any point of time entrepreneurs hold 'expectations as to the cost of output on various possible scales and expectations as to the

---

[1] Cf. Keynes, *The General Theory*, p. 161.   [2] ibid., chapter 5.

sales-proceeds of this output.'[1] These short-term expectations determine the volume of production and employment firms will provide and the prices that firms will be content to accept for their wares.

To some extent entrepreneurs can transfer some of their uncertainty about future costs of production by entering into contracts with input owners. In the case of labour, for example, the establishment of a contract for '*piece rates*' can eliminate the uncertainty of unit labour production costs; on the other hand, labour contracts specifying 'time rates' will only partially reduce the uncertainty associated with labour production costs, for labour productivity will still be a source of potential surprise. Moreover, since the 'hire-price' for most durable inputs, e.g. capital and land, as well as the opportunity cost of the finance committed is normally contracted on a time basis, the entrepreneur must maintain a residual uncertainty as to the flow production costs associated with these inputs as well.

It is on the sales revenue side, however, that most of the entrepreneurial uncertainty persists. Only for those commodities where either well-organised, public forward markets exist[2] or contracts for forward sales occur (i.e. where the customer contracts to purchase the product in the future at either a fixed price or cost-plus price before most production expense is undertaken),[3] can the entrepreneur avoid most of the burden of uncertainty as far as expected sales revenues are concerned.[4] The answer to the question, 'When this product will be finished, will its production turn out to have been worth while?' can never be known in advance by both parties to the transaction.

For any given flow of output, therefore, the entrepreneur has expectations of costs which must be covered by sales revenue, if the commitment of resources to production is to prove worth while. This association between expected costs

[1] ibid., p. 47.

[2] The theory of forward markets and its implications will be developed in Chapter 4.

[3] This may be especially important where the government is the buyer.

[4] Even if forward markets exist, the entrepreneur will have to make offers on the assumption that his costs are known with reasonable certainty and, for assembly-line production, orders can be bunched in order to minimise costs.

and outputs is the basis of Keynes's aggregate supply function which specifies the relationship between aggregate supply price or aggregate costs which the entrepreneur must expect to recover if production is to be worth while (denoted by Z) and the employment (N) offered by firms. For any given flow of production (say Q_1) and employment (N_1) per period if the aggregate demand for goods expected by entrepreneur (D_1) is greater than the aggregate supply price (Z_1), i.e. if entrepreneurs expect sales revenues to exceed the expected required costs of producing the Q_1 flow of output, they will desire to expand employment and production until they reach the point of effective demand (where $D = Z$) as determined by these expectations. Effective demand is simply that output flow where, in the aggregate, entrepreneurial expectations of sales revenue (the demand price) just equals the supply price (based on expected costs) of the same output level.[1]

Once the point of expected effective demand is determined, entrepreneurs will undertake contractual hiring commitments which, in turn, give direction to the production of goods and services, and set off a flow of contractual money payments to the owners of hired productive inputs. There will be, for example, a flow of money wage payments to workers. Rentiers who have previously entered into *contracts* with business firms to receive a fixed sum of money per period of time will also be paid. Furthermore, managers of firms will distribute some of the profits of the firms to the owners. These money flows of income to households will be used, in part, to purchase the goods and services of industries. Similarly, demands for the production flow of industry will develop from other buyers who either possess or can obtain the medium of exchange, namely investors, governments, and foreigners. Thus for any level of productive output, these various buyers – consumer households, investors, governments, and foreigners – will desire to spend a sum on the products of industry. These purchase plans ultimately became the realised sales proceeds of industry. If entrepreneurs have correctly anticipated the spending behaviour of buyers, expected sales proceeds will be realised. If not, then realised sales will surprise entrepreneurs.

[1] This definition underlies Harrod's warranted rate of growth. See Chapters 5 and 12 below.

The *actual realised* results of the production and sale of output will only be relevant to employment in so far as they cause modification of subsequent expectations . . . [each production and employment decision] will be made, with reference to this [inherited] stock, but in the light of the *current* expectations of *prospective* costs and sales proceeds.[1]

For the investment decision, on the other hand, it is long-term rather than short-term expectations which are relevant. These long-term expectations involve the entrepreneur in estimating the shape of the future income stream that can be expected from additions to his capital stock. Long-term expectations, by their very nature, are not readily checked in short periods by observing realised results. Accordingly the growth of capital in a monetary, market-oriented economy depends in large measure upon entrepreneurial expectations about points of effective demand for a large number of future periods – and these long-term expectations can not be eliminated or replaced by recent realised results. The importance of this relationship will be developed in detail in Chapter 4.

Plans and expectations are the behavioural motivating forces which link the present commitment of resources with future outputs. The inherited stock of capital is the bridge between the (usually incorrect) plans of the past, the current expectations, and the anticipation about the enigmatic future. Finally, the inherited stock of money and securities is the link between past financing decisions, the current need for a medium of exchange, and the desire to store value for the future. Any macroeconomic model that does not make those aspects central to its analysis, contains a large element of unreality. Only with the introduction of concepts that permit such relationships can economists hope to say something which is relevant for social policy.

If, for example, the inherited stock of capital is not deemed by entrepreneurs to be the most convenient for producing in line with long-run expectations of future points of effective demand, and if finance is available, then change is inevitable in such an economy, even if the current stock of capital is thought to be ideal with respect to short-period sales expectations.

[1] Keynes, *The General Theory*, p. 47.

The path of change will depend on the magnitude of the initial disequilibrium between the inherited capital stock and long-run expectations, supply conditions in the capital goods industries, depreciation conditions, the behavioural spending habits of households, and the behavioural factors underlying pricing decisions by producers and their reactions if expectations of sales proceeds are disappointed in the current period. These factors interact in a complex manner, but they must be carefully unravelled if an understanding of the real world path of economic growth is to be developed.

In any short-run production period, the original expectations which led firms to build up the current stock of capital may only be of slight relevance in determining this period's employment and supply prices. Nevertheless, once the employment and pricing decisions for this period's output has been made and carried out, two possible results can occur in a market-oriented economy – either the point of effective demand has been correctly estimated, or entrepreneurial expectations may miscarry. In the context of short-period employment analysis, erroneous expectations may not be important, particularly if one assumes, as Keynes did, that the differences between short-period expectations and realisations are very small. Accordingly Keynes felt

> It will often be safe to omit express reference to *short-term* expectation, in view of the fact that in practice the process of revision of short-term expectation is a gradual and continuous one, carried on largely in the light of realised results, so that expected and realised results run into and overlap one another in their influence. For, although output and employment are determined by the producer's short-term expectations and not past results, the most recent results usually play a predominant part in determining what these expectations are.[1]

Given this view, Keynes could switch definitions of aggregate demand in midstream from the sales revenue producers *expect* to receive from the sale of output produced by the employment of men, to aggregate demand equalling the sum of the actual propensity to consume plus the demand for invest-

[1] Keynes, *The General Theory*, pp. 50–1.

ment, and thereby implicitly assume that short-term expectations were (nearly) always fulfilled.[1] This view has been perpetuated in most macroeconomic models to the present day.

If, on the other hand, emphasis is focused on the path of growth of the economy over a number of production periods, assumptions about the continuous fulfilment of long-run expectations[2] are no longer reasonable. To limit our analysis solely to long-run equilibrium or steady-state growth models and avoid the complexities of intertemporal disappointment is to dispense with the baby and the bath water simultaneously. Disappointment means disequilibrium and in the real world disappointment is recognised by decision-makers as a potentially ubiquitous phenomenon. Consequently, if we are to understand real world phenomena, we must study disequilibrium as well as potentially equilibrium situations. Some forty years ago, Keynes announced

> But now at last we are, I think, on the eve of a new step forward, which, if it is made successfully, will enormously increase the applicability of theory to practice; namely an advance to an understanding of the detailed behaviour of an economic system which is not in . . . equilibrium.[3]

It is now time for us to take another step forward in that direction.

UNCERTAINTY AND THE CHOICE OF ECONOMIC MODEL

As Joan Robinson has pointed out, there are essentially two types of economic models which may be developed – equilibrium models and historical models. An equilibrium model builder proceeds by specifying a sufficient number of equations to determine all the unknowns in the system and then to concentrate on the simultaneous solution of the equations. The emphasis on the equilibrium position rather than the mechanism of change is the hallmark of equilibrium models. In

---

[1] Compare the definitions of aggregate demand on p. 25 with the one on pp. 89–90 in *The General Theory*.

[2] Harrod's warranted rate of growth would occur only if there was a continuous fulfilment of expectations.

[3] J. M. Keynes, *A Treatise on Money*, II 406–7.

recent years, the development of steady-state equilibrium growth models has been the equilibrium model builders' attempt to analyse the path of the economy over time. Nevertheless, all equilibrium models by their very nature of focusing on the equilibrium position are unable to handle situations of disappointment. 'A world in which expectations are liable to be falsified cannot be described by the simple equations of the equilibrium path.'[1]

Accordingly if the model builder is to provide a system which can analyse movements in the real world, an 'historical model' must be developed which proceeds by first specifying the particular set of values at a moment in time – where these values may not be in equilibrium with each other – and then shows how the interaction of forces unleashed by these non-equilibrium values lead to change, for the future is never known to those whose behaviour and interactions ultimately determine it.

The philosophy underlying the historical model view has been set by Joan Robinson as follows:

> A model applicable to actual history has to be capable of getting out of equilibrium; indeed it must normally not be in it. To construct such a model, we specify the technical conditions obtaining in the economy, and the behaviour reactions of its inhabitants, and then, so to say, dump it down in a particular situation at a particular date in historic time and work out what will happen next. The initial position contains, as well as physical data, *the state of expectations of the characters concerned* (whether based on past experience or on traditional beliefs). *The system may be going to work* itself out so as to fulfil or so as to disappoint them.[2]

This view is basic to the analysis of the following chapters. The essence of growth is dynamic change and a solid advance in the understanding of the money-securities-capital accumulation-economic growth nexus can only be made when we have developed an analysis which permits an economy to be either in or out of equilibrium and in a state of movement. Since, as Harrod has pointed out, Keynes's *Treatise on Money* is more dynamic than *The General Theory* and the former provides an

[1] J. Robinson, *Essays in the Theory of Economic Growth* (London: Macmillan, 1963) p. 25.   [2] ibid., pp. 25–6. Italics added.

analysis of an economy out of equilibrium, the analysis which follows will attempt to mix judiciously elements of Keynes's 1930 analysis, particularly with respect to money and security markets, with his 1936 classic approach to the principles of effective demand.

Some of the confusion which hitherto has prevented the combining of the analysis of the *Treatise* with the concepts of *The General Theory* can be eliminated by some recourse to micro-economic concepts – these concepts being useful for their implicit mechanisms of change, rather than for their usual role in stability analysis. If in the *Treatise*, one substitutes the Marshall-ian concept of demand price for the term 'investment,' and sup-ply price for 'savings', the terminological turmoil rising from Keynes's discussion of the disequilibrium between savings and investment is readily resolved. Thus, to recall the argument of the *Treatise*, when investment exceeds (is less than) savings – i.e. the demand price, D_p, exceeds (is less than) the short-run flow-supply price, S_p, that is, the price which just makes it worthwhile for entrepreneurs to enter into the requisite con-tractual commitments (and which includes normal profits[1]) for a given flow of output, Q_1, as in Figure 2.1 – then, in the market period, transactions occur at the demand price of p_1. This results in windfall profits (losses) as revenues exceed (fall short of) normal supply requirements. The invisible hand of the market place, operating via these windfall profits (losses) encourages entrepreneurs to expand (contract) output and em-ployment. It is the analysis of the factors which lead to a dis-crepancy between D_p and S_p which bring about the dynamic change in prices and subsequently output in the *Treatise*.

In *The General Theory* more emphasis is placed on the equilib-rium position than in the *Treatise*. This is not surprising in view of Keynes's tendency to play down the importance of short-term expectations in determining the point of effective demand. If, however, the *ex ante-ex post* conceptualisation of *The General Theory* is adopted, disequilibrium can be analysed

[1] Normal profits are defined as 'that rate of remuneration which, if they were open to making new bargains with all the factors of production at currently prevailing rates of earnings, would leave them under no motive either to increase or decrease their scale of operation.' – Keynes, *Treatise on Money*, p. 125.

when *ex ante* investment differs from *ex ante* savings. If *ex ante* investment exceeds (is less than) *ex ante* savings, then the demand quantity, D_q, exceeds (is less than) the supply quantity S_q, at

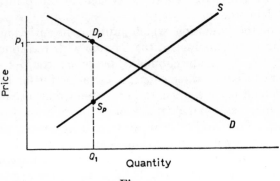

Fig. 2.1

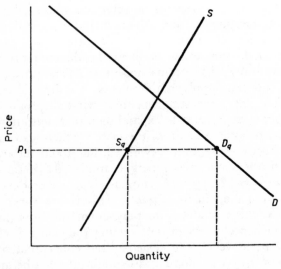

Fig. 2.2

the given supply price of p_1, as in Fig. 2.2. Market transactions occur at the price of p_1, and then the demand quantity of D_q is sold, while production is equal to the supply quantity, S_q, as inventories are drawn down. Entrepreneurs, reacting to the involuntary reduction (increase) in inventories caused by the invisible hand, are induced to expand (contract) output. Since in this latter case, the market price is equal to the flow-supply price – which is easily translated into wage units – for the given flow of output and employment, these can be no windfall profits or loss on current production. Consequently, actual savings must always equal actual investment as un-planned inventory changes play the role which windfall profits did in the *Treatise*.[1]

With *The General Theory*, however, a more subtle change in view is imparted than merely the simple transfer in concept from demand and flow-supply prices to demand and supply quantities.[2] If Harrod is correct in arguing that Keynes had concluded that his critics 'simply failed to grasp' the complexities of the 1930 analysis, then it is reasonable to believe that *The General Theory* was the result of a search for a 'simplification'. If the main breakdown is communication between Keynes and others was on the principle of effective demand, then it is not surprising that although money enters into the

---

[1] Keynes attempted to justify the change in emphasis from windfall profits to unintended inventory changes as being more realistic. Keynes, *The General Theory*, p. 51, n. 1.

[2] Modern Neo-keynesians, despite similarities in their growth models, are deriving their analysis from different Keynesian sources. Kaldor and Pasinetti are utilising Marshallian D_p and S_p conditions with market trans-actions occurring at D_p (at full employment). Since Kaldor essentially utilises demand prices as the market-clearing mechanism in his growth model, he can say 'I am not sure where "marginal productivity" comes into all this'. Productivity is relevant for the supply price and not the demand price. Joan Robinson, on the other hand, is emphasising the supply price aspect in her analysis of normal price on the rate of profit in economic growth at normal capacity. Thus, despite many similarities in the Kaldor-Pasinetti and Robinsonian Cambridge variants of growth models, there remain important differences. For example the Robinson analysis is much more involved with the relationship of technology, the money wage, and profit margins (the degree of monopoly) to 'normal' (i.e. supply) price. These items are virtually ignored in Kaldor-Pasinetti type growth models for ultimately Kaldor associates his growth model with a situation where price is determined at a point where the Marshallian demand curve inter-sects the perfectly inelastic portion of the firm's short-run flow-supply schedule. (See N. Kaldor, 'Economic Growth and the Problems of Infla-tion', *Economica*, 1959, pp. 220, 295–6.)

economic scheme in an essential and peculiar manner, Keynes purposely fitted 'technical monetary detail . . . into the background'.[1] With the supression of monetary detail, there concomitantly followed the playing down of uncertainty and incomplete information in *The General Theory* compared to the *Treatise*, for money enormously enlarges the deleterious power of uncertainty.

If Keynes's real contribution in *The General Theory* was to show that if savings are not offset by legitimate investment outlets, failure to generate a high level of employment will follow, then in winning the battle of Say's law in his 1936 volume, Keynes may have underplayed the complexities of monetary market phenomena through an oversimplified monetary analysis.

Acutally, Ohlin, with D. H. Robertson always (for company) in pursuit, was quick to seize upon the deficiencies of the truncated monetary analysis of *The General Theory*. Under their hammering, Keynes was forced to retreat and confess the incompleteness of his work in a series of exchanges in the *Economic Journal*.[2] As Keynes had already developed a more powerful and complete monetary analysis in his *Treatise*, he was immediately able to moderate his liquidity preference arguments to encompass the needs of finance, and thereby to respond to his critics with what he characterised as the 'coping-stone of the liquidity theory.' In essence, Keynes was merely restoring the theory of bearishness and the demand for capital goods as elaborated in the *Treatise* into consistency and orderliness with his liquidity preference apparatus.

Rather than a coping stone, Keynes's 1937 finance motive discussion is the Rosetta stone which makes possible the deciphering of the ancient *Treatise* hieroglyphics into modern post-keynesian terminology. In attempting to analyse the role of money in the real, non-golden age, world of economic growth, one becomes even more aware of the defects of the truncated monetary approach of *The General Theory* as against the perspicacity and elaboration of the *Treatise*'s analysis of the interrelations of commodity and security markets, and the roles

[1] Keynes, *The General Theory*, p. vii.
[2] The Ohlin, Robertson, and Keynes exchanges appear on numerous pages of the 1937 and 1938 issues of *The Economic Journal*.

played by the various financial institutions in securities markets which Keynes tends to dismiss as mere 'technical detail' in *The General Theory*. Since the *Treatise* is an analysis of 'an economy on the move', while the latter volume emphasises static equilibrium, much insight can be derived by restructuring the bearishness concepts of the *Treatise* with the more widely used classificatory scheme of *The General Theory*.

Given the deliberate ensconcement of detailed monetary analysis in *The General Theory*, it is not surprising that, thirty years after the Great Depression, the efficacy of monetary policy in promoting economic growth had been viewed, as Professor Samuelson pointed out, with scepticism by a significant portion of the academic 'Keynesian' majority of the economics establishment.[1] It will be the objective of the historical model developed below to provide a simple analysis of capital accumulation by blending the stock and flow elements in the demand and supply of (1) real capital, (2) money, and (3) securities (which are essential features of the analytical structure of the *Treatise*), with the more familiar principles and concepts of effective demand developed in *The General Theory*. Within such a framework it is possible to provide more perspective on the interplay among the organised security exchanges, corporate financing policy; investment underwriters, and the banking system in channelling the financial funds necessary for capital accumulation. Regretably this is an analysis which is virtually ignored in most 'analytical' post-keynesian models. That Keynes did not wish to ignore the financial market institutions is evident from the inclusion of Chapter 12 in *The General Theory*. Nevertheless, he considered these aspects a 'digression' which was 'on a different level of abstraction from most of this book'. While the literary content of this chapter gets high marks for brilliance, and the reader is struck by many telling phrases, the analytic portion is slim. No

---

[1] P. A. Samuelson, 'A Brief Survey of Post Keynesian Developments', in *Keynes' General Theory Reports of Three Decades*, ed. R. Lekachman (New York: St. Martin's Press, 1964) pp. 341–2. Recently, Friedman has capitalised on the 'Keynesian's' myopic analysis of Keynes's own position and he has usurped Keynes's own motto that 'money enters into the economic scheme in an essential and peculiar manner'. [Keynes, *General Theory*, p. vii] i.e. money matters.

wonder discussions of financial institutions and their impact on the economy have flowed primarily from the pens of non-keynesian scholars. Yet monetary institutions are an integral part of the real economy and a model which assumes that the monetary sector passively accommodates to the real forces must be unrealistic.

Now that over three decades have passed, it is due time that Keynesian economists were weaned from the molly-coddling liquid of liquidity preference and imbibed the stronger distillations of the *Treatise*, including its real 'non-golden' age disequilibrium approach to dynamic change.

CHAPTER 3

An Overview of Pricing and Production

BEFORE developing in detail some crucial aspects of the behavioural pattern of entrepreneurs and households, it is well to provide an overview of the workings of the historical model. For expository ease, the analysis can be initially divided into two parts: (1) the production and pricing decisions of entrepreneurs and (2) the monetary and financial relationships. In the initial discussion of Chapters 3, 4, and 5 money matters will be intentionally suppressed by assuming that entrepreneurs experience no difficulty financing any level of production they deem appropriate. In Chapters 6, 7, 8, and 9 monetary phenomena and financial institutions will be in the forefront of the analysis while real sector decisions will be relegated to a subordinate position. Finally, in the latter chapters of the book, both the monetary and real sectors will receive equal billing.

I. NEOCLASSICAL v. NEO-KEYNESIAN PRODUCTION AND PRICING DECISIONS

Our historical model assumes the existence of a monetary, market-oriented economy where production and investment activities are organised by firms acting individually, while households are the consumers of goods. These activities set up forces which interact in the market-place.

At any point of time the entrepreneur inherits a stock of capital goods from the past. This stock embodies the consequences of misguided investments made in the past. The producer, utilising this capital stock, can estimate the cost of output for various rates of flow of output over a time period which is 'the shortest interval after which the firm is free to revise its decision as to how much employment to offer'.[1] The producer must also estimate expected total revenue from the sale of these various alternative outputs.

The estimated costs for this production period have been typically viewed as falling into two categories: (1) *prime costs* which vary with output, e.g. money-wage costs, raw material and liquid capital costs, user costs of (fixed) capital equipment, and the costs of entrepreneurial effort associated with different flows of production; and (2) *fixed or supplementary costs* which do not vary with the level of output, i.e. the excess of expected annual depreciation over the user costs of capital, interest charges and other fixed charges which arise from legal contractual obligations of firms, and the normal remuneration of the owners, where the latter is a sum based on some 'normal' or expected return (or annual sum) on the net finance provided by the owners which is now embodied in the current stock of capital. This normal return is, according to Keynes, determined by the current rate of interest on loans of comparable term and risk reckoned as a percentage of the cost of the existing equipment.[2] In reality this annual sum is 'normal' only in the sense that if in any given period only this amount is left as a residual from sales revenue, *and if no changes in supply and demand conditions are expected in the future*, then there would be no market incentive to alter current production and capital stocks levels. Of course, if changes are expected, then current production and capital stock decisions will be altered even if only normal profits are currently earned.

Accordingly if, after settling all the other costs, sufficient sales proceeds are realised to just meet this normal return, at the output level decided on by the entrepreneur, then there would be no reason for the entrepreneur to alter his production decision, if he were free to relive the experiment. This normal profit is equivalent to a non-contractual short-period fixed cost (fixed as long as the net finance of owners are fixed) which is required to be left over after *all other costs* have been deducted from the expected sales revenues, if the production decision is to prove to be worthwhile. Moreover, if this expected normal return is not realised, then to the extent that current returns affect long-term expectations about future returns on the

[1] Keynes, *The General Theory*, p. 47.   [2] ibid., p. 68.

committed finance, entrepreneurs will be provoked to refuse to undertake either any further net investment or even re-placement investment in the enterprise.[1]

If on the other hand, a more than normal return is realised, then to the extent realised surprise in short-term expectations colours long-term expectations, net investment will be en-couraged. Finally, if normal profits are just being realised, and long-term expectations are based on the expected continuance of this result, then, by definition, only replacement investment will be undertaken.

To understand the production and hiring decision, it is essential to stipulate explicitly the factors which motivate entrepreneurial behaviour, for in a market-oriented, monetary economy it is the carrying out of enterpreneurial resource-hiring decisions which ultimately drives the economic system. At the beginning of each production period, entrepreneurial behaviour can be summarised via the firm's short-run flow-supply or offer-price schedule. This schedule indicates the minimum expected market price which would induce the firm to produce any given volume of output for sale during the period. Which components of the aforementioned costs enter into the short-run flow-supply price depends on the factors that motivate the entrepreneur. If, as is often assumed in neoclassical economic analysis, the producer is a short-run profit maximiser *and* if he does not value the entrepreneurial effort or already committed finance necessary to bring forth any level of output, then the short-run flow-supply price will, in a competitive economy, depend solely on the marginal prime costs of materials, labour, and user costs. This is the view of short-period supply prices adopted by Keynes in *The General Theory*,[2] and underlies the supply schedule in Fig. 2.2 of Chapter 2.

If, on the other hand, entrepreneurs offer to undertake production commitments while recognising they will not know what the level of sales will actually be until near the end of the period, then rational behaviour may be associated with

[1] Of course, they may attempt to move to another line in which they expect to earn normal profits. If, however, in the aggregate, entrepreneurs cannot conceive of lines which will generate normal profits, then the economy will decline.   [2] ibid., p. 68.

choosing some target return on standard volume. In a world of uncertainty, firms may find that experimenting with offer price changes to obtain knowledge about the revenue conditions necessary to maximise profits in each period may be very costly. Moreover they recognise that historical evidence may no longer be relevant. Under such conditions, adherence to a conventional mark-up over costs which is expected to yield a normal return for some expected or target level of output is readily understandable.[1]

If this behaviour is practiced by entrepreneurs, then the short-period flow-supply price would include 'a more or less definite rate of profits on turnover which is regarded as a 'fair' or normal rate'.[2] If this rate of profit on *turnover* or profit margin is included in the supply price and if the expected demand conditions are realised, the result will be to provide entrepreneurs with the normal rate of profit on the finance committed in that class.[3] In opposition to what is taught as the usual neoclassical position, Marshall cautioned that if entrepreneurs were willing to offer to supply a given flow of output at a price which did not include this rate of return on turnover, 'they could hardly prosper'. This neo-neoclassical view of short-period flow-supply price, which originates in Marshall's *Principles* was adopted by Keynes in his *Treatise* and underlies supply schedule of Fig. 2.1 of Chapter 2. It has also been adopted by modern Neo-keynesians such as Kaldor and Joan Robinson, and even some Cambridge, Massachusetts, scholars – at least the Harvard Square variety.[4]

According to the modern neo-keynesian (neo-marshallian?) scholars such as Kaldor, the short-period supply curve of the firm will include '. . . whatever the state of demand . . . a *minimum margin of profits* which we may call the degree of

[1] M. Fleming, *Introduction to Economic Analysis* (London: Allen and Unwin, 1969) pp. 91–5. Also see S. Weintraub, *Price Theory* (New York: Pitman, 1949).

[2] A. Marshall, *Principles of Economics*, 8th ed. (London: Macmillan, 1950) p. 617.   [3] ibid., p. 617.

[4] For example, see N. Kaldor, 'Economic Growth and the Problem of Inflation', *Economica* (1959); J. Robinson, *Essays in the Theory of Economic Growth*; O. Eckstein and G. Fromm, 'The Price Equation', *American Economic Review* (1968) and J. Robinson, 'A Reconsideration of the Theory of Value', *Collected Economic Papers*, III (Oxford: Blackwells, 1966) p. 179.

monopoly or market imperfection, or whatever we like'.[1] Thus, assuming that average and marginal prime costs are constant until capacity is reached, Kaldor draws the short-period flow-supply schedule of the firm, as determined by the 'degree of monopoly' as the line S_pS in Fig. 3.1. In this figure, the MC, APC, and ATC curves are the marginal prime costs, average prime costs, and average total costs (including 'normal' profits) cost curves of the representative firm.

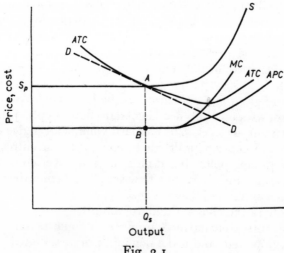

Fig. 3.1

The neo-keynesian entrepreneur can be viewed as attempting to estimate at what level of output buyers would be normally willing to pay a price per unit just equal to ATC. Thus, for example, if the representative entrepreneur expects that, in the current period, he offers to sell the commodity at a price of AQ_s, buyers will be willing to place orders for a quantity equal to Q_s, i.e. he expects to be facing the dotted demand curve DD in Fig. 3.1. Since this is the only price-output combination at which he can expect to cover average total costs,[2] he sets

[1] Kaldor, 'Economic Growth', *Economica* (1959) p. 217.
[2] If the expected demand curve intersects the ATC curve at more than one production flow-level, the entrepreneur will choose between these alternatives on the basis of some criteria such as maximising the production and sales, given the normal profit target.

Q_s as his standard volume. Hence, until the entrepreneur makes his pricing and standard volume decision based on his estimate of market demand, the ATC curve can be conceived of as depicting alternative price and production combinations which, given prime costs, will yield a normal profit on the net finance committed.

In sum, the Q_s will be his *standard* or *target volume* which will be expected to yield a 'normal' profit on the total finance committed and embodied in the existing capital stock. Accordingly he will set a *unit gross profit margin* of AB over average prime costs in making his supply offer. Consequently, the neo-keynesian entrepreneur's short-period flow-supply curve is S_pS. It will be perfectly elastic until capacity is reached as long as the prices of the factors that enter into prime costs are constant.

Accordingly, the ATC curve can be conceived as the curve which shows potential neo-keynesian flow-supply prices for any given output level, *until* standard volume for a given short-run production period is decided upon. Once the entrepreneur adopts a pricing policy based on a mark-up over costs at standard volume, the short run flow-supply schedule becomes a curve such as S_pS and, below capacity, it will intersect the ATC curve only at the chosen standard volume.

If the entrepreneur then produces standard volume (Q_s) during the period, and if the demand price associated with Q_s turns out to exceed the supply price at Q_s, then market conditions during the period could have permitted firms to realise more than normal returns. When the firm collects enough information to discover that demand price exceeds supply price, and if the firm expects this situation to continue, then there is an upward revision of long-term expectation of future returns and therefore income maximising entrepreneurs will increase their demand for capital goods.[1]

The neo-keynesian flow-supply price schedule will take into

[1] Cf. Kaldor, 'Economic Growth . . .' pp. 219–20. This view of the relationship between short-period supply and demand price is, according to Kaldor, 'perfectly consistent with Marshallian orthodoxy – looking at it as a *short-period* theory of distribution'. Kaldor insists, however, that equilibrium growth can occur only if demand intersects the inelastic segment of the short-period flow supply schedule.

account not only direct labour and material costs but also a profit margin which will provide sufficient revenue to cover a normal profit level at some expected flow of output for the short period. This expected output flow is referred to as 'normal capacity' by Joan Robinson, or 'standard volume of output' by Eckstein and Fromm. This standard volume-target return pricing approach has been found to be the predominant method used by management in such major industries as aluminium, automobiles, chemicals, and steel.[1]

A comparison of the underlying cost base of the neo-keynesian and neoclassical flow-supply prices indicates the possibility of different flow-supply responses, for any given expected price, from neo-keynesian and neoclassical entrepreneurs depending on the information they have about the type of market they operate in, in an uncertain world. In a 'produce to order' market where each sale is negotiable neoclassical behaviour may be rational, but in the case where all output is either offered or produced in anticipation of market, the neo-keynesian view would be more appropriate. In either case, however, a unique short-run supply representing the relationship between flow-supply prices and supply quantities can be developed, given the state of the arts, the inherited stock of capital, the prices of hired factors of production, and the motivational attitudes of entrepreneurs.[2]

In either case, the representative firm can then estimate its *required sales proceeds* for each rate of flow of output from a given plant by multiplying the expected short-run flow-supply price by its associated supply quantity.[3] This expected required sales proceeds (i.e. the revenue which would just make any output flow worthwhile) will obviously be different, for any

[1] W. Adams, *The Structure of American Industry*, 3rd ed. (New York: Macmillan, 1961).

[2] In the real world, cases of either near perfect information or an almost complete lack of information about market conditions are rare. Instead, entrepreneurs operate in a shadowy world of intuition, order taking, bunch processing, etc. and are likely to exhibit aspects of both types of behaviour – although as a stylised fact – the neo-keynesian mode appears more realistic.

[3] This is equivalent to points on the aggregate supply curve for the economy. For example of the derivation see P. Davidson and E. Smolensky, *Aggregate Supply*, Chapter 9 including Appendix; and S. Weintraub, *An Approach to the Theory of Income Distribution* (Phila.: Chilton, 1958) ch. 2.

output flow, if the entrepreneur is a full-cost standard volume producer than if he is a neoclassical short-period profit maximiser. In other words, for any given expectations about demand, the supply response will differ depending on the behavioural characteristics of entrepreneurs.

Given his expectations of demand conditions in the type of market he sells his wares, the entrepreneur, whether displaying neoclassical or neo-keynesian behavioural principles, estimates expected sales proceeds for each potential rate of output per period and compares this expected revenue estimate (the equivalent of the aggregate demand) with the expected required sales proceeds (the equivalent of aggregate supply) for each possible output plan. The entrepreneur will then set his production schedule at the target level of output where expected sales revenue equals required sales proceeds and he offers the output at this point of expected effective demand at a unit price equal to the flow-supply price.

In essence, therefore, the neoclassical profit-maximising firm is operating under a behavioural pattern which permits the short-run supply price to differ significantly from the long-run supply price. For an entrepreneur exhibiting this behavioural pattern, the short-run supply price will equal the long-run supply price coincidently only if (1) the excess of marginal prime costs over average prime costs at the point of expected effective demand is equal to the sum of the average supplementary, risk, and interest costs. Of course, when in some past period, the neoclassical entrepreneur undertook the purchase of construction of his equipment (i.e. when he made the investment decision), he fully expected the excess of marginal over average prime costs to cover these sums. Nevertheless, these original expectations which led the firm to acquire the capital equipment are not relevant, in the neoclassical scheme, for deciding the scale of current production.[1]

The neo-keynesian view of the representative 'full cost' producer, on the other hand, implies that the short-run flow-supply price will equal the long-run supply price *at the point of expected effective demand* (standard volume). If at the point of expected effective demand, demand price is actually greater (less than) flow-supply price, and if the short-run flow-supply

[1] See Keynes, *The General Theory*, pp. 47, 68.

price is the offer price at which suppliers will accept all orders from buyers, then the quantity demanded (D_q) will exceed (fall short of) the quantity produced at standard volume (S_q) and either inventory changes or non-price rationing (e.g. lengthening of promised delivery date) must occur. On the other hand if at standard volume $D_p \gtrless S_p$, and market clearing prices are permitted to rule, then the actual market price will differ from the long-run supply price.[1]

In reality, many manufactured products as well as most services are sold at the short-run supply or offer price of the firm rather than at market-clearing prices. In fact, market-clearing prices are likely to occur only in markets for durables which have exceedingly high carrying costs, or in spot markets for secondhand commodities which are standardised. If both spot and a forward market exists for a commodity, then the spot market is ruled by market-clearing demand prices, while the forward market is dominated by flow-supply considerations.[2]

The traditional neoclassical short-run profit maximiser, who ignored user costs and viewed his marginal factor costs as the prime determinant of his short-run flow-supply schedule tends to be the creation of a Walrasian general equilibrium view of the world. In contrast, in his *Principles*, Marshall argued that 'the true marginal supply price for short periods . . . is nearly always above, and generally very much above the special or prime costs for raw material, labour and wear-and-tear of plant which is immediately and directly involved by getting a little further use out of appliances which are not fully employed'.[3] Both Marshall and Kaldor believe that the view that

[1] In 'produce to anticipation of' markets, it is only nondurable goods which may be thrown on the market to be sold at its demand price (e.g. day-old bread, fashion-oriented goods at the end of a season) for these goods are sold in essentially spot markets. If the good is durable or if sales tomorrow are related to prices today, then user costs will enter today's offer price consideration. In other words, even in the Marshallian market period, when goods are offered for sale (on a spot market), the supplier, if he is a 'going-concern' will never sell shelf-inventory for less than the current flow-supply price of replacement less carrying costs.

[2] This will be developed in Chapter 4.

[3] Marshall, *Principles of Economics*, pp. 374–5. Keynes, in *The General Theory*, occupied a middle ground between the simplistic neoclassical view and the neo-keynesian approach for he permitted user costs to affect profit margins.

the short-run supply price should only cover marginal prime costs, *whatever the state of demand,* is a myopic one – for it does not take into account the impact that a current offer price significantly below the long-run supply price will have on future market demand. Real world producers are, according to Marshall and Kaldor, more perceptive than their Walrasian neoclassical counterparts in recognizing the possibility, in a world of uncertainty, of intertemporally related demand for a product so that a depressed current price will induce consumer resistance to higher prices in the future – a phenomenon which is labelled as 'spoiling the market'.[1]

In the real world, where producers operate under technological conditions and institutional rules (e.g. severance pay, contributions to unemployment funds, etc.) in which steady flows of production per period are less costly than temporarily varying production flows with every sale, and where producers tender offer prices to buyers for forward delivery while such offers are accepted on a stochastic basis, producers will have a cost incentive to adopt a target return on a standard volume pricing procedure and use bunch processing, delivery delays, and inventory variations to operate as buffers in the short run.

A Walrasian general equilibrium approach to price determination, on the other hand, either ignores time entirely in that it assumes that prices are set only with regard to current demand and perfectly inelastic resource endowment availability; or, if time is explicitly introduced, all future prices are assumed to be known currently and with complete certainty, and these future prices are independent of the current market price. Thus, in the neoclassical Walrasian approach, the analysis of entrepreneurial behaviour which takes time into account is nugatory.

[1] Spoiling the market implies that if the demand curve is temporarily depressed, then though the demand curve might shift out in the next period, the customers will display a very elastic response to any price increase over the current price. Accordingly, the opportunity cost of reduced future earnings as a result of offering current output at a price that will only cover marginal direct costs can be so significant as to make it 'unprofitable' to pursue such a profit-maximising policy. The neoclassical view implicitly assumes that present prices cannot affect future elasticity responses. In *The General Theory*, Keynes would permit 'spoiling the market' to enter into price offers via the user cost concept.

Whether real world entrepreneurs act in a manner which resembles neoclassical profit maximising behaviour or the Marshallian–neo-keynesian target return pricing behaviour is, therefore, not only a matter of empirical fact but is also a matter of logical reaction to the type of market a producer operates in and the institutions which are available to him to share the burdens of uncertainty when the future is unpredictable and expectations about tomorrow affect what is produced today. Nevertheless, for any situation, the effects on pricing production, income distribution, and even investment differ significantly for each behaviour pattern. Consequently, since different economic models assume different entrepreneurial behaviour patterns, the logical implications of these alternative modes of response will be traced out in the analysis of production and pricing decisions which follows.

II. TWO POSSIBLE OUTCOMES – REALISATION v. SURPRISE FOR SHORT-PERIOD EXPECTATIONS

Once production commitments are made, events will prove whether the representative entrepreneur's short term expectations are realised or not. To the extent that sales realisations are the basis of future short term *and* long term expectations,[1] Table 3.1 compares the responses that neoclassical and neo-keynesian entrepreneurs will exhibit to either correct or surprised expectations. In Table 3.1, D_p is the demand price, MC is marginal prime costs, S_p is the short-run flow-supply price, I is investment, ED is effective demand, Q_s is standard volume and $LRSP$ is the long-run supply price. For both neoclassical and neo-keynesian systems, unit $LRSP$ may be defined as

$$LRSP \equiv \frac{TPC}{Q} + \frac{TSP}{Q} \tag{1}$$

[1] In other words, when entrepreneurs' current realisations are used as the best estimate of next period's market conditions. If, on the other hand, growth is normally expected, then Table 3.1 should be interpreted as indicating entrepreneurial behaviour over and above what would be undertaken to meet the expected, 'normal' rate of growth (on the Harrod-type assumption that expectations about the normal *rate* of growth are inert with respect to current realisation).

where *TPC* is total prime costs, *TSP* is total supplementary costs, including normal profits or the expected annual return on

Table 3.1

ENTREPRENEURIAL EXPECTATIONS

Decision	Neoclassical Entrepreneur		Neo-keynesian Entrepreneur	
	Correct Short-Period Expectations	Disappointed Short-Period Expectations	Correct Short-Period Expectations	Disappointed Short-Period Expectations
Production	Unchanged	Expand if realised $D_p > MC$ Contract if realised $D_p < MC$	Unchanged	Expand if realised $D_p > S_p$ Contract if realised $D_p < S_p$
Investment	No Unique Solution Net $I \gtrless 0$, if realised $D_p \gtrless LRSP$		Net $I = 0$	Net $I \gtrless 0$, if realised $D_p \gtrless LRSP$, i.e. realised $ED \gtrless Q_s$

the net finance provided, and Q is the flow-quantity. Normal profits is, as has already been discussed, the opportunity cost of the net finance provided by owners.

A Correct Guess as to the Point of Effective Demand

If the entrepreneur guesses the point of effective demand correctly, then expected and actual sales revenues will equal required sales proceeds, and as Table 3.1 suggests, the firm will be in short-period equilibrium and the entrepreneur, be he neoclassical or neo-keynesian, will continue to produce the same amount each period if he expects future short-run supply and demand conditions to remain unchanged.

If he is a neo-keynesian entrepreneur, however, then he will be just earning his long-run supply price, so that as long as he assumes future demand conditions, technology and factor prices are expected to remain unchanged, he will merely maintain his capital stock, while if he expects to grow at some rate, he will undertake net investment at a rate which he believes will maintain both short-run and long-run equilibrium in the sense of earning a normal profit sum on net finance each period. Thus, in any neo-keynesian model, if entrepreneurs' expectations are being proved correct by events, growth can occur *only* if entrepreneurs expect tomorrow to be different from today so that although the existing stock of capital is optimal for today's events, a change will be necessary if it is to prove optimal tomorrow. Thus for example, Harrod's conception of warranted rate of growth as an equilibrium growth path implies that the 'animal spirits' of entrepreneurs will make them believe that next period's demand will be sufficiently greater than this period so that it will be profitable to install additional capital.[1]

For the neoclassical entrepreneur in short-period equilibrium, there is, as Table 3.1 suggests, no necessary relationship between realised profits and his normal return where the latter is defined as the annual profit that is expected to be made on net finance currently being invested.

Thus, in a neoclassical model there is no unique relationship between correctly anticipated short-term expectations and the long-run growth of the firm. Instead it is usually assumed that if the current realised profit is less than the expected profits on net investment, then, to the extent that these low earnings colour entrepreneurial views about the future earnings potential of the existing capital stock, this lower earnings expectations will be capitalised into the market or notional value of existing equipment. Accordingly, if the same level of gross profits minus depreciation is expected to be earned in future years, then a 'normal' profit will be earned on the downward revised notional value of existing equipment, as the owners take a once for all capital loss. The spot market price or notional value of

[1] In a conversation (31 January 1969) Harrod indicated that the warranted rate of growth occurs when entrepreneurs correctly foresee the point of effective demand each period *and* the supply price includes a normal return on standard volume. Consequently if the economy is on a warranted growth path it must mean that although at any point of time the existing stock of capital is optimal for this period's demand, the 'animal spirits' of entrepreneurs will suggest demand next period will be greater and therefore additional capital will be needed.

Joan Robinson, on the other hand, has argued that the economy will be on the warranted rate of growth path only if realised effective demand keeps 'the stock of plant over-utilised to just that extent as it grows' (see J. Robinson, *Essays in Economic Growth*, p. 84). Over-utilisation of capacity, however, would be characteristic of a situation where the neo-keynesian entrepreneur's expectations were too low, so that the system was in disequilibrium. Harrod agrees that over-utilisation means disequilibrium, and that this would be an extra stimulus to actual growth, over and above the projection of growth in demand due to animal spirits. (Kaldor, on the other hand, assumes that over-utilisation of capacity, at each moment of time, is an essential characteristic of a moving equilibrium growth model. See Kaldor, 'Economic Growth', p. 220.)

the equipment should now be less than replacement costs,[1] so that there will be no incentive to provide additions to facilities, and even replacement will be curtailed.[2] A similar mechanism would be implied for a neo-keynesian entrepreneur if he was in short-period *dis*-equilibrium.

The writing down of existing facilities can be viewed as reducing the stock demand schedule for capital goods, and given the flow supply conditions in the capital goods industry, the result is a decline in the output of the capital goods industry. If there are diminishing returns in the capital goods industry, then the decline in output results in an expected rate of return on those new capital goods actually produced (computed as the ratio of expected lower gross profits minus depreciation to the value of newly produced capital goods, where the latter is valued at a lower flow supply price than before) equal to 'nor, mal' profits, unless the total stock of capital is so redundant-that gross investment falls to zero. In the latter case, the market price of existing capital goods falls below the minimum flow-supply price of the capital goods industry, and the capital goods industry will not start up again until either the redundancy has been worked off, or expectations improve.

If, on the other hand, in the neoclassical model the resulting market price at the correctly estimated point of effective demand is greater than the long-run supply price, then the realised current rate of profit will be greater than the normal or expected rate of profit on finance embedded in past investment. This leads to a writing up of the existing facilities (if the higher earnings colours expectations about the future), so that the notional or spot market value of current plant exceeds the replacement costs of plant (valued at current flow supply prices). This increases the demand for capital goods and encourages

---

[1] Replacement cost is defined as the valuation of replacement of present (net) plant with currently produced capital goods of equal efficiency at the current short-run flow-supply price of capital goods (see Keynes, *The General Theory*, p. 71). This aspect will be discussed in more detail in Chapter 4 below.

[2] Of course if the entrepreneur expects growth in demand, and if these long-term growth prospects are inert with respect to current realisations then this expectation would offset some of the drop in the spot value that would occur if current disappointment was merely capitalised into the future potential earnings of the capital stock.

capital production to expand, so that with higher flow supply prices, higher gross profit expectations lead to expected 'normal' profits on net investment.

Incorrect Expectations About the Point of Effective Demand

If entrepreneurs incorrectly guess the point of effective demand, then whether the entrepreneur behaves like a neoclassical short-period profit maximiser or a neo-keynesian 'full-cost' producer, his decision to produce a given flow of output, Q_s, and offer it for sale at the short-run flow supply price of S_p will bring forth surprise.[1] When the firm brings the production flow to market, the producer finds that at the quoted flow-supply price, the quantity demanded (D_q) exceeds (is less than) the quantity supplied (S_q). Alternatively, the producer may view the situation as one where if he provides the Q_s output the demand price (D_p) exceeds (falls short of) the flow-supply price (S_p).

In this case of an incorrect guess about sales revenues – the correctness of the guess is determined by a stochastic process – the producer has three possible alternative market period solutions which he may adopt. These are: (1) continue to charge the supply price allowing inventories to adjust the discrepancy between D_q and S_q; (2) charge the market clearing (D_p) price for the standard volume rather than the supply price and obtain a windfall profit or loss on sales; or (3) charge the flow-supply price and allow the size of queues (i.e. the length of the delivery period) to change. In the real world, market situations compatible with any of these market period solutions may be found. In part, the solution adopted will depend on such factors as (a) the durability of the product and the expected qualitative homogeneity between future and current products, (b) institutional arrangements in the particular market and (c) legal and/or customary views on 'fair' bargaining procedures between buyers and sellers in a period of dis-equilibrium.

---

[1] If neoclassical profit maximising behaviour is only associated with 'custom building' and *if each supply price is negotiated* separately and secretly, then the entrepreneur can never be 'disappointed' about his estimated revenues unless the buyer defaults on his contract to purchase. Since, however, profit maximising behaviour is usually associated with 'produce to market' neoclassical models, neoclassical entrepreneurs can be surprised by realised sales-proceeds.

Whatever the entrepreneur's market period solution, to the extent that realisations affect current short-term and long-term expectations, entrepreneurs will reassess their production and investment decisions.

Before discussing the market period adjusting mechanisms in some detail it will be useful to illustrate with the aid of Fig. 3.2 how surprise can alter the short-period production and employment decisions.

In Fig. 3.2 the aggregate supply function (Z) shows how much sales proceeds entrepreneurs would require for any given level of employment to make them believe the resources commitment was worthwhile, while the aggregate demand function (D) indicates how much buyers would spend at any level of

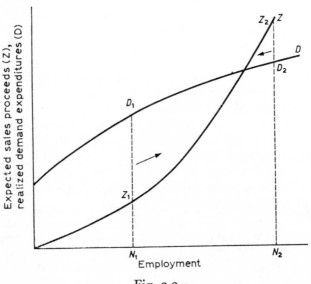

Fig. 3.2

employment.[1] Suppose at a given point of time, entrepreneurs expected sales of Z_1 (in Fig. 3.2). They would hire N_1 workers to produce a certain flow of output. If the N_1 workers are hired, however, then the total sum that all buyers would want to

[1] For a complete discussion of the derivation of the aggregate supply and demand functions, see Davidson and Smolensky, *Aggregate Supply*, chs. 9 and 10.

spend would be D_1,[1] which would exceed entrepreneurial expectations, so that entrepreneurs would be pleasantly surprised by realisations. Thus as Keynes notes, 'there will be an incentive to entrepreneurs to increase employment . . . and, if necessary, to raise costs by competing with one another for the factors of production'.[2]

In a similar manner, if entrepreneurs had expected sales proceeds of Z_2, they would have hired N_2 workers and would have been disappointed when sales realisations came out to be only D_2.[3] This disappointment would induce employers to cut back on production and hiring of decisions.

Surprise, Disequilibrium, and Market Period Adjustments
1. *The Inventory Adjustment Case.*[4] In this case, the producer maintains the flow of output at standard volume in the short-period and offers this output to buyers at the short-period flow supply price of S_p. The discrepancy between the demand quantity (D_q) and the supply quantity (S_q) is made up by accumulation or the running down of inventories from their expected levels. Thus in the case where D_q exceeds S_q, total realised sales revenue covers required sales proceeds on the production of Q_s *plus* the unexpected sales revenue on inventory. To the extent that this unexpected additional revenue alters short-term expectations about future market demand it will induce entrepreneurs to expand production from existing facilities. Moreover if this excess demand at S_p is expected to continue

[1] At this stage, aggregate demand price can be interpreted as either equal to the product of the quantity demanded by the buyers multiplied by flow-supply price $(=D_q S_p)$, or as the product of the demand price times the supply quantity $(=D_p S_q)$. Although there is no necessity for $D_q S_p$ to $=D_p S_q$, if aggregate demand exceeds aggregate supply both $D_p S_q$ and $D_q S_p$ will exceed $S_p S_q$. Whether D_1 will equal $D_q S_p$ or $D_p S_q$ will depend on entrepreneurial behaviour in the market period when disequilibrium occurs.

[2] Keynes, *The General Theory*, p. 25.

[3] In this case, D_2 can be equal to either $D_q S_p$ or $D_p S_q$, both will be less than $S_p S_q$.

[4] In *The General Theory*, Keynes believed that the inventory adjustment case was the most realistic solution. (See ch. 5, especially 51 n.) Logically inventory adjustments are essential adjuncts to 'produce in anticipation' of sales and therefore are more likely to be associated with neo-keynesian behaviour.

for a sufficient number of periods in the future then the neo-keynesian entrepreneur will be induced to expand facilities if these long-term expectations indicate that future returns will be able to cover normal profits on additional financial commitments.

If the neoclassical producer finds himself in a position where at the going market price $D_q > S_q$, then whether he will make any net investment or not will depend on whether his revised short-term expectations of higher future sales proceeds involve expanding output into a scale of production where either (i) diminishing returns (of the classical variety) involving homogeneous short-period variable input factors occur; or (ii) hiring path diminishing returns occurs – that is, where expansion requires hiring substantial quantities of less efficient heterogeneous labour inputs all of whom will be paid equal time rates, or (iii) the costs of searching out or training further labour inputs will be substantial; or finally (iv) the anticipated increased demand for labour by all entrepreneurs is expected to increase the time rate of remuneration for all labour inputs in the future.

If either cases (i), (ii), or (iii) occur, neoclassical entrepreneurs will anticipate higher short-run supply prices at the expected higher levels of effective demand. These expected short-run supply prices will tend to exceed the long-run supply price (in this area of rapidly increasing costs) as the spread between expected marginal and average prime costs increase. Accordingly there will be an incentive to increase investment.

Moreover, in all these cases, if the cost of production at some future date is expected to rise above the present cost by an amount which will cover the cost of carrying a stock of goods produced now to the date of the prospective higher short-period flow-supply price, then entrepreneurs will have an inducement to increase their current inventories of all goods including equipment – and consequently there would be an increase in aggregate investment.[1]

The analysis of the inventory adjustment situation, when D_q is less than S_q, can now be handled in less detail. If the standard volume is produced while a flow-supply price is quoted in the market, the excess supply will be accumulated in inventories.

[1] This aspect will be discussed in Chapter 9.

As a result, the realised sales revenue will be less than the required sales revenue and this result will encourage the entrepreneur to cut back his production. Obviously, this will have an impact on the notional value of existing facilities, lowering the demand for capital goods and resulting in a decline in output in the capital goods industry.

The inventory adjustment case is most applicable to a going concern producing standardised goods with low carrying costs, and/or where the costs of temporarily altering production schedules are large.

2. *The Market-Clearing Case*. In this case, the producer, realising he has incorrectly forecast the point of effective demand, sells his already produced output at the demand price to clear the market.[1] This case is only likely for perishable goods, or durables that have seasonality and/or rapid obsolescence and very high carrying costs; or where demand tomorrow is not expected to be related to sales today; i.e. there is no 'spoiling the market', phenomenon. This is most likely to be the case of 'clearance sales' where either fashion obsolescence or model year change prevents intertemporal comparisons, or the cost of carrying the commodities till next period exceeds the expected cost from spoiling the market. There are no sales from (or additions to) inventories. If the realised demand price exceeds the short-run supply price, there will be windfall profits which can encourage the entrepreneur to expect higher future sales proceeds and he will expand production from existing facilities.[2] If this expansion carries the neoclassical producer into the area of rapidly increasing costs then, as before, there will be an incentive to expand facilities; while if the neo-keynesian entrepreneur expects future sales to cover normal profits on additional finance, he will undertake net investment.

---

[1] This is the case analysed by Keynes in his *Treatise on Money*, Vol. 1, ch. 10; also J. R. Hicks, *Critical Essays in Monetary Theory*, p. 191 and utilised by Kaldor, 'Economic Growth', pp. 219–20 and L. L. Pasinetti, 'Rate of Profit and Income Distribution in Relation to the Rate of Economic Growth', *Review of Economic Studies* (Oct 1962) p. 275.

[2] This redistribution towards profits because market prices rise relative to money wages plays an important role in Kaldor's theory of growth. (See N. Kaldor, 'Economic Growth', pp. 290, 294.) Keynes also believed that an increase in realised profits relative to costs could aid economic growth. (See J. M. Keynes, *Treatise on Money*, II 153–4, 162–3.)

If, on the other hand, the realised demand price is less than the supply price then to the extent realisations affect expectations, the firm will retrench in future periods.

3. *The Changing Queue Case.* In this case, the producer continues to charge the short-run flow-supply price for the product and permits the size of the queue or the delivery date to alter.[1] In these industries, entrepreneurs will, in general, offer the same supply price (non-negotiable) to all buyers in a class. This behaviour is likely to occur in industries where either (a) production is organised on a batch processing basis and/or (b) the cost of storing the product is exceedingly high. (Batch processing techniques tend to be adopted if there are huge economies involved in large production runs.)

For entrepreneurs in these industries the length of the queue will be an important determinant of expectations of future sales, and will therefore affect both employment and investment decisions.

III. SUMMARY

1. *Production and Investment Decisions by the Neoclassical Entrepreneur*

For the neoclassical short-period profit-maximising entrepreneur, the normal or expected return on finance enters into the long-run supply price of output but not into the short-run flow-supply price. Current *realised* profits will not equal normal profits as long as the short-run supply price does not equal the long-run supply price, *even if short-period expectations about effective demand are correct*! Hence, although normal profits enter into the investment decision for the neoclassical entrepreneur, they are not a determinant of pricing or production decisions. As Keynes noted in *The General Theory*, the current production decision in response to expected supply price does not depend on the original expectation of normal profits which led the firm to acquire the equipment and inventory it presently holds, i.e. the expectation of normal profits on past investment does not affect present short-period supply decisions. These decisions 'will be made, with reference indeed to this equip-

---

[1] Machine tools, airlines, automobiles, hotels, are some examples of industries which exhibit changing length of queues.

ment and stock, but in light of the *current* expectations *of prospective* costs and sales-proceeds.'[1]

It is the expected market price implicit in the expected future points of effective demand (where the latter is based on a projection of current market and cost conditions *and expected changes in these*) that is compared to the long-run supply price at the expected future points of effective demand that determines the demand for investment goods. For every difference between realisable demand price and long-run supply price which is projected into the future, there is some rate of investment which can bring the expected next period's short-run flow-supply price to equality with the long-run supply price of the annual output which will be expected to be forthcoming from next period's capital stock. It is this rate of investment which equates next period's expected short-run flow-supply price at standard volume with next period's long-run supply price which may be labelled the *expected* or *warranted rate of investment*. This warranted rate of investment is related to Harrod's capital-requirements concept, where the latter is defined as 'that addition to capital goods in any period which producers regard as ideally suited to the output which they are undertaking in the period.'[2]

The neoclassical analysis of the firm operating in the light of expectations in an uncertain world which has been presented in this chapter is similar to, but not identical with, the view put forth by Keynes in the Appendix to Chapter 6 of *The General Theory*. In this appendix, Keynes develops the short-period supply price as the 'sum of marginal factor cost and marginal user cost' which in co-ordination with expected demand, is the prime determinant of the entrepreneur's short-period production decision. For the investment decision, on the other hand, Keynes insists that the entrepreneur must expect to cover, at least, the long-period supply price of new capital goods, that is, the sum of the discounted revenue expected to be obtained from the output over the life of equipment must cover the present short-run flow-supply price of equipment *plus* the sum of discounted expected future factor

[1] Keynes, *The General Theory*, p. 47.
[2] R. F. Harrod, *Economic Essays* (New York: Harcourt, Brace, 1952) p. 260.

costs *plus* the sum of discounted annual amounts equal to 'the current rate of interest on loans of comparable term and risk reckoned as a percentage of the cost of [new] equipment.' In other words, the long-run supply price for any piece of equipment with an expected life of m years is expected to be just covered if

$$\sum_{n=1}^{m} DTR = S_p^k + \sum_{n=1}^{m} DTC + \sum_{n=1}^{m} DNP \tag{2}$$

where DTR is discounted expected future total revenue, S_p^k is present flow supply price of equipment, DTC is discounted expected future factor cost, and DNP is discounted annual normal profits (equal to a percentage of the initial cost, S_p^k, of the contemplated investment). [It is through the DNP term that the concept of 'normal profits' enters into the investment decision.]

In a world of uncertainty, different entrepreneurs – even in the same industry – may have different degrees of confidence in their ability to foresee the future. Thus, even if all entrepreneurs have the same expectation about the future points of effective demand, they may have different degrees of confidence in their visions and hence use different rates of discount. Accordingly, for some entrepreneurs a given project may appear profitable, while for others with the same view of future markets but less confidence, it may not.

Moreover, if entrepreneurs recognise that their ability to estimate future revenues for the later years of long-lived investments 'amounts to little and sometimes to nothing,'[1] then they will tend completely to discount the expected revenues from these distance years, and use some form of 'payout period' criteria where the total cost of the project, i.e. S_p^k, plus operating expenses, etc. must be covered by expected revenues in a certain period, or, in essence

$$\sum_{n=1}^{h} DTR = S_p^k + \sum_{n=1}^{h} DTC + \sum_{n=1}^{h} DNP \tag{3}$$

where h is the number of years in the payout period.

In sum, in any short period, producers in the capital goods industries will be producing a flow of output as each entre-

---

[1] Keynes, *The General Theory*, p. 150.

preneur who can obtain finance places orders for the delivery of capital goods until the left side of equation (2) or (3) is equal to the right side on the last piece of equipment he is willing to enter into a contract for. If, in the aggregate, entrepreneurs' expectations of the future sales revenues and costs are realised over time, then, in each period the economy will be undertaking its warranted rate of investment as it moves along on equilibrium growth path. Nevertheless, future events may prove that the current rate was not warranted, for in an uncertain world, past successes are no assurance of correct forecasts.

Production and Investment Decisions by the Neo-keynesian Entrepreneur

The neo-keynesian entrepreneur, as visualised by Marshall, Joan Robinson, Kaldor and Keynes of the *Treatise of Money*, has a somewhat different behavioural pattern than the simplistic neoclassical profit-maximiser. In essence, this neo-keynesian approach views the firm as a continuous operating unit which, at a minimum, expects to perpetuate itself over time in a 'produce and offer in anticipation of market' situation. Accordingly, these authors implicitly believe it would be foolish for entrepreneurs to ever commit any finance (for either fixed, working or liquid capital[1]) to produce output for anticipated sales if there were not an expected profit on the committed finance included in the short-period flow-supply or offer price of output. In other words, if the flow-supply price is to represent the minimum revenue required by an *on going* firm to make the contractual commitments for hiring inputs worthwhile, it must include a level of profits which the entrepreneur expects will compensate for the finance committed.

In essence, therefore, the neo-keynesian entrepreneur's short-period supply or offer price will include a term for profit on expected turnover so that if expectations are realised sales proceeds will just cover the long-run supply price. If the expected volume of purchases is realised, then the producer is in long-run and short-run equilibrium simultaneously, and *if* current expectations are for a continuing of the existing situation,

---

[1] The distinction between these forms of capital and their importance will be discussed in Chapter 4.

i.e. no growth of demand is expected, then of course there
will be no desire on the part of entrepreneurs to change production from existing facilities, nor to engage in any net investment.

Thus, in the neo-keynesian scheme, if current short-term
expectations are being realised, the only reason for change will
be if entrepreneurs expect that future demand and/or supply
conditions will be different in the future than they are currently;
i.e. that current long-run expectations anticipate that future
period's short-run sales expectations will differ from current
short-run realisation. Of course, since the Cambridge neo-
keynesian school is growth-oriented in its analysis, entrepreneurial 'animal spirits' become the prime motivator for growth,
when current expectations are being realised.

If, on the other hand, demand exceeds supply at standard
volume, then the neo-keynesian entrepreneur has under-
estimated the point of effective demand. If, in the market period,
the entrepreneur were to permit the market clearing demand
price to rule, then he would make windfall profits which (1)
to the extent it alters his current short-run expectations, will
induce the firm to expand production from given facilities,
and (2) to the extent it alters long-run expectations, will induce
him to undertake new net investment.

Kaldor argues that it is 'impossible to conceive of a moving
equilibrium of growth' under any other circumstances and
hence, in his view, over-utilisation of capacity is the prime
motivator, in conjunction with a demand price in excess of the
supply price at standard volume or normal capacity, in bringing about entrepreneurial decisions for accumulation.[1]

If, on the other hand, it is possible to suggest that in the face
of this excess demand, the neo-keynesian entrepreneur adheres
to his short-run flow-supply price in the market period, he will
have to either supply the excess demand from inventories or
extend the length of the queue for his product. To the extent
that this drawing down of inventories or lengthening of queues
alter short- and long-run expectations, the entrepreneur will
expand his production and investment commitments, as short-

---

[1] N. Kaldor, 'Economic Growth', p. 220. It is difficult, however, to understand why such a growth path should be termed a 'moving equilibrium'
when it requires that firms be out of equilibrium in each period.

run disequilibrium provides the impetus for growth.

Finally, if realised demand is less than supply at standard volume, then in the market period either (a) the market clearing price will be less than the flow-supply price and less than normal profits are realised, or (b) the entrepreneur adheres to his short-period flow-supply price while absorbing the excess in inventories or reducing the size of the queue. To the extent these results affect expectations then the producer will cut back production *and* revise downward the notional value of existing facilities, thus depressing the demand for capital schedule.

The Relation between Normal Profits and the Rate of Profit

Whether we use a neoclassical or neo-keynesian framework, it is true that the expected annual profit stream on any investment project viewed over its life (or its payout period) can be converted into an expected rate of profit on the cost of the investment, if one wishes to do such a mathematical calculation. This is true simply because the marginal efficiency of capital equation contains three unknowns – present cost, future profit stream, and a rate of discount – and given any two, the third may be elicited. This mathematical property has encouraged some economists into promoting the 'expected *rate* of profit' as the prime determinant of investment. In fact, Keynes in *The General Theory* (but not in *The Treatise*) tends to encourage such habits of exposition by first discussing the relationship between the prospective future profits of a capital asset and its supply price as the *marginal efficiency of capital* and then defining the marginal efficiency as equal to the rate of discount which makes the prospective yield equal to the supply price.

In recent years, however, the economic literature has shown that when the expected profit stream is not uniform over time, the solution of the marginal efficiency equation for the rate of discount may yield two or more roots. If this result is obtained for any given income stream and investment cost situation, then it is impossible to specify a unique rate of profit, and therefore one cannot associate a unique marginal efficiency or expected rate of profit with any given expected annual profit stream.[1] Such an ambiguous result should raise suspicion about any

[1] This is just another view of the now famous reswitching controversy.

economic model which makes the rate of profit a determinant of investment and economic growth.

What is relevant for any entrepreneurial investment decision is simply a present value calculation which *for any given minimum rate of discount*[1] and expected income streams of alternative projects will always yield a unique array for the value of alternative investment projects. It is this calculation of the present value or demand price of investment relative to the short-run flow-supply prices in the capital goods industry which determines investment spending *and* the choice of technique, if finance is available. An income maximising assumption about entrepreneurs does not require the computation of the expected rate of profit in choosing either technique or the rate of investment to undertake. It merely requires the computation of the absolute difference between expected net present value of output produced per unit of capital and the flow-supply price for the production of another unit of capital[2] and the desire of entrepreneurs to choose those projects which are expected to be most rewarding. This view of investment demand will be developed in the following chapters.

[1] This minimum rate of discount represents the annual sum on finance which entrepreneurs will require over the payout period in order to induce them to take on a long-term commitment which pre-empts future courses of action. This minimum discount rate is a function of the cost of finance *plus* a premium based on their subjective disutility of being surprised in the future. It can be different for each entrepreneur.

[2] Cf. Keynes, *The General Theory*, pp. 135, 186 n. 1, 187 n. 2, 3, 213; *Treatise on Money*, 1 202 ff. Assuming that all entrepreneurs use the same rate of discount, the (notional) spot price of all existing assets will *always* adjust themselves to changes in expectations about future streams of quasi-rents until the rate of profit expected in all lines of endeavour are equal. Hence prolonged discussions relating the demand for capital to the rate of profit are, as Keynes warned, likely to be circular and misleading.

CHAPTER 4

The Demand and Supply of Capital Goods — The Building Blocks of A Theory of Accumulation

'IT is by reason of the existence of durable equipment that the economic future is linked to the present . . . therefore . . . the expectations of the future should affect the present through the demand price for durable equipment'.[1] Any demand for investment goods, however, needs to be financed and hence, the stock of money (i.e. the inherited stock plus current creations) plays an important role in connecting entrepreneurial long-term expectations with current efforts to expand plant and equipment. These links between the irrevocable past, the present, and the uncertain future interact so that the present economic situation has an impact on the future, while anticipations about the future affect current economic behaviour. Thus, any discussion about expectations and current activity must, in an uncertain world, involve monetary phenomena. For expository simplicity, at the present stage, monetary phenomena will be suppressed by assuming that the monetary authorities provide whatever finance is required.[2]

TYPES OF CAPITAL GOODS

Capital goods, which represent the embodiment of the stock of material wealth of an economy, are desired primarily for their use in the production process, i.e. for the expected stream of quasi-rents that they will yield over their useful lives. As a stylised fact, it can be assumed, at this stage, that fixed capital

---

[1] Keynes, *The General Theory*, p. 146.
[2] This assumption will be relaxed in Chapter 6.

goods are *not* desired as a store of value in an uncertain world, that is as a vehicle for transferring purchasing power over time to an unspecified date for an unspecified use, since the spot market for reselling fixed capital goods is thin, poorly organised and discontinuous, even if it exists at all.[1] In general, capital goods can be viewed as either (1) *fixed capital*, that is, goods which are very durable and therefore by their very nature provide their yields over a very long period of time for they can not be immediately consumed, or (2) *working capital*, or goods in process, i.e. durable goods which provide their entire yield in the course of a single production period.[2] Given the state of the arts, the quantity of working capital normally demanded is directly related to the entrepreneurial production and hiring decision, so that for any given short-period expectations, there is an entrepreneurial demand for a minimum stock of raw material, semi-finished, and finished products which the entrepreneurs consider necessary either to avoid the possibility of interrupting the production process or to iron out normal seasonal patterns. If, at any point of time, the stock of working capital exceeds the quantity that would normally be held for a given short-period production plan *and if there is a continuous, well-organised market* where this surplus can be readily sold, then the excess of working capital may be considered *liquid capital*. In the aggregate, therefore, stocks of liquid capital come into existence only when there is a surfeit of working capital. The analysis of such a situation will be developed in a later section.

Since working capital demand is normally associated with

[1] Discontinuity in the spot market is due to the absence of financial intermediaries who 'make' a market by operating as residual buyers and sellers of second-hand capital goods. (See Chapter 13 below.)

Producible capital goods lack the necessary elasticity properties which are required for liquidity, and therefore, by definition, for continuous well-organised spot markets. (Cf. Keynes, *The General Theory*, p. 249 n. 1, and Chapters 9 and 13 below.) In a growing economy, *average opinion* will never expect producible capital goods to be a good store of value, for the expected future spot price (net of carrying costs) must always be less than the current spot price (a condition known as 'backwardation') if the existing stock of capital is growing over time.

[2] 'Working capital is necessary because some goods take time to produce and fixed capital is necessary because some goods take time to use or consume.' – Keynes, *Treatise on Money*, I 128.

short-term production plans, *then long-term expectations can be primarily related to the demand for fixed capital goods*. Hence, unless it is specified otherwise in what follows, the demand for capital or investment decision can be considered synonymous with the demand for fixed capital.

CAPITAL GOODS AND STORES OF WEALTH

Durability is a characteristic possessed by capital goods and by money and other financial assets (e.g. stocks, bonds). This quality of *durability* makes capital goods a primary form of wealth and a capitalised source of income in a temporal view, and the demand for capital primarily as a store of value has sometimes been emphasised in the economic literature. Thus, the pre-keynesian writers as well as modern neoclassicists associated the act of savings, i.e. the decision to abstain from consumption out of current income, with the demand to store wealth in durable, producible capital goods. This view led to the neoclassical fallacy that underlies Says' Law, namely that an increased desire to hold wealth on the part of households in order to transfer command over resources to the indefinite future is the same thing as an increased desire to hold real capital goods.

It was exceedingly difficult for Keynes to dislodge this fallacy from men's minds, and although he was temporarily successful via the short-period analysis of effective demand in *The General Theory*, this sophism has reappeared in the modern growth literature.[1] It is the contention of this section that in this resurrection of the view that the demand for capital goods is a result of the desire of households to obtain a store of value lies much of the confusion in the current literature that has made much controversy barren and sterile. On the interpretation offered here, it is the peculiarity of a growing production-specialisation-exchange monetary economy where the future is uncertain that the existence of money and the development of spot financial markets which have intermediaries who 'make' the market by operating as residual buyers and sellers that assures that (1) readily reproducible capital goods will be

[1] For example, see J. Tobin, 'Money and Economic Growth', *Econometrica*, **33** (1965).

demanded primarily as a factor of production rather than as a store of value; (2) money is demanded as both a medium of exchange and a vehicle for transferring purchasing power over time; and (3) titles to capital goods and debt contracts – placements – are demanded solely as stores of value.

It is the durability of all assets – money, capital goods, and securities – which links the uncertain economic future with the present. In the obscure and oft-neglected Chapters 16 and 17 of *The General Theory*, Keynes wrestled with the problem of trying to extricate himself from the short-period framework of the rest of his book. The essence of these chapters involves the problem of financing the demand for additional investments as the real wealth of the community accumulates.[1]

Keynes noted three attributes which all durable assets possess in different degrees and which affect their desirability: (1) q, the expected money value of the output, net of the running expenses, which can be obtained by 'assisting some process of production or supplying services to a consumer' (2) c, the costs (including wastage) of carrying the asset over the period, and (3) l, the liquidity premium which arises from the power of disposal of the asset during the period.

The power of disposal over an asset involves, in a monetary economy, the expectation of being able to exchange the asset for the medium of exchange cheaply and readily in a continuous spot market at a money price which is never very different from the well-publicised spot prices of the last few transactions. For any asset which is simultaneously the medium of exchange and the store of value, the power of disposal must, by definition, be the greatest. For any other asset to be a store of value, it must possess low carrying costs and possess liquidity. In order to possess liquidity there must be a well-organised, continuous spot market for the asset; hence, liquidity can not be discussed independently of the financial institutions which make the spot market for particular durables.

With respect to liquidity premium, Kaldor prefers to treat the 'power of disposal' as a marginal risk premium, r, due to

[1] For similar views on these chapters, see J. Robinson, 'Own Rates of Interest', *Economic Journal*, **71** (1961) and R. Turvey, 'Does the Rate of Interest Rule the Roost?' in *The Theory of Interest Rates*, ed. F. H. Hahn and F. P. R. Brechling (London: Macmillan 1965).

illiquidity and to represent it as a deduction from the net yield $(q - c)$ of the asset where 'The *uncertainty* of future value (or return) in terms of money, or on account of their imperfect marketability, carries a risk premium for which this yield must compensate'.[1] Thus, for Kaldor r represents the potential cost to the holder if he attempts to convert his store of value into a medium of exchange at some unspecified and even unknown date when he may have to exercise command of resources in excess of his future income at that future time. Obviously for those assets for which no spot market exists $l = 0$ or r is infinitely large, and therefore, for these assets, ownership is irrevocable 'and indissoluble, like marriage, except by reason of death or other grave cause'.[2] Under such circumstances the asset will be held and used solely for its expected income stream. Even if a spot market exists, if it is poorly organised, the asset will be primarily held for its anticipated ability to produce income in the future. Fixed capital goods are obvious examples of this type of asset!

In sum, if an asset is to be held for possible resale (i.e. as a store of value) then there must be a well-organised, continuous spot market in the asset. Moreover, the existence of financial institutions whose primary function is to make an orderly spot market and operate as a residual buyer and seller in pursuing this objective significantly reduces but does not eliminate the risk of illiquidity as the future spot price can still change within the narrow minute-by-minute bounds set by the rules under which the financial intermediary supporting the market operates. If, of course, the financial institution pegs the spot price and is expected to maintain, always and unhesitatingly, the spot price at its current value, then uncertainty is reduced further and the liquidity of the asset is enhanced. Nevertheless even in this case there is a residuum of uncertainty remaining as long as there is any doubt about the ability of this institutional 'maker' of the spot market to maintain the peg for all possible contingencies at all possible dates in the future.

In Kaldor's view, therefore, the marginal risk premium of

[1] N. Kaldor, '"Keynes" Theory of the Own Rate of Interest' in *Essays on Economic Stability and Growth*, ed. N. Kaldor (London: Duckworth, 1960) p. 60. Italics added.
[2] Keynes, *The General Theory*, p. 160.

illiquidity of money must be zero (since there must, by definition, be a continuous costless spot market for money) so this
sets an unchanging standard against which all other durables
can be measured. For money q, c and r are, in modern economies, all equal to zero.

Explicit in the Kaldor formulation is the fact of a 'convenience
yield' to the holding of money. *Uncertainty* about future asset
values, *plus the imperfections* in spot market-place involving the
costs of getting buyers and sellers together, involve doubts in
holding any assets other than money as a store of value.[1] For
our immediate purpose it is a matter of indifference whether
the l concept or Kaldor's r is utilised, since they are essentially
mirror images of each other.

Returning to the attributes that Keynes associated with all
assets, there is a fourth characteristic which Keynes introduced,
a, the expected appreciation (or depreciation) in the spot
money price of the asset at the end of the period compared
with the current spot price.[2]) Obviously, as with the liquidity
premium characteristic, expected appreciation (or depreciation) is relevant only if there is a well-organised, continuous
spot market for the durable; i.e. l (or r) and a are relevant only
in the decision to hold assets for resale or store of value purposes.
For all other assets, the expected stream of quasi-rents $(q - c)$
is the only important characteristic for determining the desirability of holding the asset for its productive use. Although
Keynes tended to measure these attributes of q, c, l and a, in
a unit equal to a percentage per period of the initial cost of the
asset in order to normalise for differing life expectancies of the
various assets and differing initial costs, for most of what
follows it will be more useful to conceive of these attributes in
units of absolute dollar sums per period over the lives of the
various assets. This latter unit of measure can then be directly
converted into the demand price of the asset (in the mind of
the holder) via a present value calculation.

In an uncertain world, households may not wish to exercise
all of their currently earned claims on resources; they may

---

[1] Thus, because the future spot price of any durable besides money is
uncertain and because there are large imperfections in the spot markets
for these assets, money is *ceteris paribus*, a preferable store of value.

[2] Keynes, *The General Theory*, pp. 225–6.

prefer to defer some decisions (i.e. to save) if they are currently uncertain as to what consumption goods they will want in the future. This time preference decision of households (as to what portion of their currently received claims on resources to exercise today and what portion to hold for a future time) means that households will desire to transfer purchasing power to the future. The vehicle or vehicles they use to transfer current claims, will 'depend on their liquidity preference. (Of course, in the absence of organised spot markets for other assets, money would be the only available vehicle.)

Similarly, entrepreneurs, fearful that future events may make current capacity obsolete before it physically decays, may write-off (out of sales proceeds) the existing stock of capital at a rate which exceeds current replacement costs and, for the time being, entrepreneurs may wish to set aside this financial provision for future replacement in an uncommitted form, i.e. entrepreneurs may currently desire to make financial provision for replacement without entering into any current contractual commitment for future delivery of replacement of the capital stock as it decays. (This is especially likely to occur in industries which install physically long-lived equipment and are simultaneously threatened by rapid unpredictable technological progress.[1]) Thus, firms also will require a vehicle for transferring purchasing power over time – and they will choose on the basis of their liquidity preference.

In an uncertain world, there is no certain way that households or firms can transfer current command over a given quantity of current resources into command of a given quantity of resources to be used for some vague or even currently unknown purposes at some future date. Households and firms

[1] Cf. Keynes, *The General Theory*, pp. 99–100. Most neoclassical and neo-keynesian growth theories ignore the problems of entrepreneurial sinking funds which exceed the actual ordering of replacement capacity by dealing only in net income, net investment, and net savings concepts and thereby implicitly assuming that replacement investment and 'replacement savings' will always match. For the neoclassical economists, this view comes about because of the assumption of malleability, while for the neo-keynesians it is due to the assumption of tranquillity. Keynes, on the other hand, did not ignore this question; nor has Harrod, in recent times. For example, see R. F. Harrod, 'Replacements, Net Investment, Amortisation Funds', *Econ. Jour.* **80** (1970) pp. 24–31.

can attempt to make financial provision for the future, but this does not assure economic provision for the future. Saving households and firms will, therefore, endeavour to transfer control of resources via those durables in which they have the most confidence that these assets will be either stable or appreciate in value in spot markets in terms of that standard (a) in which future liabilities will fall due, (b) in which offers to sell producible goods and services, in future periods will be stated, and (c) in which, *ceteris paribus*, it will be least costly to convert back into such a standard. In a monetary economy, where production takes time and money contracts are essential for specialisation, such a standard is money. Accordingly, savers are not primarily interested in capital goods for the same reasons that investors are, i.e. for the future flow of services and associated quasi-rents to be derived from the capital goods; rather savers are merely interested in either money or the titles to the capital goods as a store of value for the latter may have continuous spot markets, while the former, by the very nature of fixed capital, will not be dealt with on such markets!

Investors are, by definition, not primarily interested in title to real capital goods as a store of value; their object is to acquire the services of real capital as inputs for the production process for they believe they possess the skill, knowledge, and time required to co-ordinate short-run production decisions in their pursuit of a stream of money income. To obtain the services of capital goods, it is true that normally investors must acquire the physical presence of the capital stock; but what is relevant to the firm's cost calculations is the *marginal unit supply price of the service* of the capital factor. Investors do not necessarily want title to the stock of capital. (Similarly, firms do not care whether they own their labour force [slaves] or allow others to hold title to the factor called labour; what is relevant is the marginal supply price of labour services.)

In sum then, what savers are interested in is protecting and possibly increasing the spot value of their wealth holdings for the future when they may wish to convert their wealth to the medium of exchange in order to buy goods and services. Since there are only two basic types of durable instruments that link the uncertain economic future with the present – durable equipment and monetary claims (i.e. financial assets including money) neoclassical economists have argued that savers must store the value in these instruments and have suggested that savers will ultimately choose producible durables.

Since all durable goods possess some q, c and l (or r) attributes, it would seem that they all might serve equally well as a store of value. Nevertheless, as long as spot markets for physical assets are poorly organised (if they exist at all), l is normally very small (r is very large) as compared to the liquidity premiums associated with the titles (financial assets) to these capital goods; titles will normally be preferred to the capital goods as a store of value. For as long as there are organised, continuous securities markets, there is – as explained below – less of an imperfection in the 'titles' market than in the spot market for capital goods itself. As a consequence, financial assets will be more attractive to wealth-holding households,[1] for the asset-titles will be more liquid and therefore have a premium which exceeds the yield minus the carrying cost of the physical asset itself. Thus the value of the title to the capital good tends to exceed the value of the capital good itself if the spot market for titles is better organised (less imperfect) than the spot market for purchasing the use of physical capital goods.

Thus, although the value of the future revenue productivity of a capital good ordinarily exceeds its costs over its useful life, its liquidity premium is negligible. Consequently, if a saver possessed a physical capital instrument and intended to convert his store of value (e.g. a sausage machine) into future consumption goods in a different time pattern than the stream of anticipated earnings over the life of his physical capital asset, he would, at some point of time, have to find a sausage-machine buyer. In selling, he would almost certainly disrupt the machine's physical (and value) productivity yield and incur delivery costs, if he must physically dismantle and transport the equipment to the buyer. Moreover, since real capital assets are normally large, indivisible physical units, the saver may be required to search out a buyer of the whole unit, in a future period, even if he desires only to increase his consumption in that period by some amount smaller than the expected value of the whole physical asset. The smaller the unit of asset,

[1] If the expected yield on capital goods is equal to the expected yield on titles to capital.

ceteris paribus, the greater its saleability is likely to be. Thus, as Makower and Marschak have shown, sales of large units 'not only increase the dispersion of future yields, but also reduce their actuarial values'.[1]

Accordingly, the problem of finding a buyer for a machine is likely to be complex and costly. It is here that financial titles rather than the physical assets are superior. The existence of a spot market (whose continuity is usually assured by the existence of a financial institution who acts as a residual buyer and seller[2]) assures that with a minimum of search costs for a buyer, and without disrupting productivity and incurring delivery costs, the title to either the entire asset or to some fraction of the asset can be transformed as the saver's needs arise. Hence, he will, *ceteris paribus*, be better off.

Obviously, the development of placements, i.e. equity and loan securities, and organised spot markets to deal in these securities have thus allowed savers to store value over time in small saleable packages, with a minimum of fuss and costs. Hence, the liquidity premium attached to fractionalised titles to capital goods exceeds the liquidity premium of the physical capital goods themselves. Accordingly, in economies with developed securities markets, money and 'placements' become the most desirable stores of value. Real capital is thus freed for service as an input in the production process. The development of markets for placements, however, has not been without some major side effects, for 'finance-capitalism' has severed the link between the demand for capital decision (involving production control or management of the services of the factor) and the portfolio balance decision (involving ownership of the factor). Here, of course, is the major institutional conflict of managerial capitalism.[3]

Since savers are interested in titles to wealth only as a store of value, while entrepreneurs desire the flow of productive services from capital goods, wealth-holding or portfolio balance decisions and investment decisions will look out towards different price levels. Capital investment decisions depend on the

---

[1] H. Makower and J. Marschak, 'Assets, Prices, and Monetary Theory', *Economica*, 5 (1938) p. 279.   [2] See Chapter 13 below.

[3] Galbraith's scathing indictment of *The New Industrial State* develops from this institutional conflict.

market demand price relative to the minimum flow-supply of capital goods. Financial accumulation, however, depends on the price of securities. The sole direct relationship between them consists of the interest rate and discount rate mechanism.

The analysis in the rest of this chapter concentrates on the investment decision for *it* is the one which determines the rate of capital accumulation! The portfolio balance or wealth holding decisions of households will be discussed in detail in later chapters. At this stage it will simply be assumed that all increments in household wealth are retained only in money or placements and that the Monetary Authority acts so that a shortage of finance is never a constraint on the rate of investment.

THE DEMAND AND SUPPLY OF CAPITAL GOODS IN A GROWING ECONOMY

The very nature of most fixed capital goods produces conditions which would create significant imperfections in any second-hand or spot market for capital goods. In general, each unit of second-hand capital (1) lacks standardisation (so that each unit would have to be physically inspected to obtain a reliable judgement about its ability to provide future services); (2) its value relative to bulk is likely to be low so that delivery costs will be large; and therefore (3) there will be significant obstacles which will prevent financial intermediaries from making a continuous spot market in such goods, and hence it will be even more difficult to obtain information about the location and behaviour of potential buyers and sellers. Consequently, the liquidity premium and expected appreciation in spot market prices associated with most fixed capital goods will be negligible; the demand for fixed capital can be viewed, therefore, as a safe first approximation, as solely due to the desire of entrepreneurs to use them to obtain the expected quasi-rents over their useful lives.[1] The demand price for fixed capital

---

[1] For the moment we are ignoring the possibility of expectations of price inflation (or deflation) which might make the expected money yield of capital goods $= (a + q - c)$. Such inflationary expectations can induce the accumulation of liquid capital goods for inventory speculation reasons, and accelerate the rate of installation of new capacity, so that expectations of inflation could be viewed as an increase in the demand price of capital goods. This aspect will be dealt with later in this chapter and in Chapter 9 below.

goods can therefore be associated solely with the sum of the discounted values of $(q - c)$.

If, at any point of time, the demand price for any reproducible physical asset exceeds the minimum short-period flow-supply price which is necessary to bring additional units of that asset forward, then these capital items will be newly produced. If, on the other hand, the demand price is less than the supply price, there will be no current production of that asset.

This simple mechanism of comparing the demand price with the flow-supply price of capital goods has for the most part been neglected in the economic literature in favour of a comparison of the expected rate of return on capital relative to 'the rate of interest'. This latter view has not only been unproductive but it has encouraged many economists into a delusive search for a factor (such as the marginal productivity of capital expressed as an annual percentage) which *determines* the *rate of return* on capital goods. Despite the fact that Keynes utilised the concept of the marginal efficiency of capital (which was defined as equal to a rate of discount), it is obvious that Keynes always viewed the production of investment goods in a monetary economy as depending on the comparison of the demand price with the flow-supply price ('or replacement costs'). For example, besides his continual use of demand price relative to supply price in the chapter on The Marginal Efficiency of Capital in *The General Theory*, in an extensive appendix on Marshall's views on the rate of interest, Keynes provides running comments in a series of footnotes in which he insists that 'the equality between the stock of capital goods offered and the stock demanded will be brought about by the *prices* of capital goods, not by the rate of interest'.[1] Moreover Keynes was adamant in arguing that if there was, for example, a large increase in the demand for capital goods which could not be immediately met by the output of the capital goods

[1] Keynes, *The General Theory*, p. 186 n. also see pp. 135–7, 147, p. 187 n. 2, n. 3, 224. Also see Keynes, *Treatise on Money*, I 202. If the production process is continuous, while sales are expected to occur at discrete points of time, the rate of interest will, via the demand price calculation, determine the investment in fixed and working capital so that production can be organised 'in the most efficient manner compatible with delivery at the dates at which consumers demand is expected to become effective'. (*The General Theory*, pp. 215–16.)

THE DEMAND AND SUPPLY OF CAPITAL GOODS 71

industry, there would be 'a rise in the supply price of capital goods sufficient to keep the marginal efficiency of capital in equilibrium with the rate of interest without there being any material change in the scale of investment'.[1] In other words, it was changes in the demand price relative to the flow-supply price of capital which was the mechanism determining the rate of investment, and alterations in the demand and supply prices would then bring about changes in the expected return at the margin, which is known as the marginal efficiency of investment. Accordingly, this Keynesian demand price–supply price mechanism deserves some elaboration.

THE DEMAND AND SUPPLY OF CAPITAL IN A GROWING ECONOMY

As firms require the services of capital goods as inputs in the production process, they must acquire the physical capital goods. Accordingly, the firms' demand for the flow of capital services leads to a *demand for a stock of capital goods*, and for any given set of contemplated circumstances firms will visualise a stock of capital which they feel is most convenient given their long-term expectations. This demand for capital goods for a given firm is readily determined, for as Keynes indicated, the estimated prospective yield, $Q_r = (q - c)_r$, for each unit of capital at time r is multiplied by d_r, which is the present value of $1 'deferred r years *at the current rate of interest*, [so that] $\sum Q_r d_r$ is the demand price of the investment.'[2] Plotting these estimated demand prices on the ordinate axis and the quantity of capital (K) on the abscissa will yield the stock demand curve for capital for a given firm.[3] The aggregate demand for capital

---

[1] ibid., p. 187. This view permitted Keynes to denigrate the importance of marginal productivity theory (pp. 139–40 including n.) for capital theory many years before modern Cambridge economists such as Joan Robinson, Kaldor, and Pasinetti were able to make the grand effort of dislodging marginal productivity theory from economists' minds. Nevertheless, it did lead Keynes into a semantic argument with D. H. Robertson on the importance of productivity and thrift on interest rate determination. This latter aspect will be dealt with in Chapter 7.   [2] ibid., p. 137.

[3] This assumes that the stock of capital can be aggregated along the abscissa by homogeneous physical units – an obviously unrealistic assumption. The alternative would be to provide separate demand and supply

goods is derived from the summation of the demand curves of all firms. Thus in Fig. 4.1 (a) a capital-stock demand curve, D_k (for a given set of quasi-rent expectations and the rate of discount), relates the maximum quantity of the capital good desired to be held by firms to alternative market price of capital goods. This stock demand curve for capital, D_k, includes the Wicksteedian reservation demand of holders of existing capital at each moment of time. The demand function can be specified as

$$D_k = f_1(p_k, i, \phi, E) \qquad (1)$$

where D_k is the stock demand for capital, p_k is the market price of capital goods, i is the rate of discount,[1] ϕ is a set of expectations about the growth in demand and the consequent future stream of quasi-rents which can be expected to be earned by each unit of capital, and E represents the number of entrepreneurial investors who can obtain finance for their demand for capital goods, where

$$f'_{1p_k} < 0, f'_{1i} < 0, f'_{1\phi} > 0, f'_{1E} > 0.$$

Underlying the conception of a demand curve for capital goods specified by equation (1) is the assumption that entrepreneurs – whether they act in a neoclassical or neo-keynesian pattern – view investment choices in a manner so that they

---

curves for each type of homogeneous capital goods – an unnecessary complication, as long as we discuss investment in a demand price $v.$ supply price context, and not by reference to 'the rate of profit on physical capital'. Thus we are assuming some composite capital good. Keynes, on the other hand, suggested that 'for each type of capital we can build up a schedule' (ibid., p. 136). Instead, for expositional simplicity the analysis that follows is based on a concept of a representative capital good.

[1] The symbol i represents the average subjective rate of discount used by entrepreneurs in evaluating any expected future income stream. For each entrepreneur the rate of discount used may differ (even if they are in the same industry) but the actual rate used will always exceed 'the rate of interest' on borrowing by a premium which is the minimum the entrepreneur feels is necessary to overcome the disutility of having to take on additional commitments and face the prospect of potential surprise. In essence this subjective premium which the entrepreneur wants before he will enter into a contract for the purchase and use of capital goods is a measure of 'the doubts in his own mind as to the probability of actually earning the prospective yield for which he hopes'. (Ibid., p. 144.)

always prefer the expected more profitable project to the less profitable alternative, that is, they prefer, *ceteris paribus*, quasi-rents that have higher present values per dollar of finance

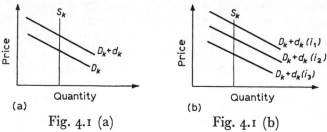

(a)

Fig. 4.1 (a)

(b)

Fig. 4.1 (b)

committed to those that have lower present values per dollar of finance committed.[1]

Writing the demand for capital goods as equation (1) may suggest an undue precision to the reader unless he is made aware of the complexities and interdependencies underlying the symbols. Essentially,

> the demand-price of capital goods . . . depends on *two* things – on the estimated net prospective yield from fixed capital (estimated by the opinion of the market after such allowances as they choose to make for the uncertainty of anticipation, etc.) measured in money, and on the rate of interest at which this future yield is capitalised.[2]

Nevertheless, changes in any one of the independent variables can affect the others. For example, changes in the market rate of interest may affect the demand for capital not only via altering the rate of discount used in capitalising the expected yield, but also by creating new expectations about (a) future sales (affecting ϕ) and (b) future interest rates (affecting E).[3]

Hence, in an uncertain world, changes in any of the independent variables in equation (1) may induce changes in expectations about the future which can alter the magnitudes of the

[1] Cf. Robinson, *Essays in Economic Growth*, p. 45.

[2] Keynes, *Treatise on Money*, I 202.

[3] If current changes in financial conditions are considered temporary rather than permanent these expectations will affect the timing of investment projects, as well as affecting, via the organisation of the financial markets, the willingness of banks to make loans and underwriters to float new issues. These aspects of financial markets will be discussed in Chapters 10 and 13.

other 'independent' variables. Thus, variables on the right side of equation (1) (and of many of the other equations presented here) are independent only in the sense that any value, positive or negative, of one, is compatible under the appropriate circumstances, with any value positive or negative of the other and therefore the values of any of the independent variables can not be inferred from one another.

At any point of time, the existing stock of capital happened to be whatever has been inherited from the past. Accordingly, the stock supply schedule for capital goods (S_k) can be drawn as vertical in Fig. 4.1 (a). Thus, *at any point of time*,

$$S_k = a_k \qquad (2)$$

where S_k is the stock supply of capital and a_k is a predetermined constant at any instant of time.

Barring production or depreciation of capital goods (e.g. in a pure exchange economy), the resulting market price would, of course, be whatever is necessary to allocate the stock without remainder among demanders. The resulting price can be conceived of as the spot price of capital goods. For a production economy, however, flow considerations must be added to the stock analysis of capital. A stock is a *quantity* measured *at an instant of time*, while a flow can be viewed as the rate at which a stock quantity changes *per unit of time*. Under these definitions, the flow demand for capital is attributable to the actual using up (or depreciation) of the existing capital stock per unit of time. For simplicity we will assume that depreciation is a (small) fraction, n, of the existing stock of capital per unit of time. Hence, the flow demand for capital is

$$d_k = nS_k = na_k \qquad (3)$$

where d_k is flow demand (depreciation) and $0 < n < 1$.

Combining equations (1) and (3) yields the total market demand for capital over the period,

$$D_k + d_k = f_1 (p_k, i, \phi, E) + na_k \qquad (4)$$

which, because of our simplifying assumption about the rate of depreciation, implies that the market demand curve, $D_k + d_k$, is parallel and to the right of the stock demand curve in Fig. 4.1 (a). The horizontal difference between the two curves represents depreciation.

The flow supply schedule of capital goods indicates the output quantities which will be offered on the market by the capital-goods industry at alternative expected market prices, i.e.

$$s_k = f_2(p_k) = I_g \qquad (5)$$

where s_k denotes the flow-supply of capital and I_g represents gross investment. As we have already developed in Chapter 3, the short period flow-supply schedule of the representative firm (and therefore of the industry) will depend on whether entrepreneurs behave according to neoclassical or neo-keynesian principles.

If the capital goods producers exhibit neo-keynesian behaviour then the flow-supply curve will be composed of marginal prime costs plus a gross profit margin calculated to yield normal profits at standard volume. If, for example, marginal prime costs are relatively constant till capacity, the flow-supply curve can be represented by the dotted reverse L-shaped curve, $s_p s_k$ in Fig. 4.2, where s_p represents the normal short-run supply price (which equals the unit long-run supply price at standard volume).

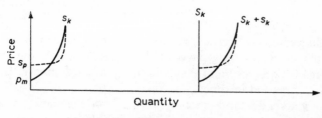

Fig. 4.2

If, on the other hand, entrepreneurs display traditional neoclassical behaviour patterns, the flow-supply schedule, in a competitive environment, will reflect short-run rising marginal costs because of diminishing returns in the investment-goods industry, i.e. $f'_{2pk} > 0$. This neoclassical flow-supply curve, $p_m s_k$, is represented by the upward sloping curve in Fig. 4.2. The minimum flow-supply price p_m in Fig. 4.2 (it would be s_p for neo-keynesian entrepreneurs) represents the shutdown price for the neoclassical industry. If the market price falls below this minimum flow price, that is, if buyers are not willing to accept offer contracts at a price of p_m or greater, no production offerings will be made, as capital goods producers find that given their expectations and objectives shutting down involves smaller losses than attempting to produce for market. Obviously therefore the supply responses in the capital goods industry for any given expected market price will differ depending on whether the entrepreneurs are more neoclassical or neo-keynesian in behaviour. For simplicity of exposition as well as for some reasons developed below, the supply response of capital goods producers will be discussed primarily in terms of neoclassical behaviour. (For comparability and as guide to the reader, some comments on the supply response of a capital goods industry operated under neo-keynesian principles will be provided, but it is hoped that the reader can at this stage, readily develop a complete neo-keynesian capital goods producing model if he so desires. As has been suggested in Chapter 3, the supply response of capital goods producers will depend on the available information about buyers' behaviour.)

The market supply situation can be obtained by laterally summating the stock and flow schedules (Fig. 4.2), i.e. by combining equations (2) and (5) to obtain

$$S_k + s_k = a_k + f_2(p_k) \tag{6}$$

The horizontal difference between the stock supply schedule and the market supply curve in Fig. 4.2 represents the gross output of the investment-goods industry at each market price in a given period of time.

The market demand function $(D_k + d_k)$ and the market supply function $(S_k + s_k)$ are combined in Fig. 4.3. If, at the beginning of the short-period, the demand price (i.e. the spot price) for the existing stock of capital $(p_s$ in Fig. 4.3) exceeds the minimum flow-supply price, p_m, investors have long-term expectations of profit opportunities which are sufficiently great to encourage them to place some orders for newly producible capital goods.[1] In the real world, the market for plant and equipment is often

[1] This can be true even if there is no current overutilisation of capacity. In other words, net investment can be conceived as having two important – but independent – origins: (i) *a stock adjustment process* if the current equipment is being overutilised and the current level of demand is projected over the future life of the net investment; and (2) *an expected growth in demand* or 'animal spirits' which induces net investment even when there is no current overutilisation.

organised on a 'custom building' or 'to contract' basis, that is, because of the specific nature of certain aspects of *fixed capital* (e.g. site location and industrial specification characteristics) contracts for orders are often placed on an individual basis prior to actual production and delivery. The actual flow of

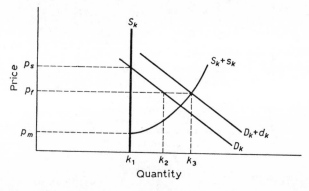

Fig. 4.3

output in the capital goods industry will, therefore, be able to be carried out, as Keynes argued, to the point where the demand price for the period equals flow-supply price[1] so that, in each period, capital goods producers tend to be in short period equilibrium as

$$(D_k + d_k) - (S_k + s_k) = 0 \qquad (7)$$

Accordingly, actual orders for future delivery of capital goods are a leading indicator of the flow of output that will be forthcoming from the capital goods industry.[2]

[1] Keynes, *The General Theory*, p. 137.

[2] Since delivery occurs at some future point of time (the end of the period) after an offer contract is accepted by the buyer, there is a time dimension-units problem in placing the stock *and* flow demand and supply curves on the same 'timeless' quadrant as in Fig. 4.3. (This same time dimension-units problem exists in all Marshallian short-period diagrams but is traditionally ignored in a Marshallian timeless analysis. In Walrasian systems a similar dimensional problem exists.) Since delivery will take place at the end of the period, the present value or demand price for all units of capital goods which must be ordered must be less than the demand price for a similar unit which can be obtained immediately by an amount equal to the current period's net yield. Thus, the stock demand D_k of Fig. 4.3 should be drawn with a discontinuity at the point where it intersects

If the capital goods market is organised on a 'custom building' or 'to contract' basis, there is more reason to expect the behaviour of the producers of capital goods to approximate

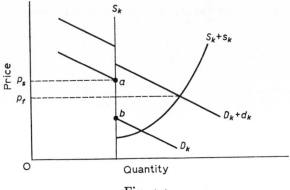

Fig. 4.4

that of short-period maximising neoclassical entrepreneurs, than if the industry is organised on a 'offer or produce in anticipation of market' basis as many firms in the retail stage of a non-integrated chain are. The existence of a 'custom building' arrangement permits, as was discussed in Chapter 2, the producer to shift some of the uncertainty about the 'worthwhile' aspect of production decisions to the buyer, while reducing the uncertainty (unless the buyer violated the contract) about the level of sales revenue over the period, especially if the seller can control delivery. Hence, the producer in the 'custom building' capital goods industry may have substantial information about the market demand he is facing before he makes many current major short-period commitments to hire resources. The entrepreneur under such an arrangement can, therefore, be much more confident about his ability to maxi-

---

the stock supply curve, S_k, as shown in Fig. 4.4, so that the vertical distance ab represents the foregone expected net yield for the current period if delivery is obtained at the end of the period. Thus in Fig. 4.4, p_s is the spot price at the beginning of the current period, and p_f is Marshallian short period flow-supply price or offer price for delivery of currently produced capital goods at the end of the current period. Since nothing fundamental will be changed by ignoring the units problem, for reasons of expositional simplicity in most of what follows, diagrams similar to Fig. 4.3 rather than Fig. 4.4 will be utilised.

mise profits in the short period via his estimate of the point of effective demand than the 'produce in anticipation of market' entrepreneur who has little objective information about the current demand curve which underlies his short-term revenue expectations, while he faces the usual uncertainties about costs of production that all firms do.

Given the greater uncertainty, *ceteris paribus*, of the 'produce in anticipation' firm, it is reasonable to expect that the latter's marketing strategy will be to make an offer to sell to any and all buyers (whose specific identities are likely to be unknown at the beginning of the period when production commitments are made) at a price based on an expected standard volume which if correct will yield a normal profit. Given the obvious stochastic nature of actual sales in such a market, the 'produce in anticipation' entrepreneur is unlikely to know with any degree of certainty as to whether his estimate of effective demand was correct until he is at the end of the period.[1] The 'custom building' producer, on the other hand, knowing that he does not have to make major short-period production commitments until he has firm contractual orders, has more confidence in his ability to determine the profit maximising pricing and production position implicit in the current *known* market conditions and is therefore more likely to follow neoclassical behavioural rules. Under these neoclassical rules, the capital goods producer will be in short-period flow-equilibrium in each period, even though he may not be earning 'normal' profits on the net finance provided by the owners, while the neo-keynesian entrepreneur will never be in short-period flow equilibrium unless normal profits are earned. Thus, the position of equilibrium is dependent, *ceteris paribus*, on the behavioural views of entrepreneurs.

Given the arguments developed above, it may seem appropriate to emphasise neoclassical as well as neo-keynesian supply

[1] Thus, in a note on p. 47 of *The General Theory*, Keynes associates the short-period expectations with 'the shortest interval after which the firm is free to revise its decision as to how much employment to offer. It is, so to speak, the minimum effective time.' Given the length of contractual obligations to hired variable inputs, revisions of decisions are most likely to occur, in an uncertain world, only after the entrepreneur has collected sufficient information about current sales to recognise that his original expectations are incorrect.

behaviour in the capital goods industry even though Chapter 3, which discusses industry decision behaviour in general, suggested the predominance of neo-keynesian entrepreneurs in modern economies. Industries at or near the retail stage, which constitute the majority of the firms selling 'final products' in a developed market-oriented monetary economy, are more likely to have a 'produce to anticipate market' orientation which encourages, in an uncertain world, a neo-keynesian entrepreneurial behaviour. Thus, although an aggregative model of fully integrated firms may suggest, rational entrepreneurial behaviour is more closely related to neo-keynesian principles, a sectoral analysis of industry may suggest certain industries, such as the fixed capital goods industry, where neoclassical deportment can be reasonable. In reality, in an uncertain world where some contracts are individually negotiated and others are offered openly to all buyers, entrepreneurial behaviour will be a mixture of the stylised conduct associated with profit-maximisers and those associated with neo-keynesian entrepreneurs. In certain circumstances, short-run marginal costs will be the prime determinant of offer prices and in other situations target return pricing practices will predominate.

In any case, in any particular short-period, net investment will be going on, that is the quantity of the stock of capital will be changing, if $s_k - d_k \neq 0$, for the difference between flow-supply and flow-demand (i.e. excess flow-demand) represents a current addition to or depletion of existing stocks.[1] In Fig. 4.3 for example, at the short-period flow price of p_f, the gross output of the capital goods industry will be $k_3 - k_1$, while depreciation equals $k_3 - k_2$. The value of net investment $(p_n I_n)$ is equal to the difference between the flow-supply and demand quantities multiplied by the market price, i.e.

$$p_k I_n = p_k (s_k - d_k) \tag{8}$$

In Fig. 4.3, while net investment output equals $k_2 - k_1$, capital growth during the period will be $(k_2 - k_1)/k_1$.

[1] The stock of capital can be changing each period even though it is fixed at each instant of time. A procedure which relates stock supply functions to excess flow-demands and a time variable is 'mandatory if one wishes to conduct a systematic inquiry into problems of "capital accumulation" '. See D. W. Bushaw and R. W. Clower, *Introduction to Mathematical Economics* (Homewood: Irwin, 1957) p. 22.

Any increase in the stock-demand for capital goods will, *ceteris paribus*, raise the spot market price, and the quantity demanded at the flow-supply price, and consequently lead to an increased flow of output of capital goods, as the producers of investment goods respond to the market. Investors determine the stock quantity of capital goods they desire by computing the present value (or demand price) of the expected future earnings of the future flow of productive services of the stock of capital. It is the expectations of investors about future quasi-rents relative to the current rate of discount and their ability to obtain finance – in order to execute this demand – which determines the position of the stock-demand curve and, given the rate of depreciation, the market-demand curve in Fig. 4.1 (a).

A higher rate of discount, with any given set of expectations about the prospective money yield of capital, will entail a leftward shift in the stock demand for capital schedule in Fig. 4.1 (a). Thus, given entrepreneurial expectations and the rate of depreciation, there is a different demand for capital schedule for every possible rate of discount (Fig. 4.1 (b)). Given expectations of entrepreneurial investors, the existing stock of capital and its rate of depreciation, the market price for the capital stock depends peculiarly on the current rate of interest.[1] If this price exceeds the minimum flow-supply price of capital goods, p_m, new gross investment will be undertaken. The rate of capital accumulation will thereby depend on the rate of capital depreciation and the elasticity of supply in the capital goods industries. As Keynes observed: 'A fall in the rate of interest stimulates the production of capital goods not because it decreases their costs of production but because it increases their demand price.'[2]

It is the effect of a change in the rate of interest on the discounting process, and hence on the demand for capital schedule,

[1] This approach highlights Keynes's insistence that knowledge of the prospective yield of capital is *not sufficient* to determine the rate of interest; rather, the rate of interest is an exogenous variable in determining the demand for capital. See ibid., p. 137. The rate of discount will be related to the rate of interest; if the latter changes, *ceteris paribus*, the former will change. Thus the rate of interest can be used as a proxy for the rate of discount as a variable which explains investment.

[2] Keynes, *Treatise on Money*, I 211.

which links the money rate of interest to the level of investment output. Hence the money rate of interest rules the roost – the activity in the capital goods sector – in the short run by limiting the demand for capital.[1]

In summary, the growth of the capital stock depends on the long-run entrepreneurial expectations of future effective demand, the net money yields from the future flow of capital services, the rate of interest, the ability to obtain finance, the pre-existing stock of capital and its rate of depreciation, and the flow-supply elasticity of the capital goods industry. It is the long period expectations of the users of physical capital assets in combination with the flow-supply offers of the producers of capital goods which determines that rate of discount or marginal efficiency which can be calculated to make the stream of prospective yields equal to its *current flow supply price*. Changes in either expectations about the stream of earnings or the supply offers of capital goods producers alters the value of the resultant marginal efficiency of capital or expected internal rate of return; similarly, changes in either the expected stream of quasi-rents or the flow-supply prices of capital goods, or the rate of discount will alter the actual rate at which capital goods are produced per period. Hence, in a monetary economy, these aspects of entrepreneurial long-term expectations, finance, wearing out and supply elasticities become the essential building blocks in constructing an understanding of accumulation and growth phenomena.

DEMAND AND SUPPLY OF CAPITAL IN THE STATIONARY STATE– THE RELATIONSHIP BETWEEN SPOT AND FORWARD MARKETS

As long as net investment is positive, the stock of capital will increase each period. If either: (1) there is no change in the stock-demand schedule for capital over time, that is if there is no change in profit expectations (ϕ), or the rate of discount (i), or the number of entrepreneurial investors (E), or (2) the stock supply schedule shifts out more rapidly over time than the demand schedule, then ultimately a stationary state will be

[1] With imperfections in loan markets, the lack of finance may also be an important element affecting activity, i.e. 'availability' may become as important as interest charges. (See Chapters 9 and 13.)

reached where the gross output of the capital goods industry will equal the rate of depreciation of the capital stock. This situation is represented in Fig. 4.5 (a). This stationary state is, of course, completely compatible with a less than full employment level of effective demand. (If the units are corrected for the passage of time during the period, then Fig. 4.5 (b) is the relevant figure.)

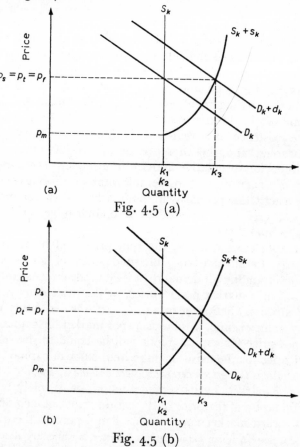

Fig. 4.5 (a)

Fig. 4.5 (b)

At the stationary state price of p_t in Fig. 4.5 (a), accumulation is absent. The short-period flow-supply price, p_f, must, of course, be equal to the long-run flow-supply price, p_t in the capital goods industry, for otherwise the short-run flow-supply curve would shift as firms entered or left the industry. For all reproducible capital goods then, as long as excess flow-demand is positive in a period, the capital stock will be increasing, as the short-run supply price, p_f exceeds the long-run supply price, p_t, while if excess flow demand is negative, the short-run supply price, p_f is less than p_t and net disinvestment is occurring.[1] Moreover, as long as the market price exceeds p_m some gross investment will be undertaken.

Spot and Forward Markets

For any durable, there is the possibility of two separate, but related markets existing side by side, namely: (1) *a spot market* which deals in transactions for the immediate payment and delivery of the good and (2) *a forward market* which deals in contractual arrangements which require payment *and* delivery at some specified future date.

The existence of a well-organised, continuous spot market in durables, and the presence of uncertainty, are essential conditions for speculative activity in a modern economy. In a world of uncertainty, considerable human effort is expended on such activities, primarily in spot markets where an institution has been created to operate as a residual buyer and seller in order to 'make' the market.[2]

If a spot market exists, the spot price will be whatever is necessary to allocate the inherited stock of goods without remainder among all demanders. (The spot price is equivalent to Marshall's market period price, or the price determined by the Walrasian auctioneer in a pure exchange economy.) Thus, at any point of time, if there is a spot market for capital goods the spot price for capital goods will be equal to the stock demand price for the existing (inherited) stock of capital, that is, *the spot price is that price where excess stock demand is zero* $(D_k - S_k = 0)$.

A spot market, by its very definition, deals solely with the determination of the price of the existing stock of a commodity. The forward market, on the other hand, permits the quantity

[1] For a neo-keynesian capital goods industry, a stationary state implies that the point of current effective demand is *at standard volume* with short-run unit supply price equal to long-run unit supply price with normal profits just being earned. Under these conditions, unless a change is expected in the future, the economy will merely replace the capital stock as it wears out.

[2] The importance of these institutions is discussed in Chapter 13.

of goods to be augmented by short-period flow-supply. The forward price for a future date corresponding to the normal length of the production process can never exceed the short-period flow-supply price associated with that gestation period, for if it did it would be possible to make a profit by placing an order with a producer of the good to buy the commodity at the future date at its short-period flow-supply price and simultaneously selling a forward contract to deliver at the higher forward price at the future date. Hence, the short-period flow-supply must always provide an upper limit for the forward price.

Any market which is organised in a manner where buyers enter into contracts to make payments in the future while suppliers agree to make delivery at future specified dates is, in essence, a forward market. Most transactions for the flow of output of the capital goods industry occur via such contractual agreements and therefore it permits the entrepreneur in these industries to operate as if he was in a 'custom building' environment. The existence of a well-organised, freely competitive forward market would permit, of course, the entrepreneur to operate as if he was a price taker in the traditional neoclassical competitive market place. He could observe the forward price and compare it to his short-period flow-supply schedule to determine his short-period production decision. If the forward price

> shows a profit on his costs of production, then he [the entrepreneur] can go full steam ahead, selling his product forward and running no risk. If, on the other hand, this price does not cover his costs (even after allowing for what he loses by temporarily laying up his plant), then it cannot pay him to produce at all.[1]

In the real world, of course, most newly produced capital goods are sold via forward contracts, but the forward market is neither freely competitive nor well-organised, nor are the forward prices always public information. Consequently, although the output of capital goods producers are typically sold

[1] Keynes, *Treatise on Money*, II 142–3. Even if the entrepreneur did not accept a forward contract, he could use the current forward price as the best estimate of the spot price that would prevail on the delivery date.

via forward contracts, the price may be agreed upon by nego-
tiation, or via sealed bids, or via publicly announced prices as
available to all buyers with or without any quantity restrictions.
In these cases, the entrepreneur will have to make flow-supply
offers before he is certain of the buyer's responses; consequently
he still may adopt a neo-keynesian flow-supply production
decision pattern. Nevertheless, since entrepreneurs who operate
via forward markets can avoid major short-period production
commitments (unless the costs associated with changing production scale are very large) until he has a firm contractual
order, such entrepreneurs can permit short-period marginal
costs to bulk more heavily in their offer strategy than the representative neo-keynesian entrepreneur who produces in anticipation of market would.[1]

Since the costs underlying the short-period supply schedule
are partly a function of the length of the period between when
production begins and when delivery is made,[2] then if the forward price is associated with a future date when the flow-supply
can be delivered, it must be equal to that price at which the
market demand price equals the supply price. Thus, the short-
period equilibrium condition is given by equation (7), namely
that the flow of investment is carried out to the point where
demand price equals supply price, $(D_k + d_k) - (S_k + s_k) = 0$. This
will determine the forward price except for any situation where
the capital goods industry is not in short-period equilibrium.
There are two cases where the latter may occur: (1) when the
future date is so close to the present date that technology
prevents any flow-supply from coming forth, or (2) when there
is such a redundancy in the existing stock, that there is no incentive for entrepreneurs to make any commitments to produce
any new capital goods during the period (i.e. gross investment
is zero). The first situation we will eliminate by treating it

---

[1] The ability to bunch process orders with the existence of negotiated
contracts and non-publicised prices will further encourage the use of short-
run marginal cost in determining *some* offer prices. Thus phenomena such
as secret price discrimination have always been considered important by
economists interested in 'industrial organisation' but have usually been
ignored by economic theorists who abstract from the institutional setting
of markets.

[2] A. Alchian, 'Costs and Output', in *The Allocation of Economic Resources*,
M. Abramovitz *et al.* (Stanford: Stanford University Press, 1959).

under the spot market analysis, while the second will be treated in the analysis of contango in the next section, and therefore at this stage we can treat the forward price as synonymous with the short-period flow-supply price.

In order for well-organised spot and forward markets to exist, the commodity must have certain characteristics namely: (1) The good must be an article of general demand; (2) the commodity must be capable of standardisation; (3) there must be a high degree of substitutability between old and new items; (4) the existing stock must be relatively large compared to annual flows; (5) the good must be durable; and (6) it must be valuable in proportion to bulk.[1] Furthermore, continuity of markets, in an uncertain world, requires (7) the existence of a financial institution which 'makes' the market by acting as a residual *buyer or seller* when necessary.

Obviously, different goods may have these features in different degrees. Conditions (4) and (5) are necessary conditions for spot and forward markets to develop, while conditions (1), (2), (3), (6), and (7) will be important factors in determining on how well-organised or perfect markets will be if they exist.

The degree of organisation of spot and forward markets for different goods vary depending on the magnitude of these characteristics they possess. Thus many raw material or working capital goods, because they are durable and capable of standardisation may have well-organised spot and forward markets, while second-hand fixed capital, by its very nature, becomes, as it ages, to some extent destandardised and hence the spot market for fixed capital is likely to be poorly organised if it exists at all.[2] Actually, few second-hand markets in fixed capital goods do exist, but for expository purposes at this stage, it will be useful to discuss all markets for fixed capital as if they existed. In reality, of course, the spot market for most fixed capital goods will be notional.

If at the beginning of a period, the stock demand or spot price for the existing stock of capital p_s in Fig. 4.6 (a), exceeds

---

[1] Cf. N. Kaldor, 'Speculation and Economic Growth', *Rev. Econ. Stud.* (1939) reprinted in *Essays on Economic Stability and Growth* (London: Duckworth, 1960) p. 20. All references are to reprint.

[2] The spot market for placements, on the other hand, should be very well organised. See Kaldor, ibid., pp. 22–3 for a more complete discussion.

the short-period equilibrium (flow-supply) price or forward price, p_f in Fig. 4.6 (a), then, in the language of the market there is *backwardation*. In periods where there is no surplus of capital, backwardation is normal. In a period where backwarda-occurs, the flow of output during the period will exceed (or just equal) the quantity used up in the production process and net investment will be positive (or zero). Thus, backwardation is associated with accumulation and a growing economy (or, at the limit, with a stationary economy).

If, on the other hand, at the beginning of any period, the spot price is below the forward price, there is a contango in the market, the inherited stock of capital is redundant and a running down of existing stocks will occur during the period. Two possible conditions in the capital goods industry are compatible with a contango market, either (1) the existing stock is expected to be redundant only to the extent that normal 'wearing-out' will remove the surplus before the period is over, so that gross investment over the period is positive while disinvestment is occurring, or (2) the inherited stock is expected to be so redundant that even at the end of the period, a surfeit of capital is expected. In the latter case, gross investment will be zero and disinvestment will be equal to the rate of depreciation.

Fig. 4.6 (b) illustrates the contango situation (1). In Fig. 4.6 (b), the spot price (p_s) is less than the short-period equilibrium flow-supply or forward price (p_f) which in turn is less than the long-run supply price (p_t) while the forward price is greater than the minimum flow-supply price (p_m).

In Fig. 4.6 (c), which illustrates contango situation (2), the existing stock is so redundant that the spot price is so far below the minimum flow-supply price ($p_s < < p_m$) that the combined stock and flow demand curve does not intersect the combined stock and flow supply curve and therefore a short-period equilibrium flow price can not be readily defined.[1] In this case the forward price (which can never exceed the short-period equilibrium flow price) must be less than the minimum flow-supply price, p_m, or else some producers of

---

[1] In this case, the marginal efficiency of capital is negative, even if fixed capital goods are physically productive. This illustrates that it is the scarcity of capital and *not* its physical productivity which is relevant to an analysis of accumulation. (Cf. Keynes, *The General Theory*, pp. 213–15.)

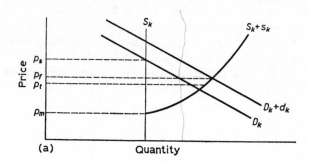

Fig. 4.6 (a)

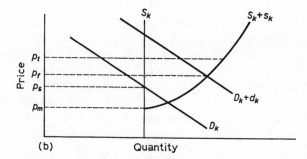

Fig. 4.6 (b)

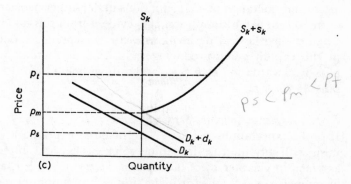

Fig. 4.6 (c)

capital goods would be willing to enter into forward contracts. Accordingly, in contango situation (2), the forward price, i.e. the price for delivery at the end of the period, while being below p_m will depend solely on the *expected* spot price at the future date when delivery is required as forward contracts reflect speculation about the value of the remaining surfeit of capital at the end of the period. Since the determination of expected spot prices at the end of the period involves speculation, the discussion of this aspect will be delayed until the next section.

Finally, Fig. 4.5 (a) can now be reinterpreted via our spot and forward market framework. In the stationary state, the spot price will equal the forward price which will equal the long-run supply price. (Actually the spot price will exceed the forward price by an amount just sufficient to cover the expected net yield that will be earned from the present date to the delivery date, as illustrated in Fig. 4.5 (b).) Thus even in the stationary state, there will be an amount of backwardation equal to the difference in the net yield that is expected to be earned by having immediate delivery as compared to delivery at the end of the period for a small marginal increment in the stock of capital. If the difference exceeds this amount, then there will be a significant amount of accumulation during the period.

Table 4.1 summarises the relationships between the spot, forward and long-run supply prices for various backwardation and contango market situations under either neoclassical or neo-keynesian assumptions. It is evident from this table that whether neoclassical or neo-keynesian entrepreneurs operate in the capital goods-producing industries, accumulation implies backwardation as $p_s > p_f$, and disinvestment involves contango, or $p_s < p_f$.

Keynes, Keynesians, and the Stationary State

If profit expectations (i.e. $q - c$) are taken as expected to diminish with any increase in capital stock (as Keynes implicitly assumed in Chapter 17 of *The General Theory*) while q, c, and a for money are zero, then it is the liquidity premium of money which 'rules the roost' in the long run, in the sense that it ultimately checks the output of capital by checking demand for

Table 4.1

SUPPLY PRICES UNDER DIFFERENT ASSUMPTIONS

Market Situation	Neoclassical Behaviour	Neo-keynesian Behaviour
1. Accumulation-Backwardation	$p_s > p_f > p_l > p_m$	$p_s > p_f \geqslant p_m = p_l$
2. Stationary State*	$p_s = p_f = p_l > p_m$	$p_s = p_f = p_l = p_m$
3. Disinvestment-Contango		
(a) Gross Investment Positive	$p_s < p_f < p_l$ $p_s \lessgtr p_m < p_f$	$p_s < p_f = p_m = p_l$
(b) Gross Investment Zero	$p_s < p_f < p_m < p_l$ no short-period flow equilibrium price	$p_s < p_f < p_m = p_l$ no short-period flow equilibrium price

Symbols:

p_s = spot price

p_f = forward price

p_l = long-run flow-supply price

p_m = short-period minimum flow-supply price

* actually in the stationary state $p_s = p_f + (q - c)_{t_0}$

capital goods. The logic of the stationary state unfolds if the long-run supply price of capital goods is given and the positive constraint on the yield on money (since $l > c$) limits the demand curve for capital, no matter how much the supply of money increases. The consequent fall in the spot and forward prices of capital relative to the long-run supply price, as accumulation occurs, tends ultimately to reduce the flow of new capital goods produced, until only replacement demand remains. In other words, as fixed capital becomes less scarce, its prospective yield in terms of a future income stream falls relative to its flow-supply price, even if capital goods have not become less productive in the physical sense. Hence, at some state, unless the prospective money yield relative to money flow-supply price can be raised, the accumulation of capital will cease.[1]

Since the interest rate is confined to the range of positive value, if the economy is to avoid the stationary state, then the ultimate source of capital accumulation for an income maximising, market-oriented economy lies in investors believing in the continuous growth of profit opportunities over time (animal spirits), so that capital goods continue to be scarce. Profit expectations depend primarily on the expected *value* productivity of capital services or net money yield of capital goods

[1] Cf. Keynes, *The General Theory*, p. 165.

over time relative to their current flow-supply price. There is no natural law of diminishing value productivity over time as long as either the demand for new consumer goods (or fashions) can be continually stimulated, and/or the income elasticity of demand for all existing goods equals unity, and/or the populations of buyers (including governments, foreigners, etc.) *and* their exercised total purchasing power per period grows at least as rapidly as potential output, or technical change reduces costs of production, or some combination of these factors. In other words, profit expectations, in large measure, are determined by expectations that effective demand will grow through time. It is this view which underlies the Cambridge Neo-keynesian belief that in a golden age there is a positive relationship between entrepreneurial animal spirits, the growth of effective demand, and profits. Such an outlook supports the notion that there is no necessary reason to expect either a decline in the rate of return on capital over time as an economy accumulates nor is there any *a priori* reason to believe in the inevitability of the stationary state as long as profit expectations are enlarged over time.

Keynes, on the other hand, following the logic of his assumptions noted that as the stock of physical assets increased over time, given long-term expectations, excess flow-demand would fall until the forward price fell below the supply price where 'it no longer pays to produce them [additional capital goods] *unless the rate of interest falls* pari passu'.[1] At this point, if the rate of interest is at its practical minimum, we have reached the true stationary state. At that stage, any further increase in the stock of capital goods will induce a contango in the market and yield a negative marginal efficiency of capital.

The imminency and inevitability of the stationary state in *The General Theory* derives from the static framework on which it is based. Keynes clearly recognised that changes in technique, tastes, population, and institutions can still lead to progress.[2] Yet from the orthodoxy of the time he reflected the fear of a fundamental tendency for a decline in the prospective yield of capital goods relative to their flow-supply price, i.e. a fall in the rate of profit with accumulation.

[1] Keynes, *The General Theory*, p. 228.   [2] ibid., pp. 220–1.

REDUNDANT CAPITAL – A PROBLEM IN ABSORPTION AND SPECULATION

If, in any period, the forward price is below the minimum short-run flow-supply price, then gross investment will be zero. If the forward price exceeds the minimum short-period flow-supply price, while it is above the current spot price, there is a surfeit at the beginning of the period which is expected to be eliminated before the end of the period. In either case, entre-preneurial long-term expectations about sales-proceeds have brought about a contango in the capital goods market and the result will be disinvestment during the period.

In reality, the spot markets for most fixed capital goods are very poorly organised, if they exist at all, since fixed vintage capital, by its very nature tends to be destandardised. This lack of uniformity even among units of a given vintage of fixed capital implies very high transactions costs and therefore it is a deterrent preventing any non-governmental financial in-stitution from acting as a residual buyer and seller in the spot market. Hence, in those second-hand fixed capital spot markets which do exist the spread between the bid and asked can be exceedingly large, indicating the large imperfections and dis-continuities in these markets. Thus in an uncertain world in which there are well-developed spot markets for securities, wealth owners will always find placements a more desirable store of value relative to the holding and using of fixed physical capital goods. Thus as long as wealth holders can store value in securities and/or money (both having exceedingly well-organised and continuous spot markets)

the alternative of purchasing actual capital assets cannot be rendered sufficiently attractive (especially to the man who does not manage the capital assets and knows very little about them), except by organising [spot] markets wherein these assets can be easily realised for money.[1]

[1] Keynes, *The General Theory*, pp. 160–1. On the other hand, Professor Friedman has insisted that physical reproducible commodities (e.g. fixed capital goods and consumer durables) are very good substitutes for money as a store of value. Accordingly, Friedman argues that exogenous increases in the quantity of money *must* increase the demand for resources directly as wealth holders adjust their stores of wealth by ridding themselves of

The market for the sale of newly produced fixed capital goods is generally organised on a forward contract basis.[1]

Entrepreneurs who wish to expand their plant and equipment facilities because they expect the discounted net yield of the additional capacity to equal or exceed its current flow-supply or offer price are much more likely to place contracts for forward delivery rather than purchase second-hand equipment.[2] It is therefore very unlikely that there will be a sufficiently large and steady volume of transactions to maintain a continuous spot market for most fixed capital goods; hence the spot price for fixed capital at any point of time is more likely to be a *notional* value than an actual observable market price.

To the extent that well-developed spot markets for capital goods actually exist, they are more likely to involve working (or liquid) capital than fixed capital for the former typically have the characteristic of standardisation which is essential for minimising transaction costs and thereby permitting institutions to 'make' a well-developed market. Economic growth, on the other hand, is more closely associated with the accumulation of fixed capital than working capital for it is in the nature of the former that it takes time to exhaust its contribution to the production of goods and services. Hence, if the rate of production flow is to increase, the stock of fixed capital, by its very nature, must *pari passu* increase. Since growth is one of the main focal points of this monograph, rather then delving deeply into the theory of the demand for working capital via the analysis of

---

their excessive cash holdings and ordering from suppliers additional producible durables to be held as part of the wealth holders' portfolios.

The lack of spot markets for such producible durables, however, would make it economically irrational for wealth holders, in a world of uncertainty, to behave in a way that Friedman proposes. (This will be discussed in greater detail in Chapters, 6 and 9 below.)

[1] This does not deny that some types of fixed capital goods may be sold out of 'shelf inventory'. Nevertheless, if the supplier of these 'shelf-inventory' fixed capital goods operates as an on-going concern, the cost of ordering replacement for the inventory as sold will be the short-period flow-supply price, and this will determine the offer price of the supplier of shelf-inventory goods.

[2] In abnormal times, that is, in periods of redundant capacity, the spot market for fixed capital may become active as individual entrepreneurs who wish to expand facilities purchase second-hand equipment from firms via bankruptcy proceedings at less than the flow-supply price.

organised spot and forward markets, it is desirable at this stage merely to adopt these aspects of the theory which will shed light on the problems of accumulation. This can be readily accomplished by employing a notional concept of a spot market in co-ordination with an analysis of an actual forward market for fixed capital.[1]

Expected Future Spot Prices and Current Forward Prices

The previous analysis has implied that it is only in spot markets that fluctuation in demand necessarily result in *pari passu* fluctuations in market prices. Neoclassical general equilibrium analysis tends to emphasise changes in prices responsive to changes in demand for, in essence, this approach involves viewing price determination as occurring in an economy where spot markets predominate and where flow-supply considerations are irrelevant (or at least unimportant). In the real world, however, spot markets actually exist for only a very few standardised durable goods; moreover most commodities which have spot markets also possess forward markets where flow considerations are relevant in determining price, and the prices in the two markets are inter-related.[2] Moreover, the forward (or flow-supply) price is normally the best estimate of the spot price at the future date.

Observation of statistical series of forward prices has shown that these series exhibit a random walk pattern. Working has developed the economic meaning of such random walks as follows:

> Pure random walk in a futures price is the price behavior that would result from perfect functioning of a futures market, the perfect futures market being defined as one in which the market price would constitute at all times the best estimate

[1] The analysis of this section is derived in large measure from Chapter 24 of Keynes's *Treatise* and from Kaldor, 'Speculation and Economic Growth'. Aspects of the theory of the *demand for liquid capital* solely for speculative purposes will be developed below; speculative activities in general will be discussed in Chapters 8 and 9 below.

[2] For all reproducible goods for which no spot market exists, flow-supply factors *are* important and for industries operating under neo-keynesian principles flow-supply considerations are primary in determining market price.

that could be made, from currently available information, of what the [spot] price would be at the delivery date of the futures contracts . . . the observation that the behavior of futures prices correspond closely to random walk thus led to the economic concept that futures prices are *reliably* anticipatory; that is, that they represent close approximations to the best current appraisals of prospects for the future.[1]

In Fig. 4.7 (a) the relevant spot and forward (or flow-supply) prices in the current period, t_1, are p_s^1 and p_f^1 respectively. With these prices, the stock of capital at the beginning of the t_2 period will be k_2 and therefore the stock supply schedule at time t_2 can be represented by a vertical line at k_2. If there has been no change in entrepreneurial long-period expectations, then the stock demand schedule (the D_k curve) at the beginning of the t_2 period will be unchanged, and therefore the spot price at the beginning of t_2, p_s^2, will be equal to the forward price in t_1, namely p_f^1. Consequently, as long as the factors underlying the stock-demand schedule and the short-period flow-supply schedule are expected to remain unchanged, and if no redundancy is expected in the t_1 period, the current flow-supply price will not only be the forward price, p_f^1, but it will, in the current t_1 period, reflect, as Working has indicated, the 'best current appraisal' of the expected spot price, p_s^2, in t_2.

If, of course, there was a sudden change in expectations at the beginning of t_1, this will be reflected in a shift in the stock-demand schedule. For example, if there is a change in expectations about future points of effective demand such that it is believed that capital goods will have higher net yields than was expected in the t_0 period, then the stock demand curve and therefore the market demand curve will be further to the right than previously. This new market curve, $D_k' + d_k'$, is shown in Fig. 4.7 (b). Working's statement can now be readily demonstrated via Fig. 4.7 (b). (In order not to clutter this latter diagram, the original market demand curve, $D_k + d_k$, has not

[1] H. Working, 'New Concepts Conerning Futures Markets and Prices', *Amer. Econ. Rev.* **52** (1962) pp. 446–7. Working continued: 'Conceiving the fluctuations of futures prices to be mainly appropriate responses to valid changes in expectations produces a great change in thought regarding them, as compared with regarding the price movements as mainly lacking economic justification.'

been drawn in, but the original spot and forward prices as well as the original k_1, k_2, and k_3 values have been transposed from Fig. 4.7 (a).) As a result of the rightward shift in the market demand curve due to this change in expectations, the forward price in t_1, $p_f^{1'}$, is greater than the forward price under the original expectations (p_f^1) and consequently the rate of accumulation will increase, and the stock of capital at the beginning of t_2 will be greater, i.e. $k_2' > k_2$, and therefore the spot price in t_2 will be $p_s^{2'}$ ($= p_f^{1'} > p_s^2 = p_f^1$).

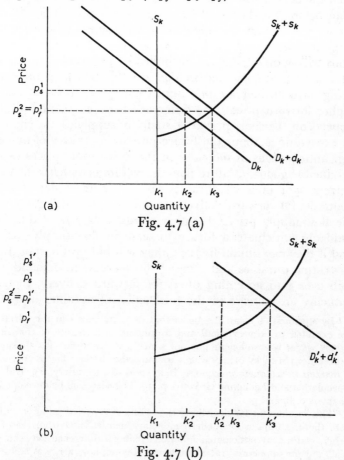

(a)

Fig. 4.7 (a)

(b)

Fig. 4.7 (b)

Accordingly, our analytical approach has demonstrated that the forward price at any point of time is the best estimate that can be *made with the information currently available*, as to the spot price at a future date. Ultimately the link between forward (current flow-supply) price, and expected future spot price is based on a belief in the stickiness of flow-supply prices (and therefore ultimately the expectation of stickiness in the money wage rate).[1] If, for example, at any moment expectations about future money wages suddenly change, e.g. if money wage rates are expected to rise (relative to productivity) in the next period, then the current *and* expected future spot price will be greater than before, for there will be an expected appreciation in the money value of the durable good at the point of time when the wage increase is expected (i.e. $a > 0$). This change in expectations will manifest itself in an increase in current demand for capital such as suggested in Fig. 4.7 (b), which in turn will bring forth an increase in output from $k_3 - k_1$ to $k_3' - k_1$ and a higher forward price. The difference between $p_f'^1$ and p_f^1 will depend on the short-period elasticity of supply. Thus changes in expectations about the future purchasing power of money, e.g. anticipations of increases in the flow-supply prices of re-producible goods in future periods, will immediately affect the current spot price of durables and the current demand for contracts for forward delivery of durables and thereby affect the flow-supply price.[2] In other words, if buyers of durables suddenly anticipate a future increase in flow-supply prices, and if they can obtain finance, they will bid up the spot price of existing durables and some of this increase in demand will spill over into accepting offers for forward delivery, thereby inducing an increase in the production of durables until the

[1] By stickiness, I mean the belief that period changes in the variables are expected to be very small and continuous, a zero rate of change in money wages is a sufficient but not a necessary condition for stickiness. Expectations of sticky money wages are important to the efficient operation of markets in a monetary economy in a world of uncertainty, e.g. Kaldor, 'Speculation and Economic Growth', p. 35. This view will be developed in Chapters 6, 8, and 9.

[2] This mechanism for describing the effects of expected inflation differs from the one utilised by modern monetary neoclassicists who, following Fisher, claim that anticipated inflation creates a difference between the 'real' and the 'monetary' rates of interest. Keynes, however, was adamant in his belief that Fisher's mechanism of a difference between real and monetary rates of inflation was hopelessly misleading in analysing cases of expected inflation. See Keynes, *The General Theory*, pp. 142–3.

increased flow-supply price and the carrying costs of the additional durables equals the expected savings obtained by accelerating the ordering of the durables. Hence, in a growing economy, when the flow-supply prices of producible durables are expected to be sticky, then current short-run flow-supply or offer prices are the most reliable estimate of the cost of buying such goods *either* spot or forward *at any future date*. Consequently, the current short-run flow-supply prices are the set of prices which individuals will use in their calculations to determine the future purchasing power of money and therefore the desired real quantity of cash balances they will need for any future expenditure plan.[1]

Redundant Capital, Spot and Forward Prices

If, at the beginning of period t_1, the stock of capital is redundant, the spot price (which may be notional) will fall below the forward price as a contango is established. The two possible contango markets are illustrated in Fig. 4.8 – contango with positive gross investment in Fig. 4.8 (a) and contango with zero gross investment in Fig. 4.8 (b).

In Fig. 4.8 (a) the spot price of p_s^{t1} is below the forward (flow-supply) price of p_f^{t1}, the redundancy is expected to be worked off before the end of the period, and the economy will begin period t_2 with a capital stock of k_2^a and an (expected) spot price of p_s^{t2} which is equal to the current flow-supply price. In Fig. 4.8 (b) gross investment is zero as the redundancy is expected to exceed depreciation, so that the economy will begin period t_2 with an inherited capital stock of k_2^b. Hence the expected spot price in period t_2 will be p_s^{t2}, which will therefore be the forward price, p_f^{t1}, in period t_1. The spot price in t_1, p_s^{t1}, will, of course, be less than the forward price. Fig. 4.8 (b) has been constructed so that although the stock of capital (k_2^b) at the beginning of t_2 is still redundant this surfeit is

---

[1] Accordingly, if individuals are to utilise money as a temporary abode of purchasing power either because they have already contracted for future delivery and payment or because they desire a vehicle for transferring purchasing power to the more remote and indefinite future, then such individuals must expect flow-supply prices of producible durables to be relatively sticky over time so that no matter how far the current spot price may be momentarily displaced, the market price at a future date will be at some anticipated level.

expected to be absorbed before the end of t_2, so that gross investment in t_2 is positive and the forward (flow-supply) price in t_2 is $p_f^{t_2}$. Thus at the beginning of period t_3 the economy is expected to inherit a capital stock of k_3^b, and the spot price at that time is expected to be $p_s^{t_3}$, which is equal to the forward price of $p_f^{t_2}$ in period t_2.

In Fig. 4.8 (a), the (expected) spot price of the t_2 period is equal to the flow-supply price in t_1, while in Fig. 4.8 (b) the (expected) spot price in t_3 will be equal to the flow-supply price of t_2. Thus, in any case of redundancy, the spot price at any time must fall sufficiently below the anticipated flow-supply price that is expected to exist in that period when the redundancy will be worked off in order to 'provide the carrying charges through the period[s] which is [are] expected to elapse before the redundant stocks are completely absorbed'.[1]

These carrying costs include (1) expected deterioration in quality or quantity; (2) warehouse and insurance charges; (3) interest charges; (4) any expected change in the money value of the goods due to expected changes in factors underlying the flow-supply schedule over the period in which the redundancy is being eliminated; and (5) the costs of transactions and brokerage fees if it is expected that the commodity may have to be sold before the surfeit is eliminated. (These costs are readily associated with the c, a, and l attributes which Keynes associated with durable goods in Chapter 17 of *The General Theory*.) Hence if it is expected to take n periods to work off the redundant stock, and if the total carrying cost per period is reckoned as x per cent of the expected short-period flow-supply price when the capital goods industry recovers, then the current spot price must be nx below the expected flow-supply price in the nth period, in order to provide the expectation of a normal profit for anyone to buy, hold, and ultimately utilise the capital goods over their useful life. Thus in contango the actual spot price (or notional spot price for durables where organised spot markets do not exist) declines sufficiently below the flow-supply price in order to make it worthwhile for the buyer (holder) of capital goods to hold them until a future time when they can be profitably

[1] Keynes, *Treatise on Money*, II 136.

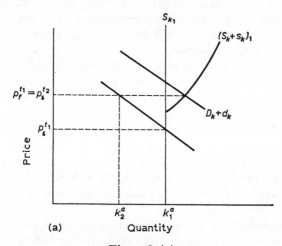

Fig. 4.8 (a) ·
Contango with Positive Gross Investment at time t_1

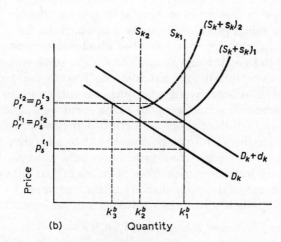

Fig. 4.8 (b)
Contango with Zero Gross Investment at time t_1

used. If, of course, n or x is so large that the product of n times x exceeds 100 per cent for any capital good, it would be abandoned by its owners, and the commodity would become a free good until such time as the redundancy has been reduced sufficiently so that $nx < 100$ per cent. Nevertheless once the one-shot capital loss due to the redundancy has been established in the notional or spot market valuation of capital goods, as long as $nx < 100$ per cent, these goods can be held and ultimately used with the expectation of earning a normal profit on the *current* spot valuation.

Thus, this scarcity theory of the demand for capital goods is compatible with both positive and negative expected rates of return on fixed capital goods even when such goods are still physically productive, a criterion which Keynes believed that only 'a correct theory' of capital accumulation would be able to meet.

Whenever there is a contango in the capital goods market, then previous investment decisions were, according to current expectations, grossly over-optimistic; and any attempt to employ labour with the entire current stock of capital to produce commodities for forward delivery at a date which is most *physically* efficient is expected to be uneconomical. In this situation the desire on the part of the community to postpone consumption and avoid exercising its current income claims is so strong that it produces a situation in which the full utilisation of the capital stock would require a volume of production of new capital goods so great that the capital stock will continue to be redundant. In this situation, as Keynes pointed out, a production process would become advantageous to society *merely* because it was lengthy 'in which event we should employ physically inefficient processes provided they were sufficiently lengthy for the gain from postponement to outweigh their inefficiency . . . [and] *short* processes would have to be kept sufficiently scarce for their physical efficiency to outweigh the disadvantage of the early delivery of their product'.[1]

In sum, when a contango exists in a durable good market,

---

[1] Keynes, *The General Theory*, p. 214. Thus, if it were not for the Vietnam war, American attempts to explore Mars, or Jupiter, the fruits of which cannot be had for decades, may be more socially advantageous to the United States than attempts at further exploration of the moon.

the current (actual or notional) spot price will be below the current forward price, which in turn will be below anticipated flow-supply price associated with that period when the surfeit of capital is expected to be entirely absorbed. The magnitude of the decline in spot price below the normal flow-supply price (which will equal the expected spot price in the period after the redundancy is removed) will depend on the number of periods till a normal market is expected to emerge plus the expected costs of carrying the durable till that future date. Thus:

> If the stocks are expected to be absorbed within a year, the present spot price must fall (say) 20 per cent below the anticipated future spot price, but if the stocks look like lasting for two years, then the present spot price must fall (say) 40 per cent.[1]

ABSORPTION, SPECULATION, AND TITLES TO CAPITAL: A PREVIEW

Working capital goods are essentially durables in the form of raw materials or semi-finished products which provide their entire yield in the course of the single period when they are utilised as an input in the production process. Since some goods take time to produce, working capital is a necessary adjunct to the production process. *Liquid capital* is that portion of the existing working capital stock which exceeds the quantity that normally would be held for a given short period production plan and which can be readily sold on a spot market. In essence, liquid capital is superfluous to the requirements of a given production plan.[2] Every unit of the existing stock of liquid

---

[1] Keynes, *Treatise on Money*, II 144.

[2] In fact, some working capital goods in excess of a given production plan may not be very liquid because well-organised spot markets for these goods do not exist. In these cases, surplus working capital is similar to redundant fixed capital when changes in notional valuation occur.

capital, however, must be expected to compete as an input with a unit of working capital that will be produced and sold at its expected flow-supply price at some future date. In a period of surplus working capital stocks therefore, the actual (or notional) spot price of working capital must decline sufficiently below the expected future flow-supply price for such goods in order to encourage the buyer that it is worth while to hold an existing unit to that future date when it is expected to be a competitive input to a newly produced unit.

It is through the spot price mechanism that the economic system which abhors the existence of a stock of redundant capital which is a result of past miscalculation, generates powerful forces to discourage any new production until the existing surplus is absorbed. Thus, as Keynes noted. 'the efforts to get rid of surplus stocks aggravate the slump, and the success of these efforts retards the recovery'.[1] Miscalculations, there-fore, which are almost inevitable in a world of uncertainty, leave their imprint on the employment and production history of the economy. Obviously, therefore, miscalculations aggra-vated by speculative excess can readily alter the output path of the economy.

For fixed capital goods, the situation is only somewhat more complex since these durables provide their yields only gradually over a succession of future production periods. An existing unit of fixed capital, therefore, will have to compete over a number of periods during its useful life with future newly produced fixed capital goods sold at expected flow-supply prices in a succession of future periods. When the existing stock of fixed capital is found to be redundant because of previous misjudge-ments, then the spot price must fall sufficiently to allow the existing units to be profitably held for future production. Since spot markets for the *hire-purchase* (or use) of fixed capital goods are not well-developed due to the lack of standardisation, the decline in the spot 'hire' price is likely to be notional in nature. Nevertheless, previous over-optimistic errors in forecasting the current requirements for fixed capital will reduce the demand for the hire of capital in the forward markets, and therefore impinge on the historical growth path of the economy. Thus the actual rate of accumulation in a world of uncertainty is

[1] Keynes, *Treatise on Money*, II 145.

unlikely to follow the rules of growth developed by economists using models based on certainty (or tranquility) postulates.

Although second-hand units of fixed capital goods are de-standardised, fractionalised titles to either units of fixed capital or aggregates of fixed capital can be standardised, thereby permiting the development of organised spot and forward markets for such titles.[1] In a world of uncertainty the existence of such security markets as well as the existence of spot and forward markets for titles to working capital goods – commodity markets – permit speculative activity in titles to all types of capital goods. Although a thorough discussion of speculation in 'capital titles' will be developed in Chapters 9 to 11, some useful insights can be presented at this stage.

The Impact of Speculation on Economic Activity
Contractual arrangements for the purchase of titles to capital can be important in linking speculative activity to production activity. Since spot and future contracts for the purchase of title to working capital calls for the *delivery* of the physical goods, which when used will be entirely consumed in one production period, while spot and future contracts for the purchase of titles to fixed capital do *not* normally require delivery (hire purchase) of physical capital (which even when used will require many production periods to consume) the former represent inextricable commitments for both ownership and control of a relatively short-lived durable while the latter permit – and encourage – the separation of ownership from use of a long-lived productive asset. Speculation in commodity contracts inevitably affects the production and use of these specific short-lived goods, while speculation in titles to fixed capital does not directly affect the production and use of such goods; it affects the demand for hire purchase and therefore accumulation only to the extent that it affects financial conditions. (A discussion of financial aspects is undertaken in Chapters 11 to 13.)

Since the future is always uncertain, if a contango has developed say for working capital, no one can be sure when

[1] Thus it is important to distinguish between spot and forward markets for titles to fixed capital and notional spot and forward markets for the hire purchase of fixed capital; a distinction not required for working capital.

the redundant stock of goods will be absorbed in the production process, but since such goods are short-lived, once the redundancy is over, replacement demand will be the major proportion of current demand. Any individual who believes he has a better insight than the market into the number of periods (n) necessary to absorb the surplus, can speculate on his ability to outguess the market. If, for example, the market believes that $n = 4$, while an individual speculator believes that $n = 2$, then the current spot price will appear to the individual to undervalue the good. The speculator, although he has no desire to utilise the raw materials in production in the future, expects he can make a profit in excess of his carrying costs, if he buys (and takes delivery) spot and then resells his holdings two periods hence when events prove him correct and the large shortages he expects develop. Alternatively because of the existence of a well-organised forward market, the speculator can buy a forward contract for delivery two periods from now and since the market expects the redundancy to persist for more than two periods, this forward price will be below the expected future minimum flow-supply price. If in two periods, the surplus has been absorbed, then the spot price must be above the forward price and therefore the minimum flow-supply price of that period, and our speculator can sell the goods delivered under his forward contract at the higher spot price in the $n = 2$ spot market.

Similarly, if the individual believes that $n = 6$, while the market evaluates n at 4, the speculator can make a profit if he sells a forward contract for delivery at $n = 4$ at the forward price (which is equal to or above the minimum flow-supply price) even though he does not plan to engage in the production of the good during the interim. The speculator will be required to buy spot at $n = 4$ in order to make good on his promised delivery, and if events prove him correct, the stock will still be redundant so that the spot price will be below the minimum flow-supply price and a profit will be made.

The speculator, as opposed to the investor (buyer or hire-purchaser of fixed or working capital goods) and the producer of capital goods, is not interested in either utilising the goods in further production or organising the flow of production of new capital goods. The speculator is merely interested in utilising the legal *title* to such goods as a store of wealth which will increase his financial claims on the future. Most speculators, if they were required to take possession *and use* of either working or fixed capital goods would have neither the knowledge, the time, nor the ancillary facilities necessary in order to utilise these in the further production of goods for ultimate consumption. It is only when a well-developed spot market for titles to capital goods exists, that the items actually traded in the spot market become subject to speculation.[1] Since spot and forward contracts for titles to working capital call for physical delivery ('hire-purchase'), while the markets for titles to fixed capital call for delivery of legal titles but *not* physical goods (no necessary hire-purchase), the ability of speculative excesses in the market for working capital to disrupt the flow of production of goods that use certain working capital commodities as inputs is much greater and more direct than speculative excess in the market for titles to fixed capital goods.

If a speculator anticipates that the spot price at a future date of any durable is going to be greater than the existing forward price, he will 'buy' a forward contract. For working capital goods, the acceptance of forward contracts by speculators permits the producer to enter into hiring commitments, assured of his sales-revenue; while the speculator has, he hopes, used the forward contract as a purely financial means of transferring values from others to himself at the future date, for he anticipates he will be able to profitably sell spot at that time to those who wish to utilise the commodity in further production. If, however, no well-organised spot market for the durable exists – as is the case for hire-purchase of fixed capital goods and certain working capital goods – then a forward contract for hire-purchase of the good will be useless to the speculator, for even if he is correct he will have no mechanism readily available to convert the notional spot value into a financial claim.

It is because of the development of spot markets for some working capital goods that forward contracts in commodity markets are often 'used chiefly as purely financial rather than merchandising contracts',[2] since the speculative buyers (sellers)

---

[1] Such well-developed spot markets require a financial institution which assures continuity by 'making' the market.

[2] Working, 'New Concepts', p. 433 n.

of forward contracts do not expect to take possession (organise production) of the good. Instead, the speculator buyers (sellers) plan to sell (buy) the commodity spot on the delivery date. The speculator is venturing on the difference between the existing forward price and his expected spot price at that future date.

Speculation which can play such an important part (a) directly in encouraging or discouraging production of specific working capital goods, and (b) indirectly via financial circumstances in the market for the hire purchase of fixed capital, could only occur in an uncertain world, where changes in factors underlying all demand and supply schedules can never be anticipated with certainty. Thus the historical path of employment, output, and accumulation for any real world economy are inextricably tied to conditions of uncertainty.

The speculator is gambling on his specialised skills and abilities to foresee changes in future demand and supply factors which the rest of the market does not expect. The speculator believes that, in an uncertain world, he can foresee future events better than the best estimate the market can make with the currently available information. Such behaviour would, of course, be illogical in a Walrasian world of perfect certainty. Yet such behaviour is common in the real world where well-organised spot markets for titles to capital goods exist.

If speculators are more bullish than the 'market' about the future, they will increase the demand for titles. In working capital (commodity) markets this will directly increase the demand for the future production of the commodity producing firms and will therefore directly stimulate the demand for resources. In the markets for titles to fixed capital goods, on the other hand, this increase in demand by speculators does not increase the acceptance of forward contracts from producers of fixed capital goods – for the speculators have no spot market in which they can resell the actual capital goods! Thus speculative activity in titles to fixed capital goods will have an effect on the demand for resources only to the extent that it alters financial conditions and the ability of entrepreneurs to externally finance new investment.

Thus the more bullish speculators are, relative to 'normal' market buyers of working capital titles, the greater the possible future redundancy of durable commodities, if future events prove the speculators wrong. These future redundancies will, of course, set up strong spot price movements relative to flow-supply prices (at the future dates) which will depress economic activity in the working capital industries when the errors of the speculators are recognised. Excessive bullish speculation in titles to fixed capital goods, *to the extent they affect financial conditions*, can stimulate additional net investment which can lead to a future redundancy, if future events prove entrepreneurial long-period expectations were wrong.

If, on the other hand, speculators are proved correct in working capital markets, the economy will start a future period with a stock of working capital which is more appropriate for its production plans in that period than what would have been available had the economy depended on the normal market forces of earlier periods to foresee the future. Similarly, if the speculative demand for titles to fixed capital goods provides easier financial conditions which stimulates additional net investment in fixed capital goods, and if these entrepreneurial expectations prove correct, then the current activity of speculators will be advantageous to the future.

If speculators have bearish expectations, on the other hand, their activity in the titles markets will depress the forward price for certain working capital goods, as well as tighten financial conditions, *ceteris paribus*, in the money markets. The ultimate impact in either case will be to discourage producers from entering into hiring commitments to produce additional capital goods. If these bearish sentiments are proved incorrect by events, a shortage of capital will occur in the future, altering the time path of accumulation. If speculators prove right, on the other hand, then they have provided the economy with a 'better' guide to the proper rate of accumulation than normal market forces.

The more uncertain the future is, the more likely human miscalculations become. The institutional arrangements for spot and forward markets in some working capital goods and in titles to fixed capital which exist in developed capitalist economies encourage men to develop proclivities towards trying to outguess the average view. In the normal course of events in such capital markets 'speculators may do no harm as bubbles on a steady stream of enterprise. But the position is serious when enterprise becomes the bubble on a whirlpool of speculation'[1] for 'it is enterprise which builds and improves the world's possessions'.[2] Thus, when the future is unknown, speculation may run rampant in these markets, causing, for example, either 'rational' producers of working capital goods to bring forth additions to total supply tomorrow, which in the dawn's early light, may prove to be a blunder, or easier financial conditions which encourage entrepreneurs to install excess capacity. The resulting effort of the economy to rectify the error in the shortest period of time can have a substantial impact on employment, output, prices, and the distribution of windfall losses and/or gains.[3]

[1] Keynes, *The General Theory*, p. 159.
[2] Keynes, *Treatise on Money*, II 148.
[3] Since the spot market for the hire-purchase of fixed capital goods is unlikely to be as well developed as the spot market for working capital, speculative activity in this former market is likely to be held to a minimum because of the high transactions costs of bringing buyers and sellers together. Hence, the spot market for the hire purchase of fixed capital is likely to be active only during periods of bankruptcy where firms are required to liquidate these assets at below notional values in order to meet contractual obligations. Speculation in titles to fixed capital can, however, via finance, affect the forward market for the hire purchase of fixed capital.

CHAPTER 5

Accumulation and Growth in Effective Demand

IF the process of accumulation is to be left to free and independent decisions of firms operating in a market-oriented, monetary economy, then continuous steady rates of growth require that entrepreneurs (a) expect constant rates of growth in effective demand over time, and (b) these expectations are not disappointed.[1] In reality, of course, these provisions are not likely to be continually met, but at an early stage of analysis it may be useful to explore the circumstances that would be necessary to bring these conditions about.

In the traditional short-run Keynesian analysis of Chapter 3, the point of effective demand is defined as the intersection of the aggregate supply and demand functions. It can be shown[2] that the point of effective demand at a time t_o is given by

$$Y_o = \left[\frac{1}{s_w(\alpha) + s_c(1 - \alpha)} \right] [A^{t_o} + I_g^{t_o}] \qquad (1)$$

where

Y_o is effective demand at t_o

s_w and s_c are the marginal propensities to save out of wages and gross profits respectively

α is the wage share in gross national product

$I_g^{t_o}$ is gross investment at time t_o

A^{t_o} is all other autonomous (or not related to current income) expenditures.

---

[1] Or if current results disappoint long-term expectations of current sales-proceeds, these realisations do not feed back on long-term beliefs, i.e. long-run expectations are inert with respect to short-run movements.

[2] See Appendix.

In Fig. 5.1, the point of effective demand, Y_o, is given by the intersection of the aggregate supply function, Z^t_o and the aggregate demand function, D^t_o at time t_o. The equilibrium

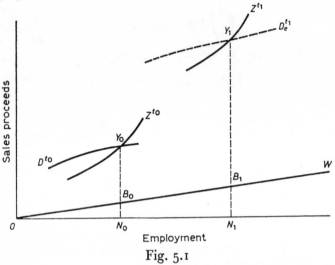

Fig. 5.1

level of employment is N_o. Given the money wage rate, the OW line represents the money-wage bill for alternative levels of employment.

If effective demand is to grow over time, then both productive capacity and the demand for goods must, *pari passu*, increase. Growth in effective demand in a simple two sector model ultimately depends on increases in that process which generates additional income – namely gross investment. It follows from equation (1) that

$$\Delta Y = \left[\frac{1}{s_w(\alpha) + s_c(1 - \alpha)} \right] \Delta I_g \qquad (2)$$

where

ΔY is the change in effective demand from t_o to t_1, and

ΔI_g is the change in gross investment from t_1 to t_o

The investment in the t_o period helped create the capacity on which the aggregate supply curve Z^{t_1} of the t_1 period in Fig. 5.1 is based, while the gross investment undertaken in period t_o depended on expectations about effective demand points not only in t_1, but also t_2, t_3, etc. If expectations are continuously met, then connecting the points of effective demand such as Y_o, Y_1, etc. traces out the growth path of the economy. In order to keep the exposition simple, it will be assumed that the anticipated profits associated with any unit of physical capital is the same in t_1, t_2, etc. over the life of the unit. Thus, the analysis can focus primarily on comparisons of the t_1 and t_o period.

In order to have decided to install $I^{t_o}{}_g$ in the t_o period, entrepreneurs must have had some expectation of total quasi-rents relative to the money wage bill in period t_1 (and the subsequent periods), i.e. if entrepreneurs were motivated by the desire to make profits on their financial commitments, they must have had some expectation about future points of effective demand. For example, in the aggregate, they may have expected the dotted aggregate demand curve $D_e^{t_1}$, as shown in Fig. 5.1. Hence, given the point of effective demand Y_1 in t_1, the increase in gross profits (quasi-rents) which induced the expansion in the capital stock between t_o and t_1 which is implicit in the gross investment component of the aggregate demand function of t_o can be obtained from Fig. 5.1 as

$$\Delta P = (Y_1 N_1 - Y_o N_o) - (B_1 N_1 - B_o N_o) \qquad (3)$$

where ΔP is the change in gross profits from t_o to t_1, $(Y_1 N_1 - Y_o N_o)$ is the change in total sales-proceeds, and $(B_1 N_1 - B_o N_o)$ is the change in the wage bill, under the simplifying assumption of a constant money-wage rate.

In each period, however, realised gross profits at the point of realised effective demand can be shown[1] to be

$$P^t = \left[\frac{1}{s_w\left(\dfrac{\alpha}{1-\alpha}\right) + s_c} \right] [A^t + I_g^t] \qquad (4)$$

where P^t is gross profits in the tth period.[2] Changes in gross profits, therefore are

$$\Delta P = \left[\frac{1}{s_w\left(\dfrac{\alpha}{1-\alpha}\right) + s_c} \right] [\Delta I_g] \qquad (5)$$

---

[1] See Appendix.

[2] In equilibrium, when commodity markets are clearing, gross profits equals gross investment plus all other autonomous spending plus consumption by profit recipients less workers' savings. Cf. J. Robinson, *Essays in Economic Growth*, p. 45.

Hence while it is expectations of changes in gross profits which induce entrepreneurs to undertake net investment in t_o, actual changes in profits will depend on actual changes in investment expenditure over time. Accordingly, if long period entrepreneurial expectations are ultimately to be justified by future events, entrepreneurs, in the aggregate, must have correct and consistent forecasts of the changes in sales-proceeds over time which will be associated with changes in gross investment spending[1] which will actually be undertaken. In other words, for entrepreneurs to be satisfied with their rate of installation of newly produced capital goods, they must advance their contractual acceptances for capital goods each period at a rate sufficient to generate growth in aggregate demand to match the increased sales expectations which led to their desire to increase capital. If this harmonious state of affairs happens to exist, then the economy is on its warranted rate of growth path. If not, then actual growth will differ from the warranted rate of growth.[2] In an uncertain world where 'growth is the aggregated effect of a great number of individual decisions'[3] and since individual decisions are based on trial and *error*, it is unlikely that an economy will be able to maintain an unchanging warranted rate of growth as errors and inconsistent entrepreneurial forecasts are almost inevitable. If the increment in actual sales over time differs significantly from expectations, then the rate of capital accumulation undertaken by entrepreneurs depends, in large measure, on how these realisations will alter their future expectations, and whether changes in expectations induce spending behaviour which brings about economic forces which permit these new hopes to be fulfilled. Thus a decentralised capitalist system operating in an uncertain world will typically follow a wobbly growth path except in the unlikely case where there is a mechanism which assures that entrepreneurs will maintain their long-run expectations even in the face of surprise by current events. An uncontrolled capitalist economy is, in fact, essentially unstable.

[1] Actually with changes in all autonomous expenditures.

[2] Harrod defines the warranted rate of growth as 'the condition in which producers are content with what they are doing', while actual growth is the actual 'increment in output in any period'. See R. F. Harrod, *Towards Dynamic Economics* (London: Macmillan, 1948) pp. 77–85.   [3] ibid., p. 76.

INVESTMENT, INDUCED CONSUMPTION, AND GROWTH
IN THE KEYNESIAN SYSTEM[1]

Hiring and production decisions in a market-oriented economy ultimately depend on expected short-period sales proceeds. Consumption outlays are generated by current hiring decisions and current profits (or recent past profits).[2] Thus, if current consumption is primarily a function of current income for wage earners and profit recipients and if aggregate profits and employment in any period depends on gross investment in that period, then, in a sense, *'supply decisions generate the consumer outlay sums'*.[3] Since warranted growth necessitates concomitant increases in purchasing activity and productive capacity, then dynamic equilibrium requires, in a simple two sector model, induced increases in consumption spending to be in a 'proper' relation to increases in gross (and net) investment. Hence, if different groups of households have different consumption propensities, the distribution of income becomes an important variable in determining the condition necessary for a steady-state warranted rate of growth.

Given depreciation per period, and given the savings propensities of various groups, continuous growth in output requires current net investment plans being justified by future points of effective demand (which embody future investment

[1] Much of the following analysis is based on S. Weintraub, *A Keynesian Theory of Employment, Growth, and Income Distribution* (Philadelphia: Chilton, 1966), esp. pp. 30 ff.

[2] Kalecki argues that current consumption by profit recipients is a function of last period's profits. See M. Kalecki, *Theory of Economic Dynamics*. Revised ed. (London: Allen and Unwin, 1965) p. 53.

This view tends to draw an arbitrary distinction between the variable which induces consumption spending and the source of finance of that spending. For example, if wage earners were to get paid at the end of each week, then, in general, they would finance this week's spending from last week's wages – but, in a monetary economy, this necessarily means that this week's consumption is a function of last week's income. If a fairly long period of clock time is chosen as the interval – say one year – this distinction between the variable inducing spending and the source of finance for this endogenous spending becomes less relevant, although 'life cycles' and 'permanent income' hypothesis suggests that even annual income magnitudes are inappropriate.

[3] S. Weintraub, *A Keynesian Theory*, p. 128. Cf. Kalecki, *Theory of Economic Dynamics*, p. 54.

commitments). Nevertheless, even in an economy where the supply and demand for output are growing in step, there is no necessity for the growth of effective demand to keep pace with the growth of the effective labour force.[1] In other words, in Fig. 5.1, the equilibrium levels of employment in each period (e.g. N_0 and N_1) may be equal to, or less than, the supply of labour in each period. In fact, given the money-wage rate, warranted growth merely requires, the effective demand points in Fig. 5.1 (e.g. Y_0 and Y_1) to move in a northerly direction over time, and not necessarily in a northeasterly direction. Hence it is possible to have growth with growing unemployment, as technological progress[2] leads to a growth in output per head in excess of the growth in demand per head.

In Chapter 2, it was indicated that Keynes altered the definition of the aggregate demand function from one involving producers' expectations of buyers' expenditures at alternative levels of employment to one involving potentially realised expenditures of buyers' at alternative employment levels, on the assumption that, for production and hiring decisions, the differences between expectations and realisations are never very large. Once long-period expectations underlying investment decisions are made the focal point however, intertemporal disappointment can no longer be ignored. If, for example, in period t_1, the 'realised' aggregate demand function as given by $D_r^{t_1}$ in Fig. 5.2. is less than the one that was expected $(D_e^{t_1})$ when investment was undertaken in the t_0 period, then

---

[1] Some economists, notably Kaldor and Pasinetti, have assumed a pricing mechanism where commodity prices are more flexible than money wage rates *and* investment spending is always sufficient to ensure full employment to develop growth models where demand grows at full employment. (For example, N. Kaldor, 'Some Fallacies in The Interpretation of Kaldor', *Rev. Econ. Stud.*, 1970, p. 6 and L. L. Pasinetti 'Rate of Profit and Income Distribution in Relation to the Rate of Economic Growth', *Rev. Econ. Stud.* 1962.) Other economists, notably the modern neoclassicists such as Solow, Patinkin, Friedman, Tobin, etc. have assumed flexible wages and prices – and therefore (as we demonstrate in Chapters 6 to 9) a barter economy, in order to provide a model of growth at full employment.

[2] Actually, technological progress and/or a change in the composition of demand toward products whose labour inputs are very low can create 'technological unemployment'. For a complete discussion of potential capital-output and capital-labour ratios see Weintraub, *A Keynesian Theory*, pp. 33–8.

entrepreneurial long-run expectations will be disappointed at time t_1. If this bad luck is taken to be only a temporary and random fluctuation[1] which will quickly be compensated for, and no change is anticipated in the long run path of future

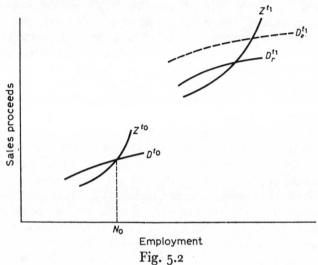

Fig. 5.2

points of effective demand (so that long-term expectations are inert) then planned capital installations can proceed unchanged, and if finance is available, growth can continue uninterrupted – until entrepreneurs are convinced by a series of surprising events that their initial long-term expectations were wrong.

If, on the other hand, entrepreneurs interpret a current sales-proceeds realisation which is less than the current revenue which was expected in the previous periods (when capacity was being installed to meet anticipated current demand), as symptomatic of a continuing deficiency in demand in future periods[2] then part of the existing stock of capital at the beginning of t_2 will be considered redundant. A contango will

[1] 'It is of the nature of long-term expectations that they cannot be checked at short-intervals in the light of realised results'. Keynes, *The General Theory*, p. 51.

[2] Actually this is a more stringent requirement than is required to move the economy off its previous warranted growth path. A sufficient condition is that current realisations induce a belief that previous expectations of growth were either overoptimistic or underoptimistic.

develop in the market for capital goods[1] and until the surplus capital stock is expected to disappear either because of physical wearing-out or an expected increase in demand at some future date,[2] gross investment will fall to zero. As a consequence, the realised aggregate demand function in t_2 will be below its counterpart in t_1. This reduction in realised effective demand in t_2 may, in turn, increase the belief in capital redundancy in t_3, (even after depreciation) and therefore induce a continual self-fulfilling feeling of pessimism as once-wounded entrepreneurs become more gun-shy.

Alternatively, disappointed current sales proceeds realisations may be interpreted by entrepreneurs as indicating that effective demand will continue to grow – but at a much slower rate than previously expected. Consequently, the existing capacity may not be viewed as redundant at the beginning of t_2; instead addition to capacity may still be required, but the desired rate of expansion may be lower than previously. Entrepreneurs will therefore still enter into contracts for the ordering of new capital goods in t_2, but at a slower rate than in t_1. Net investment in t_2 can still be positive, but it will not be growing at the same rate as before and it may even decline. Consequently, the actual rate of growth between t_1 and t_2 will decline, even if economic activity does not slump. The economy may experience either a sluggish rate of growth (as compared to the historical growth path) or even a recession. These results may then feed back into self-fulfilling entrepreneurial feelings of pessimism and stagnation, unless or until some future events revive the flagging long-run expectations of entrepreneurs.

In a similar manner, if the realised aggregate demand function in t_1 exceeds expectations, and this pleasantly surprising result induces entrepreneurs to increase their long run sales expectations, then gross investment will rise even more rapidly creating boom conditions which can continue only until such time as expectations outrun resource constraints, or shortages of finance

[1] See Chapter 4.

[2] Given technology, the rate of discount used by firms to evaluate the worthwhileness of investment projects, will determine how far in advance of the expected increase in demand firms will order the new equpiment necessary to provide additional capacity to meet the expected increment in demand.

(particularly in inflationary conditions) chokes off investment.[1]

This latter view of volatile long-period expectations when actual growth of demand is different from the warranted or expected growth underlies Harrod's argument that when expectations are not satisfied, 'there will not be any tendency to adapt production towards G_w [the warranted rate of growth], but on the contrary, a tendency to adapt production still further away from it, whether on the higher or lower side'.[2] This view has often been mislabelled Harrod's knife-edge in the literature.[3]

In sum, if long-period expectations about future points of effective demand are inert, economies may maintain warranted steady rates of growth over time, until entrepreneurs ultimately loose faith in their previous expectations of the growth of demand. If, on the other hand, long-term expectations are impetuously and disproportionately based on the facts of the existing situation, then in a world of uncertainty, where disappointment is inevitable, maintenance of any steady warranted growth path is unlikely. In either case, of course, the actual rate of growth need not generate sufficient demand to employ the entire labour force over time, or at any point of time.

TWO NEO-KEYNESIAN VIEWS ON GROWTH

Using essentially the same conceptual building blocks,[4] but utilising them under somewhat different assumptions, Joan

---

[1] Problems of finance and inflation will be dealt with in the following chapters.　　　　[2] Harrod, *Towards Dynamic Economics*, p. 87.

[3] Knife-edge connotes a fine balancing point which if not obtained causes the system to fall *rapidly* away from the warranted path. The degree of falling away, in Harrod's model depends on the sensitivity to change long-run expectations on the basis of current facts. Harrod has argued that there are a number of built-in frictions in the system and suggests the top of a shallow dome as more accurate representation of the situation than a knife-edge. R. F. Harrod 'Harrod after Twenty Years', *Econ. Jour.* (1970) pp. 740–1.

[4] The intellectual antecedents of these building blocks are to be found in Marshall, Keynes, and Kalecki. Essentially, equations (1) and (2) are from Keynes, while equations (4) and (5) are from Kalecki. For example, see Kalecki's *Theory of Economic Dynamics*, chapter 5.

See Chapter 2 for a discussion of the Marshallian underpinnings of the neo-keynesian theories. Walras, and the the traditional neoclassical general equilibrium approach is viewed as a snare and a delusion by the Neo-keynesians.

Robinson, on the one hand, and Kaldor and Pasinetti, on the other, have developed neo-keynesian growth models which reach similar – but not identical – conclusions. Thus Cambridge growth models, which appear to many outsiders as a monolithic 'Anglo-Hungarian-Italian' view, are two distinct variants of the aggregate supply and demand model developed by Keynes in *The General Theory*. The advocates of these neo-keynesian (or neo-kaleckian) models believe that they highlight certain policy aspects which would otherwise be buried in the traditional Keynesian approach.

In these neo-keynesian models, equation (4), which indicates that gross profit in any period is a multiple of gross investment[1] is made the focal point of the model. This keystone equation is interrupted as indicating that, in equilibrium, gross investment spending will generate a level of effective demand which produces a level of absolute profits equal to what entrepreneurs expected when they undertook short-period production commitments.

In Joan Robinson's model, individual firms, operating in a tranquil world, but producing in anticipation of market, have to make a pricing and production decision in advance of actual sales. Hence each firm settles on a price level (relative to prime or wage costs) which entrepreneurs expect will yield a normal return on the standard or target volume of production to be undertaken in the period. With tranquillity, expectations will be realised, and this 'normal return' will just cover an annual sum which will cover overheads including depreciation and yield a normal profit on the committed finance. The choice of standard volume at 60 per cent of plant capacity, or 80 per cent, or any other level, ultimately depends, in the Robinsonian view, on entrepreneurs having correct expectations of the demand conditions facing the firm[2] relative to the average total cost curve (as illustrated in Fig. 3.1 of Chapter 3).

Given the money-wage rate and unit prime costs, entrepre-

---

[1] More generally, gross profits are a function of autonomous expenditures, i.e.

$$P = \left[\frac{1}{s_w\left(\dfrac{\alpha}{1-\alpha}\right) + s_c} \right] [I_g + (G - T) + (X - M)]$$

where G is government expenditures on goods and services, T is tax revenues, X is export receipts, and M is import expenditures.

[2] See J. Robinson, 'A Further Note', *Rev. of Econ. Stud.*, **36** (1969) p. 260.

neurs therefore set profit margins and hire workers based on their short-term expectations of market demand conditions and their need to earn a return on the committed finance. If, in the aggregate, the sum of the profit margins multiplied by standard volume in each firm just equals aggregate profits as determined by equation (4) above, then entrepreneurs will have, in the aggregate, correctly forecast the point of effective demand, and they will be satisfied with the outcome. Thus, in a tranquil world where equilibrium is achieved (in the Robinsonian model), whatever the volume of investment spending, the level of prices relative to money wages in the consumption and investment sectors and the level of employment in each sector must be such that given the savings propensities of workers and profit recipients and entrepreneurial investment commitments, the quantity demanded in each sector must equal the standard volume produced.[1] Accordingly, the level of employment is determined in the short-run by the technique of production embodied in existing plant and the entrepreneurial view as to the standard volume at which a normal return can be obtained. Thus, the greater the expected standard volume (and therefore the smaller mark-up necessary to generate normal profits), the greater the short-period level of employment. Moreover, as long as entrepreneurs, in the aggregate, have short-term expectations which sum up to a level of profits which is just equal to that determined by equation (4), then no matter what price and standard volume (and therefore employment level) is adopted, entrepreneurial short-term expectations will be realised. If, on the other hand, normal profit views either exceed or fall short of the level of profits determined by equation (4), then short-term entrepreneurial expectations would, in the Robinsonian model, always be disappointed, *no matter what margins or price levels are chosen*, since product markets will never clear in the sense of the flow of demand for products just equalling the flow of output at

---

[1] Or as Joan Robinson puts it on p. 40 of her *Essays on Economic Growth*: 'Whatever the rate of investment may be, the level and distribution of income must be such as to induce the firms and households, between them, to wish to carry out savings at an equal rate . . . the level of prices relative to money wages is such, in equilibrium conditions, as to provide sufficient profits to call forth a rate of savings equal to the rate of net investment'.

offer prices for standard volumes. Such a result would be a disequilibrium one – and can not be readily handled by the steady-state growth models of the Neo-keynesians.

A comparison of the similarities and the differences between the earlier Keynes growth model (as developed by Harrod and Weintraub) and the Robinsonian view can be readily observed, once the latter has been presented into an aggregate supply–aggregate demand format. Since the behavioural aspects of entrepreneurial pricing and production decisions is different in the Robinsonian model from that pattern hypothesised by Keynes in *The General Theory* (i.e. target return pricing in the former, profit-maximising in the latter), the Robinsonian aggregate supply function must be conceptually different from its Keynesian counterpart. In the Robinsonian model, the aggregate supply function can be *initially* conceived as the aggregate analogue of the average cost curve, ATC, of the representative neo-keynesian firm (as depicted in Fig. 3.1 of Chapter 3). This aggregate function relates the aggregate supply price or expected total sales proceeds entrepreneurs would require in order to hire alternative levels of employment, where the expected sales revenue would just yield a normal profit, in the aggregate, for any given level of employment. Accordingly each point on this initial aggregate supply function is given by the sum of the wage bill associated with the level of employment plus a fixed annual sum which equals the quasi-rents necessary to cover overheads and yield a normal expected return on the committed finance.

In Fig. 5.3, therefore, the AZ_b curve is the aggregate supply function; it indicates alternative expected aggregate supply prices or sales-proceeds which would leave entrepreneurs contented for the alternative quantities of workers which they could hire in the period. Given the money wage rate, OW is the wage bill line, while the normal profits expected on the committed finance in the period is equal to the vertical distance OA in Fig. 5.3. The vertical distance between the aggregate supply curve and the wage bill line is, by construction, unchanged; hence, the greater the equilibrium level of employment in the period, the larger the wage share as a proportion of total sales revenue or gross national product. If the expected aggregate demand function is ED_e in Fig. 5.3, then the point of expected effective demand is B and in the aggregate, N workers will be hired by entrepreneurs to produce the standard volumes of output in the various industries. At this employment level, aggregate consumption receipts are expected to be NG (assum-

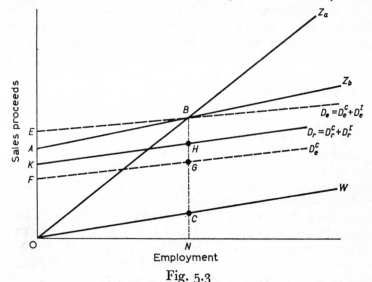

Fig. 5.3

ing FD_e^c is the expected aggregate consumption function[1]), and sales revenue in the capital goods industries is expected to total BG. If an aggregate sales revenue of BN is realised, then actual gross profits of BC will equal that level, OA, which entrepreneurs expected. Thus, if entrepreneurs actually spend BG on new capital goods, and if they have correctly forecast the market demand for goods generated by this level of investment plus induced consumption spending, then the expected and the realised profits of BC will be related to gross investment of BG by the relationship specified in equation (4).

At this stage, the major difference between this neo-keynesian aggregate supply function and the one conceptualised by Keynes in *The General Theory* is that this supply relationship (AZ_b) is constructed to represent potential alternative sales-proceeds-hiring decisions *before* a price policy is adopted by the firms while the traditional Keynesian function is developed

[1] Where workers' consumption spending is a function of the wage bill line, and capitalists' consumption is a function of gross profits.

given the particular price policy of the firms. Accordingly, it is possible to construct a second, more conventional, aggregate supply function (OZ_a in Fig. 5.3) which is the macroanalogue of the Marshallian short-period flow-supply curve (S_pS in Fig. 3.1 of Chapter 3). The OZ_a function shows alternative sales-proceeds that can be expected to be forthcoming after prices and profit margins had been decided on, by neo-keynesian firms, for alternative output decisions. At the point of expected effective demand both the Z_b and Z_a functions coincide. Thus the difference[1] between the supply behaviour implicit in AZ_b and that in the more conventional OZ_a becomes important only if the realised aggregate demand function differs from the expected, e.g. if in Fig. 5.3 KD_r represents realisable demand expenditures for alternative levels of employment. It is, therefore, when short-run expectations are disappointed that differences appear between the Robinsonian and the conventional Keynes model.

In the Keynes model, if, at a given level of employment, realisable aggregate demand (point H in Fig. 5.3) is less than expected effective demand (point B), then given the level of gross investment, supply responses,[2] and spending propensities, the short-run level of employment will decline. Thus short-run adjustments to disequilibrium occur primarily via changes in output and employment, and only secondarily via changes in income distribution and/or prices which are associated with alternative levels of employment.[3]

The neo-keynesian models of Robinson, Kaldor and Pasinetti, which are more directly derived from Kalecki's work and Keynes's *Treatise on Money*, on the other hand, lay

[1] For example, the OZ_a curve suggest a constant wage share whatever the level of employment, while the AZ_b curve indicates an increasing wage share if employment is higher.

[2] Keynes, of course, recognised that results could alter short-term expectations and that induced changes in short-term expectations will have different effects on employment depending on the length of time necessary to permit entrepreneurs to minimise the costs of altering production schedules. To avoid these conceptual complexities Keynes assumed that the current expectations were forseen sufficiently far ahead so that short-period hiring commitment can be carried out. See Keynes, *The General Theory*, pp. 47–9 including footnotes.

[3] For a more complete analysis, see P. Davidson and E. Smolensky, *Aggregate Supply and Demand Analysis*, ch. 9–13.

emphasis on changes in the distribution of income and prices as the primary adjusting mechanism to short-period disequilibrium, and adjustments via changes in employment and output are considered either to be of secondary importance or assumed away.

In Joan Robinson's model, if realised aggregate demand is below expected demand, then it is assumed that competition brings down market prices (and profit margins) *at the normal or standard volume of output*; thus, the entire short-period output associated with employment level of N in Fig. 5.3 is sold[1] at the market-clearing or Marshallian demand price. In the short-run, firms realise total revenues equal to NH in Fig. 5.3, the wage bill is NC, and realised gross profits are CH instead of the expected CB. Thus, in the Robinsonian model the initial adjustment to disequilibrium comes via a difference between expected and realised profit income rather than via change in output and employment, since short-period employment is 'more or less closely determined by available plant'[2] and not, therefore, by realised aggregate demand.

This neo-keynesian view that short-period adjustments are made via demand prices, profit margins and income distribution ultimately is based on a belief that profit margins are more flexible than either money wage rates or employment levels in conditions of disequilibrium. This conception of income redistribution and profit margin flexibility is a convenient supposition which permits Mrs Robinson to use the current *realised* lower quasi-rents on existing plant as the basis for new projections of future quasi-rents on new projects. If a lower steady rate of growth is to be established from this short-period disappointment of entrepreneurs, then realised lower current gross profits for a given level of employment and standard volume of production must reduce long-term expectations and reduces entrepreneurial desires to accumulate. Entrepreneurs adjust their sights to a new level of prices relative to money wages which will yield a lower gross profit per period per unit of equipment, if steady growth is to be re-established once current facts have proven past expectations wrong.[3] Ultimately

---

[1] J. Robinson, *Essays in Economic Growth*, pp. 46–7. [2] ibid. p. 47.
[3] ibid. p. 47. Also see p. 41. If instead entrepreneurs attempted to re-adjust profit margins to recover the originally expected normal profit sum

therefore short-term sales disappointments cause the degree of monopoly, in the Kalecki sense, to decline as accumulation and the rate of growth is lowered, while neither plant utilisation or current labour hiring is affected.[1] Unlike Joan Robinson's model where the ON employment level may be equal to or less than full employment, Kaldor and Pasinetti analysis assumes that full employment at each point of time is a necessary condition.[2]

In essence, Kaldor and Pasinetti visualise a vertical short-period aggregate supply function at N in Fig. 5.3 where N is assumed to be full employment.[3] With employment and output fixed at each point of time by assumption, adjustment to disequilibrium can only take place via prices. Kaldor and Pasinetti implicitly assume that there is a higher degree of price (profit margin) flexibility than money wage flexibility so that if realised aggregate demand is different than expected, it is the income distribution between wages and profits which is the adjusting mechanism. Thus Kaldor notes

> According to the 'Cambridge' theory, the labour market does not behave in accordance with the postulates of neo-classical theory. With a rise in the demand for labour [i.e if realised demand exceeds expected aggregate demand at

by choosing another point on the AZ_b function of Fig. 5.3, they will be disappointed again since the realised demand function does not intersect AZ_b.

[1] Cf. J. Robinson, 'Harrod After Twenty Years', *Econ. Journal*, **80** (1970) p. 735. Mrs. Robinson continually insists that her analysis is applicable only for comparisons between economies on equilibrium paths with different rates of growth, degrees of monopoly, etc., and not for analysing the effect of a change in a variable on the path of a single economy. Nevertheless, Mrs. Robinson does lapse into making such comparisons on occasion (e.g. *Essays in Economic Growth*, pp. 41, 46–7), while Kaldor and Pasinetti have less qualms about discussing the traverse of a single economy.

[2] For example, see N. Kaldor and J. A. Mirless 'A New Model of Economic Growth', *Rev. Econ. Stud.* (1962) p. 175. N. Kaldor, 'Some Fallacies on the Interpretation of Kaldor', *Rev. Econ. Stud.* (1910) p. 6; L. L. Pasinetti, 'Rate of Profit and Income Distribution in Relation to the Rate of Economic Growth', *Rev. Econ. Stud.* (1962) pp. 268, 276, 279.

[3] Interestingly, Kaldor and Pasinetti have assumed the same short-period aggregate supply function as Patinkin – despite their distaste for neoclassical economics. See D. Patinkin, *Money, Interest and Prices*, 2nd ed. (New York: Harper and Row, 1965) p. 211.

full employment] there is a rise in the share of profit and a fall in the share of wages, and not the other way round.[1]

Interpreting this passage in terms of the situation depicted in Fig. 5.3 if there is a fall in the demand for labour, i.e. if $D_r < D_e$, the wage share will increase from an expected value of NC/NB to a realised NC/NH, while the profit share declines, and the full employment level of output is sold.

In sum then, both Robinson and Kaldor–Pasinetti rely on income redistribution via profit margins relative to money wages at a given level of employment[2] to adjust when short-period entrepreneurial sales forecasts are proved incorrect, while in *The General Theory*, Keynes suggested that changes in the level of employment were the primary short-period adjustment mechanism, with income distribution playing a less important role.[3] If equilibrium growth is to be restored in the neo-keynesian models, entrepreneurs must adjust their normal profit requirements to a level which will be compatible with a different rate of gross investment. If equilibrium growth is not restored, then these neo-keynesian models are inapplicable.

The applicability of these neo-keynesian models to questions of short-period adjustments depends on the empirical question whether, in fact, prices or employment levels are more flexible. In the following chapters, the argument will be developed that it is an *essential* characteristic of a monetary economy that offer prices and money wages should have short-period stickiness and hence employment levels *must* be more adjustable to disequilibrium conditions. Hence, these neo-keynesian models will be seen to be deficient in terms of their discussions of monetary aspects. Nevertheless, the authors of these models recognised the limitations of their efforts and have continually stressed that their analyses are basically concerned with long-run steady rates of equilibrium growth. These models were primarily designed to analyse and explain the necessary real aspects of uniform and constant growth rates in conditions of

[1] Kaldor, 'Some Fallacies in the Interpretation of Kaldor', *Rev. Econ. Stud.*, 1970, p. 5.

[2] Kaldor and Pasinetti have the more stringent requirement that the short-period demand for labour must equal the supply of labour.

[3] For example, see Keynes, *The General Theory*, pp. 92, 96, 262.

tranquility where expectations are never disappointed.[1] Accordingly, assumptions about underlying mechanisms are built into the analyses so that the rate of investment undertaken can never be severely jarred by internal events. For example, Kaldor and Pasinetti merely assume that the level of investment will always be sufficient to guarantee full employment, while Joan Robinson supposes an accommodating monetary system so that there will never be any financial constraints to investment, except in cases of inflation (normally at or near full employment).[2] In essence therefore, this neo-keynesian view of equilibrium growth

> require[s] a state of finance which has been built into the equilibrium system, in such a way that the deterrent influence on investment of the difficulty and cost of financing investment, and of the attraction of alternative methods of laying out financial resources, just matches the stimulating influences of profit expectations. The rate of interest, and all that goes with it in the financial sphere, has accommodated itself to the rate of profit and neither the rate of profit nor the rate of interest can be regarded as independent influences on investment.[3]

In sum, the neo-keynesian growth models in their present stage of development can be viewed as assuming that, given the minimum rate of discount entrepreneurs require in order for them to believe that the expected future stream from a new capital project is sufficient for them to undertake long-term commitments, financial conditions are such that (1) the level of new investment projects undertaken in each period will be

[1] See R. F. Kahn, 'Exercises in the Analysis of Growth', *Oxford Economic Papers* (1959) pp. 149, 153. As Joan Robinson puts it 'for equilibrium to persist it must turn out that expectations were correct. Equilibrium in this sense involves past history', *Essays in Economic Growth*, p. 35.

[2] Pasinetti, 'Rate of Profit', pp. 268, 276, 279; Kaldor, 'Some Fallacies', pp. 5–6; J. Robinson, *Essays in Economic Growth*, p. 44.

[3] Kahn, 'Exercises in the Analysis of Growth', p. 153. In private correspondence about this statement Mrs. Robinson has insisted that these neo-keynesian models are presented merely to make explicit 'the necessary conditions for steady growth and *not* as a prediction of what will happen in actual history. They are set out in order to show why they will *not* be realised.'

sufficient to generate a level of effective demand which justifies the entrepreneurial decisions underlying short-period production decisions, and simultaneously (2) the present value of the marginal investment undertaken in each period is equal to the current cost of producing the investment.

If, however, the level of gross investment necessary to generate sufficient effective demand to vindicate short-term expectations involve some investment projects whose present value is less than present costs, or if there are potential borrowers who are unable to obtain finance to contract for new projects even if the present value exceeds present costs, then financial constraints and/or 'animal spirits' can prevent the system from an attainment of equilibrium growth. These possibilities are excluded in the neo-keynesian system only by assuming entrepreneurs are endowed with sufficient 'animal spirits' so that they believe in the inexorable growth in demand, and that the monetary system will always create conditions to accommodate the steady rate of growth.[1]

PATH ANALYSIS IN THE NEO-KEYNESIAN WORLD

Figs. 5.4 (a) and 5.4 (b) indicate how the two neo-keynesian variants can be formulated via aggregate supply and demand diagrams within an equilibrium growth context. To keep these diagrams simple only small segments of the supply and demand functions associated with time periods t_1, t_2, and t_3 have been included. Fig. 5.4 (a) represents the Robinsonian model and 5.4 (b) the Kaldor–Pasinetti analysis, the sole difference being that the short-period aggregate supply functions in the latter is assumed to be vertical *at the full employment level* associated with each period. The money wage rate is, for simplicity, assumed constant over time. Thus Y_1, Y_2, and Y_3 are the points of effective demand and are associated with N_1, N_2, and N_3 employment levels over time. Connecting these effective demand points traces out a Golden Age growth path for Kaldor

[1] Joan Robinson suggests that financial constraints are only operative in cases of wage-price inflation at or near full employment. See J. Robinson, *Essays in Economic Growth*, p. 54. Kaldor indicates that his model is only applicable if market conditions are favourable for continuous full employment growth. N. Kaldor, 'A New Model of Economic Growth', *Rev. Econ. Stud.*, **29** (1962) p. 175.

and Pasinetti (Fig. 5.4 (b)), while the path of effective demand need not be a Golden Age in Mrs Robinson's model. She has in fact suggested colourful names to describe the alternative possible paths of a growing economy. Table 5.1 provides a catalogue of some of the more important paths in Mrs Robinson's model.

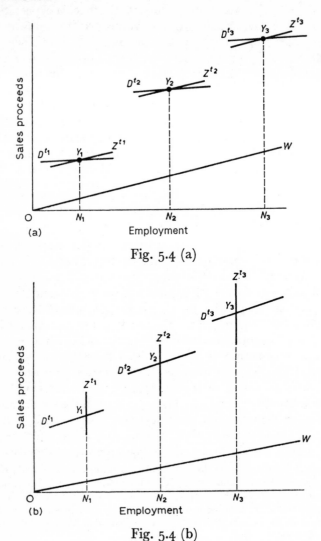

Fig. 5.4 (a)

Fig. 5.4 (b)

If net investment is occurring, then the committed finance in the enterprise is rising over time. Accordingly entrepreneurs must be anticipating that annual net profits will be increasing as effective demand grows over time. Expected gross profits

Table 5.1

ALTERNATIVE ROBINSONIAN GROWTH PATHS

Name of Path	Description	Cause
Golden Age	Growth at full employment	Demand for labour grows at full employment
Limping Golden Age	Growth at less than full employment	Ratio of unemployed to labour force in each period is greater than zero
Leaden Age	Growth with rising rates of unemployment	Labour supply growth outrunning labour demand
Restrained Golden Age	Desired growth exceeds resource base growth which in turn leads to financial constraints	Financial constraints hold down growth in demand for labour relative to supply
Galloping Platinum Age	Growth starting at a position of less than full employment with investment sector expanding rapidly until full employment is obtained	High 'animal spirits' of entrepreneurs
Bastard Golden Age	Financial checks prevent higher rates of accumulation even though there is unemployment	Threats of wage-price inflation before full employment create financial restraints to faster growth

Source: J. Robinson, *Essays in Economic Growth*, pp. 52–9.

will therefore be increasing over time,[1] and therefore the absolute difference between the point of effective demand and the wage bill line OW in Fig. 5.4 will increase, i.e. later Y points will lie relatively further to the north of the OW line than earlier ones. According to equation (5), however, realised gross profits will increase only if gross investment is rising at an

[1] Unless technical changes are being adopted of a form that lowers annual amortisation changes per worker per period by an amount which exceeds the increase in the expected net profit per worker.

equal pace and thus the neo-keynesians conclude that steady equilibrium growth requires simultaneous proportionate increases in profits and the stock of capital, and therefore results in a constant rate of profits.

If, for any reason, the rate of increase in gross investment spending is altered at any point of time, then the previous rate of growth in profits can not be maintained and entrepreneurial forecasts which have extrapolated past history will be incorrect. At that point, short-term adjustments must occur which will, unless long-term expectations are very inert, feedback on decisions about the accumulation of capital in the future.

PATH ANALYSIS v. A COMPARISON OF ECONOMIES

These neo-keynesian models, when combined with the analytical concepts developed in Chapter 4 can be utilised to provide useful insights into growth phenomena even when past errors have been embodied in the current stock of capital i.e. even in the absence of tranquillity.

Mrs Robinson has cautioned that these neo-keynesian models are only applicable to economies growing at constant rates through time and that in the current state of the economic arts these formal models could not readily explain how economies traverse from one growth rate to another, or how adjustments to disequilibrium are made when tranquillity conditions are disturbed.[1] Accordingly, the Cambridge philosophy is to use these models to make comparisons between economies each growing at a uniform but different rate in conditions of tranquillity rather than[2] to attempt disequilibrium path analysis. For example, in Fig. 5.5. the growth path of two economies, α and β, are represented. It is assumed that at time t_1, each economy employs the same number of workers at the same money-wage rate, and exhibits the same class savings propensities. The entrepreneurs in β, however, expect to receive (and

---

[1] 'In reality, disturbing events occur on disequilibrium paths. The resulting turbulence is beyond the skill of model builders to analyse.' Robinson, *Essays in Economic Growth*, p. 27.

[2] In private correspondence, Mrs. Robinson suggested the phrase 'as a preliminary to' instead of 'rather than'.

have received in the past) a higher annual profit sum per worker than their counterparts in α as β has grown at a faster rate in earlier periods. Accordingly, Y^1_α and Y^1_β in Fig. 5.5 represent the points of effective demand in t_1 in α and β

Fig. 5.5

respectively. In order to maintain equilibrium growth in t_2, t_3, etc. gross investment in β in t_1 will be greater than in α and hence, according to equation (4), gross profits will be higher. This relatively higher gross investment and profits situation in β will occur in every future period, if the equilibrium rate of growth in each economy is to be maintained. More gross investment in β, *ceteris paribus*, must imply more net investment in β than α, it must mean a greater increase in output per worker, i.e. a higher rate of growth of output in β. If *the rate of profit* is defined as the *expected increase in annual profits income per period per dollar of expenditure on currently produced capital goods*[1] then, it follows that entrepreneurs in β who are installing more equipment must have a higher expected rate of profits than their counterparts in α. Thus, the economy which exhibits the greater

[1] That is the annual profit sum per period per dollar over the life of the new facilities.

rate of growth must possess entrepreneurs who have higher expected rates of profit, while, the realisation of this higher rate of profit can only occur if there is a higher rate of growth.[1]

It also follows that unless expectations have always been realised throughout the historical path up to the present period (i.e. all past changes in circumstances have been properly foreseen and past capital installations have been planned so that they physically decay exactly in step with both technological change and the rates of gross and net investment necessary to keep growth in aggregate demand and productive capacity in step), the *current realised rate of profit*, which is defined as the ratio of current annual profits (net of depreciation) to the net historical cost of capital goods (or net finance committed) will *not* be equal to expected rate of profits on new investment projects. If, however, at any point of time, profit expectations were disappointed and if entrepreneurs believe that current realised profits per unit of equipment is the best estimate of future annual profits to be earned per unit of *existing* equipment and finally, if the current *rate of profit* is defined as the ratio of current realised profits to the *value* of capital as established on the 'spot' market for existing capital goods,[2] then as the (notional) spot price of capital instantly adjusts the 'current' rate of profit on the stock of capital will equal the expected rate of profit on new investment.

Empirically, economists attempt to measure 'the rate of profits' as the ratio of current annual profits to the net historical value of the existing capital stock. In an uncertain world, this measure must certainly be wrong. Yet for businessmen, faced with the need to continually make decisions about commitments for new capital goods, this measure is unimportant and even irrelevant. Only if the existing stock of capital *could be instantly revalued* in the light of future expectations *in a real spot market* will the rate of profits on the value of the existing stock have relevance on the decision whether to buy newly produced capital goods or to buy pre-existing facilities in the spot market from others for use in production processes. Such spot markets are not well-developed even when they exist, and hence the proper measure of the rate of profits on the existing capital

[1] Kahn, 'Exercises in the Analysis of Growth', p. 153.
[2] Assuming the spot price of capital goods exceeds zero.

stock under non-tranquil conditions is a theoretical conundrum which perplexes and confuses economists, but the insolubility of the problem in no way inhibits business decisions.

In the real world, it would be astonishing if the existing stock of capital did not contain the fossils of many past investment errors. Accordingly neither neoclassical capital theory which requires malleability for the determination of the rate of profit on the capital stock nor the neo-keynesian analysis which assumes no past errors in accumulation can provide *practical* conclusions about 'the rate of profits'. If, in fact, concepts such as the rate of profit on the capital stock are theoretical enigmas which, however, never mystify practical business decisions, then such concepts are not only irrelevant to the understanding of a sequence of actual economic events they 'are unnecessary. And indeed, as soon as one makes the attempt, it becomes clear . . . that one can get on much better without them.'[1] That is why the previous chapter's analysis of the demand and supply of capital goods has been formulated in terms of present values calculated by using minimum acceptable discount rates rather than utilising the more traditional variable of the rate of profits for the former is merely a formal way of explaining entrepreneurial desire for action rather than inaction, while the latter concept encourages a delusive search for a 'real' determinant – other than entrepreneurial dreams.

It is, of course, true that the existence of either a notional or a real spot market for second-hand capital goods provides a modicum of 'economic malleability' and therefore a tinge of flexibility for the use of physically immutable long-lived structures in alternative production processes. Re-evaluations of second-hand capital reduces the impediments disgorged by investment fossils and permits economic production processes to continue once the once-over capital losses or gains are digested, so that expectations of being able to earn a normal return on the revalued stock permits production to continue.

If, of course these capital gains or losses could be readily assimilated without altering long-term expectations, then steady equilibrium growth paths would be easily attainable and practical conclusions could be drawn from models based on tranquillity assumptions. If, on the other hand, these capital

[1] Keynes, *The General Theory*, p. 39.

stock re-evaluations feedback on to long-term expectations (that is, if variable ϕ in equation (1) of Chapter 4 is a function of current facts relative to past expectations regarding quasirents) then considerably more work on the formation of expectations under uncertainty remains to be done before a *complete* model can be attempted to suggest a determinant growth path over a long period of time can be developed. Nevertheless, even at the present state of the economic arts, it should still be possible to provide an understanding of economic behaviour and the resulting direction of movement that occurs when the economy finds itself in disequilibrium conditions. With the aid of these more modest economic insights it will still be possible to suggest shock-absorbing policies and institutions which will limit socially undesirable economic movements.

The implicit faith in the constancy of long-period expectations and the belief of unchanging entrepreneurial confidence in these inert long-run forecasts which underlies most steady-state economic growth models is a tribute to economists' desire to delude themselves and the public into believing that they can make profound pronouncements about long-run rates of growth. Instead, economists should content themselves with attempting to achieve the more mundane task of providing an understanding of the detailed behaviour of an economic system which is unlikely to be on a dynamic equilibrium path.[1]

GROWTH, MAXIMUM GROWTH, AND ECONOMIC POLICY

In an economy where most incomes are still primarily generated via hiring and production decisions, a less than fully employed community must involve socially avoidable misery for the unemployed households. If, therefore, desirable objectives of social policy are to (a) maintain full employment so that no one sector of the economy suffers needlessly, and (b) to maintain a continuous rate of growth of output and desired leisure which exceeds the rate of population growth so that real incomes are rising over time, then the 'Visible Hand'[2] of public

---

[1] Cf. Keynes, *Treatise on Money*, II 407.

[2] To use Weintraub's apt phrase. See S. Weintraub, *A Keynesian Theory*, pp. 117, 130.

policy will be required to intervene whenever entrepreneurial investment commitments do not generate sufficient growth in effective demand to keep pace with the growth of productive capacity at full employment. If the government did not act when, given the savings propensities of wage-earners and profit recipients, consumption demand fails to advance at an appropriate rate, then the gap would have to be filled by increased capital accumulation (and/or foreign purchases). It is, however, highly unrealistic to expect that entrepreneurs will desire to expand their rate of capital formation, if consumption growth is not sufficient to purchase all that can be presently produced. To comprehend the methods with which the government can act as the balance wheel to the private sector in generating conditions for full employment growth, therefore, a theory of economic growth must encompass the analysis of the business cycle since:

> a recession is an egregiously unsatisfactory growth circumstance; a prosperity wave is a gratifying growth outcome. The cycle phases are not independent of the theory of growth; instead they are instances of unsteadiness in the mechanics of entrepreneurial investment action and the interconnected expenditure decisions of the major economic groups[1]

Discussions of recession and boom, however, are sensible only after the peculiarities of money and finance have been placed in their proper prospective in the analysis, a task undertaken in the following chapters. Even at this stage, however, it is possible to formulate some strictures about the economist's role in providing guidelines for social policy related to economic growth.

Joan Robinson coined the term a *Golden Age* 'to describe smooth, steady growth with full employment (intending thereby to indicate its mythical nature)'.[2] A golden age does, of course, permit the best long-run opportunity for simultaneous growth in capital, employment, and output. Given population growth, leisure-income preferences and technology, the maximum output of capital goods that can be obtained in each period is constrained by the demand of consumers out of current full employment incomes. Thus, rapid economic growth in a fully

---

[1] ibid. p. 131.   [2] Robinson, *Essays in Economic Growth*, p. 52.

employed economy can occur only if capitalists are endowed with a strong desire to accumulate and workers and capitalists either voluntarily or forcibly are constrained in their ability to exercise consumption claims on current national income.

If, however, workers and capitalists are 'bloody-minded' and 'self-indulgent' then even if full employment is maintained, the surplus available for growth can be exceedingly small. In a world of large governments and cold wars, of course, cuts in military expenditures, etc. can permit both consumption and capital accumulation to grow for some time even at full employment, but in an enterprise economy there is little point in increasing net investment, if the increase in aggregate demand will not be there when the capacity is installed.

Maximum growth, after all, is not an end in itself. A 'golden rule of accumulation' which purports to suggest an optimal growth rate which best satisfies wants over times is a ludicrous precept. Merely to suggest that one can specify a rule which can best provide for future streams of wants in a world with an uncertain future and as yet unborn generations is to indicate the absurdity of such a rubric. Instead, the more limited objectives of seeking to maintain full employment and simultaneously inducing a rate of growth of output and leisure which exceeds population growth are goals on which a social consensus could be obtained and on which economists could provide some guidelines.[1] Economists should lower their sights from esoteric, irrelevant, and useless objectives which are formulated via 'golden rules' and which promote endless controversies in the economic literature and instead discuss more mundane practical goals.

[1] For a more complete discussion of the impossibilities of making inter-generational welfare comparisons see S. Weintraub, *A Keynesian Theory*, pp. 134–6 and J. de V. Graaff, *Theoretical Welfare Economics* (Cambridge, Cambridge University Press, 1967), chapter 9.

APPENDIX

Let Z = aggregate supply price $(\equiv wN + P)$
 w = the money wage rate
 N = the level of employment
 α = the wage share in aggregate supply $\left(\equiv \dfrac{wN}{Z} \right)$
 P = gross profits
 I_g = gross investment spending
 A = autonomous spending
 D = aggregate demand
 Y = effective demand (point where $D = Z$)
 s_w = marginal propensity to save out of wages
 s_c = marginal propensity to save out of gross profits
 S = gross savings $(= s_w wN + s_c P)$

At the point of effective demand, $Y (D = Z)$

$$A + I_g = S = s_w wN + s_c P \tag{a}$$

but since

$$wN = \alpha Z \tag{b}$$

and

$$Z = \left(\frac{1}{1 - \alpha} \right) P \tag{c}$$

therefore equation (a) can be rewritten

$$A + I_g = P\left[s_w\left(\frac{\alpha}{1 - \alpha} \right) + s_c \right] \tag{d}$$

Rearranging terms

$$P = \left[\frac{1}{s_w\left(\dfrac{\alpha}{1 - \alpha} \right) + s_c} \right] [I_g + A] \tag{e}$$

and since

$$Y = Z = \left(\frac{1}{1 - \alpha} \right) P$$

$$Z = Y = \left[\frac{1}{s_w(\alpha) + s_c(1 - \alpha)} \right] [I_g + A] \tag{f}$$

CHAPTER 6

Money and Uncertainty—an Introductory View

THE NATURE OF MONEY

'Money,' Hicks has declared, 'is defined by its functions . . . "money is what money does".'[1] Harrod notes that 'Money is a social phenomenon, and many of its current features depend on what people think it is or ought to be'.[2] 'Money,' Scitovsky adds, 'is a difficult concept to define, partly because it fulfils not one but three functions, each of them providing a criterion of moneyness . . . those of a unit of account, a medium of exchange, and a store of value.'[3]

While economists have probably spilled more printers' ink over the topic of money than any other, and while monetary theory impinges on almost every other conceivable branch of economic analysis, confusion over the meaning and nature of money continues to plague the economics profession. Pre-keynesian neoclassical economists tended to emphasise the medium of exchange aspect of money, as the early quantity theorists stressed a strict relationship between the money aggregate and transactions (or income). In a neoclassical world of perfect certainty and perfect markets, with a Walrasian auctioneer assuring simultaneous equilibrium at a given point of time, it would of course be irrational to hold money as a store of value as long as other assets provided a certain positive yield.[4] In the absence of uncertainty, neoclassical theory had

---

[1] J. R. Hicks, *Critical Essays in Monetary Theory*, p. 1.

[2] R. F. Harrod, *Money* (London: Macmillan) p. x.

[3] T. Scitovsky, *Money and the Balance of Payments* (Chicago: Rand, McNally, 1969) p. 1.

[4] See P. A. Samuelson, *Foundations of Economic Analysis* (Cambridge: Harvard University Press, 1947) pp. 122–4.

no room for the store of value function in its definition of money; nor would money play any more important role than peanuts in a neoclassical world. The tatônnement process implies that no transactions occur until equilibrium is attained (i.e. recontracting is essential); hence, anyone holding money either during the auction or till the next market period is irrational. Why hold money if it is really not needed for transactions since in equilbirium goods trade for goods, and since the present and the future value of all economic goods can be determined (at least in a probability sense) with complete certainty?[1] The essential nature of money is disregarded in all Walrasian general equilibrium systems since there is no asset whose liquidity premium exceeds its carrying cost.[2] As Hahn has recently admitted *the Walrasian economy that we have been considering, although one where the auctioneer regulates the terms at which goods shall exchange, is essentially one of barter*.[3]

Keynes was the first important economist bluntly to accuse the neoclassical view of the nature of money as foolish. Keynes wrote:

> Money, it is well known, serves two principal purposes . . . it facilitates exchanges. . . . In the second place, it is a store of wealth. So we are told, without a smile on the face. But in the world of the classical economy, what an insane use to which to put it! For it is a recognised characteristic of money as a store of wealth that it is barren. . . . Why should anyone outside a lunatic asylum wish to use money as a store of wealth?[4]

His answer to this rhetorical question was clear and unequivocal; 'our desire to hold money as a store of wealth is a

[1] The introduction of production into a Walrasian model requires that all future prices of all possible quantities that could be bought or sold be known with certainty; otherwise, production involves an irreducible uncertainty since there must be a current contractual commitment to hire resources to produce products which will be available to the market at some future date.

[2] See Keynes's definition of a non-monetary economy, *The General Theory*, p. 239.

[3] F. H. Hahn, 'Some Adjustment Problems', *Econometrica*, **38** (1970) p. 3.

[4] J. M. Keynes, 'The General Theory of Employment', *Quarterly Journal of Economics*, **51** (1937) reprinted in *The New Economics* (Boston: Knopf, 1947), ed. S. Harris, pp. 186–7. All references are to reprint.

barometer of the degree of our distrust of our own calculations and conventions concerning the future . . . the possession of actual money lulls our disquietude'.[1] Distrust? Disquietude? These are states of mind which are impossible in a world of certainty.

It is in the Keynesian world where

> expectations are liable to disappointment and expectations concerning the future affect what we do today . . . that the peculiar properties of money as a link between the present and the future must enter. . . . Money, in its significant attributes is above all, a subtle device for linking the present to the future.[2]

This link can exist only if there is a continuity over time of contractual commitments denominated in money units. It is the synchronous existence of money and money contracts over an uncertain future which is the basis of a monetary system whose maxim is '*Money buys goods and goods buy money; but goods do not buy goods*'.[3]

Despite the victory of the Keynesian Revolution for many practical short-run employment policies, subsequent developments in monetary theory by Patinkin, Friedman, Tobin, and others have regressed on this crucial aspect of uncertainty. These modern monetary theorists, some of whom have been labelled neoclassical, some Keynesian, but all right-of-centre, have ignored Keynes's insistence that certain propositions were so uncertain in principle as to be incapable of having any numeral value; and they have instead substituted the concept of quantifiable, predictable risk for uncertainty.[4] At the same

[1] J. M. Keynes, 'The General Theory of Employment', *Quarterly Journal of Economics*, **51,** (1937) reprinted in *The New Economics* (Boston; Knopf, 1947), ed. S. Harris, p. 187.

[2] Keynes, *The General Theory*, pp. 293–4.

[3] R. W. Clower, 'A Reconsideration of the Microfoundations of Monetary Theory', *Western Economic Journal*, 6; reprinted in *Monetary Theory*, ed. R. Clower (Middlesex: Penguin, 1969) pp. 207–8. All references are to reprint.

[4] Risk can, via probability statements, be reduced to a certainty, uncertainty cannot. Modern monetarists fail to detect this crucial difference. Keynes, on the other hand, insisted that uncertainty was the sole intelligible reason for holding money, and by uncertainty he meant that there 'was no scientific basis on which to form any capable probability whatever. We

time, these modern monetary theorists have swung with the Keynesian pendulum towards emphasising the extreme opposite view of the primary function of money from that which the pre-keynesian neoclassicists held. For these monetary theorists, it is, paradoxically, the store of wealth function of money which is highlighted in their models of complete certainty. Thus, for example, Tobin declares 'The crucial property of "money" in this role is being a store of value',[1] as he emphasises asset choice or portfolio balance among a menu of assets all with *certain* yields. Friedman defines money as 'anything that serves the function of providing a *temporary abode for general purchasing power*'[2] while simultaneously assuming that in equilibrium there is no uncertainty since all 'permanent' anticipated real values are unchanged during the period under analysis, i.e. all changes are foreseen from the beginning.[3]

Similarly, the well-known real balance effect of Patinkin's model is based on the store-of-value aspect of money. The flexibility of money wages and prices, which is essential to the generation of a real balance effect and the equilibrium position, requires certainty conditions[4] and therefore removes the need

---

simply do not know' (Keynes, *The New Economics*, pp. 184–5). Thus, true uncertainty, in the Knight-Keynes sense, does not obey the mathematical laws of probability. Keynes, who spent a substantial part of his early years studying and analysing the concept of Probability, believed that certain propositions (or events) were incapable of possessing a measurable value in terms of probability statements or decision weights (see R. F. Harrod, *The Life of J. M. Keynes*, pp. 653–4). Nowadays, Shackle comes closest to expressing the Keynesian view when he indicates that uncertainty involves doubt or disbelief of all conceivable outcomes; the complete set of subjectively determined eventualities need not have decision weights that sum to unity or any particular total. Nor is it necessary when changing decision weight for one eventuality or recognising the possibility of a new and different outcome to alter the weights of the other events. (See G. L. S. Shackle, *Uncertainty in Economics*, pp. 9–10.)

[1] J. Tobin, 'Notes on Optimal Growth', *Journ. Pol. Econ.*, **76** (1968) p. 833.

[2] M. Friedman, *Dollars and Deficits* (Englewood Cliffs: Prentice-Hall, 1968) p. 186.

[3] M. Friedman, 'A Theoretical Framework for Monetary Analysis', *Journ. Pol. Econ.*, **78** (1970) p. 223; also see M. Friedman, 'Monetary Theory of Nominal Income', *Journ. Pol. Econ.*, **79** (1971) pp. 326–9.

[4] D. Patinkin, *Money, Interest and Prices*, 2nd ed. p. 275. Patinkin permits uncertainty to enter the front door via the assumption that during the 'period' the individual is uncertain as to when he receives payments or is

for money as a store of value. Patinkin succinctly epitomises the modern monetarist view of money being concerned 'with the *utility of holding money*, not with that of *spending* it. This is the concept implicit in all cash-balance approaches to the quantity theory of money; and it is the one that will be followed explicitly here.'[1] Furthermore, Patinkin continues:

> our concern . . . is with the demand for money that would exist even if there were perfect certainty with respect to future prices and interest. Uncertainty does play a role in the analysis, but only uncertainty with respect to the timing of payments. Thus one by-product of the following argument is the demonstration that dynamic or uncertain price and/or interest expectations are not a *sine qua non* of a positive demand for money. . . . The general approach of the following argument is in the Keynesian spirit of analysing the demand for this asset as one component of an optimally chosen portfolio of many assets.[2]

But how can an analysis of portfolio decisions which irretrievably dispenses with uncertainty and faulty expectations – as does much of what passes for advanced monetary theory in the current literature, be in the 'spirit of Keynes'? The music of this lively if mislabelled 'Keynesian' gavotte which emphasises portfolio balance in a world of certainty may be the melody to which most modern monetarists trot, but surely it is not attuned to Keynes's majestic monetary dirge for Say's Law. It is only in a world of uncertainty and disappointment that money comes into its own as a necessary mechanism for deferring decisions; money has its niche only when we feel queasy about undertaking any actions which will commit our claims on resources onto a path which can only be altered, if future events require this, at very high costs (if at all).

Recognition of this desire to avoid the commitment of claims on resources provides the insight necessary to describe the social institutions associated with money as well as the elemental and

---

required to make payments, while simultaneously kicking uncertainty out of the back door by asserting synchronisation of payments by the end of the period, in equilibrium (e.g. pp. 14, 80).

[1] D. Patinkin, *Money, Interest and Prices*, 2nd ed. p. 79.

[2] ibid. p. 80–1.

peculiar properties which are necessary to fulfil the two equally important functions of money, namely, a generally accepted medium of exchange, and a store of value in a modern, monetary, market-oriented, but uncertain world.

These necessary properties of anything which will fulfil the functional definition of money are:

(1) a zero (or negligible) elasticity of productivity, so that if individuals, uncertain about the future, want to defer additional commitments of resources, their increased demand for money as a mode for postponing action will not encourage entrepreneurs to employ additional resources in the production of additional quantities of the money commodity.

(2) a zero (or negligible) elasticity of substitution, so that if individuals want to preserve additional options for action for the future, the increase in the price of money induced by an increase in the demand for money as a store of value does not divert people into substituting other assets, which have high elasticities of productivity, as a store of value. Hence the demand for a store of value, in an uncertain world, does not generate the demand to commit resources. Thus the virtuous interaction between supply of resources and the demand for resources which is succinctly expressed via Say's Law is broken.

(3) the cost of transferring money from the medium of exchange function to the store of value function or vice versa must be zero (or negligible) so that individuals do not find it expensive to defer decisions or to change their minds. Minimising their transactions costs requires the existence of at least two economic institutions: (a) Offer and debt contracts dominated in money units and (b) legal enforcement of such contracts. An additional contribution to the minimising of such transactions costs is the presence of an institution, namely a clearing system, which permits using private debts in the settlement of transactions as long as it is expected that the private debt can be promptly converted into the form of money which is enforceable in the discharge of contracts.

In sum then, in an uncertain world, a monetary system is associated with at least two and usually three institutions – namely, contracts, enforcement, and clearing. The thing which becomes the money commodity will have two properties, a zero (or negligible) elasticity of productivity and a zero (or negligible) elasticity of substitution between it and any other good which has a high elasticity of productivity.

It is a failure by many able but wrong-headed economists to comprehend the importance of these three institutions and two properties which are peculiar to money in a monetary economy, which has led to the shunting of much of modern monetary analysis onto a wrong line.

Any model of a monetary, market-oriented economy which attempts to provide insights about the real world should have the following characteristics:

(1) Decision making by firms and households who are fully aware that human judgement is fallible.

(2) The existence of contractual agreements, enforceable by acceptable legal institutions, which permit the sharing of some of the burdens of uncertainty between the contracting parties.

(3) Different degrees of organisation of spot and future markets for all sorts of real goods and financial assets. In many cases, either only a spot or a future market exists for a particular item because of difficulties of organising a market in a world of incomplete information; and even in markets which do exist, there may be significant and increasing transactions, search, and information costs.

(4) Money buys goods in these markets, and goods can buy money, but except for some relatively small – but not necessarily unimportant – markets, goods never buy goods.[1] As an immediate corollary to this condition it follows that demand involves want plus the ability to pay and therefore financial conditions can affect real markets.

(5) The various institutions which develop in organising a market can affect the price path in the market as it reacts to a disequilibrium situation.

(6) There is a generally available clearing mechanism for private debts which permits the existence of a fractional reserve banking system. There are also non-bank financial institutions which because they lack a generally avaliable clearing mechanism independent of the banking system cannot

[1] Goods should be interpreted as including financial assets as well as real commodities and services. In some markets such as organised exchanges, assets may clear against assets, without resort to money as a medium of exchange. Cf. Clower, 'A Reconsideration', pp. 207–8.

create a medium of exchange. Nevertheless, these financial intermediaries can affect financial flows and hence market demands.

(7) There is 'confidence' in the monetary and financial system.

Thus the main characteristics of a real world monetary economy are Uncertainty, Fallibility, Covenants, Institutions, Commerce, Finance, and Trust. These are the Seven Wonders on which the Modern World is based. Simultaneously, these are the sources of the outstanding faults of a modern, monetary, free market economy, namely 'its failure to provide for full employment and its arbitrary and inequitable distribution of wealth and incomes'.[1]

THE NATURE AND IMPORTANCE OF MONEY

Hicks has observed that although 'monetary theory is less abstract than most economic theory, it cannot avoid a relation to reality'.[2] Yet, much of the current literature on monetary theory, based on Walrasian general equilibrium foundations (to which Professor Hicks has provided much impetus), is unrealistic. In the real world, money is not created like the manna from heaven of a Patinkinesque world or dropped by helicopter as in Friedman's construction. In the real world, money 'comes into existence along with debts, which are contracts for deferred payment, and Price-lists, which are offers of contracts for sale or purchase'.[3] Contracts are therefore essential to the phenomenon of money, and the existence of institutions which can enforce the discharge of contractual commitments for future action are essential in providing trust in the future operation of the monetary system. Thus, the existence of institutions, normally operating under the aegis of the State, provides assurances of the continuity between the present and the future which is necessary if one is going to hold money as a store of value. It is with the development of such State sponsored institutions, that the government appropriated to itself the right to define what is the unit of account and what *thing* should answer that definition. Thus the State

[1] Keynes, *The General Theory*, p. 372. [2] Hicks, *Critical Essays*, p. 156.
[3] Keynes, *Treatise on Money*, 1 3.

'claimed the right to not only enforce the dictionary but also to write the dictionary'.[1] Only if the community loses confidence in the ability of State institutions to enforce *contracts*, does the monetary system break down, and the community reverts to barter practices. For a developed interdependent economy where production takes time and contractual commitments for the hiring of resources must occur some time before everyone can possibly know how valuable the outcome will be, barter practices are so wasteful of resources, and so costly, that most members of society will cling to any ray of hope in the government's ability to enforce contracts in the future. Hence most communities reveal a preference to use even a crippled monetary system rather than revert to barter. It is only when the situation has deteriorated to such an extent that everyone is completely uncertain of the meaning of contractual commitments, that a catastrophic breach in the continuity of the system is inevitable. Such a catastrophe, by wiping out all existing contracts simultaneously, provides a foundation for developing a new monetary unit of account which can be utilised in denominating new contractual commitments.

Thus, as Keynes insisted so many years ago, money and contracts are intimately and inevitably related. Money as a numeraire is *not* merely a device to help the neoclassical economist specify the relationship among diverse goods – it is not merely a lowest common denominator. The very institution of money as a unit of account immediately gives rise to at least two types of contracts – contracts which offer to provide goods and services in exchange for money (i.e. offers to buy money via the production and delivery of goods at some moment of time after the offer is made) and offers to provide money for goods (i.e. offers to deliver money at some point of time after the offer is made). If money was simply a neoclassical numeraire, then goods could buy goods without the intermediation of money.

The numeraire is not money; it is not even a partial money; it is not even assumed that it is used by the traders themselves as a unit of account. It is not more than a unit of

[1] Keynes, *Treatise on Money*, I 5.

account which the observing economist is using for his own purpose of explaining to himself what the traders are doing.[1]

It is the synchronous existence of money as a unit of account and the presence of 'offer contracts' and 'debt contracts' which are denominated in money units which forms the core of a modern monetary production economy. Money is and must be the thing which is ubiquitously involved on one side or the other of all contracts if these contracts are to be enforceable in a viable monetary system. Money is that thing that by delivery discharges contractual obligations. Money can function as the medium of exchange only because it is a general tenet of the community that acceptance of the monetary intermediary as a temporary abode of general purchasing power involves no risks (only uncertainties), since the State will enforce enactment of all future offer contracts which may be entered into, in terms of the unit of account.

In a world of uncertainty where production takes time, the existence of money contracts permits the sharing of the burdens of uncertainties between the contracting parties whenever resources are to be committed to produce a flow of goods for a delivery date in the future. Such contractual commitments (e.g. hire contracts and forward contracts) are, by definition, tied to the flow-supply price. Ultimately, underlying the flow-supply price is the relationship between the money-wage rate and productivity phenomena. If individuals are to utilise money as a temporary abode either because they expect to accept delivery of reproducible goods in the very near future, or because they desire a vehicle for transferring immediate command of resources to the more remote and indefinite future, then these economic units must have *confidence* that no matter how far the current spot price for any producible good may be momentarily displaced by spot market conditions, the market price for the good will not be above some anticipated level at a future date.

As long as the flow-supply prices are expected to be sticky,[2]

---

[1] Hicks, *Critical Essays*, p. 3.
[2] Sticky flow-supply prices mean that the annual rate of change in the money-wage rate relative to the rate of change in productivity is expected to be comparatively small.

coherent, and continuous, each individual 'knows' he can, at any time, accept a contract offering future producible goods at a delivered money price which does not differ significantly from today's flow-supply price. Moreover, in an economy where production is going on, sticky flow-supply prices imply relatively stable forward prices of producible goods since the latter will never exceed (and will normally equal) the flow-supply prices associated with the same delivery dates.[1] Since these forward prices reflect the best current expectations of the spot prices at the future delivery dates[2] they are the best estimates of the *future* costs of buying such goods either by currently accepting a contract for forward delivery or by waiting until the future date to buy them spot. Hence, the current set of forward prices (and therefore flow-supply prices) are the best measures of the purchasing power of money at any future date; they are the prices individuals will use in calculating the *real* balances they wish to hold. Ultimately then, in a viable monetary–production–specialisation economy, expectations of sticky money wages combined with the public's belief in the sanctity of contracts for future performance encourages the public to accept, as a temporary abode of purchasing power, either the thing the State terms as money, or any private debt contract for which there is a clearing mechanism and for which there is public confidence in the ability

[1] By definition the price that buyers are offering to pay for forward delivery can never exceed the flow-supply price since the latter is the money-price required to call forth the exertion necessary to produce any given amount of the commodity for any given delivery date. (Cf. N. Kaldor, 'Speculation and Economic Activity', reprinted in *Essays on Economic Stability and Growth*, pp. 34–5.)

If, for example, the public suddenly changes its views about the rate of inflation in future flow-supply prices and if they act on the basis of such anticipations, they would immediately bid up the current spot price of all durables *and* they would place additional orders for forward delivery (of producible goods) at the current flow-supply price associated with the greater production flow. In other words, changes in the expected rate of inflation of producible goods will affect the current spot prices of all assets and the marginal efficiency of capital goods, while the resulting forward price of output will *not* exceed the current flow-supply price associated with the induced greater effective demand. (Cf. Keynes, *The General Theory*, pp. 142–3, 231.)

[2] H. Working, 'New Concepts Concerning Futures Markets and Prices', *American Econ. Rev.*, 52 (1962) pp. 445–9.

of any individual immediately to convert it into legal money without costs.[1]

Any economy which uses such a medium of exchange has a tremendous advantage over a similarly endowed hypothetical economy which permitted only barter transactions – for the cost of anticipating the needs of trading partners and then searching out such partners greatly exceeds the resources used in bringing buyers and sellers together in a money economy. It is only the presumed existence of the costless Walrasian auctioneer which permits general equilibrium models to reach a Walrasian equilibrium solution.[2] The assumption of zero transactions costs, Hicks reminds us:

> is hopelessly misleading when our subject is money. Even the simplest exchanges are in fact attended by some costs. The reason why a well-organised market is more efficient than a badly-organised market . . . is that in the well-organised market the cost of making transactions is lower.[3]

The desire on the part of rational economic men to minimise all costs – including transaction costs, leads to the discovery that while the introduction of a medium of exchange reduces transaction costs over a barter system, the process of clearing titles to money rather than taking delivery of the intermediary commodity itself can lower transaction costs even further.

Bank money is, of course, simply evidence of a private debt contract, but the discovery of the efficiency of 'clearing', that is the realisation that some forms of private debt can be used in settlement of the overlapping myriad of private contracts immensely increased the efficiency of the monetary system. Three conditions are necessary in order for such a private

---

[1] 'In other words, expectation of a relative stickiness of wages in terms of money is a corollary of the excess of liquidity-premium over carrying-costs being greater for money than for any other asset.' – Keynes, *The General Theory*, p. 238.   [2] Hicks, *Critical Essays*, p. 6.

[3] ibid. p. 6. What Hicks fails to realise is that, in an uncertain world, there will only be an accidental matching of buyers and sellers in any spot market at any point of time – no matter how well organised. Thus, unless there is a residual buyer or seller who is willing to step in and make a market whenever one side or the other of the market temporarily falls away, the spot price can fluctuate violently. Such fluctuations are incompatible with individuals' desires to hold such items as a store of value.

debt to operate as a medium of exchange: (1) the private debt must be denominated in terms of the monetary unit; (2) a clearing institution for these private debts must be developed; and assurances that uncleared debts are convertible at a known parity into the legally enforceable medium of exchange.

The development of an institution to clear specific types of private debts and an institution to prevent the misuse of these private debt facilities not only permits but assures – because of the lower costs of transactions – that these private debts will replace state enforced legal money as the main medium of exchange in most transactions. Thus any form of private debt can become a medium of exchange if institutions are created which permit increases in clearings while preventing mis-application of these private debt facilities. What prevents other kinds of private debt (e.g. trade credit, commercial paper) from becoming part of the medium of exchange is either the absence of a specific clearing institution that deals in the specific type of debt under consideration, or if such an institution exists its facilities are not available for most of the transactors in the community.[1] Thus, for example, the ability of businessmen to enlarge their demand for the hire purchase of capital goods by arranging for increased clearings of debts outside the banking system is, in the short run, extremely limited, and hence financial constraints on investment demand may restrict investment purchases even when the present value of additional capital goods greatly exceeds the flow-supply price of these goods. Thus the lack of a sufficient quantity of the medium of exchange can restrain the economy even when there are owners of idle resources who would be willing to enter into offer contracts at the going money wage rate.

What permits money to possess purchasing power is, ulti-mately, its intimate relationship to 'offer contracts' in general and contracts involving labour offers specifically. Thus it is the money-wage rate, that is the number of units of the money-

[1] Of course, some forms of private debt may discharge commitments for small closed subsets of transactors within the community via a clearing mechanism, if there is a large number of continuous offsetting flows of goods and debts traded restricted to this subsector, e.g. stock market clearings. Nevertheless this private debt is not generally acceptable and therefore is not money.

of-account which labour is willing to buy for a given unit of effort, which is the anchor upon which the price level of all producible goods is fastened. It is because changes in the quantity of money are inevitably tied to changes in the stock of existing contracts, and the fact that the offer prices for contractual commitments for the forward delivery of all reproducible goods are, *when money buys goods*, constrained by money flow-supply prices whose principal component is ultimately the money-wage rate, that changes in the quantity of money, changes in the level of employment of resources, changes in the money-wage rate and changes in the price level are inevitably inter-related.

It is only in the Walrasian general equilibrium world where the quantity of money is (a) conceived to be independent of the level of contracts[1] and (b) provided to the community like manna from heaven, that the general equilibrium theorist finds no secure anchor for the level of absolute prices which are indeterminate in his system. Having cut the connection between money, labour offer contracts, and flow-supply prices, these modern Walrasians conclude that the level of prices is whatever it is expected to be, for if it were not money holders would, with the co-operation of the ubiquitous Walrasian auctioneer, simply bid up or down the price level until the purchasing power of money was at the level they wanted it to be, while resource utilisation (full employment) would be unaffected.[2]

In the real world, money is among the most ancient of man's institutions. Barter economies are more likely to be the figments of economists' minds, than the handmaidens of human transactors. A description of activity in a barter system may be useful as a benchmark for observing the effects of money on the system, but the results of such comparative anatomy should never be taken seriously as indicative of real world alternatives. The barter transactions implicit in the Walrasian approach

[1] Since recontracting is not only permitted but is required for Walrasian equilibrium to occur.

[2] See D. Patinkin, *Money, Interest, and Prices*, 2nd ed. pp. 44–5. Also Hicks, *Critical Essays*, pp. 9–10 and J. Tobin, 'A Dynamic Aggregative Model', *Journ. Pol. Econ.*, **63** (1955) p. 105. Thus many modern neoclassicists are in essence providing a bootstrap theory of the price level of goods in place of a bootstrap theory of the price level of bonds.

can only be meaningful as an analysis of the immediate ex-change of pre-existing goods. The majority of important trans-actions in a modern mass-production economy, however, involve the contractual commitment of resources for the pro-duction of goods and services to be delivered at a future date. Modern neoclassical monetarists, finding that the real world does not possess the perfect certainty, or a fixed quantity of labour hirings, or flexible wages and prices, or the ability to recontract of their theoretical framework, 'resemble Euclidean geometers in a non-Euclidean world who, discovering that in experience straight lines apparently parallel often meet, re-buke the lines for not keeping straight – as the only remedy for the unfortunate collisions which are occurring'.[1]

MONEY, FINANCIAL INSTITUTIONS, AND ECONOMIC GROWTH – AN OVERVIEW

In the absence of a money with the requisite zero elasticities, each income receiving unit would have to plough its savings into commodities, for without such a money, the decision of what reproducible thing to buy with the thing being sold can-not be postponed. In such a mythical neoclassical economy, income receiving units must store value in those physical goods which they believe are most 'productive'. Even if decision-making units are ignorant about the future they must 'override and ignore this ignorance'.[2] Say's Law prevails, and the alloca-tion of resources between consumption and capital goods will depend entirely on the savings propensities of the income receiving units.

With the existence of a non-reproducible money and appro-priate financial institutions for clearing, a mechanism is pro-vided which permits (but does not require) the efficient transfer of current command over resources (as long as resource offer contracts are denominated in terms of money) from economic units that wish to spend less than their income to those units that wish to spend more. Moreover the existence of a clearing system which permits private debt to discharge contracts, makes it possible for those who want to spend more than their

[1] Keynes, *The General Theory*, p. 16.
[2] G. L. S. Shackle, *The Years of High Theory*, p. 290.

income to obtain immediate claims on resources, while those who wish to spend less do not have to surrender their immediate claims. Such a system, however, does not guarantee that the abstaining economic units will be able to obtain command, in the future, of as much of the services of resources as they have decided not to use at the present time. Nor does it require that those who abstain gain title to the increment of real wealth which such abstinence permits.

If abstinence exceeds the desire of other units to spend in excess of their income, and if savings can be stored in a form which does not require resource utilisation, i.e. the item which is utilised as a store of value has a zero elasticity of productivity, then the potential services of some real resources will be wasted as their offer contracts are not accepted. If, on the other hand, the aggregate desire to spend exceeds abstinence when resources are already fully employed, then the creation of additional units of the medium of exchange by financial institutions can permit some decision-makers to outbid or outrace others in accepting resource offer contracts; as a consequence, some income recipients may be forced to relinquish command over real resources involuntarily. These questions of voluntary and forced abstinence, the ownership of titles to real wealth, and the ability to make economic provision for the future are fundamental aspects of the problem of economic growth.

Since the creation of private debt by financial institutions does not by itself require the use of resources, jobs are not created merely by the process of increasing certain forms of private debt such as bank money. Job creation will depend on what the increment in bank money is used for. The immediate (first round) purpose will, of course, depend on why individuals were willing to go into debt. If individuals desired more money either to hold as a store of value or to demand other things that have a zero elasticity of productivity (e.g. titles or other non-monetary forms of private debt), then this increment of money is immediately enmeshed in the 'financial circulation'[1] and though it may change hands from time to

[1] Since organised security exchanges develop institutions which permit the 'clearing' of securities for securities among a closed set of transactors, the stock of money involved in circulating financial balances is kept to a minimum and the volume of such 'active' balances will be relatively

time it will not create jobs unless it moves (in a subsequent round) into the 'industrial circulation' where it will be used to accept offer contracts for new production.[1]

If, on the other hand, the initial user of the increment of bank money desired it to *increase* his acceptances of offer contracts for new goods and services – the finance motive for demanding money – then new jobs will be created on the first round and on subsequent rounds as portions of the increment of money remain in the 'industrial circulation' as the income generating multiplier process works its way through the economy. The increment of money that remains in the industrial circulation is often referred to as 'active balances' to distinguish it from the money in the financial circulation which is somewhat misleadingly labelled as 'idle balances' since the latter nomenclature suggests a zero velocity. Financial balances may still change hands while remaining in the financial circulation if individuals alter their bear position, while the community maintains its position.

In a monetary economy, many financial non-bank intermediaries evolve which provide links between the financial and industrial circulations. These non-bank financial intermediaries can affect the level of aggregate demand by removing the medium of exchange from either the bear hoards of abstaining households or by borrowing newly created money from commercial banks, and then making these funds available to economic units who want to accept offer contracts for new goods and services in excess of their current incomes.

These nonfinancial intermediaries are able to extract the medium of exchange either from bear hoards and/or directly from commercial banks by providing a store of value in the form

---

independent of the activity involved in the churning of the security portion of individual portfolios. Nevertheless, since certain financial institutions maintain money balances in order to 'make a market' in securities, it is possible that the quantity of money needed to maintain such markets may rise slightly with expansion of the securities market (especially with geographical distance between transactors).

[1] It may move into the industrial circulation by improving financial conditions and/or reducing interest rates and thereby inducing entrepreneurs to increase their demand for fixed capital, or by increasing the demand for delivery of working capital goods thereby calling forth additional supplies.

of a debt contract which promises (1) a greater yield than money, (2) greater confidence in the reliability of the intermediary to meet its obligation when it comes due than the confidence that would be generated by the debt contract of the economic unit which wishes to spend in excess of its income, (3) greater confidence in the future parity between the intermediary's debt and the medium of exchange (if conversion is required before the maturity date of the debt contract) than is expected from other securities and (4) very low transactions costs in converting the non-bank intermediary debt into the medium of exchange at any date in the future.

The difference between the liabilities of non-bank financial intermediaries and commercial bank liabilities is that clearing institutions exist for the latter which permit them to be a perfect substitute for legal money both as a medium of exchange and as a store of value, while no such similarly accessible clearing institution exists for the former. Hence liabilities of non-bank financial intermediaries, while being a good substitute for money as a store of value, cannot be used in settlement of an obligation. As a consequence there will always be some transactions cost involved in converting non-bank financial intermediary liabilities which are used as a store of value into the medium of exchange – a cost which does not exist for legal money or bank money.

In sum then, therefore, the difference between non-bank financial intermediary liabilities and commercial bank liabilities is that although both are evidence of private debt, only the latter can be generally used to discharge a contract. Accordingly, given the stock of money, increases in non-bank financial intermediaries' liabilities can raise aggregate demand for new goods and services only to the extent that (a) it replaces existing legal money or commercial bank liabilities in the bear hoards of economic units and (b) these balances which are released from bear hoards are channelled to potential buyers who have the want, but without these channels of finance would not have the ability to accept the offer contracts that are available in the market place.

Any increase in commercial bank liabilities, on the other hand, because of the existence of clearing institutions, provides either an additional store of value or an additional medium to settle debts and contracts – a costless option for the holder. To the extent these bank debts are made to potential buyers of additional goods and services, aggregate demand is, of course, expanded.

As long as full employment is a social objective, and as long as a 'work requirement' is a condition for earning income for propertyless households so that full employment becomes a humanitarian as well as an economic objective, then monetary policy should be geared to always increasing the supply of money available to all potential buyers of producible goods who are willing to spend in excess of their income, as long as the point of effective demand is less than full employment. If, and only if, effective demand exceeds full employment volume, then monetary policy should, as a matter of fairness, become restrictive in order to thwart potential buyers who have pre-ferential access to bank facilities from forcing abstinence on other income recipients, whose monetary income is relatively fixed and who do not have similar ease of access to bank credit.

A simple rule for expanding the money supply will not per-mit the efficient operation of such a monetary policy because exogenous changes in the desired portfolio composition between money and other financial assets will alter the quantity of money available to the industrial circulation; and, in a mone-tary economy, only money can buy goods, and goods can buy money. Any 'shortage' of money from the industrial circula-tion can be viewed as either frustrating potential buyers from obtaining goods, or preventing sellers from finding takers for their offer contracts. It is to a detailed study of these matters to which we turn in the following chapters.

CHAPTER 7

The Demand for Money as a
Medium of Exchange

THE fundamental question for monetary theory is why do people hold money which is barren rather than interest bearing securities or 'productive' physical goods? The answer must involve uncertainty!

In *The General Theory*, Keynes distinguishes between three motives for holding cash '(i) the transactions-motive, i.e. the need for cash for the current transaction of personal and business exchanges; (ii) the precautionary-motive, i.e. the desire for security as to the future cash equivalent of a certain proportion of total resources; and (iii) the speculative-motive, i.e. the object of securing profit from knowing better than the market what the future will bring forth.'[1] Keynes recognised that

> money held for each of these three purposes forms, nevertheless, a single pool, which the holder is under no necessity to segregate into three watertight compartments for they need not be sharply divided even in his own mind, and the same sum can be held primarily for one purpose and secondarily for another. Thus *we can* – equally well, and perhaps, better – *consider the individual's aggregate demand for money in given circumstances as a single decision though the composite result of a number of different motives.*[2]

In essence, then, there is only a *single* demand for money although for purposes of exposition, it is desirable to study each motive for holding money 'as if' it was separate and independent of the others, even though, in reality it may not be.

---

[1] Keynes, *The General Theory*, p. 170.
[2] ibid. p. 195. Italics added.

Moreover, in both the *Treatise* and *The General Theory*, Keynes did suggest that these three categories formed an exhaustive set and that all other reasons for holding (e.g. the income motive or the business motive) are merely subcategories of these three major divisions.

Keynes's triumvirate analysis of the demand for money is 'a study in depth of a magisterial quality not matched in the present century'.[1] It represents the most important breakthrough in our insight into the operations of money in a modern market-oriented economy. Yet, it may be argued that the liquidity preference theory of 1936 represents a retrogressive movement from the monetary analysis of the *Treatise*, where, in the latter, Keynes's 'views about all the details of the complex subject of money are . . . to be found',[2] and 'it is a paradox that the man whose world-wide fame during most of his lifetime arose from his specific contributions to monetary theory, which were rich and varied, should be studied mainly in one of his books which contains little about money as such'.[3] In the monetary analysis presented in the following chapters, an effort at a judicious blending of *The General Theory* and the *Treatise* approaches is attempted.

THE DEMAND FOR MONEY AS A MEDIUM OF EXCHANGE[4]

At various places in the *Treatise* and *The General Theory*, Keynes discusses the transactions demand for money as the motive for holding money in order 'to bridge the interval between the receipt of income and its disbursement'.[5] Underlying this motive for spanning institutional and contractually determined time intervals is (1) the behavioural pattern of households to avoid the embarrassment of insolvency between the time they expect to receive money as a result of contracting

[1] R. F. Harrod, *Money*, p. 151.

[2] R. F. Harrod, *The Life of John Maynard Keynes*, p. 403.

[3] R. F. Harrod, 'Themes in Dynamic Theory', *Economic Journal*, **73** (1963) p. 442.

[4] Much of this section is based on P. Davidson, 'Keynes' Finance Motive', *Oxford Economic Papers*, 17 (1965) and 'The Importance of the Demand for Finance', *Oxford Economic Papers*, 18 (1966).

[5] Keynes, *The General Theory*, p. 195. Also see *Treatise on Money*, I 34–5, 43–7, ch. 24.

for the sale of goods and services and the time they have met all their anticipated contractual commitments incurred while buying goods for money during the period, and (2) the behaviour of entrepreneurs to eschew bankruptcy from the point of time they will be required to redeem their promises to pay for inputs to the production process with money and the time when they receive money receipts from the sale of goods produced by these inputs. In *The General Theory* Keynes referred to the behaviour of households as the income motive and the entrepreneurial reaction as the business motive, while in the *Treatise* he refers to the money being held for these motives as income deposits and business deposits respectively.[1] In the *Treatise*, the quantity of income deposits held by households depends on (a) the length of time between well-established contractual pay intervals, and (b) the *anticipated* household *expenditures* during the period; while the quantity of business deposits held depends on (a) the payments period, (b) the degree of integration of the firms, and (c) the *expected expenditures* of businesses during the period.

In the truncated monetary analysis of *The General Theory*, however, Keynes, while defining the transactions motive as the 'need for cash for the current transaction of *personal* and *business exchanges*',[2] tends to encourage viewing this demand for money as a medium of exchange solely from the householders' position while neglecting the business motive. Since in the Keynesian system, planned household expenditures are primarily a function of *income*, it is not surprising therefore that many 'Keynesians' have been misled by this cursory treatment, in *The General Theory*, of the medium of exchange function of money into incorrectly specifying the demand for transactions balances function as showing 'the *desired* volume of active or "transactions" cash balances at various levels of income Y'.[3] Moreover, this mis-specification is compatible with a popularised misrepresentation of Keynes's system which is pedagogically

---

[1] Keynes, *The General Theory*, p. 195, *Treatise on Money*, I 34–5. Actually Keynes subdivides business deposits into two categories – A and B – and only business deposits A are used for transactions purposes, ibid. I 244.

[2] Keynes, *The General Theory*, p. 170. Italics added.

[3] A. Hansen, *Monetary Theory and Fiscal Policy* (New York: McGraw-Hill, 1949) p. 61.

centred about the Bastard Keynesians' familiar 45-degree diagram[1] (Fig. 7.1 below) where the latter, by definition, prohibits the analysis of nonequilibrium positions (i.e. positions off the 45-degree line). In such circumstances it is not surprising that this deficient representation of Keynesian monetary theory has been open to the charge that

> In a dynamic [nonequilibrium] context, the loanable funds theory definitely makes more sense [than the mis-specified Keynesian transactions-motive based theory]; and the sustained resistance of Keynesians to admitting it, evident most notably in the prolonged defense in the English literature of the proposition that an increase in the propensity to save lowers the interest rate only by reducing the level of income, is a credit to their ingenuity rather than their scientific spirit.[2]

Mis-specification, in the traditional Bastard Keynesian analysis of the transactions (income) motive, is the cause of the in-

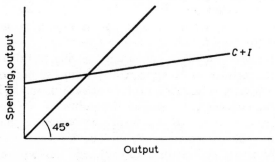

Fig. 7.1

[1] Had an alternative geometrical apparatus using aggregate supply and demand functions (as developed by Weintraub) been adopted, the omission of the finance motive and the incorrect specification of the transactions demand for money function would probably not have occurred. With Weintraub's scheme, it would have been obvious, I believe, to relate the demand for money schedule with the demand for goods function. See S. Weintraub, *An Approach to the Theory of Income Distribution*, ch. 2.

[2] H. G. Johnson, 'The General Theory After Twenty Five Years', *American Econ. Rev. Pap. Proc.* (1961) p. 7. Johnson, a neoclassical monetarist, is correct in his indictment of the right-of-centre Bastard Keynesian school; but his criticism is not applicable to Keynes's own model.

applicability of this theory to disequilibrium analysis, but this fault can be redressed by appeal to Keynes's subsequent analysis of the finance motive and his earlier *Treatise* approach.

Hansen's writings can be chosen as a familiar example of this Bastard Keynesian transactions-motive analysis. Hansen specifies the demand for transactions balances as

$$L_t = kY \qquad (1)$$

where k is a constant. He thereupon plots the function as the straight line L_t emanating from the origin (Fig. 7.2). The im-

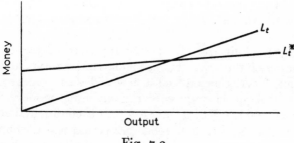

Fig. 7.2

plication of Hansen's diagram is that the demand for transactions balances is a function of the 45-degree line (i.e. the output identity line). In other words, Hansen has made the quantity of money demanded for transactions purposes a function of the *actual* level of output at each level of output (and employment).

Hansen was, however, merely expounding on a simplification of Keynes's when, for the purpose of analysing a specific situation, Keynes decided it was a 'safe first approximation' to write the demand for transactions (and precautionary) balances as $L_1(Y)$.[1] This specification for the demand for money as a medium of exchange conflicts with the *Treatise* view of money needed to meet expected personal and business *expenditures* during the contractual income period, since in a disequilibrium situation in a monetary economy, aggregate expected expenditures during the period need not equal aggregate income over the period. In other words, a correct

[1] Keynes, *The General Theory*, p. 199.

and complete specification of the demand for transactions balances based on the *Treatise* would make the quantity of income and business deposits a function of *planned*-consumption and investment expenditures during the payments period. It was only Keynes's search for a simplification when he had concluded that his critics 'simply failed to grasp' his elaborate analysis of the Treatise[1] that led to the less rigorous monetary specification in *The General Theory* as 'technical monetary detail falls into the background'.[2] As indicated in Chapter 2 this deliberate ensconcement of monetary analysis led Keynes into loosely specifying the transactions demand, and encouraged the right-of-centre Keynesians to develop a 'Bastard Keynesian Model' which was a perversion of Keynes's own system.

In 1937, Ohlin quickly spotted the error of Keynes's simplification of the transactions demand. In reply to Ohlin's criticism, Keynes introduced a new and what appeared to be a somewhat novel purpose for demanding money, namely the *finance motive*.[3] Keynes argued that if contractual commitments to buy new capital goods per period was unchanged in each period, then the money held to 'finance' investment was more or less constant and could therefore be lumped under a subcategory of the transactions motive, where capital goods transactions are involved. In other words, entrepreneurs typically hold some cash balances between payments periods to assure themselves that when they enter into forward contracts for the purchase of capital goods that will be produced during the period, they will be able to meet these obligations. The level of cash balances needed to meet forward capital hire-purchase contracts will be unchanged as long as planned (contractual) investment expenditures are unchanged in each period; therefore for any given output flow, there will be a certain volume of planned investment transactions for which transactions balances will be maintained.

'But', Keynes argued, 'if decisions to invest are (e.g.) increasing, the extra finance involved will constitute an addi-

[1] Harrod, *Life of John Maynard Keynes*, p. 435, also see p. 437.

[2] Keynes, *The General Theory*, p. vii.

[3] J. M. Keynes, 'Alternative Theories of the Rate of Interest', *Economic Journal* (1937) **47**, pp. 241–52.

tional demand for money.'[1] Thus, for example, if profit expectations are exogenously increased, then at the given flow of output and rate of interest, entrepreneurs would desire to enter into more forward contracts for capital goods then before and consequently the demand for money to use to pay for the hire-purchase of these goods would increase.[2]

To clarify the essence of the finance motive, and to indicate why it is not properly taken into account in the discussion of the transactions motive, Keynes wrote:

> It follows that, if the liquidity-preferences of the public (as distinct from the entrepreneurial investors) and of the banks are unchanged, an excess in the finance required by current ex-ante output (it is not necessary to write 'investment', since the same is true of *any* output which has to be planned ahead) over the finance released by current ex-post output will lead to a rise in the rate of interest; and a decrease will lead to a fall. I should not have previously overlooked this point, since it is the coping-stone of the liquidity theory of the rate of interest. I allowed, it is true, for the effect of an increase in *actual* activity on the demand for money. But I did not allow for the effect of an increase in *planned* activity, which is superimposed on the former. . . . Just as an increase in actual activity must (as I have always explained) raise the rate of interest unless either the banks or the rest of the public become more willing to release cash, so (as I now add) an increase in planned activity must have a similar, superimposed influence.[3]

Considering that Keynes felt that the finance motive was the coping-stone of his liquidity preference theory, it is surprising to see that the concept has practically disappeared from the literature.

There was, however, a very clear practical illustration of this point offered by Keynes about a year later when his attention was devoted to the imminent rearmament programme and

[1] ibid. p. 247.
[2] Cf. J. Robinson, *The Rate of Interest and Other Essays* (London: Macmillan, 1952) pp. 20–2.
[3] J. M. Keynes, 'The Ex-Ante Theory of the Rate of Interest', *Econ. Jour.* **47** (1937) p. 667.

the prospect of war. In a letter printed in the 18 April 1939 edition of *The Times*, Keynes elucidated his reasoning still further. The immediate question was how to finance the pending additional government expenditures for rearmament. Keynes argued that 'If an attempt is made to borrow them [the savings which will result from the increased production of non-consumption (war) goods] before they exist, as the Treasury have done once or twice lately, a stringency in the money market must result, since pending the expenditure, the liquid resources acquired by the Treasury must be at the expense of the normal liquid resources of the banks and of the public'. In other words, an increase in planned governmental expenditures will normally result in an increase in the aggregate demand for money function, even before the expenditures are undertaken.[1]

It is therefore evident from the writings of Keynes in the *Treatise* and in his notes on finance that the view that demand for money as a medium of exchange is directly related to income [i.e. $L_1(Y)$] is merely a gross and somewhat misleading simplification. The introduction of the finance motive concept involves relating the demand for transactions balances to *planned*, *contractual*, or *expected* spending propensities during the period, i.e. it is a function of the aggregate planned demand for goods (the $C + I$ line in Fig. 7.1) which is, in turn, partly exogenous and partly a function of the level of output. Thus the finance motive concept is associated with *shifts* in the transactions demand function, or *changes* in demand for the medium of exchange as the planned demand for goods change and it permits the rate of interest to change if there is a change in the demand for money even *before* there is any accommodating change in the flow of output. If, on the other hand, the Monetary Authority and the banking system attempt to maintain the rate of interest by increasing the money supply in response to an increased demand for additional finance, then the money supply will endogenously expand *before* there is any change in the rate of flow of production and the level of employment.

The correctly specified Keynesian transactions demand

---

[1] Thus Keynes anticipated and explicitly responded to Johnson's criticism of the conventional Bastard Keynesian model of interest rate determination almost a quarter of a century before Johnson presented it in his analysis of 'The General Theory After Twenty-Five Years'.

concept will relate transactions balances with, in the simplest two-sector case, the summation of the consumption function and the investment demand function. If we assume that the quantity of money demanded for transactions balances is equal to some constant fraction of the aggregate planned demand for goods at each level of output, then the transactions-demand-for-money function would be drawn as L^*_t rather than L_t in Fig. 7.2 (since it is related to the $C + I$ line rather than the 45-degree line in Fig. 7.1).[1]

Much more is involved here than merely a geometric mis-representation of the demand for transactions balances, for it now becomes obvious that the relationship between the quantity of money demanded for transactions and the level of output is a 'function of a function', rather than the simple direct relationship. Thus to trace out the change in the quantity of transactions money demanded for a given change in output it is necessary to obtain the change in the quantity demanded of transactions balances for a given change in aggregate demand and the change in aggregate demand for a given change in output.[2] In other words, the change in the quantity of money demanded for transactions purposes depends not only on changes in output, but also on the relationship of the change in the level of aggregate demand with a change in output (e.g. given the level of investment, on the marginal propensity to consume). Furthermore, given the customary contractual payments period in the economy, it follows that if consumers and/or

[1] Keynes, of course, recognised that the demand for transactions balances was not only related to the aggregate demand function, but also via 'the business motive' to the parameters of the aggregate supply function (i.e. to the price of inputs, production functions, degree of industry integration, and the degree of monopoly). To make the following analysis comparable to the usual post-Keynesian treatments of liquidity preference, however, we shall make the explicit assumption (which is implicit in the works of others) that, either (1) there is no change in the aggregate supply function, or (2) any change in the quantity of money demanded for 'the business motive' occurs only *pari passu* with changes in the aggregate demand function. Accordingly, we can focus our attention entirely on aggregate demand.

[2] Symbolically this can be stated as

$$\frac{dL^*_t}{dY} = \frac{dL^*_t}{dD} \cdot \frac{dD}{dY}$$

where D is aggregate demand.

investors decide to spend more at any given flow of income (an upward shift in the aggregate demand function), then there will be an increase in the demand for money for the purchase of goods at each *level of output* (an upward shift on the L^*_t function). Thus, the finance motive involves changes *in the demand* for money as a medium of exchange which are *not* induced by changes in output, while the traditional transactions motive involves changes in the quantity of money demanded as a medium of exchange which are induced by changes in the flow of income and output.

Let us summarise symbolically the argument as developed so far. The demand for transactions balances should be written as

$$L^*_t = \alpha C + \beta I \qquad (2)$$

where α and β are constants $(0 < \alpha < 1; 0 < \beta < 1)$ whose magnitudes depend primarily on the frequency of payments and the overlapping of payments and receipts in the system, and C and I are the consumption and investment commitments which are *expected* to fall due during the period. Assuming linear functions for C and I (merely for algebraic simplicity) the consumption function may be written as

$$C = a_1 + b_1 Y \qquad (3)$$

when a_1 is a constant (> 0) and b_1 is the marginal propensity to consume. The investment commitment function, given the supply schedule in the capital goods industry, may be written as

$$I = a_2 - b_2 i \qquad (4)$$

where a_2 and b_2 are constants and i is the rate of interest. Combining equations (3) and (4) into (2) we get the demand for transactions balances function as

$$L_t^* = \alpha a_1 + \beta a_2 + \alpha b_1 Y - \beta b_2 i \qquad (5)$$

If we assume a constant rate of interest (which is implicit in the usual 45-degree diagram), then the fourth term on the right-hand side of equation (5) is a constant; thus, equation (5) appears to be similar to Hansen's equation (1) except that the function does not emanate from the origin.

There is, however, a significant analytical difference between equations (1) and (5). In Hansen's system, the parameter k of equation (1) depends only on the customary length of the payments period in the economy, and consequently, the equation is entirely *independent* of the behavioural parameters of the real sector [equations (3) and (4)]. Thus, as long as the conventional payments period is unchanged, the magnitude of k is fixed, and therefore Hansen's transactions demand for money function is stable – even if the parameters of the aggregate demand-function change. On the other hand, equation (5) shows that some of the parameters (the a's and the b's) are common to both the transactions demand for money function and the real consumption-and-investment-demand functions. Thus, according to equation (5), even if the payments period is unchanged (i.e. α and β are constant), any change in either the investment demand or the consumption functions will result in a shift of the entire transactions demand for money schedule; or as Keynes noted, any 'increase in planned activity' will result in an increased demand for money *at each level of output*. Accordingly, any change in the parameters of the aggregate-demand function (contrary to Hansen's system) will result in a shift on the L^*_t function. The demand for money function is *not* independent of changes in the real sector.

It is the shift in the L^*_t function induced by a change in spending propensities that Keynes was describing when he discussed the finance motive.[1] Whenever there is a shift in the aggregate-demand function, there will be a concomitant shift in the demand for money schedule. Consequently, when there is an increase in planned investment, for example, the equilibrium quantity of money demanded will ultimately increase for two reasons: (1) a shift in the L^*_t function (i.e. the finance motive), and (2) a movement along the new L^*_t function as output increases and induces further spending via the multiplier. It is the shift in the L^*_t function which puts additional pressure on the rate of interest.[2]

[1] In the case of war finance, discussed by Keynes in 1939, what was involved was an increase in the government component of aggregate demand which was to be financed by borrowing before the actual spending occurred.

[2] As we will show below, it was this aspect that led D. H. Robertson to utter the triumphal note that Keynes had at last restored productivity 'to something like its rightful place in governing the rate of interest from the side of demand'. See D. H. Robertson, 'Mr. Keynes and "Finance" ', *Economic Journal*, **48** (1938) p. 317.

Thus, every upward shift of the aggregate-demand function (the $C + I$ line in Fig. 7.1) implies the prevalence of a 'finance motive' as spending units switch over from one money-demand function to a higher one. Once this change has occurred, spending units will maintain larger transactions balances than before *at each level of output*. At that point the dynamic finance motive merges with that static concept of the transactions motive. The finance motive thus evolves as one of the dynamic elements in the static Keynesian model; its major contribution is in macroeconomic disequilibrium path analysis rather than in comparative statics.

Implication of the Analysis

It is useful to distil three important implications of the analysis before elaborating on it. These are:

1. Since the demand for money function is not as stable as Hansen's formulation implies (i.e. it varies every time the aggregate-demand function shifts), and since it does not emanate from the origin, *even if the rate of interest is a constant*, there is no reason to expect a constant relationship between the demand for money for transactions purposes and the level of output. In other words, and in the language of monetary theorists, we should *not* expect the income velocity of money to be constant. The recognition of the 'finance motive' concept prepares us for some clearer understanding of monetary phenomena.

For example, Friedman, recognising that the income velocity of money is a demand-oriented phenomenon, has attempted to estimate the income elasticity of demand for money. He has found that observed short-run variations in income velocity imply an income elasticity less than unity, whereas secular evidence indicates an elasticity which exceeds unity. In a novel (and perhaps somewhat forced) explanation, Friedman tries to reconcile these conflicting short-run and secular estimates of elasticity by imputing differences between 'permanent' income and prices and measured income and prices.[1] Our finance motive analysis, however, suggests a much simpler

[1] M. Friedman, 'The Demand for Money: Some Theoretical and Empirical Results', *Journ. Pol. Econ.* **67** (1959) pp. 328–38. Permanent incomes and prices represent expectational levels which, it is assumed, will be realised since there is no uncertainty in Friedman's model.

explanation which is entirely consistent with Friedman's short-run and secular estimates. If the short-run demand for transactions-balances function has a positive intercept and is either a straight line or concave to the abscissa, then:

$$\frac{dL^*_t}{dY} < \frac{L^*_t}{Y}$$

It therefore follows that the income elasticity of demand for transactions balances will be less than unity along the entire function.[1] In other words, given the normal aggregate consumption and investment functions and the rate of interest, we would expect Friedman to find out that as the economy moved toward equilibrium, short-run movements in output will be accompanied by less than proportional changes in the quantity of money demanded by spending units.

Observed secular changes in the quantity of money demanded, on the other hand, are most likely the result of viewing particular demand points on different L^*_t functions as the latter shifts through time in response to changes in the parameters of the system. The 'income elasticity' calculated from observations which cut across short-run L^*_t functions will obviously be larger in magnitude than the elasticity measured along any one L^*_t function and might easily result in estimates which exceed unity. This secular 'elasticity' measurement, however, has little or no relationship to the usual concept of income elasticity which assumes a given preference scheme (i.e. given behaviourial parameters).

Friedman has made the assumption that 'the elasticity of demand for money with respect to real income is approximately unity' the foundation for his latest 'superior . . . method

[1] Letting E_m represent the income elasticity of demand for money, the elasticity can be defined as

$$E_m = \left(\frac{dL^*_t}{dY}\right)\left(\frac{Y}{L_t}\right).$$

It follows therefore that the income elasticity of demand for money is greater than (equal to, less than) unity, when (dL^*_t/dY) is greater than (equal to, less than) L^*_t/Y.

Keynes believed that the income velocity was not constant, and furthermore, he suggested that the elasticity of demand for money would normally be less than unity at less than full employment. See *The General Theory*, pp. 201, 299, 304–6.

of closing the theoretical system for the purpose of analysing short-period changes'.[1] The present analysis has shown, however, that a unit elasticity would be compatible only with the Bastard Keynesian case where L_t is a straight line emanating from the origin (Fig. 7.1). A unit elasticity of demand for money is incompatible with Keynes's finance motive analysis – and is therefore inimical to the view that the money supply may be endogenous. It is not surprising, therefore, to see Friedman assert that all changes in the quantity of money 'can be regarded as completely exogenous';[2] hence when members of the Monetarist school observe a statistically significant relationship between changes in the quantity of money and changes in GNP, they insist that the former *must* have (by hypothesis) caused the latter. Recognition of Keynes's finance motive concept, however, means that causality cannot be determined by any empirical relation between these variables. Thus, as Chapter 10 will analyse in greater detail, changes in the quantity of money can be either exogenous or endogenous; and hence the Monetarist school view is not applicable to the real world where finance is important.

A shift in *any* component of the aggregate demand for goods function will induce a concomitant shift in the transaction demand for money function. Thus, when Keynes linked the finance motive with changes in the decision to invest, he was, as he readily admitted, discussing 'only a special case' of the finance motive. Keynes's justification for linking the finance motive to changes in planned investment was his belief that planned investment is 'subject to special fluctuation of its own'. In his discussion of war finance, however, Keynes was generalising the finance motive to other exogenous components of aggregate demand. Thus any change in exogenous planned spending behaviour will result in a shift in the transactions demand for money function, and if the banking system responds, changes in the money supply will be endogenously determined. Generally speaking, the finance motive will be involved whenever the aggregate demand function is changed. For example, if we add a government spending function (assuming, for the moment, no change in the $C + I$ line in Fig. 7.1) then we would

[1] M. Friedman, 'A Monetary Theory of Nominal Income', *Journ. Pol. Econ.* (1971) pp. 324–5.   [2] ibid. p. 329.

have to shift up the $L*_t$ function (in Fig. 7.2) to include government's demand for transactions balances. Furthermore, to the extent that the quantity of money demanded per dollar of consumption is different from the quantity demanded per dollar of planned investment (i.e. $\alpha \neq \beta$) or planned government spending (or planned foreigners' purchases for that matter), then the total demand for transactions balances will depend upon the composition of aggregate demand (at each level of output), while the latter, in turn, will depend at least in part on the distribution of income. To illustrate, if income is redistributed from spending units which have high liquidity needs to units which have lower liquidity needs to carry out a given volume of planned expenditures, then even with the same level of aggregate demand for goods, the quantity of money demanded will be reduced. For example, to the extent that consumers have less leeway in matching their receipts to their obligations (because of less flexible consumer credit institutions), consumers may require higher balances per dollar of planned expenditures than business firms. Thus, the composition of aggregate demand as well as the level of output may be an important determinant of the demand for cash balances.

At the level of public policy, as well as correct theory, it thus appears that once the $L*_t$ function is related to the components of the aggregate demand function, rather than to the 45-degree line, some important insights appear. For example, if the economy is initially at some output level, say Y_1, and if the government decides to increase its purchases of new goods and services by x dollars (on the assumption that the supply of money is unchanged), the magnitude of the impact on the rate of interest at the original Y_1 level (as well as at any other Y level) will depend on whether the government 'finances' the increased expenditure by borrowing or by taxation.[1] (This was noted earlier in the revealing quotation from Keynes regarding war finance.) This suggests that even before an expansionary activity occurs, a planned increase in government spending will affect the money market through the demand for new balances to finance and fund the projected outlay. Assuming investment demand to be relatively inelastic to changes in the

[1] In either case, of course, the equilibrium rate of interest and the equilibrium level of output will rise.

rate of interest, the magnitude of the impact on the money market will be greater if the government borrows rather than increases taxes to finance the expenditure, since borrowing will result in the addition of the government component to the aggregate demand function; while financing via income-taxes, for example, will reduce the consumption component while elevating the government component. Thus, in the latter case, we should not expect the aggregate demand curve to be elevated as much as in the former case: the shift in the L^*_t function will be less with taxation than with borrowing. (Hansen's L_t function, on the other hand, portends a complete absence of impact on the money market until after the increase in economic activity actually occurs.)

If the demand for transactions balances is related to the aggregate demand function, then a straight-line L_t function which emanates from the origin has an income elasticity of unity and it belongs to the world of Say's Law – a world where the aggregate demand function coincides with the 45-degree line,[1] i.e. a world where the aggregate demand function is linear and homogeneous with respect to the flow of output. In such a world, however, 'money is but a veil' and there exists a dichotomy between the real and monetary sectors so that there can be no monetary obstacle to full employment for the real and monetary factors are completely independent.[2] Once, however, it is recognised that the demand for transactions balances is a function of aggregate demand, which, in turn, *is not homogeneous with respect to output*, then the demand for money function is not homogeneous with respect to output. It therefore follows that the system cannot be dichotomised into independent monetary and real subsets since the scale of activity is an important determinant of the level of planned aggregate demand and, therefore, of the quantity of money

[1] The case where the aggregate demand function is a straight line emanating from the origin at an angle other than 45 degrees is a trivial case, since the only solution to the system occurs at a zero level of output.

[2] In a world of Say's Law (e.g. a barter economy) the commodity price level, if one can be conceived of, will be independent of monetary analysis. It is therefore significant to note that in Professor Friedman's latest formulation based on a unity income elasticity of demand for money, Friedman finds that his monetary analysis is unable to say anything directly about changes in the supply of money and changes in the price level.

demanded. (Certainly, Keynes believed that the analytical separation of the real and monetary sectors was wrong.)

The Finance Motive and the Interdependence of the Real and Monetary Sectors

The inappropriateness of attempting to dichotomise the system into independent real and monetary subsets can be clarified by utilising the more general Hicksian $IS-LM$ framework where both the rate of interest and the level of output are simultaneously determined, rather than relying on the 45-degree diagram which assumes a constant rate of interest. The $IS-LM$ system has the advantage of showing both the real sector and the monetary sector on the same diagram; consequently, interdependence can be visually observed if when one function shifts, the other is concomitantly displaced. It has the disadvantage of being based on a Walrasian general equilibrium approach. Thus the following analysis is merely a pedagogical exercise to suggest that even within the traditional Bastard Keynesian neoclassical approach to macroeconomics, recognition of the finance motive concept will alter the traditional results.

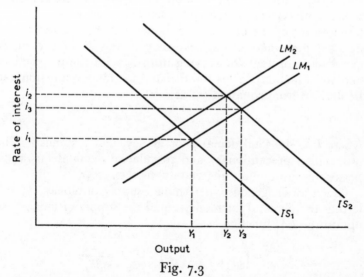

Fig. 7.3

In Hicks's system, the basic determinants of the IS-function are the investment demand schedule and the aggregate consumption function, while the *LM*-function is based on the money demand and supply functions.[1] The *IS*-function may be derived by combining equations (3) and (4) with the output identity $Y \equiv C + I$

$$Y = a_1 + b_1 Y + a_2 - b_2 i \tag{6}$$

or

$$Y = \left(\frac{1}{1 - b_1} \right) (a_1 + a_2 - b_2 i) \tag{7}$$

Equation (7) is the *IS*-function; it traces out all the values of output and the rate of interest which are compatible with the investment demand and consumption functions. In Fig. 7.3 it is plotted as the downward sloping IS_1 line, since as the rate of interest declines, according to equation (7), the level of output will rise.

The demand for money equation can be derived by adding the speculative and precautionary demand functions to the demand for transactions-balances function. Since we are only interested in the implications of the demand for money as a medium of exchange at this point, we do not have to specify the forms of the demand for money as a store of value, i.e. the precautionary and speculative demands for money. These latter forms of the demand for money will be assessed in the next chapter; at this stage we may merely assume them as given and constant (or varying directly with the transactions demand function). Thus the demand for money function can be derived from equation (5) as:

$$L = \alpha a_1 + \beta a_2 + \alpha b_1 Y - \beta b_2 i + \sigma \tag{8}$$

where L is the total demand for money, and σ stands for the unspecified precautionary and speculative demand functions, possessing substantial 'uncertainty' factors.

Given an exogenously determined supply of money, $\bar{m}$, and letting the demand for money equal the supply of money, we obtain the *LM* function as;

$$i = \frac{a_2}{b_2} + \left(\frac{\alpha}{\beta b_2} \right) (a_1 + b_1 Y) - \frac{1}{\beta b_2} \bar{m} + \frac{1}{\beta b_2} \sigma. \tag{9}$$

---

[1] J. R. Hicks, 'Mr. Keynes and the "Classics": A Suggested Interpretation', *Econometrica*, **5** (1937) pp. 147–59.

Thus, given α and β, and the a's and the b's, once outside of the liquidity trap, the LM function is plotted as upward sloping (see LM_1 in Fig. 7.3) since, as Y increases, the rate of interest rises. The values of I and Y which satisfy both (7) and (9) simultaneously are revealed as the equilibrium rate of interest and the equilibrium level of output of the system (i_1 and Y_1 in Fig. 7.3).

The interdependence of the money market [equation (9)] on the real sector [equation (7)] is now easily demonstrated. For example, suppose an outward shift of the investment demand function [equation (4)] is posited. In other words, assume a_2 increases. It follows from equation (7) that at each rate of interest, the Y ordinate of the IS function will increase by an amount equal to the change in a_2 multiplied by $1/(1 - b_1)$; this means simply that the IS function moves outward to IS_2 in Fig. 7.3. Observe that whereas in Hansen's system, the LM function would remain unchanged when the IS curve shifts, it can be seen from equation (9) that when a_2 increases, the i ordinate of the LM function will increase by an amount equal to the change in a_2 multiplied by $(1/b_2)$ at each output level. Thus, the whole LM function shifts upward to LM_2 in Fig. 7.3, so that the new equilibrium level of output and rate of interest (Y_2 and i_2 respectively) are higher than before.[1] In

---

[1] Since normally $b_2 > 1$, while $1 - b_1 < 1$, a change in a_2 will have a larger impact on the IS function (7) than on the LM equation (9), that is the IS curve will shift more than the LM curve so that the new intersect will always be to the north-east of the original intersection.

In Hansen's traditional system, since the LM curve is not displaced, the new equilibrium level of output and rate of interest is Y_3 and i_3 respectively.

For completeness, it should be pointed out that the traditional (e.g. Hansen's) algebraic formulation of the LM function can, given a restrictive and highly unrealistic assumption, be resuscitated by reinterpreting it as representing the loci of equilibrium points (a sort of long-run equilibrium path) traced out as both the short-run IS and LM functions shift in response to changes in the parameters of the spending propensities. In the following Appendix, it is demonstrated that if, and only if, $\alpha = \beta$ (that is, if the additional quantity of transactions money demanded for an additional dollar of planned consumption is always equal to the additional quantity of transactions money demanded for an additional dollar of planned investment spending, or planned government or planned foreigners' purchases), then a money sector function based on equation (8) being written in the traditional algebraic form of $L = kY + \sigma$ (where $k = \alpha = \beta$) describes an

a similar manner, equivalent simultaneous shifts in the *IS* and *LM* functions can be demonstrated whenever any of the parameters of the consumption or investment demand functions change.

The inevitable conclusion is that even this neoclassical-Bastard Keynesian system cannot be dichotomised into independent real and monetary subsets; consequently, it is not correct to separate monetary economics from real economics as has often been done. It is important to note that the interdependence of the real and monetary sectors does not require the fine theoretical point (which may have little practical significance) of a real balance effect. That so much controversy about the possible independence of the real and monetary sectors has appeared in the post-Keynes literature is surprising in view of Keynes's warning that the 'division of Economics between the Theory of Value and Distribution on the one hand and the Theory of Money on the other hand is, I think, a false division'.[1] Had the interconnection between the finance motive, the transactions motive, and the aggregate-demand function been understood originally, much of this barren controversy could have been avoided.

Once the finance motive concept is understood, it is easy to demonstrate the correctness of Keynes's *obiter dictum* that an overdraft system is an 'ideal system for mitigating the effects on the banking system of an increased demand for ex-ante finance'.[2] For example, if there is an outward shift of the *IS* function from IS_1 to IS_2 as profit expectations rise, and if the resulting increase in demand for cash to finance the additional investment plans can be furnished by overdrafts, then the supply schedule of money will endogenously increase *pari passu* with the increase in the demand for money function. Consequently, the *LM* function will not shift; rather it will remain

---

equilibrium path which cuts across shifting *LM* curves, when the latter are displaced as a result of shifts in the *IS* function.

(I am extremely grateful to Sir Roy F. Harrod for bringing this possibility initially to my attention, and to Helen Raffel for providing me with a basic mathematical proof for clarifying this point.)

[1] Keynes, *The General Theory*, p. 293.

[2] Keynes, 'The Ex-Ante Theory of the Rate of Interest', *Econ. Jour.* **47** (1937) p. 669.

firm as LM_1 so that the equilibrium level of output will expand to Y_3 while the equilibrium rate of interest increases only to i_3 (Fig. 7.3). Consequently, as Keynes noted, 'to the extent that the overdraft system is employed and unused overdrafts ignored by the banking system, there is no superimposed pressure resulting from planned activity over and above the pressure resulting from actual activity. In this event the transition from a lower to a higher scale of activity may be accomplished with less pressure on the demand for liquidity and the rate of interest'.[1]

The Role of Productivity and Thrift: a Digression

With the aid of Fig. 7.3, it is now easy to demonstrate that much of the controversy between Robertson and Keynes on the role of productivity and thrift in determining the rate of interest is mainly a semantic confusion between movements along the demand schedule for money and shifts in the schedule.[2] An increase in the productivity (i.e. expected profitability) of capital would induce an outward shift in the *IS* curve (from IS_1 to IS_2 in Fig. 7.3) and, as we have already argued, a concomitant shift in the demand for money schedule so that, given the supply of money, the *LM* curve is elevated from LM_1 to LM_2. Since LM_2 lies above LM_1, Robertson was correct when he argued that an increase in productivity will *ceteris paribus* raise the rate of interest (at each level of output) as the demand for money function shifts.[3] On the other hand, Keynes was correct when he stressed that, given the supply of money, the increase in the equilibrium quantity of money demanded (due to the finance motive shifting the $L*_t$ function 'superimposed' upon a movement along the $L*_t$ schedule as output increased) caused the equilibrium rate of i interest to rise from i_1 to i_2. Since Keynes was discussing a movement from one equilibrium rate of interest to another in *The General Theory* he stressed changes in spending propensities and output as the producer of changes in the equilibrium quantity of money

[1] ibid. p. 669.

[2] Since we have demonstrated that the economy cannot be divided into independent real and monetary subsets, it should not be surprising to find that the 'real' variables of productivity and thrift have an impact on the monetary sector.

[3] D. H. Robertson, *Essays on Monetary Theory* (London: Staples, 1940) pp. 10–12.

demanded and in the rate of interest; whereas Robertson was essentially viewing the impact of changes in 'productivity' on the entire demand for money schedule.

The discussion of the role of thrift was similarly enshrouded. An increase in thrift (i.e. a downward shift of the consumption function) would result in an inward movement of the IS function (say from IS_2 to IS_1) and a reduction in the demand for money schedule, so that the LM curve would be depressed (say from LM_2 to LM_1). Here again, we can see that Robertson, in arguing that an increase in thrift lowers the rate of interest (at each level of output), is emphasising the shift in the entire demand for money schedule, while Keynes stressed the fall in the equilibrium rate of interest from i_2 to i_1, which resulted from a decline in the equilibrium quantity of money demanded as spending propensities and output fell.[1]

THE SUMMARY OF THE DEMAND FOR THE MEDIUM OF EXCHANGE

The mis-specification of the transactions demand and the disregard of Keynes's finance motive analysis in the modern monetary literature of the neoclassical and Bastard Keynesian schools has led to some omissions and some confusions, making for wrong theoretical constructions and an incomplete understanding of certain policy implications of money supplies in a growing economy where finance must be provided or deflationary pressures emerge via the monetary system.[2]

In order for business firms to be able, as well as willing to expand, two conditions are necessary. These are: (1) firms must have expectations that demand will be greater in the future when planned new investment will come 'on-stream' i.e. entrepreneurs must show strong 'animal spirits' and (2) entrepreneurs must be able to obtain a sufficient quantity of money so that they can accept forward offer contracts for additional capital goods with little fear of not being able to meet these contractual obligations when they come due.[3] If firms can obtain

[1] Cf. Keynes, *The General Theory*, pp. 98, 183–5, 372.

[2] Cf. Harrod, *Money*, ch. 7.

[3] After years of debate and acrimony, Friedman has recently adopted Keynes's mis-specified demand for money function and has therefore failed

sufficient finance, they will be able to 'command' resources (at the going offer price) to produce goods which come forth during the period in a form which is not 'available' for current consumption.

Thus an additional demand for 'non-available' capital goods involves a prior increase in the demand for money as the medium of exchange. In the aggregate, entrepreneurs will be able to obtain these additional funds only if either (1) households are simultaneously reducing their liquidity preference either via (i) a lower transactions demand for money or (ii) a lower demand for holding money as a store of value, or (2) the quantity of bank money is increased *and* made available to entrepreneurs, or (3) entrepreneurs 'outbid' some households for access to the existing stock of bank money thereby either bidding up the rate of interest or causing credit rationing among other borrowers.[1] If none of these events occur, then entrepreneurs will be limited in the volume of offer contracts they can accept per period, and stringent financial conditions will limit expansion despite strong 'animal spirits' which foresee additional potentially profitable investment projects. Thus the banking system, by controlling the quantity of bank credit, and financial institutions, by restricting availability of finance, can constrain the level of economic activity, even when there are idle real resources.

In sum, then, the growth of real capital and output in the economy ultimately depends on: (1) the behaviour of the banking system, financial institutions and the liquidity desires of households,[2] and (2) the animal spirits of entrepreneurs as reflected in the present values of investment projects relative to the costs of production of such projects.

A COMPARATIVE ASSESSMENT

It is provocative, at this stage, to speculate briefly how this Keynes approach compares with other views of the importance

---

to permit changes in planned spending to affect the demand for money. (See Friedman, 'A Monetary Theory', pp. 325–6.)

[1] Given the organisation of financial markets. This latter aspect is especially important to developed capitalist economies such as the United States and the United Kingdom. See Chapter 13 below.

[2] This is discussed in detail in Chapter 13.

of finance in the theory of economic growth. For example, in the neoclassical world of Gurley and Shaw, the growth of non-monetary intermediaries will reduce the growth in the demand for money by spending units, and consequently 'reduces the required growth of the money stock' necessary for a policy of expansion. Furthermore, Gurley and Shaw claim that 'a favorable climate for the growth of non-monetary intermed-iaries is one in which there is an expansion of national output based primarily on private expenditures . . . that are financed to a great degree by external means'[1] since such circumstances will induce the expansion of financial intermediaries and ulti-mately lower the demand for money.

Gurley and Shaw's thesis can be made more specific by using our Fig. 7.3. If when profit expectations improve, so that the IS schedule shifts from IS_1 to IS_2, in the absence of either an overdraft system, or financial intermediaries, or specific action by the Monetary Authority, the supply of money would be unchanged, and the new equilibrium levels will be i_2 and Y_2. If financial intermediaries are in the system and *if* they are induced to expand their activities *pari passu* as output expands, then the ultimate equilibrium level of output will be higher than Y_2 and the rate of interest will be lower than i_2 (say, Y_3 and i_3 in Fig. 7.3). This movement from the original equilibrium values of Y_1 and i_1, to Y_3 and i_3 can be looked upon as occurring in two stages. In the first instance, the outward shift of the IS function has increased the demand for money function as planned spending increases. The resulting increase in economic activity, if Gurley and Shaw are correct, stimulates the growth of non-bank financial intermediaries who may be able to reduce the liquidity needs of households by providing them with assets which have such high liquidity as to fill a gap in the liquidity spectrum of available financial assets, so that households feel secure enough to reduce the quantity of money they hold as a store of value at any given rate of interest. Thus, in the second stage, the demand for money function is reduced as the inter-mediaries grow. The final result on the demand for money function depends upon the magnitude of these two counter-vailing forces. As a first approximation, we may assume that

[1] J. G. Gurley and E. S. Shaw, *Money in a Theory of Finance* (Washington: Brookings, 1960) p. 228.

they just neutralise each other, so that despite the constancy of the money supply the relevant LM function may be LM_1 instead of LM_2. Thus, Gurley and Shaw's system of non-monetary intermediaries suggests a somewhat different, and perhaps more difficult, path than Keynes's overdraft system for avoiding shortage of liquidity as plans for expansion are made; for unless the public is willing to accept the less liquid debts of the financial intermediaries as a store of value instead of money, then expansions can not occur – even if the public would be willing to save a sufficient quantity of future income to equal the desired increase in capital goods. As Keynes has cogently argued:

> if there is no change in the liquidity position, the public can save ex-ante and ex-post and ex-anything-else until they are blue in the face, without alleviating the problem in the least – unless, indeed, the result of their efforts is to lower the scale of activity to what it was before.[1]

As an alternative to the financial intermediaries' debts providing an almost as liquid substitute for money in households' holdings it may be argued that non-bank financial intermediaries are able to obtain additional bank credit which would not be made directly available to entrepreneurs because of imperfections in the money market. In this latter case, there is an endogenous effect on the money supply volume similar to Keynes's overdraft scheme, but the trail of debt contracts left in expanding the money supply will be different under the two schemes.

Keynes's analysis highlights the view that ultimately:

> the banks hold the key position in the transition from a lower to a higher scale of activity. If they refuse to relax, [i.e. to provide endogenous additional finance] the growing congestion of the short-term loan market or the new issue market, as the case may be, will inhibit the improvement, no matter how thrifty the public purpose to be out of their future income. On the other hand, there will always be *exactly* enough ex-post saving to take up the ex-post investment and so

---

[1] J. M. Keynes, 'The Ex-Ante Theory of the Rate of Interest', *Econ. Journ.* **47** (1937) p. 668.

release the finance which the latter had been previously employing. *The investment market can become congested through shortage of cash. It can never become congested through shortage of saving. This is the most fundamental of my conclusions within this field.*[1]

Thus, Keynes's analysis emphasises the importance of banking and financial institutions on the operation of the real economy. If, for example, institutional barriers, imperfections in the money market or operations of financial institutions restrain changes in the rate of interest which would otherwise be associated with changes in the demand for finance, at any given level of employment and output (assuming the money market cleared before the increase in demand for finance occurred), then credit rationing will prevail, and individual firms are prevented from making their 'wants' for increased capital goods per period effective in the market by their inability to borrow money to use to pay for delivery on offer contracts.[2] Queueing for finance, *even* at the initial level of output, is a readily understandable phenomenon in the Keynes system which emphasises[3]

. . . in what sense a heavy demand for investment can exhaust the market and be held up by the lack of financial facilities on reasonable terms. *It is to an important extent the 'financial' facilities which regulate the pace of new investment.* Some people find it a paradox that, up to the point of full employment, no amount of actual investment, however great, can exhaust and exceed the supply of savings. . . . If this is found paradoxical, it is because it is confused with the fact that *too great a press of uncompleted investment decisions is quite capable of exhausting the available finance*, if the banking system is unwilling to increase the supply of money and the supply from existing holders is inelastic. It is the supply of available finance which, in practice, holds up from time to time the onrush of 'new issues'. But if the banking system chooses to make the

[1] J. M. Keynes, 'The Ex-Ante Theory of the Rate of Interest', *Econ. Jour.*, **47** (1937) pp. 668–9. Italics added.   [2] See Chapter 13 below.
[3] The literature on 'availability' is remarkably confused or naive or both on this aspect. Chapter 13 deals with problems of credit rationing in some detail.

finance available and the investment projected by the new issues actually takes place, the appropriate level of incomes will be generated out of which there will necessarily remain over an amount of saving exactly sufficient to take care of the new investment. *The control of finance is, indeed, a potent, though sometimes dangerous, method for regulating the rate of investment* (though much more potent when used as a curb than as a stimulus).[1]

APPENDIX[2]

In the traditional (e.g. Hansen's) formulation, the demand for transactions (L_t) [and precautionary (L_p)] balances are usually taken as a linear function of the level of output,

$$L_t + L_p = kY \tag{10}$$

while the speculative demand function (L_s) is assumed to be inversely related to the rate of interest (outside the liquidity trap). If, for algebraic simplicity, we assume a linear relationship, then the speculative demand for money balances can be written as:

$$L_s = \lambda_1 - \lambda_2 i, \text{ for } i > i_0 \tag{11}$$

where i_0 is the liquidity trap value of i. Combining equations (10) and (11) with an exogenously determined money supply, $\bar{m}$, the traditional *LM* function can be written as

$$i = \frac{\lambda_1 - \bar{m}}{\lambda_2} + \left(\frac{k}{\lambda_2}\right)Y \tag{12}$$

Equation (12) is traditionally interpreted as indicating the rate of interest in the money market which will bring the total

[1] J. M. Keynes, 'Alternative Theories of the Rate of Interest', *Econ. Journ.* **47** (1937) p. 248. Italics added. Of course, if there was some queueing initially (before the increase in the demand for finance), then the length of the queue will increase as planned transactions rise as a result of entrepreneurs attempting to finance more investment projects than before.

[2] This appendix is based on a mathematical proof provided for me by Helen Raffel. Any errors occurring in the interpretation of this proof are mine alone.

demand for money into equilibrium with the total supply of money for any given level of output.

The equilibrium level of output for the economy is obtained by solving equations (6) and (12) simultaneously as

$$Y^* = \frac{\lambda_2(a_1 + a_2) + (\bar{m} - \lambda_1)b_2}{\lambda_2(1 - b_1) + kb_2} \tag{13}$$

where the equilibrium rate of interest is

$$i^* = \frac{k(a_1 + a_2) + (\lambda_1 - \bar{m})(1 - b_1)}{\lambda_2(1 - b_1) + kb_2} \tag{14}$$

With the finance motive system stressed in this paper, on the other hand, the transactions demand for money is related to the aggregate demand function, i.e.

$$L_t = \alpha C + \beta I \tag{15}$$

Substituting the consumption and investment demand function [equation (3) and (4)] into equation (15) yields

$$L_t = \alpha(a_1 + b_1 Y) + \beta(a_2 - b_2 i). \tag{16}$$

Combining equation (16) with equation (11) and equating the sum to the exogenously determined supply of money, the *LM* function can be written as

$$i = \frac{\alpha a_1 + \beta a_2 + \lambda_1 - \bar{m}}{\beta b_2 + \lambda_2} + \frac{\alpha b_1}{\beta b_2 + \lambda_2} Y. \tag{17}$$

Solving equations (6) and (17) simultaneously, the equilibrium level of output in this system is given by

$$Y^* = \frac{\lambda_2(a_1 + a_2) + (\bar{m} - \lambda_1)b_2 - (\alpha - \beta)a_1 b_2}{\lambda_2(1 - b_1) + \beta b_2 + (\alpha - \beta)b_1 b} \tag{18}$$

while the equilibrium rate of interest for the entire system is

$$i^* = \frac{\alpha a_1 + \beta a_2 + (\lambda_1 - \bar{m})(1 - b_1) + (\alpha - \beta)a_2 b_1}{\lambda_2(1 - b_1) + \beta b_2 + (\alpha - \beta)b_1 b_2} \tag{19}$$

A comparison of equations (13) and (18) shows that, if, and only if $\alpha = \beta = k$, then the equilibrium level of output in both the traditional and finance motive systems will be identical. This result can be interpreted with the help of Fig. 7.4.

If, as we have argued in this paper, the demand for transactions balances is a function of the aggregate demand for goods, then when IS_1 shifts to IS_2 (in Fig. 7.4) the LM_1 function shifts

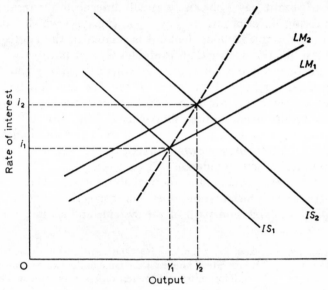

Fig. 7.4

to LM_2, and the equilibrium values for Y and i rise from Y_1 to Y_2 and i_1 to i_2 respectively. The locus of equilibrium points which will be derived for given shifts in the IS and LM functions is given by the dashed line in Fig. 7.4, and would be algebraically represented by equation (12). This implies, however, that the traditional interpretation of equation (12) is incorrect. This equation does not show the rate of interest in the money market which brings the demand for money into equilibrium with the supply of money for any level of output; rather, if $\alpha = \beta = k$, equation (12) indicates the various combinations of rates of interest and output levels which will bring about simultaneous equilibrium in both the commodity and money markets, given specified changes in the real behavioural parameters of the aggregate demand function.

On the other hand, in the more realistic case where $\alpha \neq \beta \neq k$, the equilibrium level of employment of the traditional system as derived via equation (13) will be different from the result obtained via (18), once the finance motive is recognised. Consequently, when $\alpha \neq \beta$, the traditional approach tends to suggest that for a given shift in *IS*, the resulting equilibrium level of output (say Y_3 in Fig. 7.3) will differ from the resulting equilibrium level of output (say Y_2 in Fig. 7.3) which would occur, if the transactions demand is related to the aggregate demand function rather than to the level of output.[1]

Consequently, only in the case where $\alpha = \beta = k$, can the traditional algebraic formulation of the *LM* function be salvaged by reinterpreting it as a sort of long-run growth path which results from shifting short-run *IS* and *LM* functions. (This analogy to the micro-concepts of short-run and long-run curves is admittedly somewhat forced, but it may help clarify my position to some readers.)

In the more general (and more realistic case) where $\alpha \neq \beta$, the traditional formulation does not correctly describe the equilibrium expansion path of the system, and should, therefore, be discarded.

[1] A similar comparison of equations (14) and (19) indicates that when $\alpha = \beta = k$, the equilibrium rate of interest is the same in the two systems, but when $\alpha \neq \beta \neq k$, the equilibrium rate of interest differs in the two systems.

CHAPTER 8

The Demand for Money as a Store of Value

THAT portion of the money supply which is being used to satisfy the needs for a medium of exchange as determined by households' desire to use money to buy producible goods and entrepreneurs' desires to use money to buy services of the factors of production will consist of 'active' bank deposits. The use of these active balances was termed the *industrial circulation* by Keynes in his *Treatise on Money*, as opposed to the use of the portion of the money supply which is involved in the business of distributing titles or stores of wealth, the *financial circulation*. The industrial circulation as developed in the last chapter, depends primarily on the length of the contractual payments period, the aggregate planned demand for producible goods, the money rates of remuneration of the factors of production employed, and the degree of industrial integration. In this chapter we shall discuss the determinants of the quantities of money demanded for the financial circulation where by finance

> we mean the business of holding and exchanging existing titles to wealth . . . including Stock Exchange and Money Market transactions, speculation and the process of conveying current savings and [windfall] profits into the hands of entrepreneurs.[1]

In *The General Theory*, money held for financial circulation is associated with the speculative and precautionary motives. At the time of *The General Theory*, Keynes felt that the speculative motive 'needed a more detailed examination than the others, both because it is less well understood and because it is particularly important in transmitting the effects of a[n

---

[1] Keynes, *Treatise on Money*, I 243.

exogenous] *change* in the quantity of money'.[1] Hence Keynes highlighted the speculative motive – not because he thought it more important than the precautionary motive – but because of his belief in a general lack of understanding in the mechanism of how open market operations affected portfolio decisions.

Since 1936, however, the speculative motive has received predominant attention, while, until very recently, the precautionary motive has been virtually ignored.[2] Although both the precautionary and speculative demands for money have been linked in the literature via the concept of idle balances, they are normally dealt with as if they were separate and independent phenomena, with the speculative demand concept dominating changes in 'idle' cash holdings.

The *necessary* conditions for both the speculative and precautionary motive is uncertainty about the course of future economic events. The speculative motive whose objective was described by Keynes as 'securing profit from knowing better than the market what the future will bring forth'[3] requires uncertainty about the future spot price of assets *and* a well-organised, continuous spot market in which these assets can be dealt with. Obviously then, 'depending on social practice and institutions',[4] different assets in different times and in different economic systems may have been the alternatives to holding money as a store of value. Those assets with low carrying costs, very low elasticities of production and substitution (compared with producible assets), and whose spot markets are the best organised in any economic system will (by definition) possess the greatest degrees of liquidity.[5] Hence, in modern

---

[1] Keynes, *The General Theory*, p. 196. In the real world, increases in the quantity of money can only be a result of either (a) an income effect, i.e. increase in the supply of money is induced by an increased borrowing from banks in order to increase the demand for goods, or (b) an open market effect by the banking system. In the last part of this quoted passage Keynes is merely suggesting the importance of the speculative motive for understanding open market operations.

[2] See Harrod, *Money*, pp. 171–3.

[3] Keynes, *The General Theory*, p. 170.   [4] ibid. p. 240.

[5] Even if a well organised spot market for fixed capital goods existed, if the forward price of fixed capital is, as Chapter 4 indicated, a reliable estimate of the expected spot price at the delivery date, then if there is

societies, it is uncertainty about the future spot price of debt securities and other titles of wealth and not the future spot price of hire-purchase of producible capital goods that stimulates speculative activity and permits wealth to be stored not only in the form of money but also in financial (non-reproducible) assets.

Uncertainty is also a necessary condition for the precautionary motive for holding money where the latter is defined by Keynes as holding money 'To provide for contingencies requiring sudden expenditure and for unforeseen opportunities of advantageous purchase';[1] thus strongly suggesting human recognition of the fallibility of predicting the future. It is simply because tomorrow's events are uncertain and 'to err is human' that there is a weighty advantage 'to hold an asset whose value is fixed in terms of money to meet a subsequent [contingent] liability fixed in terms of money';[2] a gain which is evident in the uncomparable liquidity premium associated with money.

In the absence of organised spot markets for placements and/or other non-reproducible assets, money would be the sole durable that could be used as a vehicle for deferring decisions on the current commitment of resource claims and 'liquidity preference due to the precautionary-motive would be greatly increased'.[3] The existence of organised spot securities markets however, permits each decision-making unit to vary widely the quantity of money they hold as a vehicle for transferring purchasing power over time as uncertainty about the future spot price of placements affects money holdings; while the total portfolio of money plus securities which are used as vehicles for the transfer of general command over time (rather than entering into contracts for current or forward delivery) is related to wealth-holders' inability to know the date of all their economic needs at each date in the future.

Were it not for the indisputable fact that members of any economy (a) recognise the capricious element in the course of future events and (b) simultaneously believe in the continuity over time of overlapping offer and debt contracts denominated

---

growth in the stock of capital going on (backwardation), the market for fixed capital must be assuming that these goods are poor objects for speculation since the spot price will decline as the stock is augmented.

[1] Keynes, ibid. p. 196.   [2] ibid. p. 196.   [3] ibid. p. 170.

in monetary units, there would be no asset in the economy which could command a liquidity premium which always exceeded its carrying costs. (In a world of certainty, since it would be possible to enter into forward contracts for the entire 'life cycle' consumption patterns at the time of birth, there would be no need for liquidity.) The absence of any asset whose liquidity premium always exceeds its carrying costs is, as Keynes noted, 'the best definition' for the neoclassical concept of a non-monetary economy.[1] Uncertainty and money contracts are therefore necessary attributes of money economies; or, more precisely, in a world of uncertainty where production takes time, an interdependent community must create rules and institutions for governing money and money contracts – as long as human nature fears the making of commitments which future events may prove undesirable. In the real world, a non-monetary or barter economy is a contradiction in terms for there can be no developed interdependent market-oriented economic activity in the absence of money and related institutions except under the most stationary conditions and stationary expectations.[2]

Since, in point of fact, uncertainty dominates human life and economic activity, decisions by households or business firms about what forms to utilise to store economic wealth for the desired purpose of transferring present command over resources into future command must be based on the belief that the date when future command will be required can never be known with complete certainty. Even if there is a spot market for an asset, the cost of converting any store of value other than money into the medium of exchange if a contingent liability should come due in the *near* future will normally exceed the earnings from the purchase of an income yielding asset; hence it will always be preferable to hold *some* wealth in the form of money to cover possible contingent short-period liabilities.[3] The more clouded future events appear, the more contingencies

---

[1] Keynes, *The General Theory*, p. 239.

[2] Or in a regimented economy where everything is decided on and fixed at the centre, e.g. the military or a kibbutz.

[3] Cf. J. R. Hicks, 'A Suggestion for Simplifying the Theory of Money', *Economica*, **2** (1935), reprinted in *Critical Essays in Monetary Theory*. All references are to the reprint.

that may be anticipated to occur during the interval, the more desirable, therefore, it will be to minimise costs by storing wealth in the form of money rather than securities. The fundamental behavioural desire to minimise transaction costs in moving from a store of value to a medium of exchange when unforseen occurrences are expected in the ordinary course of events is an important aspect of human behaviour which affects the operation of a market-oriented economy in the real world.

Since the costs of purchasing and selling securities are independent of the length of time they are held (and normally increase at a decreasing rate as the value of the purchases rises), while the income earned on securities is closely related to the passage of time, it normally is uneconomic to invest transactions balances for the short period between the point of income receipts and the intended or expected time of payment.[1] Thus money may be held as a temporary abode of purchasing power within the contractual payments period to meet both the expected needs for the medium of exchange and the precautionary reserves which are required to lull our fears of becoming illiquid as unpredictable events occur during the period.

Transactions costs (of holding alternative assets) in the broadest sense – that is including the *fear* of rapid *unpredictable* rates of change in spot prices, and operating in a thin spot market where no financial institution will act as a residual buyer and seller – are basic to the transactions, precautionary and speculative demands for money; the magnitude of such costs are therefore associated with the degree of organisation and the existence of financial institutions who 'make' spot markets and who thereby assure reasonable moment-to-moment stickiness in spot prices.

UNCERTAINTY, ORGANISATION OF SPOT MARKETS, AND THE STORE OF VALUE FUNCTION

Keynes in his luminous way, lists eight subjective motives for refraining from exercising current command of resources, i.e. for savings. In his words these motives are: 'Precaution,

[1] ibid. pp. 67–8. The length of the period will be, *ceteris paribus*, related to the transactions costs facing the holder.

Foresight, Calculation, Improvement, Independence ["without a clear idea or definite intention of specific action"], Enterprise, Pride and Avarice.'[1] These motives can readily be sub-divided among those plans associated with definite expected future commitments, and those plans which are obscured by uncertainty and imprecise future patterns of action. Thus, an individual's decision to refrain from utilising current resources requires a second decision as to whether he should store value in 'the form of immediate liquid command . . . [or leave] it to *future* [spot] *market conditions* to determine on what terms he can, if necessary, convert deferred command over specific goods into immediate command over goods in general.'[2]

Any durable good – an automobile, a lathe, even an overcoat – has a store of value quality in the sense that it can be carried over to the future. Nevertheless, since the spot market for most durables (especially fixed capital and consumer durables) are so poorly organised and discontinuous (if they exist at all) because of destandardisation, high carrying costs, and the absence of a financial institution to 'make' the spot market, that the costs of converting such durables into money at any future date are very high *and* uncertain. It would be patently foolish to store value in any specific physical durable good, even if its notional value was expected to increase at an annual rate which exceeded the rate of interest on riskless bonds, if at some future date, when the holder wished to utilise his deferred command by accepting an offer contract for goods he found either (1) the spot market for the durable was so poorly organised that transactions cost reduced the expected capital gain below what could have been expected to be earned on interest-bearing securities, or (2) the spot market was thin and discontinuous so that the holder had no notion what he could get for the asset in the spot market, or (3) there is no spot market in which the durable can be resold for money at its notional value (or any other value). The growth of well organised, continuous spot markets for securities dealing in standardised, fractionalised titles to physical goods and private debts has, in comparison, reduced the cost of con-

---

[1] Keynes, *The General Theory*, p. 108.
[2] ibid. p. 166. Italics added.

verting 'paper' stores of value to the medium of exchange (and vice versa) far below the potential costs of moving between money and the underlying fixed capital goods.

Even if a well-organised spot market for reproducible fixed capital goods existed, however, these durables would be less desirable objects or speculative activity compared to money, debts, or titles, especially in a growing economy. As Chapter 4 has indicated the indivisibility of physical capital and its large delivery costs, as well as the costs of obtaining the necessary technical knowledge to utilise physical capital as an efficient input in the production process, are always going to make fixed capital goods inferior objects vis-à-vis titles, as long as there is a well-organised spot market in titles. Moreover, in a growing economy, where capital goods are scarce (i.e. in the absence of a contango) the elasticity of the short-period flow-supply schedule tends to prevent the current spot price from greatly exceeding the forward price, while the high costs of carrying physical capital for non-production (speculative) purposes will require expectations of large increases in future spot prices compared to the current price, if such durables are to be seriously considered as profitable speculative objects. Thus, as long as the flow-supply price is expected to be sticky, producible durables will not be important objects to hold for speculative purposes – as long as production of these durables is currently going on.[1] In sum, in a growing, developed

---

[1] At any point of time, as long as there is backwardation in the durables market, then the forward price will be, as Chapter 4 demonstrated, equal to the short-period flow-supply price, and it will, by definition, be less than the current spot price. Since this forward price also reflects the market's best estimate of the spot price at the delivery date, then *even if there is a well-organised spot market,* unless individual speculators believe the market is grossly in error and expect the flow-supply price in the future to rise sufficiently to cover the heavy and increasing carrying costs of holding fixed capital goods (these costs rise rapidly as the quantity of capital increases vis-à-vis holding additional titles), speculators will not hold fixed capital goods as a store of value. Consequently, expectations of exceeding by large and rapid increases in the flow-supply price of capital goods would be necessary to stimulate significant speculative activity in fixed capital in a growing economy; that is, expectations of rapidly rising money-wage rates (relative to productivity increments) may encourage such speculative activity. Nevertheless, if such expectations become widespread, then the market will immediately re-establish a backwardation by bidding up the

monetary economy, money, titles to physical capital, and debt contracts (that is, money and securities) are the major stores of value for their low transactions costs and continuous spot markets make both assets useful vehicles for the transfer of purchasing power, and thereby render the elasticity of substitution between them very high. Moreover, the high or infinite costs of converting producible capital goods into the medium of exchange via discontinuous or non-existent spot markets makes such durables inferior stores of value and consequently the elasticity of substitution between fixed capital and securities or money is negligible.

Although the right-of-centre Monetarist and neoclassical and Bastard Keynesian schools pay lip service to the importance of money, these schools ignore the peculiarity of the high substitutability between money and securities, and the resultant low substitutability between financial assets and real capital. Tobin, for example, constructs models in which only money and real capital are stores of value – and are therefore good substitutes.[1] Friedman has used the assumption of a high substitutability between money and all producible durables as the keystone mechanism for explaining how exogenous changes in the quantity of money induce changes in aggregate income.[2]

---

spot price and increasing orders for new deliveries. (Cf. Keynes, *The General Theory*, p. 231.)

If, on the other hand, the market for producible durables is currently in a contango situation, then the spot price may decline far enough to compensate the individual for the heavy carrying costs on existing instruments, and hence there may be some speculation in existing fixed capital goods in such circumstances – but speculators would not place new orders for speculative purposes, since the minimum short-period flow-supply price will be above the forward price. (See Chapter 4 above.)

Finally if a well organised spot market for fixed capital exists, and if an individual believes that the market has over-estimated future quasi-rents, the individual would sell his current holdings. He would not, however, hold the receipts in the form of money (as a store of value) unless he also thought that the price for titles had also been overvalued. (Cf. Keynes, *The General Theory*, p. 170, n. 1.)

[1] J. Tobin, 'Money and Growth', *Econometrica* (1965) **33**.

[2] M. Friedman and A. J. Schwartz, 'Money and Business Cycles', *Review of Economic Statistics* (1963), supplement **45**, pp. 59–62. A high elasticity of substitution between money and producible durables is central to the Monetarist position. If the Monetary Authority engages in open

Thus, a fundamental conceptual difference between all the right-of-centre schools and Keynes's school of economic thought involves the magnitude of the elasticity of substitution between financial assets and real capital.

The decision as to whether to store deferred command in either securities or money or both – the so-called portfolio balance decision – involves both the precautionary motive and the speculative motive, for the wealth-holders can never be certain either as to when a contingent liability will come due, or as to the spot market price of securities on the date when such a liability must be met. The lack of, indeed the impossibility of, obtaining complete statistically reliable date which convert these future events into actuarial certainties generates a speculation demand for cash which, from a Keynes's school viewpoint, cannot exist separately from the precautionary motive.

Actuarial Certainty and the Speculative Motive
The modern monetary theory of the neoclassical and Bastard Keynesian schools treats the portfolio balance decision as one involving only the speculative motive. In such a view, the decision-maker wishes to maximise his utility, given his risk-income preferences. It is assumed that (a) the individual can assign a probability weight to each eventuality, that is, to each possible future spot price of securities at each possible

---

market operations, then, according to Friedman, wealth-holders find the composition of their portfolios laden with money as they sell securities for capital gains. These wealth-holders will, according to Friedman, alter the composition of their portfolios and purchase other assets including producible consumer durables and capital goods, thereby creating a demand for resources in the current period.

Since in Friedman's analytical scheme, capital gains via open-market operations could not be viewed as part of the household's permanent income, it cannot be the size of the capital gain which induces additional consumption demand for durables. Rather it must be that households prefer consumer durables to additional money holdings as a store of value! Of course, unless there is a well organised spot market in consumer durables, the cost of moving, sometime in the future, from command of these specific consumer goods to immediate command of goods in general will be prohibitive. Thus, the Monetarist position must implicitly assume well organised, continuous spot markets in all second-hand durables. (This will be discussed in further detail in Chapter 9.)

realisation date; (b) the sum of these decision weights equal unity; and (c) the individual will commit his wealth-holding to money and/or securities in order to maximise his utility given these probability statements about future events. Since wealth holders can calculate the probability[1] of any possible monetary outcome and since it is assumed that the probabilities must sum to unity, the existence of uncertainty about future events is eliminated from the system by using the mathematical laws of probability to calculate an actuarial pay off (which in operational terms is similar to a certainty equivalent) that is, the individual can make his portfolio decisions as if he had no doubt about the probable outcome.

1. *The No Risk Aversion Case.* If the decision-maker has no risk aversion, i.e. if risk does not create any disutility, this approach leads to the maximisation of the capital values of the portfolio at a given date, where by capital value we mean interest plus capital gain plus initial capital value.[2] If, for example, the actuarial pay off from holding securities is positive, i.e. the certainty equivalent of the future spot price plus interest earned (net of transactions costs) exceeds the current price, the individual will hold only securities, and thereby achieve the maximum increase in the capital value of his portfolio. If the pay off is negative, he will hold only money whose capital value (in terms of itself) will not change over the period.

In essence, at time t_0 a portfolio manager will decide to hold any asset till time t_1 only if the sum of net yield plus the difference between the expected spot price in t_1 and the spot price at t_0 (net of spot market transactions costs) exceed the sum obtainable from holding money (which is zero), i.e.

$$(q - c) + (p_s^{t_1} - p_s^{t_0}) - T_s > 0 \qquad (1a)$$

or

$$y + G - T_s > 0 \qquad (1b)$$

where

q is the expected money income which can be obtained by holding the asset from t_0 to time t_1

c is the carrying costs of the asset over that period

---

[1] The probability of any particular outcome is defined as the limit which its frequency is supposed to approach as the number of observations increases. [2] Hicks, *Critical Essays in Monetary Theory*, p. 117.

y is the net yield ($= q - c$)

$p_s^{t_1}$ is the expected spot price of the asset at time t_1

$p_s^{t_0}$ is the actual spot price of the asset at time t_0

G is the expected capital gain ($= p_s^{t_1} - p_s^{t_0}$)

T_s is the total spot market transactions costs

Given expectations about future spot prices, those individuals who believe that $y + G - T_s > 0$ are bullish and, if they are confident about their expectations and are risk 'neutral', they will buy securities spot; while those who believe $y + G - T_s < 0$ are bearish and will sell their security holdings. The current spot price will, therefore, rapidly adjust relative to expectations about the future spot prices until, *ceteris paribus*, the quantity desired to be held by the bulls just equals the quantity that the bears decide to release.

In the absence of risk aversion and uncertainty, this 'neo-classical' approach to the motive for wealth-holding decision-making suggests that the choice of money or securities in one's portfolio depends solely on a direct comparison of the net income yield with the change in the actuarially expected future spot price of placements (net of transactions costs of purchases and sales) at the realisation date compared to the current spot price. Thus the demand for money in this simple case can be written as

$$D_m^w = f_2(i_c, \lambda, \bar{\delta}, \bar{e}, \bar{V}) \tag{2}$$

Where D_m^w is the demand for money as a store of wealth, i_c is the current rate of interest, λ is a set of expectations about the rate of change between the future spot prices of securities and the current price (net of transactions costs), δ is the period of time till the future date of realisation or conversion of securities to the medium of exchange, e represents the number of wealth owners and the distribution of wealth among them, V is the value of public's existing store of wealth,[1] and the bar over a symbol indicates that its value is exogenously determined.

[1] The inclusion of the variable V in the demand for money as a store of value function indicates that there is a 'wealth effect' on the demand for idle balances. Thus savings out of current income – a flow variable – will increase wealth and therefore induce a flow demand for idle balances; that is, there is a marginal propensity to hold idle balances out of current (household) savings which is less than unity and greater than zero. (In

At any given i_c, given expectations, individuals who sell securities and hold cash for speculative purposes, under this view, must be expecting, in the actuarial sense, the rate of decrease in the (net) price of securities till the realisation date to exceed the current annual rate of interest. These individuals are called *bears* in a financial sense. Those individuals, on the other hand, who expect the rate of decline in security prices to equal the rate of interest should be indifferent between holding money and securities as a store of value; while those who expect (net) security prices to either rise or to decline at a rate less than the current rate of interest would buy and hold only securities; they are the financial market's *bulls*.

The simplistic view underlying equation (2) requires each individual, except those on the margin of indifference, to be either a complete bull or a complete bear; to hold all wealth only in securities or in money depending solely on the certainty equivalent calculation underlying his specified probability distribution of future events. The current spot price of securities must be at such a level that the quantity of securities demanded by the bulls in exchange for money which they either have at hand or can obtain from a bank is just staisfied by the supply of securities which the bears are willing to sell in order to increase their *money* holdings as a store of value.

A stable equilibrium in the spot market for securities requires differences in expectations about future events. The future must, therefore, ultimately disappoint the bulls or the bears, or both. Stability in the spot market over time (or rather

---

Chapter 12 below it will be shown that both the neoclassical and neo-keynesian schools assume that this marginal propensity is zero.)

Household wealth may also increase if the current rate of interest declines, i.e. if the current spot price of securities rises. This second type of wealth effect merely reinforces the traditional interest rate effect on the demand for money – namely at higher rates of interest, *ceteris paribus*, households desire to hold less idle balances partly because of their expectation of greater capital gains to be obtained from holding other financial assets *and* partly because the total value of household wealth is reduced. Accordingly, except where otherwise explicitly specified in what follows, we shall subsume this second wealth effect due to changes in the spot price of securities to be handled via the i_c variable in equation (2). Cf. A. P. Lerner, 'Alternative form Formulations of the Rate of Interest' in *The New Economics*, pp. 647–9 and S. Weintraub, *An Approach to the Theory of Income Distribution*, pp. 156–8.

stickiness) – a desirable characteristic if the asset traded is
going to be used as a store of value – requires a variety of
differences in expectations on both the bull and bear sides;[1]
and consequently, the future will always surprise almost all
of the bulls and bears who trade in this spot asset market. It
is, however, this difference in views about the perfidious future
and the consequent surprise experienced by most of the players
which account for the active participation of much of the community not only in security markets but in other important
human institutions such as horse races, marriages, divorces
(or for the modern generation experiments in sharing a
domicile). None of these institutions could long exist without
differences in views – and therefore the recognition by all of
possible disappointment, and even disaster. Of course, those
most uncertain about the future are unlikely to be lured into
participating in any of these speculative activities at any price.
In an uncertain world, there may be many who are completely
unresponsive to market incentives, who fear to take a chance –
the permanent bear, the celibate bachelor, the non-gambler –
but there is no room for such 'irrational' behaviour in the world
of actuarial certainty of the 'neoclassical' schools of political
economy.

2. *The Capital Risk Aversion Case.* The complete bear–complete
bull result of equation (2) is patently unrealistic, for cursory
observations would show that most wealth owners hold both
money and securities in their portfolio. To provide a more
realistic solution to the portfolio balance problem, Tobin
added a quadratic utility function concept for capital loss risk
averters. These risk averters maximise utility by requiring a
risk premium plus an actuarial certainty of a positive pay off
before they are willing to purchase securities.[2] The demand

---

[1] And even the existence of financial institutions to 'make the spot
market'. (See Chapter 13 below.)

[2] J. Tobin, 'Liquidity Preference as a Behavior Towards Risk', *Review
of Economic Studies* (1958). Also see H. M. Markowitz, *Portfolio Selection,
Efficient Diversification of Investments* (New York: Wiley, 1959). The quadratic
utility function is not necessary for portfolio theory. Nevertheless if one uses
the standard deviation as a measure of *risk*, it implies either a quadratic
utility function or a normal probability distribution of all possible outcomes
or both. Actuarial certainty may not be explicitly postulated by the theory
but it must be assumed if risk is to be measured operationally.

for money function could therefore be written as

$$D_m^w = f_3(i_c, \lambda, \beta, \bar{\delta}, \bar{e}, \bar{V}) \qquad (3)$$

where β represents the public's aversion to capital risk and other symbols are the same in equation (2). For any given set of expectations (λ), and current rate of interest (i_c), Tobin assumes that risk aversion increases with the quantity of assets held for resale on the spot market. Thus the size of the risk premium would vary with the amount of risk undertaken.

In Tobin's model all wealth-holders are capital-loss risk averters, i.e. they find any probability of a decline in the future spot price of placements repugnant and therefore they require a risk premium above an actuarial zero change in capital value of securities before they are indifferent as to whether to hold money or placements as a store of value. Gambling on future spot security prices, even when the probabilities are known, is therefore distasteful and an individual will prefer to hold money whose capital value must, by definition, be unchanged at any specified future date rather than any other asset whose actuarial capital value is unchanged at that date. The more distasteful gambling is, or the more risks undertaken, the greater must be the expectation of positive gain in order to induce a wealth-holder to augment his security holdings. Thus by assuming that capital risk aversion was a ubiquitous human trait that is described by a quadratic function, Tobin was able to design a model which, even in the absence of uncertainty in the Knight–Keynes sense, ensured (1) that most wealth-holders would hold mixed portfolios, and (2) with given expectations, a normal downward sloping speculative demand curve for money as a function of the current rate of interest can be derived.

3. *The Capital and Income Risk Aversion Case.* In an analysis which is more general than Tobin's in the sense that a quadratic utility function is not necessary and is therefore closer to Keynes's emphasis on differences in expectations rather than the shape of the utility function, Kahn has suggested that wealth-holders are subjected to two risks – a capital risk and an income risk.[1]

---

[1] R. F. Kahn, 'Some Notes on Liquidity Preference', *The Manchester School* (1954). This seminal article was also one of the first to insist on the inseparability of the speculative and precautionary motives.

As in Tobin's model, those who hold securities and who feel that at some specified date in the future they will have to convert their store of wealth back to the medium of exchange in order to purchase some of the flow of output at that date are subject to a capital risk for if the spot price of securities (net of transactions costs) at that future date had declined at an annual rate which exceeds the current rate of interest, they will be required to realise a net capital loss on their store of value over the period. These individuals could not, of course, suffer a capital loss if they held money, since the cost of converting money from the store of value to the medium of exchange is zero.

For these individuals, on the other hand, who were absolutely certain that they would never 'live off their capital', but only desired to spend the income from ownership of any asset at a specific future date, maximisation of expected utility would be tied to the maximisation of income earned from any store of value. These individuals often caricatured as 'widows and orphans' who invest solely for income, are subject solely to income risk. As long as some securities have some probability of paying interest, or dividends, these wealth-holders would never hold money – whose income is normally zero – as a store of value. In reality, of course,

> For each person it is a question not of whether he is subject to the one kind of risk or the other, but which is the stronger, the feeling of income risk meaning, taken by itself, that it is income which matters and that the fear of some loss of income is not balanced by an actuarially equal prospect of gain, while the feeling of capital risk, taken by itself, means that it is capital which matters, and the prospect of some loss of capital is not balanced by any actuarially equal prospect of gain of capital.[1]

Here the demand for money as a store of value may be written as

$$D_m^w = f_4(i_c, \lambda, \beta, \gamma, \bar{\delta}, \bar{e}, \bar{V}) \qquad (4)$$

where γ is the public's aversion to income risks, and all other symbols are the same as in equation (3). In this neo-keynesian view, all other things being equal, the greater capital risk the

[1] Kahn, *ibid.* p. 240.

more money demanded, while the greater the income risk the less money demanded as a store of value.

Both capital risks and income risks are vexatious and an individual will divide his wealth into money and bonds depending upon his disposition at the margin to bear these risks. At each possible current rate of interest and for any given set of expectations, each individual may appraise the disutilities associated with these risks differently. Thus, if different individuals have different expectations for any given rate of interest and/or differences in their desires to avoid capital and income risks, these wealth-holders will divide into two groups – the bulls who desire to absorb securities by giving up money and the bears who desire more money balances by unloading securities. For any given division of bullishness and bearishness on the part of the general public, there is some current spot price of securities (i.e. some rate of interest) which will bring about equilibrium in the countervailing tug-of-war of the bulls and the bears. At any higher spot placement price, the bears will predominate in the market and at any lower price level, the bulls will predominate. Stability or stickiness in the price of securities, in this model, therefore will depend on

(1) differences in individuals' probability distribution of the future spot price of securities relative to the current rate of interest and the spot price of securities and/or

(2) differences in individuals' tolerances of income and capital risks.

4. *Transactions Costs and Risk Aversion.* The existence of transactions costs limits the scope for altering portfolio composition with each change in expectations. With a zero cost of dealing in securities, only expectations as to prices of securities at the next moment would be important and all expectations relating to dates further into the future would be irrelevant. If transactions were costless, portfolio behaviour would be determined entirely by what is expected to happen 'between today and tomorrow, and expectations about later dates do not become directly relevant until tomorrow, when behaviour is decided afresh in the light of tomorrow's expectations about the day after tomorrow'.[1]

―――――――――

[1] Kahn, ibid. p. 251. Cf. J. Robinson, *Essays in the Rate of Interest.* Of course, as long as financial intermediaries operate as residual buyers and

Nevertheless, since the expected yield on a security is a function of time, while transactions costs are not, then the existence of such costs reduces the net expected yield more the nearer in the future is the date of realisation. Thus the portfolio demand for money can be written as

$$D_m^w = f_5(i_c, \lambda, \gamma, \beta, \delta, \bar{T}_s, \bar{e}, \bar{V}) \tag{5}$$

where T_s is the transactions costs of moving between money and securities and δ is the period of time to the date of expected realisation.

The further in the future the date of planned realisation, the greater the expected net yield of a security and therefore the more eager the wealth-holder should be, *ceteris paribus*, to reduce his money holding to obtain additional placements in his portfolio. Alternatively the closer the date of expected realisation, the lower the net yield, and the less desirable it will be to hold securities relative to money.[1]

Finally, it should be noted that the costs of moving between placements and money is a function of the degree of organisation of security markets. Such costs are, therefore, normally assumed to be an institutionally determined exogenous factor. Any reduction in transactions costs, of course, will, *ceteris paribus*, reduce the demand for money.

Actuarial Certainty v. *Uncertainty: Are the Laws of Probability Relevant?* Until this point, the analysis of portfolio behaviour which dominates modern monetary (portfolio theory) neglects problems of uncertainty in the sense that Knight used the term. Knight suggested that the degree of confidence economic

---

sellers in spot security markets in order to maintain an orderly, continuous market the spot price at the next instant of time can never be very different from the current price. Thus, the level of transaction costs vis-à-vis the magnitude of the financial intermediaries' expected commitment to orderliness will be a significant social practice in determining the liquidity of various durable assets.

Similarly, since brokerage and other transactions costs often increase at a decreasing rate as the size of transaction increases, the relevant holding period for a liquid asset will differ between buyers of large blocks and purchasers of small quantities.

[1] It is, of course, the nearness of dates when obligations resulting from normal expenditures for goods and services out of income come due which accounts for the transactions demand for money.

decision-makers have in their estimates of the future affects their actions, but since the degree of confidence was a reflection of uncertainty about the future, it could not be subjected to any scientific probability statement: 'An uncertainty which can by any method be reduced to an objective, quantitative determinate probability can be reduced to complete certainty.'[1] Yet 'if we are to understand the workings of the economic system we must examine the meaning and significance of uncertainty'.[2]

In the preceding discussion of modern monetary theory, the assignment of known (even if subjective) probabilities to all eventualities about future events and the manipulation of such probability distributions via the mathematical laws of probability reduced 'uncertainty to the same calculable status as that of certainty itself'.[3] This probabilistic view of the future is, for the Keynes school, particularly misleading when one is analysing wealth, for it is a contradiction in terms to discuss the holding and accumulation of wealth and the laws of probability at the same time. In reality, according to Keynes:

> We have, as a rule only the vaguest idea of any but the most direct consequence of our acts. Sometimes we are not much concerned with their remoter consequences . . . but sometimes we are intensely concerned with them, more so, occasionally than with the immediate consequences. Now of all human activities which are affected by this remoter preoccupation, it happens that one of the most important is economic in character, namely, wealth. The whole object of the accumulation of wealth is to produce results, or potential results, at a comparatively distant, and sometimes at an *indefinitely* distant, date. Thus, the fact that our knowledge of the future is fluctuating, vague and uncertain renders wealth a particularly unsuitable subject for the method of the classical economic theory. . . .
>
> By 'uncertain' knowledge, let me explain, I do not mean to distinguish what is known for certain from what is probable. The game of roulette is not subject, in this sense, to

[1] F. H. Knight, *Risk and Uncertainty*, 1937 reprint ed., p. 231.
[2] ibid. p. 199.
[3] J. M. Keynes, 'The General Theory' in *The New Economics*, p. 184.

uncertainty. . . . The sense in which I am using the term is that in which the prospects of a European war is uncertain or the price of copper and the rate of interest twenty years hence, or the obsolescence of a new invention, or the position of private wealth-owners in the social system in 1970. *About these matters there is no scientific basis on which to form any capable probability whatever. We simply do not know.*[1]

Keynes's view of the demand for money as a store of value (sometimes referred to as L_2 in the literature) must therefore involve an analysis of the speculative motive under conditions of uncertainty, for as Keynes observed, '*Uncertainty* as to the future course of the rate of interest is the sole intelligible explanation of the type of liquidity preference L_2 which leads to the holding of cash M_2.'[2] True uncertainty has an essential characteristic which violates the mathematical laws of probability, namely that there is doubt or disbelief about any possible outcome and therefore, uncertainty about some possible alternative outcomes cannot be reduced to a quantitative fraction whose magnitude is between zero and unity.[3] Accordingly, when uncertainty exists, the complete set of subjectively determined eventualities need not have any decision weights (probabilities) that sum to unity (or any particular total) nor is it necessary when either changing a decision weight for any one eventuality or recognising the possibility of a new and different outcome to alter the weights associated with the other events.[4]

If an economic model limits itself to mathematical statements about the numerical values of the theoretical probabilities which may be computed for an idealised set of events, then the model is *not* discussing a decision process under uncertainty. The model is simply demonstrating the validity of purely logical propositions which were derived from specific axioms – and the model is completely dependent on these axioms.[5] Such a model can provide a useful benchmark for

[1] ibid. pp. 184–5. Final italics added.
[2] Keynes, *The General Theory*, p. 201.
[3] No matter what the outcome resulting from a turn of the roulette wheel, there can never exist any disbelief in it.
[4] G. L. S. Shackle, *Uncertainty in Economics*, pp. 9–10.
[5] See W. Fellner, *Profits and Probability* (Homewood: Irwin, 1965) p. 3.

the understanding of certain economic behaviour under idealised circumstances, and consequently it can provide useful insights into economic processes. Nevertheless, the differences between the 'ideal' case in theory and reality can be particularly misleading when dealing with questions of money and stores of wealth where the predictions must be made about *single* events which will occur at some vague date in the future, when the more vague the situation the more desirable it is to defer commitments and maintain flexibility as long as possible. Theoretical monetary models of portfolio balance based on the laws of probability related only to idealised experiments and must be modified if they are to be applicable to a world of uncertainty – the real world.

Once the date of expected realisation is made an explicit variable in the analysis of portfolio decisions, the importance of uncertainty can no longer be suppressed. The further into the future the date of realisation, the less conviction an individual will have in his ability to describe correctly his expectations via a subjective probability distribution of future eventualities; and, in fact, if we are to be honest, few would claim any ability to reliably predict security prices a year hence or even a few weeks from today.[1] Thus, the further in the future the date associated with a set of expectations, the less confident we must be that the hypothesised probability distribution has been derived from the unknown universe of events which *will* exist at that future date. Moreover, if the current hypothesised probability distribution is not drawn from the correct future universe, then the future will be fraught with surprise, and decision-makers can never dismiss the unforeseen as impossible. In such circumstances, the portfolio balance schools might attempt to salvage some of its theoretical structure by suggesting that it is possible to assign (subjective) quantitative probabilities to the probability that, at any specified future realisation date, the underlying universe of events from which the current probability distribution is drawn will be the relevant one in the future. That is, one could have a subjective probability statement about the subjective probability of any future event. In such a world, however, the sum of the probabilities for all conceivable events would not equal unity –

[1] Instant riches awaits such a person.

unless it is assumed that the decision-maker is *absolutely* certain that the future underlying universe has been properly foreseen[1] – and therefore the fundamental conceptual differences between the neoclassical way of handling uncertainty and the Knight–Keynes views remains unbridgeable.[2] Ultimately, any economic model which recognises the fact that decision-makers realise that predicting the future is a treacherous activity must involve an analysis of wealth-holding decisions which can not be reduced to simple mathematical statements about a unique, quantitative, and unchanging course of human behaviour.[3]

To complicate matters even further, once the possibility of contingent liabilities is recognised even the date of realisation is uncertain. Since unforeseen events are basic to the precautionary motive, a realistic analysis of portfolio decision-making requires the simultaneous analysis of the precautionary and speculative motives to hold money as a store of wealth.

THE INTERACTION OF THE SPECULATIVE AND PRECAUTIONARY MOTIVE

Once uncertainty about the date of realisation, transaction costs in moving between the store of value and the medium of exchange, and the lack of complete confidence in the probability distribution of foreseeable eventualities, are explicitly introduced into the analysis of the demand for money as a store of value, then it becomes obvious that the precautionary motive will alter the choice of the most desirable portfolio composition from what it would have been under conditions of completely predictable eventualities, i.e. where

[1] Uncertainty is arbitrarily assigned a quantitative value equal to the difference between unity and the sum of the probabilities of all the specified events.

[2] Cf. Harrod's Appendix to his *Life of John Maynard Keynes*, which is entitled 'Note on "Treatise on Probability" ', pp. 651–6.

[3] 'Nor does Keynes ignore the fourth degree of sophistication which acknowledges that men cannot describe their expectation in the form of a probability distribution at all but are merely aware that there are a range of possibilities, some of which appear more plausible than others; he makes as little use as possible of precise measures of expectations, and talks instead of such psychological states as bullishness, bearishness, and uncertainty.' D. G. Champernowne, 'Expectations and the Links Between the Economic Future and the Present' *Keynes General Theory Report of Three Decades*, p. 187.

the sum of the probabilities of all alternative events equals
unity. Thus if it is possible to recognise true uncertainty, then
the quantity of money held as a store of value ultimately
would involve (1) the public's disposition towards income
and capital risks; (2) the current rate of interest (or current
dividends and the current spot price of securities); (3) the
probability distribution of expected spot prices of securities
at some future realisation date; (4) the confidence wealth-
owners have in their subjective probability distribution; (5)
the length of time until the expected date of realisation (given
transactions costs); (6) the confidence wealth-owners have in
their expectations as to the date of realisation. Thus, the public's demand for money as a store of value (i.e. money used
in the financial circulation) can be expressed as

$$D_m^w = f_6(i_c, \lambda, \beta, \gamma, \delta, \kappa_\lambda, \kappa_\delta, \overline{T}_s, \bar{e}, V) \qquad (6)$$

where κ_λ is the public's ordinally measured degree of confidence
in the rate of change in security prices and κ_δ is the degree of
confidence in the estimated time interval until the date of
realisation, and the other symbols are the same as before.

Table 8.1 summarises the implied *ceteris paribus* effects for
each of the major independent variables in equation (6).
For example, if the degree of confidence in the probability
distribution of future spot security prices declines, then the
public's demand for money (bearishness) as a store of value
will increase even if, for example, there is no change in either
the subjective probability distribution of future eventualities
or risk preferences, while if the degree of confidence increases,
the quantity of money demanded decreases, i.e. the public is
more bullish.

It follows from Table 8.1 that the actual quantity of money
held as a store of value is the resultant of the interplay of many
factors, some associated with the speculative motive, some
with the precautionary motive, and some with the organisation of the market for securities. Moreover since the precautionary motive factors – the degree of confidence in λ and δ –
are related to the expectations embodied in the speculative
motive, the two motives are interdependent in the sense that
if some factor underlying one motive changes, it may alter
an element underlying the other motive.

In other words, in an uncertain world, changes in an 'independent' variable in equation (6) may induce changes in the magnitudes of the other 'independent' variables. For

Table 8.1

CHANGE IN FACTOR EFFECTS ON
THE DEMAND FOR MONEY

Factor	Increases the Quantity of Money Demanded (Bearishness)	Decreases the Quantity of Money Demanded (Bullishness)
(1) Current rate of interest (i_o)	decrease	increase
(2) Expected rate of change in security prices (λ)	decrease	increase
(3) Capital risk aversion (β)	increase	decrease
(4) Income risk aversion (γ)	decrease	increase
(5) Time period till realisation (δ)	decrease	increase
(6) Degree of confidence in expectations (κ) about λ or δ	decrease	increase
(7) Transactions costs (T_s)	increase	decrease
(8) Value of store of wealth (V)	increase	decrease

example, if the date of realisation is pushed further into the future, then the degree of confidence in given future price expectations will decrease, thus unleashing countervailing tendencies on the demand for money as a store of value.

Variables on the right side of equation (6) are, therefore, independent only in the analytical sense that any value, positive or negative, of one, is compatible under the appropriate circumstances with any value positive or negative of the other and therefore the values of any of the independent variables cannot be inferred from one another.[1] To paraphrase a conclusion of Kahn's, if this analysis demonstrates anything it demonstrates how difficult it is to identify the actual quantity of money held on account of the speculative motive as something different from the actual quantity held because of the precautionary motives. The two motives need not act additively: the demand for money is a complicated and complex outcome of their interplay.[2]

[1] This limited meaning of independent variables is basic to our demand for fixed capital goods as well (see Chapter 4 above). Also see Keynes, The General Theory, p. 184.

[2] Kahn, 'Some Notes on Liquidity Preference', p. 243.

As Table 8.1 suggests, some wealth-owners may be observed to demand money as a store of value even if they expect security prices to increase because either (a) they abhor capital risks and/or (b) they have no confidence in their expectations and/or (c) they fear they may need the medium of exchange in the very near future. In reality, the wealth-holders are not likely to be able to identify what portion of their money holdings they are using for each motive. As Kahn concludes:

> Sufficient has been said to demonstrate the unsuitability of thinking of a schedule of liquidity preference as though it could be represented by a well-defined curve or by a functional relationship expressed in mathematical terms *or subject to econometric processes.* Keynes himself often gave way to the temptation to picture the state of liquidity preference as a fairly stable relationship, despite his intuitional horror of undue formalism, but his treatment at least can be justified by the need at the time for a forceful and clear-cut exposition of it if it was to carry any weight at all.[1]

For certain expositional purposes, the formal treatment of the demand for money may be exceedingly useful, and should be continued to be used, but accurate description of real world phenomena will require an analysis which not only binds the speculative and precautionary motives together, but also relates them to the specific organisation and institutions of the money and security markets. An analysis of institutions in the financial markets will be developed in Chapter 13. Before we can evaluate the operations of the financial markets, however, it will be necessary to discuss in somewhat greater detail the peculiar characteristics of money and financial assets that set them apart from other goods, and their markets in the economy. Although these matters have already been discussed as needed at various stages of our argument, it is desirable to develop and present these aspects more systematically and in one place, at this time.

[1] Kahn, 'Some Notes on Liquidity Preference', p. 250. Italics added.

CHAPTER 9

The Peculiarity of Money

A NON-MONETARY or barter economy is a figment of economist's minds – a phantasm which is incapable of practical
working in a interdependent, production-oriented world. In
such a mythical non-monetary economy, household decisions
to save for future consumption, if they are executed, must
automatically increase the stock of capital. In a monetary
economy, on the other hand, this is no longer true, for households may, for example, decide to use current income to increase their wealth-holdings in the form of money or other
financial assets thereby forcing other economic units such as
business firms, or governments to provide these either by
drawing down either their cash balances or net placement
holdings, or by inducing the banks to increase the supply of
money; the increased wealth-holdings by households does not
automatically augment society's wealth. It is the introduction
of money, financial assets which are traded on an organised
spot market, and a clearing system for private bank debt
(based on fractional reserves) into the economic system which
permits the separation of the investment decision from (1) the
savings decisions and (2) portfolio choices for individuals,
although for a closed economy as a whole no such independence
of savings, investment, and portfolio choice exists. This idea,
of course, is a fundamental tenet of Keynesian economics; that
is, there is an essential difference between real world monetary
economies and mythical non-monetary systems and, therefore,
there is a dichotomy of analyses for the two worlds, but in a
monetary economy, a dichotomy between the real and monetary sectors is simply illusory.[1] It is the peculiarity of money

---

[1] Keynes has indicated that the traditional neoclassical economic theory
dealt only with non-monetary 'real-Exchange Economies', while he wished
to develop a 'monetary theory of production'. See J. M. Keynes 'On the

which makes the results of barter or 'real exchange' economy analysis irrelevant. Money and monetary institutions are an inseparable part of the real sector of the real world.

THE SPOT AND FORWARD PRICES OF MONEY

By utilising a stock-flow, spot-forward market analysis for money much of the terminological confusion and sterility of the discussion of the role of the money rate of interest on investment expenditures, the controversy over the notion of a liquidity trap, and the role of money in a growing economy can be avoided.

The aggregate money demand function can be specified as

$$D_m = f, (\phi, w, T, i_c, \lambda, \alpha, \beta, \delta, \kappa_\lambda, \kappa_\delta, e, V, T_s) \qquad (1)$$

where D_m is the total quantity of money demanded, ϕ is the contractual payments period, w is the money rate of remuneration to factors of production, T is planned or committed transactions, i_c is the current rate of interest, λ is expectations about the rate of change in the rate of interest or the expected rate of change in future spot prices of securities, α and β are indices of the public's aversion to income and capital risk respectively, δ is the expected date of realisation, κ_λ and κ_δ are indices reflecting the public's degree of confidence in expectations about λ and δ, e represents the number of wealth-holders and the distribution of wealth among them, V is the value of the public's wealth-holdings, and T_s is the transactions costs of moving between securities and money. Given $\phi, w, T, \lambda, \alpha, \beta, \delta, \kappa_\lambda, \kappa_\delta, e, V$ and T_s, the demand for money function can be represented by the downward sloping D_m curve in Fig. 9.1. This function includes the familiar flow demand for active cash balances (D_m^T) necessary to meet contractual commitments for the industrial circulation during the payment period plus the stock demand for idle balances (D_m^s) or financial circulation, i.e.

$$D_m = D_m^T + D_m^s \qquad (2)$$

where
$$D_m^T = f_3(\phi, w, T) \qquad (3)$$

and
$$D_m^s = f_4(i_c, \lambda, \alpha, \beta, \delta, \kappa_\lambda, \kappa_\delta \ e, V, T_s) \qquad (4)$$

Theory of a Monetary Economy', reprinted in *Nebraska Journal of Economics* (1963) pp. 7–10.

The supply curve of money, S_m, in Fig. 9.1 is entirely a stock schedule – a datum created from the past and, in economics utilising bank money, primarily the result of past actions of the Monetary Authority.

Thus

$$S_m = \bar{m} \qquad (5)$$

where $\bar{m}$ is the historically determined money supply.

Essentially, we are devoid of a 'flow-supply' schedule for money because *an essential property of money is that it should have a zero* (or negligible) *elasticity of productivity*. This rules out a supply flow.[1]

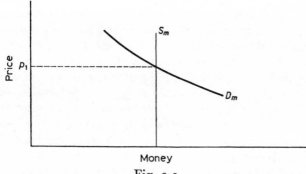

Fig. 9.1

Fig. 9.1 can be identified with the familiar liquidity preference diagram of the Bastard Keynesian school. Keynes, however, explicitly assumed that (a) the money asset cannot have a flow-supply schedule, and (b) the ordinate axis represents the rate of interest on money which is 'nothing more than the percentage excess of a sum of money contracted for forward delivery, e.g. a year hence, over what we may call the "spot" or cash price of the sum thus contracted for forward delivery'.[2] Thus, at the origin in Fig. 9.1, Keynes would place the spot price of money in terms of itself; the spot price of one dollar

---

[1] If there is no commodity which had a zero elasticity of productivity, then Fig. 9.1 would be modified to introduce a highly inelastic flow-supply schedule for that commodity which had the lowest elasticity of productivity, where by elasticity of productivity we mean the proportionate change in output in any industry for a given proportionate change in the variable inputs induced by a change in demand.

[2] Keynes, *The General Theory*, p. 222.

is one dollar, which, in effect means that the sale of the asset store of value, money, on the spot market to obtain money as the medium of exchange can be done without costs. Money, therefore, is the *fully liquid asset* in the sense that it is *immediately* convertible at a fixed rate of exchange into the medium of exchange without costs; therefore both the *spot price of money* and the *long-run money supply price of money* is located at the origin in Fig. 9.1 since the value of money can never change in terms of itself as long as it remains the medium of exchange.

The intersection of the demand and supply schedule in Fig. 9.1 yields the forward or market price for borrowing a unit of money (on an annual or period basis) in a perfect market, i.e. in a market where there is no unsatisfied fringe of borrowers. This interpretation of the price ordinate highlights the fact that the price for borrowing money, that is, the price for delivery of money at the end of the period can never be less than the spot price (and the expected long-run supply-price) of the sum of money contracted for forward delivery as long as the liquidity premium of money (which, as Chapter 6 explained, arises from the power of disposal of the asset) exceeds its carrying costs. Hence, in an uncertain world, where flexibility of action in the face of possible unforeseen events is desirable, money will be used simultaneously as a store of value and the medium of exchange and its resulting liquidity premium must exceed its carrying costs. *There can never be a contango in the spot market for money* for if it were possible for a contango to occur for money, then, unlike all other assets the forward price would be lower than both the spot *and* the long-run supply-price (the intersection would occur in the fourth quadrant) and it would be profitable to borrow money by providing an offer contract to deliver less money at some future date. In the absence of some scheme for explicitly making the carrying cost of money exceed its liquidity premium and thereby creating a non-monetary economy, such a contango cannot occur.

In sum, *there can never be a surplus stock of money in a monetary economy, the forward price of money can never be below both the spot and the long-run supply-price of money*. This, of course, is the logical basis of Keynes's argument that the 'pure' rate of interest can never be negative.[1] Imperfections in the market place prevent the effective rate of interest on borrowing money from declining below some positive rate (i.e. there is the usual liquidity trap).[2]

THE ACCUMULATION OF WEALTH, FIXED CAPITAL, AND THE FORWARD PRICE OF MONEY

Although in most neoclassical, Bastard Keynesian, and even neo-keynesian portfolio preference models it is implicitly assumed that changes in aggregate wealth-holdings by the public do not change the public's demand for money as a store of value, i.e. $f'_{4V} = 0$, there is no reason to believe this is necessarily so.[3] In fact Keynes argued 'that the inactive demand for liquidity partly depends on the aggregate wealth',[4] i.e. $f'_{4V} > 0$. Thus, as wealth accumulated and income grows, the D_m curve in Fig. 9.2 will, *ceteris paribus*, shift outwards for two

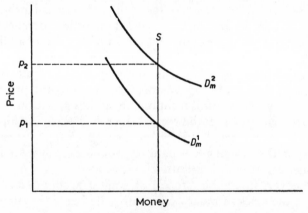

Fig. 9.2

reasons: (1) with a rise in planned transactions the demand for money in the industrial circulation will rise; and (2) with an increase in wealth-holdings, the demand for money as a

[1] Keynes, *The General Theory*, p. 218. [2] ibid. pp. 208, 141.

[3] F. P. R. Brechling, 'A Note on Bond-Holding and the Liquidity Preference Theory of Interest', *Rev. Econ. Stud.*, **24** (1957) p. 193 and Chapter 12 below.

[4] J. M. Keynes, 'The Ex-Ante Theory of the Rate of Interest', *Economic Journal*, **47** (1937) p. 668.

store of value will increase.[1] Thus, in Fig. 9.2, the D_m curve shifts from D_m^1 to D_m^2. The price of borrowing money increases from p_1 to p_2 while, assuming money wages and productivity are unchanged (or changing at the same rate), the purchasing power of money in terms of accepting offer contracts for the flow of new production will be unchanged.

In Chapter 4 it was shown that the present value of any capital good depends on the rate of discount used by entrepreneurs to capitalise the expected money value of output (net of operating and carrying costs) which could be obtained from the productive employment of the asset over its useful life. As long as spot and forward prices of fixed capital exceeds the long-run supply-price, then, in each period, the stock of capital will increase, i.e. the S_k curve of Chapter 4 would shift rightward over time. If the rate of discount which entrepreneurs use to capitalise future net revenues and long-run expectations oabut these revenues remain unchanged, then the stationary state will be approached as the spot and forward prices for capital goods decline in each period in order to reflect the lower capitalised value of the expected money value of additional output associated with the marginal increment in the stock of capital. Given the long-run supply-price of capital goods (e.g. p_t in Fig. 4.5 (a) of Chapter 4), the forward price will decline each period until it ultimately equals p_t. At that stage, any further increase in the capital stock will place the forward price for capital goods below the long-run supply-price and activity in the capital goods industry will necessarily be reduced until net investment is negative.[2]

Moreover, if, as this process of capital accumulation proceeded, the stock of money created by the banking system did not expand, then the money rate of interest would rise as the demand for money increased relative to the supply. If this higher rate of interest induced entrepreneurs to use a higher rate of discount in capitalising future expected revenue from plant and equipment (or if there is a resulting decrease in the number of entrepreneurs who are able to obtain finance),[3]

---

[1] Cf. R. Turvey, 'Does the Rate of Interest Rule the Roost?' in *The Theory of Interest Rates.*

[2] Cf. Keynes, *The General Theory*, pp. 217–18.

[3] See the analysis of when money markets do not clear below.

then the demand curve for capital, the $D_k + d_k$ curve in Chapter 4, would shift inwards while the capital stock supply curve was shifting outwards over time. These countervailing movements in the demand and supply curves of capital would accentuate the decline in the spot and forward prices of capital goods.

Alternatively, if the supply of money increased rapidly enough not only to meet the needs of increased planned transactions, but also, because of a deliberate open-market policy of the Monetary Authority, to meet and exceed the desired increment in bear hoards (at the current rate of interest), then the rate of interest could be pushed towards zero even with capital accumulation. Nevertheless, as long as the liquidity premium for money exceeds its carrying costs and there are transactions costs in bringing borrowers and lenders together, then the price of borrowing money for forward delivery must exceed the value of money in terms of itself, i.e. there cannot be a contango for money. The demand for capital schedule will, therefore, be constrained by some minimum positive rate of interest.

Inevitably, under these assumptions, there is a stage at which it no longer pays to increase the stock of capital goods since the short-period flow-supply price of capital goods will ultimately equal the (stationary state) long-run flow-supply price. At this point 'the further production of new capital assets will come to a standstill'.[1]

> It is much preferable to speak of capital as having a yield over the course of its life in excess of its original costs, than as being *productive*. For the only reason why an asset offers a prospect of yielding during its life services having an aggregate value greater than its initial supply price is because it is *scarce*. . . . If capital becomes less scarce, the excess yield will diminish, without it having become less productive – at least in a physical sense.[2]

Thus, given unchanged expectations about the future net revenues and carrying costs of all assets, and the costs of moving between assets and the medium of exchange, as the stock of assets in general increases that asset whose spot and forward

[1] Keynes, *The General Theory*, p. 228. [2] ibid. p. 213.

prices decline most slowly relative to its long-run supply-price 'will eventually knock out the profitable production of each of the others'.[1] As the market price of each capital good approaches its long-run supply-price, it is no longer profitable to enlarge the stock of it. Finally there is only one asset alone which, even if its stock was to be increased would not be redundant. The yield on this asset thus rules the roost. Acknowledging the impossibility of a contango in the money market, this asset must be money.

Of course, to the extent that the stock of money is not augmented as the demand for it expands, while the stock of all producible durables increases with growth, then the inevitable date when unchanging long-period entrepreneurial expectations are no longer sufficient to stimulate entrepreneurs to undertake additional investment commitments is hastened. Since the elasticity of productivity of money is zero, the 'invisible hand' can not be expected to assure that the supply of money is endogenously expanded with every increase in demand for money. Consequently, if capital accumulation is believed to be in the social interest, there must be a deliberate social policy to make sure that the Monetary Authority does nothing which will hamper the 'animal spirits' of those who, in a decentralised market economy, desire to undertake contractual commitments for the forward delivery of additional capital goods.

To summarise then, what matters in determining the level of production of capital goods at any point of time is the relationship between the demand price curve for these goods, the minimum flow-supply price and the short-run elasticity of supply of capital goods. The (notional) spot price for the hire-purchase of existing capital goods is determined by the intersection of the stock demand (D_k) and stock supply (S_k) schedules of capital, while the relationship between the short-run market – or forward – price (p_f) and the long-run supply-price (p_t) determines whether the stock of capital will be augmented or not during the period. The short-run market price p_f, is determined, as was explained in Chapter 4, by the intersection of the market demand curve for hire-purchase $(D_k + d_k)$ and the summation of the stock supply and short-run flow-

[1] Keynes, *The General Theory*, p. 229.

supply curves of capital $(S_k + s_k)$. This short-run flow-supply price of capital goods is the price at which producers of plant and equipment are currently offering the flow of output from their factories to potential buyers.

Since the spot markets for the hire-purchase of most fixed capital goods are either non-existent or very poorly organised and discontinuous, and since therefore the carrying costs of real capital typically greatly exceed their liquidity premium, it is possible for the (notional) spot and forward prices of such durables to be more than, equal to, or less than the long-run flow-supply price. While all other physical durable assets can become redundant, as long as there can never be a contango in the money market, money can never be in surplus supply; and hence the return on money rules the roost.

In a non-monetary economy, i.e. 'an economy where there is no asset for which the liquidity-premium is always in excess of carrying costs',[1] on the other hand, that asset whose market price declines least relative to its long-run supply-price, i.e. that asset whose elasticity of productivity was, *ceteris paribus*, the lowest would be 'the' rooster in the sense that as other assets become redundant, the public would turn more to that asset as a form for accumulating wealth.[2] In such a barter economy (a) all assets are perishable *and* reproducible; (b) there is no liquidity trap and people will always exercise all their current claims on resources in each period by purchasing newly produced goods for either consumption or store of value purposes, and (c) Say's Law prevails as there is no barrier to the full employment of available resources.

THE ESSENTIAL PROPERTIES OF MONEY

What then is so peculiar about money which enables it to occupy this strategic position in the roost? Secondly, is there something that rules the rooster? These vital questions deserve to be fully explored.

[1] ibid. p. 239.
[2] In such a mythical non-monetary economy, carrying costs for even this asset can rise rapidly as its stock increases so that ultimately even an increase in its stock can be expected to yield a zero (or even negative) return.

Keynes noted that the two essential properties of money must be that it has 'zero (or negligible) elasticities both of production and substitution'.[1] Thus Fig. 9.1 was drawn devoid of flow-supply schedule of money. As Keynes noted, unlike the case of commodities in general, 'labour cannot be turned on at will by entrepreneurs to produce money in increasing quantities as its price rises'.[2] Accordingly, if the demand for money rises from D_m^1 to D_m^2 in Fig. 9.2, there will be no increase in supply so that the price of money for 'forward delivery' will rise from p_1 to p_2.

In a world of uncertainty, there will be many times when income recipients are either temporarily satiated, or completely occupied with their current economic goods, or even involved in noneconomic matters, and are unable or unwilling to predict what specific goods they will need at specific dates in the future. They will, therefore, feel queasy about undertaking any actions which will commit their current claims on resources onto a path which can be altered, if future events require, only at very high costs, if at all. Thus, if the elasticity of productivity of money is near zero, and if at any point of time individuals, uncertain of the future, want to defer additional commitments of resources, their increased demand for money as a mode for postponing action will not encourage entrepreneurs to employ additional resources in the production of the money commodity.

With a rise in the price of money as the demand for money increases, there will be a tendency to substitute placements (which also have a negligible elasticity of production) for money as a store of value. This process of substitution, between money and financial assets, however, was *not* what Keynes had in mind in calling attention to the low elasticity of substitution for money. He was discussing the substitutability of reproducible assets (i.e. assets with elasticities of production greater than zero) for the particular money asset. If there was a high elasticity of substitution between money and any other assets which have high elasticities of production, then when individuals who are uncertain about the future wish to defer additional commitments of resources, their increased demand

[1] Keynes, *The General Theory*, p. 234. Keynes pointed out that 'A zero elasticity is a more stringent condition than is necessarily required', ibid. p. 236 n. 1.   [2] ibid. p. 230.

for money as a store of value will raise its price and induce a spill-over of demand for reproducible assets and result in an increase in employment in these goods-producing industries.

Obviously, then if the elasticity of substitution between money and producible physical durables was high, then when the forward price of money increased as wealth-owners increased their demand for money as a vehicle for transferring purchasing power, the offer or forward price of producible goods would become relatively cheap, and if these producible durables were capable of 'doing money's duty equally well',[1] then involuntary unemployment would not be a significant problem for market-oriented, monetary economies as any increase in the demand for money as a store of value would rapidly spill over into an increase in the demand for reproducible goods.[2] As Chapter 4 has already noted, it will not normally pay to demand physical capital as a store of value as long as there is an organised spot market for titles to the capital goods, and there is no similar well-organised spot market for capital goods. The lower the transactions costs in a continuous spot market for 'titles' the larger, *ceteris paribus*, the elasticity of substitution between securities and money, and therefore, the closer to zero the elasticity of substitution between financial assets and producible durables.[3]

[1] ibid. p. 234.

[2] Friedman asserts that the elasticity of substitution between financial assets and consumer durables is very large (see M. Friedman and A. J. Schwartz, 'Money and Business Cycles', *Review of Economics and Statistics Supplement* (1963) p. 60. Consequently, full employment is an inevitable outcome of Friedman's analysis since, by hypothesis, there is no way that society, in the aggregate, will defer the use of current claims on resources.

[3] Furthermore even an increase in the purchasing power of money will not encourage the substitution of any other good for money in its role *as a medium of exchange*. Unlike other durable goods, when the exchange value for money alters this does not affect its utility as a medium of exchange, which is derived solely from its purchasing power. For capital goods, on the other hand, a change in their market price alters their value as an input in the production process, i.e. it changes the price of the service of capital. Thus, an increase in the flow-supply price of capital will *ceteris paribus*, discourage entrepreneurs from installing as many capital projects as they would otherwise. Money, on the other hand, by its very definition has a negligible elasticity of substitution as a mode of settlement. In sum, reproducible commodities are not normally goods substitutes for money either as a store of value or a medium of exchange.

Since capital goods also possess a higher elasticity of production than money, then if the demand for capital increases from D_{k1} to D_{k2} (as in Fig. 9.3), the market price of new capital would rise moderately from p_{k1} to p_{k2} (instead of p_{k3} if this

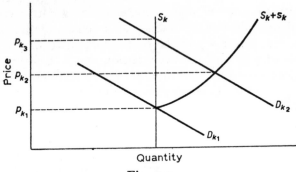

Fig. 9.3

good had a zero elasticity of production) and the accumulation of capital would increase as the number of workers hired in the capital goods producing industries rose.[1]

If the demand for money rises, since the elasticity of production is zero, no additional men can be employed to produce 'the object of desire' and therefore 'natural market forces' cannot temper the rise in price of money for forward delivery. This will mean a rise in the rate of interest which will, *ceteris paribus*, induce a leftward shift in the demand schedule for capital goods as the unchanged expected stream of quasi-rents are discounted at a higher capitalisation factor, thereby inducing a decline in both the spot and forward prices of capital goods (although capital has not become any less productive, at least in the physical sense). Thus there is a decrease in employment and output in general as a result of a *ceteris paribus* increase in the demand for money as a store of value.

The decline in the spot price of real capital, for a given set of expectations about a future stream of net money revenues, implies an increase in the expected return per dollar of current valuation of the existing stock capital. To make it worthwhile to purchase any new capital goods once the spot price of secondhand capital has declined as a result of this rise in the

[1] Cf. Keynes, *The General Theory*, p. 235.

rate of discount each firm must now expect to earn on each dollar of new capital demanded, a return at least equal to this higher opportunity cost of the alternative investment opportunity available via purchases in the spot market for capital goods.[1] In other words, the higher rate of discount has reduced the capitalised value of the unchanged expected stream of quasi-rents associated with each unit of newly produced capital relative to its flow-supply price (which, by hypothesis, is unaltered) thereby reducing its profitability. On the other hand, the higher rate of discount has reduced the spot market price of pre-existing capital sufficiently so that its unchanged expected income stream represents a higher rate of return on the revalued spot price than before. As a consequence, secondhand capital has become relatively more desirable as an input compared to new capital goods and relatively less net investment will be undertaken.

In a perfect money market, where each firm is able to borrow any sum they want at the going rate of interest in order to accept forward contracts for new capital goods, income maximising entrepreneurs will purchase new capital until the discounted expected marginal return per dollar of new capital ordered equals the sum of the marginal cost per dollar of money borrowed to finance these purchases plus the marginal disutility an entrepreneur feels in undertaking a contractual commitment over the uncertain future.[2] If the cost of borrowing money increases as the demand for money as a store of value rises, then, given expectations about capital yields and animal spirits regarding the irksomeness of undertaking commitments, the demand for resources in the capital goods producing industries would decrease. The resulting unemployment effect is obvious.

Alternatively, if the demand for money as a store of value declines, and if there is a zero elasticity of production for money, there would be no release of resources from the production of the money commodity, while the fall in the rate of

---

[1] Cf. J. Robinson, *Essays in the Theory of Economic Growth*, p. 8.

[2] 'If human nature felt no temptation to take a chance, no satisfaction (profit apart) in constructing a factory, a railway, a mine or a farm, there might not be much investment merely as a result of cold calculation.' – Keynes, *The General Theory*, p. 150.

interest will, *ceteris paribus*, increase present values of newly produced capital goods (their demand price) relative to their flow-supply price thereby encouraging suppliers to produce additional quantities. Simultaneously, the resulting rise in the spot market for pre-existing capital goods means, given expectations, that its unchanged expected yield relative to the per dollar valuation of the revalued second-hand capital has declined and therefore the opportunity cost of undertaking a new investment project has been reduced. Firms are, therefore, encouraged to borrow to finance additional investment until, in a perfect market, the expected return per dollar of marginal investment actually undertaken equals the lower marginal cost per dollar of money borrowed, i.e. the annual net revenue which a marginal new investment must be expected to yield if it is to be considered worthwhile, is equal to the now lower excess of a sum of money contracted for forward delivery over the spot price of the same sum.

On the supply side, the essential property of a zero elasticity of production immediately determines the market supply behaviour of producers of the money commodity. Thus, any discussion of how changes in the money supply come about must involve the relevant institutions which bring forth changes in the quantity of money even though the elasticity of production is zero. In the real world, Keynes reminds us at the very beginning of his *Treatise on Money*, money 'comes into existence along with debts, which are contracts for deferred payment and Price-Lists, which are offers of contracts for sale or purchase',[1] i.e. the supply of money and contracts are intimately and inevitably related. Money does not enter the system like manna from heaven, nor is it dropped from a helicopter, nor does it come from the application of additional resources to the production of the money commodity. The supply of money can increase only via two distinct processes – both of which are related to contracts.

In the first case, which may be called the income generating-finance process, an increased desire to buy more producible goods per period – the finance motive – induces individuals, firms, governments, and even foreigners to initiate the process which increases the quantity of money as long as bankers are

[1] Keynes, *Treatise on Money*, I, 3.

willing to make additional bank-debt contracts available under the rules of the game (and it is in the vested interest of each banker to do so). This endogenous increase in the money supply will then be used to finance the acceptance of additional offer contracts from producers and workers. Depending on the flow-supply elasticities of the industries thus stimulated, changes in real income and/or prices will be observed to follow (with varying time lags) this endogenous increase in money.

In the second method, the portfolio-change process, the Monetary Authority and the banking system initiates action via open-market purchases to remove assets which have a zero elasticity of production (specifically securities) from the wealth-holdings of the general public by offering private bank debt contracts as an alternative store of value at a rate of exchange which some members of the public find very favourable.[1]

With the income generating-finance process, an increase in the demand for money induces an increase in supply as long as the bankers are willing and able to expand. This endogenous increase is immediately used to place additional orders for goods and thereby increases the demand for resource services, so that changes in the money supply and changes in resource utilisation can be, via this process, directly correlated. In the portfolio change process, on the other hand, changes in the supply of money are immediately used by the receiving public as a substitute for securities as a store of value. If both money and securities have zero elasticities of production, and if they are good substitutes for each other but poor substitutes with respect to all other durables that have high elasticities of production, then this exogenous increase in the quantity of money will not be associated with any increased demand for output and resources. Thus exogenous increases in the money supply initiated by the Monetary Authority can increase the demand for producible capital goods only via the usual Keynes effect of lowering the discount rate used by firms to evaluate the expected stream of future quasi-rents from potential invest-ment projects, or by reducing the amount of credit rationing to a previously unsatisfied fringe of borrowers (or perhaps even by altering long-run expectations of quasi-rents).

Friedman and other neoclassical and Bastard Keynesian

---

[1] Of course, both processes can be reversed to reduce the supply of money.

monetarists such as Patinkin and Tobin, however, believe that exogenous increases in the money supply via open market operations, may not only operate via the traditional Keynes interest rate mechanism on the marginal efficiency of capital, but it will also increase, *pari passu*, the demand for producible household durables. This alleged increased demand for consumer durables is held to be due to (i) *a real balance* or wealth effect and/or (ii) *a portfolio balance effect*. This latter effect, it is claimed, is a result of economic-decision units finding that the proportion of their portfolio that they hold as money is excessive, and therefore they display an infinite (very high) elasticity of substitution between money and reproducible durables as components of their portfolios.[1] Keynes, of course, recognised that windfall capital gains (due to open market operations) could affect the propensity to consume both durables and nondurables;[2] although there is little evidence to suggest this plays a major role in increasing the demand for consumer durables in the aggregate. On the other hand, Keynes would reject the implication of the alleged portfolio-balance effect, namely the notion that real *producible* durables are a good substitute for money as a vehicle for transferring purchasing power over time – for this violates one of the essential properties of money. Thus another fundamental conceptual difference between the monetary theory of Keynes and those of the right-of-centre neoclassical and Bastard Keynesian schools is that the former believed that the elasticity of substitution between money and producible durables is very low, while the latter believe it to be very high.

KEYNES'S REPUDIATION OF NEOCLASSICAL MARGINAL PRODUCTIVITY THEORY: A DIGRESSION

Keynes's view of tracing the impact of exogenous changes in the supply of money primarily on the money rate of interest and only then on income and employment via the effect of discount rates on the spot price of second-hand capital and the

---

[1] E.g. M. Friedman and A. J. Schwartz, 'Money and Business Cycles', *Review of Economic Statistics Supplement* (1963) pp. 60–1; also D. Patinkin, *On the Nature of the Monetary Mechanism* (Stockholm: Almqvist and Wiksell, 1967) pp. 24 ff. [2] Keynes, *The General Theory*, pp. 93, 319.

demand (price) of capital relative to the flow-supply price[1] is fundamental not only to Keynes's attack on Say's Law but also to his rejection of a purely physical or technological concept such as the marginal product of capital as the determinant of either the earnings of capital, or the rate of return on both old and new capital, or the rate of interest.

In a series of revealing footnotes on neoclassical theory, Keynes forcefully argued that

(1) the rate of investment depends on the demand – and flow-supply – prices of capital goods and Keynes noted that

> The equality between the stock of capital goods offered and the stock demanded will be brought about by the *prices* of capital goods, not by the rate of interest. It is equality between the demand and supply of loans of money, i.e. of debts, which is brought about by the rate of interest.[2]

(2) the effect of a fall in the rate of interest on the rate of investment depends on the elasticity of the short-period flow-supply schedule of the capital goods producing industries:

> Suppose, for example, that the 'extensive increase in the demand for capital in general' is due to a *fall* in the rate of interest. I would suggest that the sentence be rewritten: 'In so far, therefore, as the extensive increase in the demand for capital goods cannot be immediately met by an increase in the total stock, it will have to be held in check for the time being by a rise in the supply price of capital goods sufficient to keep the marginal efficiency of capital in equilibrium with the rate of interest without there being any material change in the scale of investment. . . .[3]

(3) the traditional views of the importance of the rate of return on the existing capital stock as the determinant of the rate of interest is misleading, circular, and confused.

Keynes approvingly quotes Marshall's warning 'It cannot be repeated too often that the phrase 'the rate of interest' is applicable to old investment of capital only in a limited sense',[4]

---

[1] As developed in Chapter 4 above.
[2] Keynes, *The General Theory*, p. 186, n. 1.   [3] ibid. p. 187, n. 2.
[4] A. Marshall, *Principles of Economics*, 8th ed. p. 593. In the previous sentence, Marshall, anticipating the current controversy involving the

and, Keynes continues, 'In fact, we cannot speak of it at all. We can only properly speak of the rate of interest on *money* borrowed for the purpose of purchasing investments of capital, new or old (or for any other purpose)'.[1] Earlier in *The General Theory*, Keynes had insisted that Marshall was 'well aware' that if we attempt to use the equality between the rate of interest and the rate of return on existing capital resulting from adjustments in the spot price of capital goods relative to their expected yield as a basis for the marginal productivity theory of the determination of earnings of capital 'we are involved in a circular argument'.[2] Nevertheless, this twisted view of the importance and relevance of the marginal physical productivity of capital as a determinant of the earnings of capital *in a monetary economy* has been resurrected and made the keystone of modern neoclassical growth analysis.[3] As a result energies and resources have been drained in continuing barren controverises involving the malleability of capital, choices of techniques of production, and reswitching.[4] Had economists followed Keynes's lead, such concepts as the marginal physical product of capital could have been dislodged from the focal point of economic models of monetary economies a long time ago, and alternative constructs which provide relevant insights to the economic problems and policies of modern monetary economies would have come to the forefront.[5]

---

malleability of capital and the determination of the rate of profit wrote 'It is only on this [malleability] supposition that we are at liberty to speak of capital in general as being accumulated under the expectation of a certain net interest which is the same for all forms'.

[1] Keynes, *A General Theory*, p. 187, n. 3.

[2] ibid. p. 140, also see p. 184.

[3] For example, P. A. Samuelson and F. Modigliani, 'The Pasinetti Paradox in Neoclassical and More General Models', *Rev. Econ. Stud.*, 33 (1966). [4] See footnote 1, p. 16, Chapter 2 above.

[5] 'For the "marginal efficiency of capital" partly depends on the scale of current investment and we must already know the rate of interest before we can calculate what the scale will be . . . what the schedule of the marginal efficiency of capital tells us is, not what the rate of interest is, but the point to which the output of new investment will be pushed, given the rate of interest.' – Keynes, *The General Theory*, p. 184.

With the recent successful attack of the Neo-keynesians on the neoclassical view that the marginal physical product of capital determined the rate of return on fixed capital, it can be anticipated that the neoclassicists

THE MONEY RATE OF INTEREST AND THE MONEY-WAGE RATE

For Keynes not only does the money rate of interest 'rule the roost', but money is also the standard in which all contracts – debts, offers, and wages – are usually fixed. The combination of properties of a low elasticity of productivity and of substitutability rendered money uniquely desirable for measuring contractually deferred, and contingent, payments for goods and for pricing labour services in an economy where goods buy money, and money buys goods, but goods never buy goods. Money possesses a large liquidity premium once contracts are fixed in terms of money, and wages are sticky in terms of money for, as Keynes noted 'the convenience of holding assets in the same standard as that which *future* liabilities may fall due and in a standard in terms of which the *future* cost of living is expected to be relatively stable is obvious'.[1]

Stickiness in the money-wage rate is a fundamental requirement for a stable, viable monetary system. In a world of uncertainty where production takes time, the existence of money contracts permits the sharing of the burdens of uncertainty between the contracting parties when resources are to be committed to produce a flow of goods for a delivery date in the future. Such contractual commitments (e.g. hire contracts and forward contracts) are, by definition, tied to such flow-supply concepts as flow-supply price. Ultimately underlying the flow-supply price is the relationship between the money-wage rate and productivity. If individuals are to utilise money as a temporary abode of purchasing power either because they expect to buy something in the near future or because they desire a vehicle for transferring command of resources to the remote and indefinite future, then they must have confidence that no matter how far the current spot price for any producible good may be momentarily displaced by spot market conditions, it will return

---

will now emphasise the concept of marginal time preference as the determinant of the rate of profit. Keynes, of course, was equally adamant that the preference for present over deferred gratification determined the propensity to consume and not, in an uncertain world, either liquidity preference or the accumulation of real wealth. (Ibid. pp. 166, 242.)

[1] Keynes, *The General Theory*, pp. 236–7. Italics added.

to some 'known' level at a future date. As long as the flow-supply price is sticky (i.e. the annual rate of change is small) individuals will be confident that they can, at any date, accept a contract offering goods at a delivered price which will not significantly exceed today's short-period flow-supply price.[1]

Accordingly, the existence of money with its peculiar properties, the possibility of contracting for future performance, and the fact that any expected changes in future flow-supply prices will always induce individuals to alter the current spot price and volume of forward orders, permit individuals, at each point of time, *confidently* to defer use of current claims on resources by using money as a store of value if they desire to do so. Abstaining economic decision-makers, confident that they can always use money at a future date to accept an offer contract at a flow-supply price similar to today's price (as long as the money-wage is sticky and annual productivity increases are small), will use money as a store of value. That is, they will use money as a store of value as long as its carrying costs are low and the transactions costs necessary to convert from the store of value use to the medium of exchange use is negligible, i.e. as long as its liquidity premium exceeds its carrying costs.

If the standard of deferred payment used in contracts had a high elasticity of productivity, then every increase in the demand for the commodity which served as this standard (including any increase in demand for a store of value) would induce entrepreneurs to increase the demand for labour to be used in its production. This increase in labour demand would, in a period of full (or near full) employment, result in the bidding up of money-wages which would, in turn, result in an increase in the (money) flow-supply price of output as a whole. Thus, a low elasticity of productivity of money is essential if an increase in the demand for money as a store of value is not to destroy the purchasing power or exchange value of that store of value through increases in the money rate of

---

[1] In a world of uncertainty, as long as the money-wage rate is expected to be sticky, today's flow-supply price will be the best available estimate of the future flow-supply price *and* the future spot price (at the delivery date) of producible goods. Hence it is these short-run flow-supply prices which are the set of current prices that the average individual will use in his calculations of the desired real quantity of money at any future date.

remuneration of labour, and therefore 'the expectation of relative stability in the future money-cost of output might not be entertained with much confidence if the standard of value were a commodity with a high elasticity of production'.[1]

Moreover, if money is to be designed as a store of value then there must be a 'normal' expectation that the value of output in general will be more stable in terms of money than in terms of any other commodity. This does not necessarily require that wages be fixed in terms of money; rather what is necessary is that wages be 'relatively *sticky* in terms of money'.[2] If wages are sticky in terms of money, then the short-run flow-supply price (in money terms) of output as a whole will, in the absence of changes in monopoly elements (i.e. mark-ups over prime costs), vary only with the law of diminishing returns in the short-run, and changes in productivity in the long-run.[3] Consequently, if money-wage rates are sticky, then the amount of money needed to order a unit of reproducible goods for delivery in near future will be relatively stable; hence the exchange value of money is closely related to changes in money wages and changes in productivity.[4] Thus in an uncertain world where the deferment of commitment can be desirable, money will be that commodity for which wages are expected to be most sticky and it

cannot be one whose elasticity of production is not least, and for which the excess of carrying costs over liquidity-premium is not least. In other words, the expectation of a relative stickiness of wages in terms of money is a corollary of the excess of liquidity-premium over carrying-costs being greater for money than for any other asset.[5]

[1] ibid. p. 237. [2] ibid. p. 268. [3] ibid. p. 237.

[4] If there was some commodity other than money for which the number of units labour was willing to buy for a given unit of effort was more stable than for money, and if the number of units of labour input per unit of output of this commodity was constant no matter what the level of output, and if, at any point of time when there was a surplus of this commodity over current demand at its cost-price, the surplus could be held without costs (so that its liquidity premium exceeds its carrying costs), then, as Keynes admits, this commodity might be set up as a rival to money. But if such a reproducible commodity existed, then it would become a primary store of value and Say's Law would reign in the economy.

[5] Keynes, *The General Theory*, p. 238.

Fiat money will thus be the money *par excellence* on the proviso that the money-wage rate is sticky *and* in particular that the money wage rate does not exhibit autonomous movements,[1] for any increase in the demand for fiat money cannot induce an increase in the demand for labour (and hence raise the money-wage) to produce money, since the elasticity of productivity of fiat paper money must be zero. Since fiat money also does not normally involve any carrying costs, there cannot be a contango in the market for fiat money. As Keynes summarised the situation:

> Thus we see that the various characteristics, which combine to make the money-rate of interest significant, interact with one another in a cumulative fashion. The fact that money has low elasticities of production and substitution and low carrying-costs tends to raise the expectation that money-wages will be relatively stable; and this expectation enhances money's liquidity-premium and prevents the exceptional correlation between the money-rate of interest and the marginal efficiencies of other assets[2] which might, if it could exist, rob the money-rate of interest of its sting.[3]

If the money wage is sticky, then the money rate of interest will rule the roost simply because a zero elasticity of production means that any change in the demand for money will not, by itself, alter the supply of money or its purchasing power in terms of money-wage rates and therefore flow-supply prices. Instead it simply raises the rate of interest, unless the banking system takes action to offset these potential increases. Changes in the money-wage rate, however, by altering the money-wage (prime cost) component of the flow-supply price of output as a whole, will alter the exchange value between money (per unit) and goods, and hence alter money's desirability as a store of value.

If the money-wage rate (relative to productivity) is expected to increase in the future, while there is little change in the

---

[1] Certainly, the money-wage should not increase before full employment.

[2] This exceptional correlation depends on the fact that without the high liquidity premium for money, the market price might fall below the long-run supply price as the stock of money increased – as happens with all other durable goods.   [3] Keynes, *The General Theory*, p. 238.

current flow-supply price of durables (perhaps because supply is very elastic in the relevant range), then although the expected exchange value of money for labour is decreased, the expected future exchange rate of those durables with higher elasticities of productivity and for which well-organised spot markets exist will decrease less than proportionately. In other words, expectations of money-wage, flow-supply price inflation relative to current flow-supply prices will cause an expectation of being able to realise a capital appreciation via future spot market of all durables (except money whose $a = 0$ by definition). Nevertheless, for most physical assets – even those which possess liquidity in the sense that there is a well-organised spot market in which they can be resold – the carrying costs of warehousing, etc. will rise rapidly and disproportionately to the increase in holdings, so that even for such assets the increase in carrying costs associated with a small increase in stocks held as a store of value can wipe out any expected capital appreciation. Thus, producible durables with high and increasing carrying costs will hardly ever be very good stores of value relative to other durables with low and relatively constant carrying costs – namely money and/or securities,[1] even if spot markets exist for the former assets. Of course, it is highly unlikely that there will be well-organised spot markets for any durable with high carrying cost; and any durable for which no well-organised spot market exists cannot be used as a vehicle for transferring purchasing power to the indefinite future. In sum, most producible capital goods are not likely to be good stores of value, even in periods of expected inflation, either because of high and rapidly increasing carrying costs and/or their lack of liquidity because of the absence of a well-organised spot market.

Inflationary expectations will, as indicated in Chapter 4, affect the demand for capital goods as an input in the production process since a piece of equipment which is ordered at the

---

[1] Of course if the spot price of equities is expected to rise proportionately to the expected inflation in the future flow-supply prices of goods, then equities will always be a more desirable store of value than fixed money-price securities, bonds, or money and the current spot price (net of transactions costs) of equities will be immediately bid up until all durables whose elasticity of productivity is negligible (e.g. bonds, money, old masters, stamps, etc.) and for which a spot market exists, are good substitutes.

current flow-supply price will, over part of its useful life, be competitive with equipment which will be ordered at higher offer prices in the future. If, for example, money-wages and flow-supply prices are expected to rise rapidly enough in the future so that the expected forward or offer price at some future date exceeds the current offer price by an amount which will more than cover the cost of carrying the additional stock from the date of delivery to that delivery date associated with the expected higher future forward price, then there will be an incentive to move to the current period – the future demand for capital goods – including expected future replacement needs.[1] This 'is tantamount to an increase in the commodity-rates of money-interest and is, therefore, stimulating to the output of other assets'[2] as the current market demand schedule for producible capital goods shifts outward relative to the current stock and flow-supply schedules of capital goods.

Thus as Keynes noted:

> The stimulating effect of the expectation of higher prices is due, not to its raising the rate of interest (that would be a paradoxical way of stimulating output – in so far as the rate of interest rises, the stimulating effect is to that extent offset) but to its raising the marginal efficiency of a given stock of capital. . . . For the stimulus to output depends on the marginal efficiency of a given stock of capital rising *relatively* to the rate of interest.[3]

In terms of our notation of Chapter 4 this means that $\sum Q_r$ will increase by a greater proportion than any increase in the current rate of discount due to an increase in the quantity of money demanded to finance real transactions, as wage-price inflation is expected. In other words, inflationary expectations can increase the demand for producible capital goods, only if

[1] Keynes, *The General Theory*, p. 228.

[2] ibid. p. 231.

[3] ibid. pp. 142–3. Thus expectations of changes in the purchasing power of money do not directly affect the rate of interest; rather the spot 'prices of *existing* assets will always adjust themselves to changes in expectations concerning the prospective value of money' (ibid. p. 142). Keynes believed that those who analysed inflationary expectations via the Fisherian distinction between real and money rates of interest merely obfuscated the problem.

it raises the expected prospective money yields to entrepreneurs relative to any increase in the current rate of discount.

If expectations of rapid wage, flow-supply price inflation are rife, and if there are some liquid capital goods whose carrying costs are not very high relative to the inflationary costs of holding money[1] – then individuals will abandon the use of money as a store of value as the economy undergoes a flight from currency so great that certain producible durables with higher physical carrying costs than money become the primary store of value as rising interest rates are 'unable to keep pace with the marginal efficiency of capital (especially of stocks of liquid goods) under the influence of the expectation of an even greater fall in the value of money'.[2] When a flight of this magnitude occurs, liquid durable goods are continually ordered and held as a store of value (inventory speculation) and ultimately the flow-supply price is driven up so high that transactions involving durables (except due to differences in speculative expectations) can grind to a halt in the economy; only non-durable goods with close to zero gestation periods (or services) will be traded. This must mean, in a modern production-specialisation-exchange economy, the ultimate breakdown of both the monetary system and contractual relationships, and a reversion towards barter practices. When the situation deteriorates to such an extent that everyone is completely uncertain about the meaning of contractual commitments, a catastrophic breach in the continuity of the system is inevitable. Such a catastrophe by wiping out all existing contracts simultaneously would provide a foundation for developing a new monetary unit which was sticky in terms of labour offerings and could therefore be used in denominating all new contractual commitments.[3] '*The importance of money essentially flows*

---

[1] These liquid capital goods will be standardised working capital, i.e. finished or semi-finished goods, which can be readily sold in spot markets. Thus expectations of rapid inflation may lead to certain kinds of inventory speculation.   [2] ibid. p. 207.

[3] Cf. Keynes, *Treatise on Money*, 1 5. As Lerner so cogently observed:

The essential superiority of a monetary economy over a barter economy is the saving of mental effort made possible by money. In a monetary economy it is not necessary to think of all the rates of exchange of every commodity for every other commodity in which one might be interested. It is sufficient to know the money price of a commodity and to use this

from its being a link between the present and the future[1] and that link can only exist if there is a continuity over time in contractual commitments in money units.

Consequently, Keynes's emphasis on a zero (or negligible) elasticity of productivity of the money asset, if money is to be a store of value is based on his belief that the money-wage rate would change primarily in *response* to changes in tightness in the labour market. With a zero elasticity of productivity, increases in the demand for money would not induce an increase in the demand for labour and consequently would not effect the money-wage and therefore the money-supply price of output as a whole. Thus, a zero elasticity would tend to encourage wealth-holders to believe that money was a safe store of value and hence contribute to the high liquidity premium on money.

If, on the other hand, money was never utilised as a store of value and only employed as a medium of exchange (or a unit of account) for current transactions, then, as most neoclassical general equilibrium analysts correctly point out, it would make no difference what commodity was used as the numeraire. It is only when money can be utilised as a store of purchasing power in an uncertain world that low elasticities of productivity and substitutability are required for the money commodity. *The low elasticities will enhance the stickiness of wages in terms of money – a necessary condition for people to have confidence in using the money commodity as a store of value over time.* Thus in a monetary economy, while the money rate of interest may be the rooster ruling the demand for all capital goods, nevertheless, *it is the money-wage rate which rules the rooster.*

The perfunctory treatment of the problems of reproducibility, durability, and the high carrying costs of most durables in the

---

price as a representative of all the other things one might have instead. *But this service can be rendered by money only if there is a sufficient stability in its purchasing power.* In hyperinflation money ceases to be able to perform this service, and the economy reverts to barter until some other monetary unit is established.

A. P. Lerner, 'The Essential Properties of Interest and Money', *Quarterly Journal of Economics* (1952) p. 191. Italics added. Lerner also noted that the much rarer hyper-deflation phenomenon could also destroy the monetary system.

[1] Keynes, *The General Theory*, p. 293.

usual neoclassical general equilibrium analysis has not only hindered the use of such an approach in solving real world macroeconomic problems but it has also misled many into ignoring the peculiarities required for a viable monetary system. Peanuts may serve as the numeraire in the usual general equilibrium analysis; it would never be the money commodity in the real world! A general equilibrium approach may be useful in considering the allocation of resources under normal economic motives in a world where all production and consumption occurs in the present, and the future is fixed and reliable in all respects. Nevertheless, in the real world,

> expectations concerning the future affect what we do today. It is when we have made this transition that the peculiar properties of money as a link between the present and the future must enter into our calculations. . . . Money in its significant attributes is, above all, a subtle device for linking the present to the future; and we cannot even begin to discuss the effects of changing expectations on current activities except in monetary terms.[1]

Once economists recognise that rapid movements in money-wage rates can, in a modern monetary economy, destroy the usefulness of money as a store of value and consequently induce a reversion to barter, the general equilibrium delusion of the unmitigated desirability of freely flexible wages and prices will be apparent.

If the economic system is to be inherently stable, then as a matter of logic (as well as fact and experience), money-wage rates must be relatively more stable than real wages. By asserting the necessity of sticky money-wage rates, Keynes was highlighting a fundamental attribute for any production-specialisation-exchange economy which has contracts and utilises money as a store of value against an uncertain future. Keynes was not utilising a handy institutional rigidity which was due to a friction or a readily correctable imperfection in the labour market to close his system.[2] A 'perfect' labour market with flexible money-wages would be incompatible with a system

---

[1] ibid. p. 294.
[2] Cf. M. Friedman, 'A Theoretical Framework for Monetary Analysis', *Journ. Pol. Econ.* (1970) p. 209.

in which there are money contracts and money is used as a store of value. If the number of units of money which labour is willing to buy for a given unit of effort, the money-wage rate, fluctuated rapidly every time there is a small change in demand, there would be no asset whose liquidity premium always exceeded its carrying cost.

In contrast to this Keynesian position of the propriety of sticky money-wages, some neoclassical economists continue to argue that changes in demand, and not cost (and particularly money-wage rates), are the primary exogenous cause of price fluctuations. They tend to argue as if all market prices were spot prices[1] and to ignore the fact that (a) the money-wage rate is a ubiquitous component of the flow-supply prices of commodities and that (b) labour costs are uniquely related to the short-run flow-supply prices of current production. It should be obvious, however, that in a profit-oriented production system any exogenous change in the demand (price) for goods will induce changes in short-run offer prices, *if there is no change in the money-wage rate or degree of monopoly* (i.e. mark-up), only to the extent that diminishing returns are present. If, on the other hand, there is an exogenous increase in the money-wage then, even in the absence of any change in demand, the resulting short-run market (flow-supply) price will be higher than before *except* (1) if the degree of monopoly decreased proportionately more than the increase in wages or (2) if the reduction in diminishing returns as the quantity declined more then offset the increase in money-wages, or some combination of (1) and (2). In the real world of changing effective demand levels at less than full employment, an *incomes policy* which controls both the money-wage and the profit margin (mark-up) will provide more stability in the purchasing power of money than will a policy which permits freely flexible wages and profit margins. Hence such an incomes policy will enhance the usefulness of money as a store of value and prevent 'flights from money', as the price level changes only to reflect the changing *real* costs of producing commodities as aggregate demands change. Fortunately, real world institutions and imperfections

---

[1] Most important economic problems, on the other hand, involve the use of resources to produce a flow of output. Spot prices are important, therefore, only to the extent that they affect flow-supplies.

have, until recently, limited wage flexibility and have therefore prevented the establishment of flexible wages and prices of 'perfect' markets, which some economists advocate as a panacea for all our modern macroeconomic ills.

As Lerner exclaimed after his valiant effort at interpretation, one of the central propositions of *The General Theory* is that 'any money which was completely cured of wage and price rigidity would not be able to survive as money'.[1] The preceding analysis has attempted to demonstrate the validity of this position, along with insights on the dependence of the process of capital formation on the rate of discount and the money-wage. These relationships were central to Keynes's preoccupation of 'own-rates' of interest which, for most Keynesians, have generally been the most obscure part of his analysis.

The most obvious consequence of this analysis is that labour unions share responsibility with the Monetary Authority for controlling the relationship between the demand to accumulate real wealth and the rate of interest. Until such times as labour unions and central bankers recognise that a stable money-wage policy must be an essential consort to a sound monetary policy which encourages economic growth, modern market-oriented laissez-faire economies will continue to follow erratic paths of economic growth.

WHEN MONEY MARKETS DO NOT CLEAR

Until now, it has been implicitly assumed that the quantity of money demanded for the industrial and financial circulations would equal the quantity of money supplied, i.e. borrowing and lending of money conforms to the principles of a perfect market so that here can never be an excess demand or supply of money at the market price for borrowing money. In such circumstances, entrepreneurs will choose among alternative investment opportunities in new or old capital goods so as to maximise, in some sense, the expected net income stream obtainable from the sum of money committed. The opportunity cost, therefore, of ordering a new capital good is the expected net return per dollar that could be spent on purchasing old capital goods on the spot market, and, given a perfectly competitive

[1] Lerner, 'The Essential Properties', p. 193.

market for borrowing money, this will equal the cost per dollar of borrowing money.

When, however, lending occurs under conditions of an imperfect market, then there is likely to be an 'unsatisfied fringe of borrowers' i.e. at the going price for borrowing money there is excess demand.[1] This phenomenon of credit rationing can occur at any time but it is likely to be particularly apropos when business is active and expanding rapidly. Under these circumstances it is the expected return (or marginal efficiency) per dollar of potential alternative new investments which comprises the opportunity cost of any new project – and with credit rationing this opportunity cost (even after adjustment for risk) exceeds the cost per dollar of borrowing.

Moreover, it is the opportunity cost or the expected return on new projects computed as an absolute profit margin at the 'standard volume' of output which enters into (a) the short-run flow-supply price of neo-keynesian entrepreneurs in any particular industry and (b) the long-run supply price of both neoclassical and neo-keynesian entrepreneurs.[2] Thus, when business is brisk, the opportunity cost of using capital in the production of any product may be the expected profit per dollar invested on other new projects which are not undertaken because of a shortage of finance, while *ceteris paribus*, if finance is readily available perhaps because business is dull, the opportunity cost of any investment project is the rate of interest that can be earned by lending money.[3] Hence in booms, it will be the expected rate of profit on new capital which cannot be ordered because of credit rationing which enters the supply price of Keynesian entrepreneurs, while in periods of recession it will be the rate of interest.

Of course, all this omits both (i) the subjective discounting premium over the borrowing rate which entrepreneurs utilise in evaluating expected streams of quasi-rents and (ii) the degree of confidence in the future which underlies wealth-owners' fears of illiquidity. Thus if economic activity is growing rapidly *and* smoothly, entrepreneurs may reduce their subjective discount premium which they require before undertaking long-term

[1] Keynes, *Treatise on Money*, I 212.
[2] See Chapter 2 above. Also see J. Robinson, *Essays in Economic Growth*, p. 8.   [3] See Keynes, *Treatise on Money*, II 45.

commitments because they are psychologically more willing to face uncertainty when recent history has been favourable to their interests; therefore, external borrowing by entrepreneurs may increase in the face of rising interest rates and even unchanged long-run entrepreneurial expectations. When business is dull, on the other hand, entrepreneurial confidence may be weak and shaken and the subjective discount premium may rise even as the rate of borrowing falls. Over the Trade Cycle, the subjective rate of discount used by entrepreneurs to evaluate expected income streams may vary inversely to the rate of interest, and consequently statisticians may find investment spending is not very responsive to changes in the *observed* rate of interest.

Similarly, if the economy has been buoyant and incomes have been rising rapidly but smoothly in the recent past, wealth-holders may subdue their precautionary tendencies and may be more willing to be illiquid, so that interest rates need not rise as much as otherwise, or vice versa in a decline. Finally, in a bank money economy, actions of the Monetary Authority can affect *both* the bank rate for borrowing *and* the volume of funds available, so that there need not be any unique, unchanging and readily observable relationship between investment spending, the market rate of interest, and the level and direction of economic activity.[1]

In buoyant economic times if credit rationing exists, *the supply of finance* can limit the rate of investment which can be undertaken per unit of time by holding down the demand price schedule for capital goods via restrictions on the number of entrepreneurs who can obtain finance (E in equation (1) of Chapter 4 above) to make their demand for capital operational in an economy where only money can buy goods. As Keynes noted, 'A member of the public, who, as a result of the credit restriction is unable to borrow from his bank, generally has no facilities . . . for obtaining the funds he requires by bidding up the price of loans in the open market, even though he is willing to pay more than the supply price'.[2]

[1] In fact, a history of rapid and relatively wide fluctuations in sales and/or profits is more likely to affect entrepreneurial spirits and their desire to undertake long-run contractual commitments, than either any 'rational' calculation of present v. deferred gratifications or calculations based on present values. [2] Keynes, *Treatise on Money*, II 255.

Although such a shortage of finance will limit the *rate* at which new investment projects are undertaken, as long as some finance is available it will act as a 'revolving-fund' to allow all the projects whose expected rate of profit exceeds the rate of discount to be ultimately undertaken as the fringe of unsatisfied borrowers is gradually eliminated. In the long run, though we may all be dead, we can take comfort in that, *ceteris paribus*, a stationary state will emerge.

MONETARY POLICY AND THE ACCUMULATION OF CAPITAL

In the short run, the Monetary Authority's ability to affect the rate of accumulation operates in two related ways, namely:

(i) via control of rediscount rates, the Central Bank is by fiat the 'governor' of the minimum rate of discount used by entrepreneurs to capitalise expected revenues from new capital goods; and

(ii) via open market trading to control the supply of the medium of exchange and simultaneously by playing on (or even, at times altering) a set of institutional rules for the operation of banks and security markets, the Central Bank can create a situation where the price for borrowing money will not increase in order to eliminate any excess demand (i.e. the money market may not clear).

Thus if the economy is at less than full employment, financial constraints created by the Monetary Authority rather than the lack of real resources can be an effective barrier to expansion of economic activity, either because at the current rate of interest, entrepreneurs cannot visualise profitable uses for additional new capital goods, or if entrepreneurs are eager to expand

the pace, at which the innovating entrepreneurs will be able to carry their projects into execution at a cost on interest which is not deterrent to them . . . depends on the degree of complaisance of those responsible for the banking system.[1]

[1] Keynes, *Treatise on Money*, II 97.

In the latter case, even if entrepreneurs have 'great expectations' (after proper discounting), if the banking system and the associated financial intermediaries fail to furnish sufficient finance for the industrial circulation, then the shortage of money may impede accumulation and growth prospects even with idle resources.[1] (Chapter 13 will deal with this aspect in greater detail.)

Why, however, should the Monetary Authority desire to restrict the supply of money which uses up no real resources in order to constrain the demand for goods, when idle resources are available?

As ultimate producer of the medium of exchange, the Monetary Authority believes it is its duty to preserve the purchasing power of money. Since the Monetary Authority has no control over the short run (flow-supply) prices of particular goods, or over money-wage rates, and since it is these prices which are relevant for the acceptance of contractual agreements about the rate of exchange between goods and money in the near future, the Monetary Authority's control over the price level must operate indirectly via management of the rate of spending per period. If money-wage rates are rising more rapidly than productivity so that the flow-supply price of output in general is increasing, then the power of the banking system can be used to create a sufficient slackness in labour and product markets to reduce both labour's truculent demands for higher money-wages per unit of effort and management's ability to acquiesce in such wage demands that remain. 'If,' however, 'there are strong social or political forces causing spontaneous changes in the money-rates of efficiency-wages, the control of the price-level may pass beyond the power of the banking system',[2] or, at least, the ability of the banking system to offset these political and social winds will be exceedingly limited. Hence, unless rules of the game are established via the political process to prevent rapid changes in money earnings per unit of effort over time, (an incomes policy), modern economies will fluctuate between the Scylla of inflation and the Charybdis of unemployment.

[1] Of course, if entrepreneurs lack 'animal spirits', then even an abundant money supply cannot stimulate accumulation.

[2] Keynes, *Treatise on Money*, II 351.

CHAPTER 10

Financial Markets, Finance, and Investment

In modern economies, the development of well organised spot markets for placements severed any direct link between the demand decision for the hire-purchase of fixed capital (involving production control or management of the services of capital) and the portfolio balance decision (involving ownership of capital). The existence of well organised security markets permits the efficient transfer of current command of real resources and thereby facilitates the achievement of high rates of accumulation for a monetary economy (within its resource base constraints) but such markets may add greatly to the instability of the system.

If the cost of disinvestment, i.e. the cost of moving from an asset which was held primarily for yield to the medium of exchange, was exceedingly high, then the purchase of an investment good to transfer purchasing power to the future would be almost 'permanent and indissoluble, like marriage, except by reason of death or other grave cause'[1] and there would be no speculative demand for money. There would, of course, still be a precautionary demand for money for as long as the liquidity premium of money exceeded its carrying costs, and in the absence of spot markets for securities (and related financial institutions) which provide liquidity, households would be less willing to relinquish current command over resources to entrepreneurs who desire to increase the stock of capital so that high rates of accumulation would be very difficult if not impossible.[2] This then is the dilemma of modern,

---

[1] Keynes, *The General Theory*, p. 160.
[2] In the absence of money, of course, accumulation would depend on the propensity to save.

monetary economies. So long as income earners are free to store their wealth-holding in money, they will be unwilling to transfer command by holding claims which are not readily convertible (without loss) into command at a future date. Yet if these claims are readily marketable, it will be exceedingly difficult to encourage wealth-holders to directly order new capital goods (especially for individuals who do not know how to manage these assets).

SAVINGS, THE TRANSFER OF COMMAND, AND INVESTMENT

In a monetary economy, an act of saving *always* relates to units of money and must, at least initially, be in terms of money. An act of savings means that the individual has decided not to exercise earned current command of resources for the production of consumer goods. In a monetary economy, a decision to save does not involve the current purchase of a consumer durable in order to obtain a stream of utility over the future; it is not a decision to 'consume any specified thing at any specified date'.[1] In a world of uncertainty, he who hesitates to spend his current claims on resources is saved to make a decision another day.

Indeed what the saver desires to buy is 'wealth', i.e. he desires a mode of transferring command generally to some unspecified future date when he will wish to buy some unspecified article.[2] The existence of money and placements – assets which have low transactions and carrying costs, and well-organised spot markets provides a format for storing wealth which is readily convertible to the medium of exchange at any future date if the necessity should arise. Moreover, since these financial assets (money and securities) do not use resources in their creation (their elasticities of productivity are zero), the mere act of savings, whether in the form of money or placements, inevitably forces another individual to transfer a potential claim to

---

[1] Keynes, *The General Theory*, p. 210.

[2] If the saver could specify every commodity wanted on every specific future date, he could enter into a contract for forward delivery of his life cycle consumption plan at birth (or even before if his parent acted as his agent).

existing wealth to the saver, while simultaneously depressing the current demand for resources.

Investment, on the other hand, always relates to the hire-purchase of new capital goods. These goods will be demanded only if (1) they are expected to yield a sufficiently large net money flow over their useful lives in excess of their original costs and if (2) finance is available at favourable terms which will permit the ordering of these capital goods. Thus, in any discussion of the demand for capital goods

> it is much preferable to speak of capital [goods] as having a yield over the course of its useful life in excess of its original costs, than as being *productive*. For the only reason why an asset offers a prospect of yielding during its life services having an aggregate value greater than its initial supply price is because it is *scarce*; and it is kept scarce because of the competition of the rate of interest on money. If capital becomes less scarce, the excess yield will diminish, without it having become less productive – at least in the physical sense.[1]

Hence, 'the value of capital goods depends on the rate of interest at which the prospective income from them is capitalised',[2] and if this value exceeds the flow-supply price, then capital goods are, by definition, *scarce*. If entrepreneurs desiring these scarce capital goods can obtain finance via financial markets and institutions, they will be able to commit themselves to accept contracts for production of additional capital goods.

Since savers are interested in wealth only as a means of storing, transferring (and hopefully, increasing) command of resources into the future, while entrepreneurial investors desire the services of scarce capital goods for their expected net money flow and *not for their liquidity*, portfolio balance (forms of wealth-holding) decisions and hire-purchase of capital goods decisions will look out to different markets and prices. The investment decision depends on the market demand price (value) relative to the flow-supply price of capital goods, while the portfolio decision depends on the current spot price of

---

[1] Keynes, *The General Theory*, p. 213.
[2] Keynes, *Treatise on Money*, II 154.

securities relative to their expected future spot price – and there is no important direct relationship between these markets other than the rate of interest (and the concomitant financial conditions). The functions of the rate of interest are: (1) in the portfolio decision to modify the spot price of securities relative to their expected future spot price in such a way as to equalise the attraction of holding securities as a deferred claim on cash compared to holding cash directly and (2) in the investment decision to set a floor on the rate of discount used to evaluate the expected flow of net revenue from the hire-purchase of capital goods so that its present value can be compared to the flow-supply price of capital goods. The existence of financial markets in which new securities can be sold permits, but does not require, the transfer of immediate command from economic units who wish to spend currently less than their income to units who wish to command resources in excess of what their current income permits.

THE MARKET FOR PLACEMENTS

At this stage it is necessary explicitly to develop an analysis of the market for securities and to tie it to the preceding analysis for the market for the hire-purchase of capital goods (Chapter 4) and the demand for money (Chapters 6–9).

At any point of time, there is a given stock of placements which, for purposes of simplicity can be assumed to be homogeneous.[1] Accordingly the stock supply schedule of placements (S_p^1 in Fig. 10.1) facing the public, at any point of time, is perfect inelastic. Moreover, the elasticity of production for securities is zero, so that if the demand for securities increases, additional resources are not automatically and directly employed to produce more placements. Instead, increases in the supply of equity or loan securities will depend primarily on entrepreneurial demands for capital goods, the necessity to finance that demand externally, and the behaviour of financial

[1] Obviously the assumption of homogeneous units of securities is unrealistic. The alternative would be to provide separate demand and supply schedules for each type of placement, an unnecessary complication as long as we discuss demand and supply in units of money. Thus we are assuming some composite or representative security.

intermediaries who float the new issues. Business firms can usually finance replacement investment entirely from depreciation allowances. Accordingly, as a first approximation, it can be assumed that it is only the net change in the stock of capital goods which must find additional financing,[1] and since a portion of this net change may be internally funded by the firm, it is only to the extent that the firm uses external sources of funding that the supply schedule of placements will shift outwards as capital accumulates.[2] Hence the stock supply schedule of securities is likely to shift even less over each time period than the stock supply schedule of capital goods.

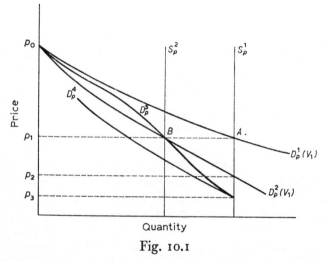

Fig. 10.1

The unit of measurement used on the quantity axis in Fig. 10.1 must be somewhat arbitrary. If every placement specified a contractual obligation to pay a given sum of money per period for each unit, then the quantity could be measured in terms of the annual income to which each security constitutes a claim, e.g. one placement is a claim to $1 per annum. For

[1] In a world of uncertainty, institutional rules may require that some proportion of all investment per period be internally funded. (See Chapter 12 below.)

[2] Cf. J. Robinson, *Essays in Economic Growth*, p. 43. Of course in periods of 'inflated' equity prices, there may be an incentive to spin off new investment projects merely to make a profit on the flotation of new securities. (This will be discussed in greater detail in Chapter 13 below.)

most equities, however, no such *contractual* income claim comes with ownership of the security. Nevertheless in order to provide an orderly method of thinking about the problem at hand, it can be assumed as a safe first approximation, that there is some quasi-contractual expected income payment per period derived from the ownership of equities so that such equities can be reduced to the same income claim unit of measure as bonds.[1] Thus, in Fig. 10.1 the quantity axis is in units of dollar income claims per period which means that at this stage we can ignore the legal and qualitative differences between types of placements. The 'rate of interest' or the cost of funding is inversely related to the market price of placements and, therefore, in essence the rate of interest is a capitalisation factor suggesting the number of years purchased of income derived from the ownership of a placement, if wealth-holders would hold securities to maturity.[2]

The stock supply of placements available to the general public (wealth-holders) at a point in time is equal to all the previously issued placements which exist net of repurchases (a_p) less those placements presently held by the banking system (a_p^b), where this latter quantity will be taken as exogenous to our model. Thus

$$S_p = a_p - a_p^b = a_p^s \qquad (1)$$

where S_p is the stock supply of placements offered to the public, and a_p^s is the effective quantity of securities at hand at any point of time.

If only a portion of net investment is ordinarily funded by selling new placements on the organised securities market, then the flow-supply of placements (s_p) offered to the public per unit of time is given by

$$s_p = f_2(p_k, I_n, g, h, p_p) \qquad (2)$$

[1] Under this view, expectations of an increase in dividends per share would have the same effect as an increase in 'short' sales; it may be viewed as an increase in effective supply. We shall ignore these problems since their introduction would make the analysis more complicated without altering the major conclusion.

[2] The price of placements relative to the expected future income claims arising from ownership of placements or 'the rate of interest (as we call it for short) is, strictly speaking, a monetary phenomenon in . . . that it equalises the advantage of holding cash and a deferred claim on cash'. – J. M. Keynes, 'Alternative Theories of the Rate of Interest', *Econ. Jour.* (1937) p. 245.

where p_k is the market or flow-supply price of newly produced capital goods, I_n is the quantity of new capital goods which represent net investment, g is the fraction of the total cost of net investment which is externally funded, h is the fraction of long-term external finance which is provided by the banking system,[1] and p_p is the spot price of placements. (Since the gestation period for the production of new placements is nil, the market price of new issues must equal the spot price of already outstanding securities.) If g and h are taken as exogenous, while the cost of net investment is defined as $p_k(s_k - d_k)$, where s_k and d_k are the flow-supply and flow-demand for capital goods per period, then equation (2) may be specified as

$$s_p = \frac{(1 - \bar{h})(\bar{g})[p_k(s_k - d_k)]}{p_p} \tag{3}$$

Given the level of net investment which must be financed via a new placement issue to the public, the quantity of placements (measured in income claim units) which must be sold to fund this level of investment declines as the market placement price increases, i.e. the flow-supply curve with respect to p_p is a rectangular hyperbola. Thus, given the contractual agreement of a fixed sum per annum per unit of security, the lower the spot price at which the market will accept deferred claims on cash, the more claims that must be sold.

The market supply of placements is obtained by summating equations (1) and (3):

$$S_p + s_p = a_p^s + \frac{(1 - \bar{h})(\bar{g})[p_k(s_k - d_k)]}{p_p} \tag{4}$$

Since both $\bar{g}$ and $\bar{h}$ are likely to be less than unity, while $d_k > 0$, placement flow-supply is normally considered to be much less important than flow-supply considerations in the capital goods market. Indeed, s_p is normally such a trifling element in the block of existing placements, that as a first approximation it is often assumed that the short-run supply of placements is completely dominated by its stock characteristics. In essence, the supply is then predetermined and can be represented by the vertical curve in Fig. 10.1. Specifically

[1] This may be provided via financial intermediaries who operate in the securities market. (See Chapter 13 below.)

if $(1 - \bar{h})(\bar{g})[p_k(s_k - d_k)]$ is negligible (e.g. if $h = 1$, or $g = 0$, or $[p_k(s_k - d_k)] \approx 0$) then

$$S_p + s_p = a_p^s \qquad (5)$$

The fact that the net investment term $p_k(s_k - d_k)$ appears in the market placement-supply equation (4) does indicate, however, that the supply of placements available to the public is not completely independent of the demand for capital goods. Though the excess flow-demand for capital $(s_k - d_k)$ may, therefore, react on the price of placements (and the price of placements on the demand for capital via the rate of interest), the existence of g and h as exogenous variables which depend partly on financial institutions' behaviour, and, in a world of uncertainty, partly on financial rules suggests that capital goods demand and the flow-supply of placements are independent 'at least in the sense that any degree, positive or negative, of the one is compatible in appropriate circumstances with any degree, positive or negative of the other'.[1] Consequently, for certain aspects of single-period analysis, which are discussed in this section, supply aspects of placements will be treated as a stock concept. In the following chapters when the relationship between finance, funding, and accumulation is analysed, the flow-supply of placements will be added to the analysis to obtain generalisations on the rate of capital accumulation, under various hypotheses about the concurrent actions of the banking system, the magnitudes of g and h and the behaviour of financial intermediaries.

The demand for placements is a demand for a liquid store of value by the public who believe that the expected future spot market in securities will determine the terms on which wealth owners can reconvert this deferred command into an immediate demand upon resources at some vague future date. The alternative to securities is to hold immediate liquid command to the future via money.

The decision on what mode to use to transfer command into the future is relevant not only in determining what vehicle to use to hold the 'current increment in wealth of individuals, but also to the whole block of their existing wealth. Indeed since the current increment is but a trifling proportion of the

[1] Keynes, *Treatise on Money*, I 145.

block of existing wealth, it is but a minor element in the matter.'[1] Thus, at each point of time, wealth-holders are required to decide how much of their postponed command of resources to hold in the form of debt obligations of firms or titles to capital goods and how much in the form of bank deposits. It is at this point that the portfolio balance decision becomes relevant. If we assume that either there is backwardation in the consumer goods market or the spot markets for such durables are so poorly organised that the general public can not expect future spot prices (net of transactions and carrying costs) to exceed the current price, then the public will not store its wealth in inventories of consumer durables and money and financial assets will be the only vehicles used to transfer generalised purchasing power over time.[2]

Wealth-holders disposition to store value between money and securities depends on all the factors previously enumerated in Chapter 8, such as households' desires to maximise or at least maintain generalised purchasing power for unspecified claims on resources over time, their fears of income and capital losses, their confidence in their ability to foresee the future, the existence of organised spot markets, etc. Given these factors, the public's demand schedule for placements (D_p^1 in Fig. 10.1) can be derived.

The public demands placements solely as a store of value, or mode for transferring purchasing power, so that the market

[1] ibid. I 141.

[2] Basic to the neoclassical schools' view is the belief that consumer durables are good stores of value (e.g. Friedman and Scwartz, 'Money and Business Cycles', pp. 59–63, Patinkin, *On the Nature of the Monetary Mechanism*, p. 26) even though carrying costs mount steeply for consumer durables after some minimum stock level per household has been obtained. Consequently, except where there is expectation of very rapid inflation in future offer prices (i.e. expectations of rapid rises in money-wages and flow-supply prices) so that expectations of rising spot prices for consumer durables are sufficient to more than offset the increasing carrying cost, the neoclassical model will be irrelevant. Such expectations, however, are incompatible with the essential properties of money and as Chapter 9 indicated, are incompatible with a viable monetary economy. Hence the neoclassical fable is only applicable to a world of perfect certainty, or to real world episodes of flight from money. These latter cases are extremely rare and it is unlikely that the neoclassical general equilibrium theories had such perverse cases in mind.

demand function may be conceptualised entirely as a stock demand at each point of time, i.e.

$$D_p = f_6(p_p, \overline{R}, \lambda, \beta, \gamma, \delta, \kappa_\lambda, \kappa_\delta, \overline{T}_s, e, V) \qquad (6)$$

where D_p is quantity of placements demanded by the public at any point of time, p_p is the market price of placements, $\overline{R}$ is the income claim per period per placement ($\overline{R} = \$1$ because of our unit of measure of placements), λ is a set of expectations about the rate of change of the future spot prices of securities, β and γ are indices of the public's aversion to capital and income risks, δ is the period of time till the expected date of realisation, κ_λ and κ_δ are measures of the public's degree of confidence in their expectations about changes in security prices and date of realisation, T_s is the cost of moving between securities and money, e represents the number of wealth-holders and the current distribution of wealth among them, and V is the magnitude of the public's total store of value at any point of time. As indicated in Chapter 8, there are two causes of a 'wealth' effect on the demand for vehicles to store purchasing power over time which operate via changes in V, namely (a) the flow of savings out of current income which induces a 'flow-demand' for securities via increases in V each period, and (b) changes in total portfolio value due to changes in the spot price of securities altering the market value of total portfolio holdings, i.e. capital gains or losses. The former may be associated with a marginal propensity to buy placements (m) out of household savings (S_h), the magnitude of this marginal propensity Keynes assumed would be between zero and unity;[1] while for the latter, one can conceptualise a marginal propensity to buy placements (j) out of capital gains or losses (G), which, may or may not equal zero.[2] The bars over the symbols R, T_s, and e in equation (6) indicate that the values of these variables are assumed to be exogenously determined.

---

[1] See Keynes, 'The Ex-Ante Theory', *Econ. Jour.* **47** (1937) p. 668. Both the neoclassical and neo-keynesian schools tend to assume that $m = 1$, that is, that all household savings are used to buy securities. Such an assumption ignores uncertainty as increases in the quantity of money are never, when $m = 1$, held as a store of value. (See Chapters 11 and 13 below.)

[2] This latter marginal propensity will be discussed in greater detail in the following chapters.

Given β, γ, δ, κ_λ, κ_δ, and V, for any given expectations λ_1, the market demand curve for placements – e.g. $D_p^1(V_1)$ in Fig. 10.1 will be downward sloping, $f'_{\delta p_p} < 0$, since if the current spot price declines relative to the expected future spot price, then the expected capital gain from purchasing a placement increases, while the (income) opportunity cost of holding money balances as a store of value increases. Hence the public will want to substitute placements for money holdings with lower current spot price of securities. The demand curve in Fig. 10.1 is depicted as intersecting the price axis at p_o indicating at that 'high' price, the quantity of placements demanded equals zero as the fear of capital loss becomes so great, while the opportunity cost of holding money is negligible. This is the traditional Keynesian liquidity trap, where every member of the public is a complete 'bear' since that spot price relative to expectations of the future spot price 'leaves more to fear than to hope, and offers, at the same time, a running yield which is only sufficient to offset a very small measure of fear'.[1]

Table 10.1 summarises the *ceteris paribus* effects, at any given placement price, of changes in each of the major independent variables in equation (6) on the demand for placements. A comparison of this table with a similar table in Chapter 8 which shows the *ceteris paribus* effects on the demand for money, indicates that except for the wealth variable V, a change in any independent variable has opposite effects on the demand for money and securities, that is, with respect to λ, β, γ, δ, κ_λ, and κ_δ, money and securities are substitutes. For changes in the value of the public's wealth-holdings, however, money and placements are complements;[2] hence any change in V partly spends itself in changes in the demand for money and partly in the demand for securities.

If, for example, individuals should increase their desire to avoid capital risks and/or they lower their expectations about the rate of increase in future spot securities prices, and/or they have less confidence in their expectations of changes in security prices or in the expected date of realisation, that is, if they should become more bearish (because of either speculative

[1] Keynes, *The General Theory*, p. 202.
[2] Compare S. Weintraub, *An Approach to the Theory of Income Distribution*, p. 157.

or precautionary factors) at any placement price level, then the public's demand schedule for securities should shift downward from $D_p^1(V_1)$ to $D_p^2(V_1)$ in Fig. 10.1. This implies that the public wish to hold less of its deferred command in the form of titles to capital and more in the form of currency or bank

Table 10.1

CHANGE IN FACTOR EFFECTS ON
THE DEMAND FOR SECURITIES

Factor	Increases the Quantity of Securities Demanded (Bullishness)	Decreases the Quantity of Securities Demanded (Bearishness)
(1) Expected rate of increase in security prices (λ)	increase	decrease
(2) Capital risk aversion (β)	decrease	increase
(3) Income risk aversion (γ)	increase	decrease
(4) Time period to realisation (δ)	increase	decrease
(5) Degree of confidence in expectations (κ) about λ or δ	increase	decrease
(6) Value of store of wealth (V)	increase	decrease

deposits.[1] If the supply of placements is constant and if V is unchanged, then the price of securities will fall from p_1 to p_2. Since, however, the total value of placements held by the public will decline as p_p falls, V will decline, reducing the demand for placements, i.e. $f'_{6V}(p_p) > 0$. In Fig. 10.1, however, the shift from $D_p^1(V_1)$ to $D_p^2(V_1)$ was due only to an increase in bearishness, with V unchanged at V_1. The resulting market demand curve when *both* the change in bearishness and the change in V are accounted for will be D_p^3 in Fig. 10.1. At any price below p_1, the value of the public's wealth-holdings has declined and therefore the quantity of placements demanded will be less than the quantity demand on the unchanged V demand curve, $D_p^2(V_1)$, while at any price above p_1, the

---

[1] This increase in bearishness may result from the fact that rapidly fluctuating stock prices may decrease the public's confidence in their expectations about the future. On the other hand, steadily increasing stock prices may increase the public's confidence and therefore increase their bullishness. Thus, changes in portfolio balance decisions may be the result of either the rapidity of fluctuations in security prices or the expected rate of change, or a combination of these factors. (Cf. Keynes, *Treatise on Money*, 1 252.)

demand quantities will be greater. The horizontal difference between D_p^3 and D_p^2 at any price will depend on the magnitude of the marginal propensity (j) to demand placements when V changes *because of a change in the market price of placements*, given the expectations about future security prices, i.e. $j = f'_6 V(p_v)$. The magnitude of j is a measure of a wealth effect, due to changes in placement prices, on the demand for placements.[1]

If $j = 0$, then D_p^3 and D_p^2 would coincide. The often mentioned 'locked-in' effect due to a security price fall implies that $j = 0$ at least for prices below the initial price p_1. Moreover, 'locking-in' is economically rational behaviour if one already possesses securities whose prices have declined, since if the security is sold immediately and the realised money used as an alternative store of value then the wealth-holder will incur a loss in future income as well as the costs of converting to money, while if the individual holds the security until the date of realisation, only the transactions costs will be incurred. Thus there is a marginal advantage to maintaining a position in securities that has already been taken, even when there is an increase in bearishness due to a decline in the market value of the public's placement holding as long as expectations of future declines in price is less than transactions costs;[2] hence j may be approximately zero at prices below p_1. Whether $j \geqslant 0$, the market price declines (from p_1 to say p_3) and the expected yield on the market value of loan and equity securities will have risen until in equilibrium the actual portfolio mix of households (which is, by hypothesis, unchanged) is the desired one. (Of

---

[1] F. P. R. Brechling, 'A Note on Bond-Holding and the Liquidity Preference Theory of Interest', *Rev. of Econ. Stud.* **24** (1957) p. 191. At the same time changes in the spot price of securities can generate a wealth effect on the demand for all consumer goods. As Keynes noted, 'A country is no richer when it swaps titles to capital at a higher price than a lower one, but the citizens, beyond question, *feel* richer' and consequently households are likely to feel less necessity to save out of normal income and therefore the consumption function is increased. [See Keynes, *Treatise on Money*, II 197.] Nevertheless, for purposes of the following discussion, it is important to note that the increment in consumption is likely to come at the expense of 'normal' savings out of income, rather than, in the aggregate, the liquidation of paper profits in the spot markets for placements.

[2] Cf. J. R. Hicks, *Critical Essays in Monetary Theory*, pp. 34–5. Hence it may not pay to buy, but it may pay to hold securities already possessed.

course, this will raise the rate of interest and therefore lower the demand for capital goods – in the traditional Keynesian manner.) *It is the flexibility of the spot market price of placements which permits each household unit to hold as many placements as it desires and to alter its portfolio as often as it desires, while in the aggregate the public holds exactly the quantity of placements and money which is made available to it.*

This decline in the spot price of placements can be offset by the commercial banks or the Monetary Authority purchasing securities and simultaneously creating bank deposits for households. In this latter case, the spot price of securities will not fall as much as in the former (and it may remain unchanged or even rise) as banks reduce the effective supply of securities available to the public (i.e. a_p^b increases), while households increase their holdings of money and decrease their holdings of placements.[1] If the banking system adopts this latter course, then the ultimate effect of the rate of interest (and financial conditions) and therefore on the demand for capital goods will be different than if the stock of money was kept constant. For example, in Fig. 10.1, we can assume that after the market price has declined to p_3, the banks buy securities on the open market, shifting S_p to the left. If the banks could purchase all the placements at the market price of p_3, then there would be no change in V (only a change in the composition of the public's portfolio holdings); and the public would be moved up a demand curve based on a constant V (D_p^4 in Fig. 10.1). Open market purchases, however, involve bidding up the price of placements and thus altering the magnitude of V at each price. Accordingly, the public will move up the varying $V(D_p^3)$ curve, and the supply schedule need be shifted to the S_p^2 line to restore p_1. Comparing points A and B on Fig. 10.1, we note that, *mutatis mutandis*, the actual portfolio holdings of the public have shifted from placements towards money as the banking system has satisfied the bearish sentiment of the public and prevented the rate of interest from rising. *Although the public has shifted out of titles to capital goods, the community need not alter its holdings of real capital goods at all.* Accordingly, the total market value of placements held by the public does not bear any particular relationship to the total stock of capital goods in

[1] Cf. Keynes, *Treatise on Money*, I 142.

the economy at any point of time.[1] The market value of securities will largely depend on the historical accidents of the past needs of firms to externally fund investment expenditures and the interaction of the current sentiment of the wealth-holding public and the behaviour of the banking system.

In summary, in an economy where the major form of money is bank deposits, portfolio decisions in combination with the operations of the banking system will determine what proportion of the community's total of real wealth is owned by households and what proportion is owned or looked after by the banking system.[2] *Portfolio decisions except to the extent that they affect either the rate of interest, or the ability of entrepreneurs to obtain finance via financial institutions, will have no effect on the demand for capital goods,* and therefore on the volume of employment and the rate of accumulation. In other words, portfolio balance can affect real investment only via the rate of interest used to capitalise the expected income stream from capital goods, or via some impact on the number of entrepreneurs who can obtain finance, or possibly the ease or difficulty of obtaining finance may alter entrepreneurial expectations of profit. Having discussed in detail in Chapter 4 how changes in the rate of discount can affect the demand for capital, we can now turn to the question of the impact of portfolio decisions at a given level of household wealth on the demand for capital goods via the number of entrepreneurs who can obtain finance or on entrepreneurial profit expectations.[3]

---

[1] Thus Kaldor's use of the valuation ratio as a determinant of long-run equilibrium growth is highly misleading since there is no necessary relationship between the market value of the outstanding stock of titles in the hands of the public relative to the value of the net finance committed to the purchase of capital goods until both the marginal propensity to buy placements out of household savings and the actions of the Monetary Authority and the financial intermediaries who 'make' spot security markets are specified. (See Chapter 13 below.) Cf. N. Kaldor, 'Marginal Productivity and Macroeconomic Theories of Distribution', *Rev. Econ. Stud.* (1966), J. Robinson, *The Accumulation of Capital*, p. 230.

[2] Cf. R. F. Kahn, 'Some Notes on Liquidity Preference', *Manchester School* (1954) pp. 237–8. Financial intermediaries may also be involved, see Chapter 13 below.

[3] The analysis of the effect of changes in household wealth due to savings and the resulting flow-demand for securities will be developed in Chapters 11 and 13.

SECURITY PRICE LEVELS, SECOND-HAND PLACEMENTS, AND THE RATE OF INVESTMENT

At any point of time, firms will have a demand for a stock of capital which will depend on the discounted expected flow of future net income resulting from the utilisation of the services of capital relative to the acquisition cost of these services. Thus, for alternative acquisition costs, there will be different quantities of capital demanded. Given the stock of capital and its depreciation rate, there will be a market price based on market demand. As we have already pointed out, if this market price exceeds the minimum flow-supply price of capital, new capital goods will appear in the market, i.e. gross investment will be positive. Given the rate of depreciation and the market-demand price above the minimum flow-supply price, the annual rate of capital accumulation will be more rapid, the more elastic the supply conditions in the capital goods industry.

Each planning period, therefore, the firm will decide on the basis of a present-value calculation based on (a) its profit expectations, (b) the rate of interest, and (c) the current spot and forward market prices of capital assets, whether its current holdings of physical capital is optimal. If the firm believes it has too much capital relative to its long-term expectations then it may sell some of its stock (if a well-organised spot market for fixed capital exists). If the firm has too little capital goods, it may either (a) buy second-hand capital on the spot market or (b) the firm may order new investment goods. Of course, if the spot and forward market prices for capital goods is below the minimum flow-supply price, no new investment goods will be produced. If above, new capital goods will be produced. All this has been discussed above.

Entrepreneurs, however, may have an alternative market – the organised securities market dealing in second-hand titles to capital goods – which can sometimes be used to gain control of the future services of capital. As Keynes pointed out, because of the absence of any precise knowledge of the prospective yield of any long-lived assets, the daily re-evaluations of equities on the organised exchanges are based on a tacitly agreed upon convention, i.e. the existing market value of equities are '*uniquely correct* in relation to our existing knowledge' and the market value 'will only change in proportion to changes in this knowledge'.[1] Thus, a wealth-owner who holds equities as a store of value 'need not lose his sleep merely because he has not any notion what his investment will be worth ten years hence.'[2] It is not surprising therefore that (a) since equity-holding households are typically individuals who do not manage or have any knowledge (or even interest) in the long-run prospective yield of the capital assets that they legally own, and (b) since market valuations are a result of a convention established on 'the mass psychology of a large number of ignorant individuals',[3] the price of equities at any point of time need bear little relationship to entrepreneurial views of future profit opportunities.[4]

It is because the spot market for securities is so well-organised in modern economies, i.e. the transactions costs of moving between money and placements are very low, that each household may feel that its store of wealth is extremely liquid while there is no such thing as liquidity for the wealth of the community as a whole. As a consequence, portfolio balance decisions are, in an uncertain world, normally oriented towards short-term capital appreciation via spot market purchases and sales, rather than the expected, but uncertain, long-term income flow derivable from the underlying capital goods or

[1] Keynes, *The General Theory*, p. 152.

[2] ibid. p. 153. If there were no costs in converting securities into money and vice versa, then the only relevant date of realisation for which expectations of future spot prices are important would be the next moment in time. The decision to buy or hold securities today would simply depend on what the individual expected to happen between today and tomorrow, and expectations about later dates would not be relevant until tomorrow when decisions can be made afresh in the light of tomorrow's expectations about the day after tomorrow. Thus, with very low transactions costs, securities are held on the basis of short-term expectations about future spot prices and not on the views of the expected yield over the whole life of the asset, even if the latter could be ascertained. (When transactions costs approach infinity – as with the actual purchase of fixed capital goods – then expectations about future spot prices are irrelevant, and only the expected yield over the whole life of the asset bulks large in the decision-making process.)

[3] ibid. p. 154.

[4] Since transactions costs in the second-hand market for real capital goods are so much larger than in the securities markets, entrepreneurs who purchase real capital goods must take a much longer-term view than the buyers of securities.

even the quasi-contractual dividend yield. In such circumstances, especially when the market value of securities is determined, not by the terms one could expect to pay for the whole block of securities, but only by the small volume which is actually traded, it is not surprising to find the total value of securities unrelated to either the market value of the underlying capital goods or the long-run expected dividend yield.

Thus, if the price of equities is depressed (perhaps because households have increased their preference for money vis-à-vis titles to capital goods due to either a more pessimistic view of the future spot price of equities, or to a lowering of their confidence in their forecasts, or to a change in risk preferences), it may be possible to buy titles to capital goods at a price below the flow-supply or replacement price of the underlying capital (e.g. market value is less than replacement value or the valuation ratio is less than unity). Then individual firms can obtain control of the flow of services from the existing capital stock more cheaply by stock take-overs (mergers, amalgamations, etc.) than either by purchasing the second-hand capital goods directly on a spot market or by ordering new capital goods.[1] Since this will reduce the number of independent demanders of capital goods (E in equation (1) of Chapter 4), depressed spot security prices can retard the rate of capital formation (independent of the effect of higher discount rates) for society by reducing the demand in the capital goods market.[2]

Depressed security prices can also retard the rate of investment, *ceteris paribus*, because financial institutions will be unwilling to float new issues in such markets. Investment bankers and underwriters, concerned with the 'goodwill' they maintain

---

[1] This is particularly likely to occur if poor management of a firm has caused equity holders to have a pessimistic view about its future earning ability. Thus, a stock-takeover by an efficient management may improve the 'productivity' of the capital goods of the firm that has been swallowed up. (Also control of the first firm's assets may come without even buying a majority of the outstanding stock.)

[2] Cf. Keynes, *The General Theory*, p. 151. Joan Robinson suggests that take-overs may depress accumulation if firms finance purchase out of their own funds and therefore 'new equipment has to be financed by borrowing which is more expensive and less eligible than an expenditure of own finance'. J. Robinson, 'Own Rates of Interest', *Econ. Jour.* (1961) pp. 599–600.

with their customers, may be reluctant to provide financial arrangements for an entrepreneur who wishes to embark on new ventures, if the previous issues that have been under-written are showing a loss on their issue price. Under such circumstances, financial middlemen may well 'try to "protect" the market for their previous issues by restricting the output of new ones'.[1] The result will be to create an 'unsatisfied fringe' of would-be borrowers at the existing market rate, as underwriters are loathe to add pressure to an already depressed market.

If, on the other hand, the price of titles to capital goods is high relative to the supply price for capital goods so that the market value of equities exceeds the replacement value of the underlying capital goods (i.e. the valuation ratio exceeds unity) because perhaps households have increased confidence in the future in which they foresee large capital gains, then entre-preneurs will find it cheaper to order new equipment rather than attempt to gain control over the flow of services from existing capital goods via the purchases of second-hand equities. Moreover, as Keynes indicated, when equity prices are high 'there is an inducement to spend on a new project what may seem an extravagent sum if it can be floated off on the stock exchange at an immediate profit'[2] so that rising secu-rity prices can encourage underwriters to float new issues, thus making it easier for entrepreneurs to obtain finance at any given rate of interest than otherwise. The profit opportunities from floating new issues in a rising securities market will en-courage financial middlemen to actively search out and en-courage entrepreneurial plans for capital expansion.[3] As a result, the number of entrepreneurial investors who can obtain finance easily may increase, raising the demand for capital goods as either (a) households wish to reduce their holdings of idle balances, or (b) the high price of securities relative to their yields implies that firms can retain profits, that is with-hold cash balances from households, or (c) the banks via financial intermediaries are willing to provide additional bank deposits to a previously unsatisfied fringe of entrepreneurial

[1] Keynes, *Treatise on Money*, II 368. This aspect will be discussed in detail in Chapter 13.   [2] Keynes, *The General Theory*, p. 151.

[3] See Chapter 13 below.

borrowers as investment is undertaken. Accordingly, although there may be no direct relationship between portfolio balance decisions which depend upon household expectations of the future spot price of securities (i.e. liquidity preference), and the capital demand decisions of firms where the latter depend upon expected future profitability of capital services and the rate of discount and current offer price of capital-goods producers, there may be some interaction via either financing ability or the ability to take over second-hand real assets via merger. The actual rate of production of new investment goods will always depend upon (a) the existence of a discrepency between the market demand price of capital and the minimum flow-supply price of capital and (b) the supply elasticity of the capital-goods industries. Thus, though there may be a link between the security market and the market for capital goods, there is also 'many a slip twixt the cup and the lip'.

Keynes used 'the term *speculation* for the activity of forecasting the psychology of the [placement] market, and the term *enterprise* for the activity of forecasting the prospective yield of assets over their whole life'.[1] Placement market activity is, for the most part, independent of both investment activity and the rate at which new securities are being floated, i.e. $g(1 - \bar{h})$ $[p_k(s_k - d_k)]$ is likely to be exceedingly small relative to the total number of transactions occurring in the securities market. Organised placement market activity, because of its low transactions costs, is focused primarily on second-hand transactions and not new issues. Stock market activity depends almost entirely on people's view about how rich they are likely to be in the near future, i.e. changes in the public's expectations of future spot security prices are much more important than the volume of new issues relative to the flow-demand for securities in affecting the level of current security prices. Because the cost of moving into and out of securities is so low, the foundation for the public's daily re-evaluations of securities is evanescent, and wealth-holders can continuously churn over their portfolios in hopes of short-term capital appreciation. Thus placement owners who are active in the security markets tend to hold securities for capital gains rather than for income.

In modern economies, security markets are organised so

[1] Keynes, *The General Theory*, p. 158.

that the majority of traders can gamble on unknown and un-knowable future changes in the conventional basis of valua-tion of securities.[1] As a consequence the market value of equities will often appear to be quite absurd to 'a rational ob-server from the outside . . . [as] the vast majority of those who are concerned with the buying and selling of securities know almost nothing whatever about what they are doing'.[2] The buyers of securities do not normally possess the technical knowledge necessary profitably to operate the capital goods which the securities give them ownership to, for they possess neither the skill nor the time, energy, and desire necessary to learn how to utilise the capital goods in a manner which will provide net revenue over time; while the professional speculator is interested only in taking advantage of the expected mis-guided views of the crowd.[3] Nor need placement buyers possess such skill as long as transactions and carrying costs are so small that the potentially profitable date of realisation, for given expectations, is near enough in the future so that the money yield on the securities and/or the underlying capital goods is relatively negligible.[4]

If wealth-holders should take a rosier view of the future and therefore accept a lower current yield on a store of equity wealth for the promise (hope? expectation?) of continuing rapid capital appreciation, while the entrepreneurial view of the prospective yield on capital goods is sombre, then stock prices can rise almost without limit[5] (as long as the bullishness persists) without directly altering the demand for capital goods except via making finance more readily available to investors. In the limiting case, where entrepreneurial investors see no new profitable opportunities while households maintain their rosy view of future placement prices, placement prices can increase, the rate of interest will decline, while the demand for capital will remain virtually unchanged.

---

[1] Keynes, *The General Theory*, p. 159, *Treatise on Money*, II 361.

[2] Keynes, *Treatise on Money*, II 361.

[3] Keynes, *The General Theory*, pp. 154–8.

[4] Thus the lower the transactions costs, the more households are likely to ignore incomes and hold for capital gains.

[5] Unless offsetting action is undertaken by financial intermediaries who make the market in securities. See Chapter 13 below.

If, on the other hand, households should require a higher present return on placements in order to give up liquidity, perhaps because the future looks worse to them than it does to the entrepreneurs, then security prices will fall while the flow of new capital goods will not be affected except if (a) the price of titles to capital falls below the flow-supply price of capital; and/or (b) firms find their ability to obtain finance reduced as individuals increase their preference for money in their portfolios, and the supply of money remains unaltered so that entrepreneurial demands for capital are aborted by higher interest charges and/or credit rationing; and/or (c) the decrease in security prices colours entrepreneurial views about future expected net revenues of capital goods.

The only unequivocal links between the portfolio balance or liquidity preference behaviour and the demand for the hire-purchase of capital goods is via the usual Keynesian interest rate effect on the discounting of expected net revenue, and on changing financial conditions which can affect the size of the Keynesian fringe of unsatisfied borrowers. The existence of an exogenous money-creating banking system permits entrepreneurs to make investment decisions which can be incompatible with the public's portfolio preferences at the current rate of interest. If entrepreneurial investors can obtain finance then they can command the necessary resources to make their investment demands operational and ultimately it will be the market price of placements which will be the adjusting mechanism which will bring the public's portfolio balance decision into harmony with the available volume of securities which represent past and present needs for external funding for the investment projects undertaken. In a monetary economy, it is finance which provides the energy fuel which permits the investment tail to wag the portfolio balance dog.

No matter what the desired portfolio holdings of the public may be, the Monetary Authority and the banking system will be the balancing factor. By operating either directly or via financial intermediaries on the spot market for securities, and, laying down rules of the game either by law or custom, the Monetary Authority and the banks can control not only the spot price of placements and the volume of securities and money available for holding by the public, but also the availability of finance.[1] Thus the banking system can permit the firms to undertake any level of expenditure on newly produced capital goods – as long as there is any viability (i.e. acceptability) in the monetary system – that is as long as the wage rate is expected to remain relatively more sticky in terms of money than in terms of anything else, so that individuals are willing to enter into money contracts.

It is the existence of money-contracts, money customs, and money understandings which are sticky for long periods of time in tandem with changing levels of employment and some changes in money-wages and prices which permit the resource requirements of investor demands (primarily resulting from short-term financing via the banking system) and consumer demands (primarily from current income) to be met out of the resource base of the community. At less than full employment, access to additional bank finance permits entrepreneurs to order additional capital goods and thereby cause employment for otherwise unutilised resources; while at full employment additional bank finance permits the bidding up of offer prices and money wages (or the lengthening of queues) forcing those either on fixed contractual incomes or without easy access to credit facilities to reduce their demands, while simultaneously encouraging some members of the community to enter the labour force and expand the resource base.[2]

---

[1] Not surprisingly, in a world of uncertainty, the spot price in the placement market need not be an equilibrium one in the sense that all potential borrowers and lenders are being satisfied at the current price. Financial intermediaries and the banking system operate as buffers by building up and/or discharging inventories of securities under certain circumstances.

[2] These matters are dealt with in Chapters 2, 3, 12, 13 and 14.

CHAPTER 11

Finance and Accumulation – A First Simplified View

AT this stage it is possible to suggest a simplified financial mechanism which links the path of capital accumulation with the supply of money as the flow-supply aspects of securities are explicitly accounted for in the model.[1]

In order to start somewhere, assume initially a mythical stationary state economy. The spot market price for fixed capital exceeds the forward price by an amount which equals the expected quasi-rents foregone by accepting capital at the delivery date rather than immediately. The forward price is equal to both the short-period and the long-run flow-supply price. New capital goods (financed internally via the business sector's depreciation reserves) are merely replacing capital as it wears out in each time period. Assuming no change in the aggregate of wealth-holders' expectations, confidence, or risk preferences, the demand and supply curves for placements are fixed and can be represented as D_p^1 and S_p in Fig. 11.1 (a). The price of placements is unchanged at a price of p_1 as the placement market clears in each period while the economy remains in the stationary state.[2] Assume that in time period t, there is an increase in profit expectations stimulated by some non-monetary factor such as a new discovery, a change in tastes, or even a change in political climate. If the demand for capital goods is to increase, it will be necessary for entrepreneurs to obtain additional command of resources. If additional

[1] A more complex view will be presented in Chapter 13.
[2] In such a hypothetical and unrealistic economy, any security transactions must represent just offsetting changing views of individual bulls and bears, while the public's aggregate bull-bear position remains unchanged.

finance is forthcoming (usually via credit creation by the banking system) then the market demand for the hire-purchase of capital goods will increase[1] (for as we always teach in courses in microeconomics, demand for any commodity implies want *plus* the ability to pay).

For accumulation to occur, two conditions must be fulfilled: (1) entrepreneurs must have the 'animal spirits' which encourage the belief in additional profit opportunities and (2) entrepreneurs must be able to command sufficient resources to put their projects into execution. Animal spirits may depend at least in part on non-monetary phenomena but the obtaining of command of resources requires the co-operation of the banking system and financial markets. If the banking system and related financial institutions acquiesce then there will be net investment as the output of the capital goods industry increases.

Since the previous level of capital demand was being adequately financed, there must have been sufficient transaction cash balances in the industrial circulation to maintain the initial level of consumption and gross investment transactions. With the improved profit expectations, however, there is an additional demand for money to finance the additional demand for capital even at the initial income level. Thus some firms will, *ceteris paribus*, require additional transaction cash balances (the finance motive) to order additional capital goods. They may engage an investment banker (or a promoter) who, after convincing himself of the correctness of the investors' expectations, will borrow funds from a commercial bank on a short-term loan to finance the increased demand for investment goods thus tying up the funds of the banks until after the new capital goods are produced and securities are floated to fund this investment. (In the case of financing increments in working capital, the firms may borrow directly from the banks, repaying the short-term loan with receipts from the sale of the final product.)

Accordingly, if the entire increase in the cost of capital goods is borrowed from the banks, who provide the money by creating additional bank deposits, then, *ceteris paribus*, the quantity of money is increased,

[1] Keynes, *Treatise on Money*, I 149.

$$\Delta M = \Delta C \tag{1}$$

when ΔM is the change in the money supply and ΔC is the cost of the increased orders for the output of the capital goods industry, that is

$$\Delta C = p_k \Delta I_g = p_k \Delta I_n \tag{2}$$

where p_k is the flow-supply price of currently produced capital goods, ΔI_g is the change in the quantity of gross investment produced, and ΔI_n is the change in the quantity of net investment goods produced.[1]

These newly created funds will immediately be used in the industrial circulation by the firms to make payments which ultimately become income to owners of the factors engaged in the capital-goods industry. There will be, therefore, an increase in the money balances of these households *pari passu* with the growth in investment expenditures as the additional capital goods move down the pipeline; hence the real wealth of the community (but not that part directly owned by the household sector) and savers' money balances increase simultaneously during the gestation period.[2] Some households who were previously in portfolio balance now find their real income *and* their money holdings have increased. They will, of course, increase their planned consumption expenditures and consequently hold some of the additional money for transactions purposes. The remainder becomes household savings (S_h) and the households must decide in what form to store wealth. This process continues over other households as the multiplier – and income velocity – works itself out. As this process progresses, the induced increased demand for consumption goods will require producers of consumer goods to finance additional

[1] Thus in the t period, $\Delta C^t = p_k I_n^t$ since the economy was in the stationary state in the $t-1$ period and therefore $I_n^{t-1} = 0$; and hence $I_n^t = \Delta I_n$. If the economy had not been in the stationary state in the earlier period, then $I_n^t > \Delta I_n$.

[2] For simplicity of exposition we will ignore, for the moment, the possibility of retained profits by the capital producing firms which can be used to finance fixed capital investments. Later the analysis will however permit retained profits to be used to finance expansion in working capital. To the extent that profits are retained for fixed capital purposes, external finance of plant and equipment as a proportion of total investment is important. This aspect will be developed in Chapter 13.

investment in working capital which, for simplicity, can be assumed to be financed by additional borrowing of short-term funds from the banks. Consequently the increased quantity of money will equal the additional net fixed capital *plus* the additional working capital expenditures.

The increments in household wealth, i.e. current household savings must, in a money economy, be initially in the form of money holdings. These savings imply an increase in the public's total store of value (V) and therefore a rightward shift in the demand for placements curve in Fig. 11.1 (b) from D^1, that is $f'_{6V_{(Sh)}} > 0$ as the flow of savings induces a flow-demand for securities. The magnitude of this shift in the demand schedule for placements depends upon m, marginal propensity to buy placements out of household savings. If $m = 1$, which is the usual assumption of the neoclassical and neo-keynesian schools,[1] then (at the initial price level of p_1) *ultimately* all savings will be held in the form of securities. If $m = 0$, on the other hand, then at the p_1 price level, all household savings will be ultimately held in the form of idle balances. There is no reason to believe that m equals either of these extreme values; Keynes argued that the $0 < m < 1$.[2] Accordingly as the multiplier (and income velocity) process works its way through the economy some of the new money is absorbed in the industrial circulation and some in portfolios.

The magnitude of the shift if $m = 1$, for example, will be such that at the original spot price of p_1 in Fig. 11.1 (b), the demand curve will move from point A to point B. This shift from A to B is indicative of an increase in demand which is just sufficient to absorb a volume of placements (at a price of p_1 per unit) so that purchases equal the increment in household wealth, i.e. $FABG$ in Fig. 11.1 (b) equals aggregate household savings. At any price below p_1, however, the total value of the public's initial holding of securities will decline; there is a capital loss effect on the demand for placements such that if $j > 0$, the

---

[1] See F. P. R. Brechling, 'A Note on Bond-Holding and the Liquidity Preference Theory of Interest', *Rev. of Econ. Stud.* **24** (1957) pp. 195–6.

[2] Keynes, 'The Ex-Ante Theory', *Econ. Jour.* (1937) p. 668. If there was no uncertainty about the future, then m would equal unity and decision-makers would never hold money as a store of value. See Keynes, *The General Theory*, pp. 208–9.

placement demand curve, at any price below p_1 will not shift out sufficiently to purchase additional placements equal to household savings even if $m = 1$. Similarly, if $j > 0$, at any price

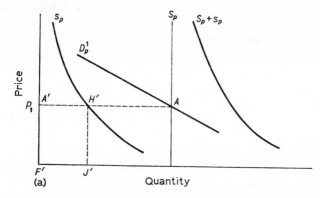

Fig. 11.1 (a)

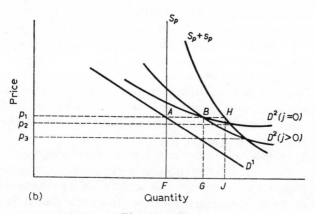

Fig. 11.1 (b)

above p_1, the demand for additional placements could exceed current savings out of household income as capital gains encourages additional placement purchases. If, on the other hand, $j = 0$, a change in the spot price of placements will not affect the demand for placements, i.e. there is no capital gain or loss effect and therefore, if $m = 1$, at any price the increase in demand for placements, i.e. the flow-demand for securities, will involve additional purchases which just equal household savings over the period. Thus, if $m = 1$, curves $D^2_{(j=0)}$ and $D^2_{(j>0)}$ in Fig. 11.1 (b) represent the two possible cases where the resulting change in demand for securities over the period has been incorporated in the new stock demand for placements at the end of the period. The $D^2_{(j=0)}$ curve will have a rectangular hyperbolic relationship with respect to D^1 since the flow-demand for securities, at any price, will, *ceteris paribus*, equal the given level of household savings in the period. Thus, if $m = 1$, the area of the rectangle obtained by taking the horizontal difference between the initial D^1 and the new $D^2_{(j=0)}$ demand curve for securities and multiplying it by the ordinate height of the price variable at any given price, will equal total household savings. (More generally, of course, the area of the appropriate rectangle will always equal the marginal propensity to buy placements out of household savings multiplied by aggregate household savings, no matter what the value of m.)

In essence, entrepreneurs normally use short-term borrowings to finance both total working capital *and* the increment in fixed capital in the period. Working capital loans will be repaid out of sales proceeds, if short-period sales expectations are met. Increments in fixed capital, it is assumed initially, will be entirely funded via the issue of new securities.[1] The quantity of placements which must be floated completely to fund any given cost of net investment in fixed capital varies inversely with the market price of placements. Assuming that in any period replacements are entirely financed internally from amortisation funds, and assuming repayment of short-term bank loans for working capital is accomplished from the current sales proceeds, and given the cost of net investment in fixed capital which is to be entirely funded by selling new issues to the public (i.e. $g = 1$ and $h = 0$) then the flow-supply function of securities as given in equation (3) of Chapter 10 reduces to

$$s_p = \frac{p_k(s_k - d_k)}{p_p} = \frac{p_k I_n}{p_p} \tag{3}$$

This flow-supply curve shows alternative quantities of placements which will have to be floated at alternative prices in

[1] The difference between internal and external funding will be discussed in Chapter 13.

order to finance a given cost of net investment in fixed capital; it is represented by the rectangular hyperbola, s_p, in Fig. 11.1 (a). Thus at the initial price level of p_1, $F'\mathcal{J}'$ securities will have to be floated to fund net investment in fixed capital, so that $F'A'H'\mathcal{J}'$ equals the given cost of net investment,[1] which is $p_k I_n$. The spot price of placements, therefore, determines the amount of securities which must be floated in order to fund a long-term capital project, whereas the amount of liquidity out of current income which the public is willing to give up (the flow-demand for securities) depends on the marginal propensity to purchase placements out of household savings.[2] The total market supply curve for the period can be represented by $S_p + s_p$ in Fig. 11.1 (a). By placing the market supply curve $S_p + s_p$ onto Fig. 11.1 (b) we can readily see what will happen in the market for securities.

Given that the total volume of net investment in fixed capital will be externally financed, *if* it is further assumed that aggregate household savings equals net investment while $m = 1$, then $FABG$ in Fig. 11.1 (b) would be equal to $F'A'H'\mathcal{J}'$ in Fig. 11.1 (a) and therefore the flow-demand for securities is, *ceteris paribus*, proceeding in step with the flow-supply of securities (new issues) at the current spot price of placements.

Of course since m is likely to be less than unity, while net investment may be partly internally financed, there is no need for $FABG$ to equal $FAH\mathcal{J}$. For example, it is possible that at the spot price of p_1, $FABG < FAH\mathcal{J}$, as shown in Fig. 11.1 (b), so that the flow-demand for securities is less than the flow-supply, i.e. excess flow-demand is negative at the original price level. If at the same time, $j = 0$, then the new market demand curve is hyperbolically related to the downward sloping D^1 curve. Since the total market supply curve has the same rectangular hyperbola relationship to the vertical S_p curve, the new intersection must occur at some lower market price, say p_2. Of course, if $j > 0$, then the intersection will occur

[1] Net investment is defined as the value of the change in the capital stock and not as the change in the value of the capital stock. In a world of uncertainty this distinction is of crucial importance. See Keynes, *Treatise on Money*, II 126 and R. F. Kahn, 'Exercises in the Analysis of Growth', *Oxford Economic Papers* (1959) pp. 143–4.

[2] Cf. R. G. Hawtrey, *The Art of Central Banking* (London: Longmans, Green, 1932) p. 327.

at even a lower market price, say p_3. The revenue from the sale of new placements at the market-clearing price will be sufficient to pay off the outstanding short-term bank loans, thus making the bank credit available again to finance another project. Of course, if the new issue underwriters had correctly foreseen the placement market conditions, they may have been reluctant to aid in the initial financing of the net investment projects, for their desire to maintain their reputation for success (and their good-will) with their customers depends on their protecting the price of previous issues.[1] Consequently, financial market conditions, which may be self-imposed by financial institutions, can restrict growth even if entrepreneurs have the proper animal spirits.

In sum, if, for example, the liquidity preference of households is such that they do not wish to plough all their current savings into securities, and if commercial banks and/or the Monetary Authority do not purchase some additional long-term securities as entrepreneurs attempt to expand the stock of fixed capital entirely via external funding, then the expected return per dollar of market value of placements will rise (as security prices fall) in order to induce households to alter their relative portfolio holdings from money to placements so that entrepreneurs can fund their current short-term borrowing. The additional short-term finances obtained from the banking system and used initially to pay for the resources committed to the increment in capital goods output becomes a revolving fund[2] which is being constantly extinguished when firms repay their bank loans and which can be immediately regenerated only if new borrowing is sufficient to maintain the current level of investment expenditure and economic activity.

If, therefore, the rate of return on placements is to be either kept constant or reduced as the stock of capital expands in a growing economy, then the banking system must absorb those titles which the public does not wish to hold currently, and the quantity of money will, in general, have to increase by an amount that exceeds the cost of net investment in both fixed and working capital.

The increase in the quantity of money in each period which

---

[1] See Keynes, *Treatise on Money*, II 360 and Chapter 13 below.
[2] Cf. Keynes, 'The Ex-Ante Theory', p. 666.

would be necessary to keep the rate of interest constant, once net investment is increasing in each period, and expectations about the rate of change of future placement prices is unchanged, will depend upon (1) the magnitudes of g and h, (2) the marginal propensity to increase active balances as planned transactions increase, and (3) m – the marginal propensity to buy placements out of household savings (which, of course, depends in part on the cost of moving between money and securities). If $g = 1$, $h = 0$, $m = 1$ and if the demand for active balances is always proportional to real output (so that, for example, there is no change in the degree of industrial integration), and if the desired ratio of fixed and working capital to the planned production flow is a constant, then the required proportionate increase in the money supply that will keep the rate of interest unchanged is equal to the proportionate change in the total cost of capital and output flow per period. If all these conditions are fulfilled, then the flow-demand for placements by households will increase at the same pace as the flow-supply of placements. If these conditions are not met – unless there are exactly offsetting influences – the rate of increase in the money supply which will leave interest rates unaltered, will not be equal to the rate of planned or warranted growth of capital goods.

Since in our example above, gross investment increased in the t period, aggregate economic activity in period t will be greater than in $t - 1$, and the economy will depart from the stationary state. The funds which are obtained by floating the new issue in period t are used to retire the short-term bank loans for fixed capital and, therefore, are available at the banks to finance the same level of gross fixed capital investment in the $t + 1$ period as in the t period.

The veracity of Keynes's dictum that 'if investment is proceeding at a steady rate, finance . . . [is] a revolving fund of a more or less constant amount'[1] is readily demonstrable. If in $t + 1$, there is no change in investment activity, then firms should have no difficulty in financing the same level of investment as in the t period via short-term bank borrowing. Thus the money for finance will be regenerated while there is, by

[1] J. M. Keynes, 'Alternative Theories of the Rate of Interest', *Econ. Jour.* (1937) p. 247.

hypothesis, no change in the quantity of money or the flow of production and income and consequently there will be the same level of household savings in the $t+1$ period as in the t period. If $m=1$, therefore, the demand for placements will increase sufficiently to absorb, at the current spot market price, enough new issues to fund the entire short-term borrowing. In such a situation, the planned net debtor position of firms has increased *pari passu* with the planned net creditor position of households (at the current rate of interest). Obviously then, finance is a revolving fund which need not be augmented *even* if net investment is positive as long as investment and economic activity are unchanged from period to period and households are willing to hold all their increments in wealth (savings) in the form of placements at the going rate of interest.[1] Of course, a constant level of fixed investment each period implies a declining rate of capital growth and economic stagnation as the level of economic activity remains unchanged.

If, on the other hand, an improvement in profit expectations in $t+1$ is posited, then there is an additional demand for money to finance an *increment* in *net* investment in $t+1$ over net investment in the tth period, and if the banks provide these additional balances via short-term credit expansion for financing the associated increments in fixed *and* working capital, then at the higher $t+1$ equilibrium level of output, the additional household savings will shift the placement demand curve out more rapidly (if $m=1$) so as to permit the flotation of a new issue large enough to fund the entire net investment in fixed capital at the current security price level. Consequently, if the rate of interest is to be kept unchanged when $m=1$, $g=1$, and $h=0$, the money supply must grow *pari passu* with the increment in net investment.

It might be helpful to inquire as to the outcome in the $t+1$ period if the banks were unable or unwilling to expand the money supply, that is if $M_{t+1}=M_t$, when firms increased their desires for capital goods as a result of improved profit expectations. (For ease of exposition that portion of net investment

---

[1] Or more precisely, if households are willing to hold the increment in wealth in the form of securities which just equals the external funding desires of firms.

which can be financed from the revolving fund will be ignored, and only the increments in net investment will be explicitly handled.) If additional finance is to be obtained, and if the banks are unwilling to create it, then some members of the public must be induced to give up some of their portfolio money holdings in exchange for securities, if entrepreneurs are to carry through their desire to increase their orders of fixed capital goods. Hence the market price of securities must initially fall (the rate of interest must rise) in order to encourage money-holding households to substitute placements for money in their desired portfolios.[1] As the additional investment projects are carried out, economic activity increases and additional money is absorbed into the industrial circulation (active balances), leaving less money permanently available for portfolio balance, so that, given liquidity preferences, security prices are permanently lower (the rate of interest is higher) than in the tth period. Of course, the equilibrium level of output in $t + 1$ will be lower and the interest rate higher than if the money supply had been expanded in pace with the additional investment demand.

Every actual increase in the level of externally funded investment will, if the money supply is unchanged, increase the quantity of placements and reduce the quantity of money permanently available as a store of value; therefore, placement prices will, *ceteris paribus*, decline. The greater the increase in net investment demanded per unit of time, the greater the quantity of active balances demanded and therefore, the greater the reduction in idle balances. Thus, the greater the growth in demand for net investment, *ceteris paribus*, the greater increase in the quantity of placements supplied relative to the increase in quantity demanded, and therefore, the greater the decline in placement prices (the more rapid the rise in interest rates). This lack of finance will ultimately limit the rate of capital accumulation as another 'liquidity trap' restrains expansion[2] since

a heavy demand for investment can exhaust the market and be held up by the lack of financial facilities on reasonable

[1] Cf. J. G. Gurley and E. S. Shaw, 'Financial Aspects of Economic Development', *Amer. Econ. Rev.* (1955) **45**, p. 525.   [2] See Chapter 8.

terms. It is, to an important extent, the financial facilities which regulate the *pace* of new investment [at less than full employment] ... too great a press of uncompleted investment decisions is quite capable of exhausting available finance, if the banking system is unwilling to increase the supply of money.[1]

Thus, in any expansion, as Keynes argued:

the banks hold the key position in the transition from a lower to a higher scale of activity. If they refuse to relax [i.e. to provide additional finance], the growing congestion of the short-term loan market or the new issue market, as the case may be, will inhibit the improvement, no matter how thrifty the public purpose to be out of their future income. On the other hand, there will always be *exactly* enough ex-post saving to take up the ex-post investment and so release the finance which the latter has been previously employing. *The investment market can become congested through a shortage of cash. It can never become congested through a shortage of saving* [or savers not *wanting* to own the titles to the real wealth (at some reduced placement price level) that has been produced]. *This is the most fundamental of my conclusions within this field.*[2]

It should be apparent, therefore, that if growth is to be sustained while liquidity preferences are unaltered, the money supply must increase as output rises. In an uncertain world, however, where expectations are volatile and unpredictable (rather than the datum assumed in our model), the relationship between the required increase in the money supply necessary to finance the increase in real wealth and to compensate for changes in liquidity preferences is much too complex to be handled by any simple rule. Money clearly matters in the process of economic growth in a monetary economy, but a simple rule can be no substitute for wise management of the money supply.[3]

---

[1] Keynes, 'Alternative Theories', p. 248.
[2] Keynes, 'The Ex-Ante Theory', pp. 668–9. Italics added.
[3] Keynes, *Treatise on Money*, I, ch. 15, esp. pp. 253–4.

FINANCE, CAPITAL ACCUMULATION, AND
PUBLIC POLICY

Our mechanism has emphasised that for increases in capital
demand to be effective, firms must be able to obtain additional
finance. Thus, for a steady rate of capital accumulation and
growth to occur, the banking system and the Monetary
Authority must play an essential role by providing the initial
funds on terms which investors deem attractive. It is at the
level of financing investment projects that the money supply
plays an essential role in stimulating economic growth in a
monetised economy, and not at the level of portfolio balances,
for the banking system is always capable of offsetting any change
in desired portfolio composition. Keynes wrote a long time ago
that 'the rate at which the world's wealth has accumulated
has been far more variable than habits of thrift have been'.[1]
To this dictum we may add 'or habits of portfolio balance'. If
we can expand Keynes's *Treatise* analogy, we might note that
the Seven Wonders of the World were not built by either
habits of thrift *or* portfolio balance; rather they were the
result of the desire for personal capital monuments by kings
and other important personages plus these people's ability
to obtain finance in order to command the necessary real
resources. (Of course, a respected government – or a feared one
– has no difficulty in finding a means of finance.[2]) Once the
active decision to increase the real wealth of the world in this
form was implemented all that the ancient households could
do was to adjust their savings and portfolios in the light of the
variables that were left open to them.

In the next two chapters, the analysis will deal with the
mechanism of how entrepreneurial desires for accumulation
interact with the behaviour of financial institutions and the
savings behaviour of different economic groups (as well
as the distribution of claims among these groups) in a
growing economy. Many of these matters have been given
special emphasis in recent years in the debates between the
Neo-keynesian and neoclassical schools, and between the
Monetarists and Bastard Keynesian schools.

[1] ibid. p. 149.
[2] J. Robinson, *The Accumulation of Capital*, p. 276, n. 1.

CHAPTER 12

Savings, Income Distribution, Growth, and Finance

IN the real sector of the economy, at any point of time, the realised level of effective demand depends on (a) the supply offerings and hiring commitments of entrepreneurs in conjunction with (b) the spending (and therefore savings) behaviour of the various economic decision-makers. Spending behaviour can be viewed as consisting of two basic types:

(1) those *endogenous expenditures* which are directly associated with currently generated monetary income, and

(2) those *autonomous expenditures* which are not constrained by, or necessarily associated with, current income. In a simple two sector economic model, the former are associated with consumption spending and the latter with investment spending.

In a monetary economy, both consumption and investment demand require the current availability of monetary claims on the output produced by the contemporary services of resources, but only the former are geared into the current period's income – and goods-generating processes, while the latter is reliant upon financial conditions and the accompanying financial rules and institutions which permit economic units to obtain claims on resource services in excess of their current monetary incomes. The financial institution may act merely as a broker between borrowing and lending economic units, that is as a financial intermediary to transfer existing monetary claims from decision units who wish to spend less than present income (savers) to those who wish to spend more (investors) on resource-using outputs; or financial institutions may create *new* claims[1] so that current household savers need not give up their immediate potential claim on resources, even though they currently do not exercise it, while investors obtain additional immediate claims which they have not earned but which they will exercise in the current period.

Given entrepreneurial expectations of future profits opportunities, it is

(1) the propensity to save out of contemporary money income of the various savings groups,
(2) the distribution of current income among savers,
(3) the relation of the savers to the financial markets (i.e. the portfolio choice of savers), and
(4) the provision of monetary claims to investors by financial institutions,

which are the 'independent' forces upon which the accumulation of capital is dependent in a modern monetary economy. If, however, there is a banking system which is willing to create and/or destroy monetary claims in pursuit of its goals, then the banking system can always offset the portfolio choices of savers and thereby remove (3) as an independent force affecting accumulation.

PROPENSITIES TO SAVE, CAPITAL REQUIREMENTS, AND GROWTH

In Chapter 5 it was demonstrated that, given the money wage rate and the productivity of labour, the resulting levels of effective demand and gross profits are primarily functions of two factors: (i) the savings propensities out of wages and gross profits and (ii) the volume of gross investment expenditures. Moreover, if entrepreneurial expectations of sales revenues are being met, i.e. if, in the aggregate, expected effective demand equals realised effective demand, then the services of resources contractually hired by firms are being paid a sum equal to their economic value in the eyes of the entrepreneurs; for neo-keynesian entrepreneurs, at least, the resulting production and sale of standard volume during the period yields 'normal' profits.

[1] Or destroy old claims.

Accordingly, if firms are in equilibrium in a period they are utilising a stock of capital goods which they believe is most convenient and desirable (least costly) for the production of the current output objective. This ratio of desired stock of capital goods to desired output flow per period is, in the aggregate, Harrod's *required capital-output ratio* (which Harrod defines as *net of replacement*[1]). The numerator of this ratio is readily derivable from the stock demand for capital schedule of Chapter 4, and is therefore a function of (i) entrepreneurial expectations of current and future points of effective demand,[2] (ii) the rate of discount firms require in evaluating the expected quasi rents associated with future points of effective demand and (iii) the flow-supply price of producible capital goods.[3] Thus, given entrepreneurial views about the growth of effective demand and the rate of discount they use to evaluate streams of expected quasi-rents, and given the inherited stock of capital and its rate of depreciation, entrepreneurs, each period, may desire to expand capacity. If they can obtain finance they will then enter into some level of contractual agreement for the acceptance of delivery of a certain volume of new capital goods – gross investment – during the period, and thereby generate a level of aggregate income as specified by equation (1) of Chapter 5. If the ensuing level of effective demand just matches this period's sales expectations, then aggregate income in the period will have been distributed between wages (or more generally contractual income) and profits (residual income) in

[1] Harrod, *Money*, p. 192. Harrod often emphasises the ratio of desired new capital to the increment in output which this net investment will sustain. This emphasis is based 'on the idea that existing output can be sustained by existing capital and that additional capital is only required to sustain additional output' – Harrod, *Towards a Dynamic Economics*, p. 82. Accordingly, it is possible to associate the required capital-output ratio with the entire stock of capital.

[2] Although Harrod tends to associate C_r with the current period's output flow, it should be obvious that since fixed capital goods, by the very nature, provide yields over a long period of time, what is deemed a convenient stock of capital must depend not only on this period's output, but the entire expected future production stream.

[3] In the typical 'Harrod'-type growth model, the rate of discount and the supply price are assumed constant. Thus, if, for example, effective demand is expected to grow at three per cent per annum, then capital requirements will grow at three per cent per annum.

accordance with the contractual expectational relationship as expressed via the wage bill line and the aggregate supply function at the point of effective demand.

Given the savings propensities out of wages (s_w) and gross profits (s_c) there is, of course, for any given level of gross income *and* its distribution, a unique level of planned aggregate savings, where these planned savings are defined in the Keynesian sense as the aggregate predilection of income recipients to defer current endogenous spending (out of current income) on newly produced (resource-using) goods, and instead, to transfer currently generated monetary claims on services of resources to some indefinite and uncertain future period. This level of planned savings, when expressed as a fraction of current aggregate income is the planned savings ratio,[1] s. In essence, s indicates that fraction of aggregate income which is not directly used by the recipients to finance their endogenous spending. For analytical convenience and simplicity, Harrod has assumed an unchanging value for this savings ratio for any given level of income, although he has recognised that there is no reason why savings need be a constant fraction of income.[2] One of the major differences, therefore, between Harrod's (and Keynes's *General Theory*) analysis and the neo-keynesian analysis of Robinson, Kaldor, and Pasinetti is that the former implicitly assume that changes in the distribution of income between wages and profits are explicitly connected only with changes in the level of employment, while the Neo-keynesians emphasise differences in aggregate savings ratios due to different distributions between wages and profits at any given level of aggregate income and employment (and for Pasinetti and Kaldor this level must be full employment[3]).

In any period, the production of the economy can be divided into two parts, namely (1) *available output* which is in a form

---

[1] Harrod includes planned savings by firms as well as the planned savings out of income by households in s. Obviously then, s is a weighted average of s_w and s_c.

[2] Harrod, *Money*, p. 192. The planned savings ratio can change if either the level of aggregate income changes, and/or the savings propensities change, and/or the distribution of income changes.

[3] For example, see N. Kaldor, 'Some Fallacies on the Interpretation of Kaldor', *Rev. of Econ. Stud.* (1970) p. 6.

which is immediately available for consumption use by households, and (2) *non-available output* which in its current state is not readily absorbable by consumers.[1] In a two-sector model, non-available output can be associated with the current flow of production from the capital goods producing industries. If the proportion of aggregate gross money income (including gross profits) generated in the capital goods producing industries differs from the savings ratio which entrepreneurs expect (or 'desire') for a given level of employment, then the realisable level of effective demand associated with that level of employment will differ from the level of effective demand which entrepreneurs will 'expect' or require if they are going to hire, in the aggregate, that level of workers. If, for example, for a given level of employment, the proportion of total sales proceeds that will be realisable in the capital goods industry exceeds the 'expected' or 'desired' savings ratio, i.e. if the demands exceed supply (or the planned savings ratio of income recipients is less than that expected by entrepreneurs), then if entrepreneurs undertake the associated hiring and production commitments they will be exhilarated by purchasers clamouring for their current flow of output. Consequently they will deem the current stock of fixed and working capital goods insufficient to sustain existing demand, much less to provide for next period's expected growth in turnover. Moreover, if entrepreneurial long-term expectations about the rate of growth of effective demand are unchanged despite the current period's surprise, i.e. if the expected rate of change of demand from the current level is unchanged, then according to Harrod, firms will desire to increase their orders for new capital goods in future periods (above what the demand for capital goods would have been if there were no surprise in the current period) so that the current conceived 'shortage' of capital can be eliminated and the total stock of capital available in the next period will be the most convenient for next period's standard volume flow of output. This additional demand for capital goods in the next period in order to eliminate the current shortage will, however, increase the actual rate of growth of effective demand even further above the 'expected' or 'warranted' rate of growth.[2]

---

[1] Cf. Keynes's use of these terms, *Treatise on Money*, I 127.

[2] Harrod, *Towards a Dynamic Economics*, p. 86.

Harrod has defined the warranted rate of growth (G_w) as

$$G_w = \frac{s_d}{C_r} \qquad (1)$$

Given the desired relationship between the stock of capital goods and the output flow per period as embodied in C_r, the warranted rate of growth in effective demand is that rate which will just 'justify' the capacity that producers are installed in each period,[1] so that s_d is Harrod's 'desired' or expected ratio of aggregate savings to income where this desired ratio is the one implicit in entrepreneurial expectations of short-period sales proceeds. Between any two periods, therefore, there is some increment in demand which will make entrepreneurs satisfied with the increased investment commitments they are currently undertaking. If the realised change in effective demand associated via the multiplier with a change in investment spending is equal to that which entrepreneurs expect, then the actual and warranted growth rates coincide as the planned and expected (or desired) savings ratios are equal. If on the other hand, $s \neq s_d$, entrepreneurs will be surprised by sales realisations and further entrepreneurial action based on current period surprise will further widen the gap between the actual rate of growth and the (assumed) unchanged warranted rate.

Finally, Harrod has developed the concept of a natural rate of growth (G_n) which is determined by the growth in the working population and the current potential for technical progress. G_n represents the potential growth in total output in the economy if it is already at full employment. In Harrod's view, G_n 'is not determined by the wishes of persons and companies as regards savings'.[2] In a free market economy, therefore, it would be fortuitous if either the warranted or the actual rate of growth equalled the natural rate. Given the factors which determine C_r, the natural rate of growth merely determines what savings ratio is compatible with growth at full employment – the aggregate savings behaviour consonant with a Golden Age. If, however, individuals in the aggregate plan to save more out of full employment income than the Golden Age savings ratio, the economy will be unable to maintain full

---

[1] Harrod, *Money*, p. 195. 'G_w is the entrepreneurial equilibrium', Harrod, *Towards a Dynamic Economics*, p. 87.   [2] Harrod, *Money*, p. 196.

employment; while if individuals plan to save less, aggregate demand will exceed aggregate supply at full employment. In the Harrod–Keynes analysis there is no automatic mechanism which assures that individual decisions result in a Golden Age. Hence, if it is socially desirable to keep the economy on a natural rate of growth path in a free market economy, and if individuals will not voluntarily maintain the Golden Age savings ratio, then government savings or dis-savings via fiscal policy can, in Harrod's view, operate as the balancing wheel. In a centrally-planned economy, on the other hand, regulation of the mark-up of market prices over production costs can provide a regulatory mechanism of the actual savings ratio similar to fiscal policy.[1]

Thus, for example, in a free market monetary economy, if the savings ratio is so great that the stock of plant and equipment which entrepreneurs deem most desirable for the flow of output which can be expected to be purchased by buyers out of full employment income is not sufficient to employ all the workers willing to offer their services on the market at the going wage rate, then even if entrepreneurs correctly perceive the situation, the warranted and actual rate of growth will be less than the natural rate. The resulting Limping Golden Age is simply due to the fact that income recipients, in the aggre-

---

[1] ibid. p. 197. Kaldor, however, has insisted that there is a mechanism that operates, even in a free market economy, which assures that the warranted rate adjusts itself to the natural rate (see Kaldor, 'Some Fallacies', p. 6). In Kaldor's view the mechanism that is basic to the Kaldor-Pasinetti variant of the neo-keynesian analysis is the greater flexibility of profit margins (mark-ups) to money-wage rates which alters the income distribution between wages and profits and brings the actual and 'desired' savings ratio into the required relationship with $G_n . C_r$. Thus, in effect, Harrod and the neo-keynesians agree on the relevance of income redistribution – at least for a planned economy – via the pricing mechanism to bring about full employment growth. (The implications of the neo-keynesian requirement of greater flexibility of profit margins relative to money wages for a capitalist-monetary economy will be discussed in detail in the next section of this chapter.)

Harrod has indicated that the simple assumption of a constant savings ratio in his initial analysis is a virtue in that at the time he was developing his ideas, it would have been undesirable 'to revert to an elaborate analysis of the conjugation of various possible profit shares with alternative growth rates'. R. F. Harrod, 'Harrod After Twenty Years – A Comment', *Economic Journal*, **80** (1970) p. 738.

gate, desire to hold from current income non-resource utilising things which are capable of transferring purchasing power to meet the uncertainties of the future and whose aggregate value exceeds the costs of maintaining and increasing the stock of capital goods that entrepreneurs believe the economy would need for its production if it was proceeding at its full employment growth potential.[1] In other words, if households desire to augment their wealth-holdings (either in the form of money or securities) at a rate out of full employment income which exceeds the needs of firms to externally finance the expansion of capital at the natural rate of growth of capacity, then growth at full employment can not be maintained.

The ability to transfer purchasing power over time in the form of money and securities which will 'keep', which involve negligible costs of storage and safe custody, which can be readily resold on spot markets, and which are not readily augmentable by applying additional resource services to their production must cause the economy to 'suffer the fate of Midas'[2] whenever the aggregate supply price of bringing the stock of productive facilities up to the level necessary to provide full employment output is less than the value of

> the aggregate desire on the part of the public to make provision for the future, even with full employment. ...This disturbing conclusion depends, of course, on the assumption that the propensity to consume and the rate of investment are not deliberately controlled in the social interest but are mainly left to the influences of *laissez-faire*[3]

Thus, for example, when the planned savings ratio is greater than the savings requirement for a growth at full employment, traditional Harrod–Keynes solution is to increase the aggregate spending via government purchases of new output financed by deficits which give the public 'marketable bits of paper'[4] which can then be held by the public as a means of transferring command over time.

[1] Harrod, *Money*, p. 198.
[2] Keynes, *The General Theory*, p. 219.   [3] ibid. pp. 218–19.
[4] Harrod, *Money*, p. 199. Harrod, of course, would not deny the possibility of altering aggregate savings behaviour by redistributing income via fiscal policy. The political feasibility of this latter approach is, however, another matter.

In sum, then, in a monetary, market-oriented economy, the savings behaviour of income recipients plays a double-edged role in determining (a) whether the economy can maintain an equilibrium rate of growth in the sense as to whether aggregate spending behaviour by the public is compatible with enterpreneurial sales expectations and (b) whether such an equilibrium rate of growth, even if attainable, will be equal to the natural rate of growth. First, given autonomous (or gross investment) expenditures in a two-sector model, savings behaviour determines total spending, and therefore realisable aggregate demand. Second, given entrepreneurial long-run profit expectations, that portion of the savings of income recipients which is transferred via financial institutions to firms is one of the major sources of financing (i.e. of obtaining exercisable claims for desired autonomous expenditure). The other major sources of monetary finance are (a) the creation of new bank debts by commercial banks, (b) the pre-existing bear hoards of economic units and (c) internal finance by firms. Since corporations are the major investors in a modern economy, and since growing corporations normally retain a significant portion of gross profits for internal financing purposes, the profits savings propensity (s_c) may play a crucial role in capital accumulation and growth as firms

> find it necessary in a dynamic world of increasing returns to plough back a proportion of the profits as a kind of prior charge on earnings. . . . This is because continued expansion cannot be ensured . . . unless *some proportion* of the finance required from expansion comes from internal sources. . . . Hence the high savings propensity attaches to profits as such, not to capitalists as such.[1]

[1] N. Kaldor, 'Marginal Productivity and Macroeconomic Theories of Distribution', *Rev. Econ. Stud.* (1966) p. 310. In an uncertain world, firms must guard against illiquidity, while lenders will fear the possibility of firms being unable to meet long-term obligations. Thus, both the entrepreneurs and the lenders are anxious to see that some proportion of net investment is funded internally. Hence, in an uncertain world, internal and external finance are complements rather than substitutes. (It is normally expected, for example, that working capital should not be financed by external funding.) Thus a firm's access to the new issue market will typically be limited by institutional rules on gearing ratios, that is, on the ratio of external funding to the value of the total capital stock.

For analytical clarity, however, it is essential to separate the public's behavioural desires to avoid committing current resource claims (time preference or savings) from the public's liquidity preference or bearishness decisions, where the latter is the decision about which vehicles to utilise to transfer claims into the future. Furthermore, in a monetary economy, it is necessary to separate such liquidity preference decisions from the decisions to commit resources to produce producible and essentially illiquid capital goods as a means of generating an expected future stream of net monetary claims, for those who undertake the purchase of fixed capital attempt to earn a future stream of claims via contractual commitments which cannot be readily undone. These savings or time preference propensities, portfolio or liquidity preference desires, and investment or accumulation or irreversible action preferences, are according to Keynes, inter-related but independent for

> although these factors react on one another, . . . [they] are independent in the sense that any degree, positive or negative, of one is compatible in appropriate circumstances with any degree, positive or negative, of the other.[1]

In order to analyse these factors 'independently', we will initially assume that financial institutions in the spot market for placements simply operate as brokers to bring savers who wish to use placements as a vehicle for transferring a portion of their command over resources into the future into contact with investors who desire capital goods whose costs exceed current income. Simultaneously we will permit commercial banks to provide, if bankers desire to do so, short-term credit to finance the costs of investment projects incurred during their gestation period. At a later stage (in the next chapter) we will also permit banks to provide short-term finance to financial institutions (e.g. investment bankers, new issue houses, stock exchange specialists, and stock dealers) who act as residual buyers or sellers in organised security markets. It is the existence of these residual buying and selling financial institutions who provide continuity in the spot market for placements, and who therefore create a degree of liquidity for securities which far exceeds any liquidity which might be associated via spot

[1] Keynes, *Treatise on Money*, I 145.

market for the capital goods of firms. Hence it is ultimately these residual buying and selling financial institutions which induce a high elasticity of substitution between money and securities and the consequent low elasticity between titles to real assets and the underlying durable goods – thus creating a schism between ownership and control of business firms and the ensuing grave consequences for a 'capitalist' society.

PASINETTI'S NEO-KEYNESIAN MODEL

In order to provide a focal point for the analysis, the following sections of this chapter will be oriented towards certain aspects of Pasinetti's 1962 model[1] and the controversy it provoked. In the pandemonium that arose from Pasinetti's startling conclusion that the 'workers' propensity to save . . . does not influence the distribution of income between profits and wages',[2] it was not recognised that this conclusion was obtained by working from postulates which are generally applicable only to a world of certainty where money is *never* used to defer decisions; Pasinetti's assumptions are not likely to be applicable to an economy where some portion of household savings is likely to be held in the form of non-resource embodying durables such as money (or securities).

Pasinetti's conclusions were based on the following assumptions:

(1) Continuous full employment,

(2) 'A price mechanism by which the level of prices with respect to the level of wages (profit margins) rise or fall according to whether demand exceeds or falls short of supply,' i.e. profit margins are more flexible than money wage rates.

(3) 'When any individual saves a part of his income, he must be allowed to own it. . . . This means that the stock of capital which exists is owned by those people who in the past made the corresponding savings',

(4) The rate of interest equals the rate of profit on real capital,

[1] L. L. Pasinetti, 'The Rate of Profit and Income Distribution in Relation to Economic Growth', *Rev. of Econ. Stud.*, **29** (1962) pp. 267–79.

[2] ibid. p. 272.

(5) Workers save the same proportion out of wages (s_w) as they do out of any profits that accrue to them.[1]

On inspection, it turns out that the seemingly innocuous third assumption will *always* be applicable only in an economy where the only available stores of value are readily reproducible (resource-using) durable goods. Such an economy Keynes defines as a 'non-monetary economy'.[2] In such an economy, when an individual saves out of current income, he must (by definition) automatically increase his ownership of the stock of producible durables, i.e. the non-available output of capital goods. Nevertheless, one of the fundamental facts of life of a monetary economy is that the increased aggregate desire for 'wealth' as such by income recipients does not require the demand for capital goods to increase for 'there is always an alternative to the ownership of real capital assets, namely the ownership of money and debts'.[3] Moreover, in a monetary economy with a developed banking system and well-organised, continuous spot market for titles to fixed capital, the creation of additional real wealth does not require that the title to this increment in wealth accrue to, or remain with, those who have abstained from spending their current income.

The addition to the accumulated wealth of the community over any given period of time depends on the decisions which are taken, mainly by entrepreneurs and financiers, during that period as to the amount of output in the shape of fixed or working capital [non-available output] and not on the

[1] Citations for these assumptions are: ibid., (1) p. 268, (2) p. 275, also see p. 269, (3) p. 270, (4) pp. 271–2, and (5) p. 273.

[2] Keynes defines a non-monetary economy as one 'in which there is no asset for which the liquidity-premium is always in excess of the carrying-costs' (*The General Theory*, p. 239). For reproducible durables, storage and other costs rise so rapidly as soon as some minimal level is held by a household that these costs will always swamp the liquidity premium. Such a non-monetary economy is, however, incompatible with a wages and profits economy in which there is a high degree of specialisation and exchange and therefore where commitments and contractual obligations must be undertaken (as a way of life) before the full result of the use of productive resources can be known. Since Pasinetti's assumptions depend on the economy operating 'as if' it was a non-monetary capitalist economy, his model has led to unnecessary obfuscations.

[3] Keynes, *The General Theory*, p. 213.

decisions of the body of individual citizens as to what part of their money incomes they will save.[1]

Thus, as Keynes argued, the accumulation of capital requires only two conditions, namely, (1) expectations of profits by entrepreneurs and (2) the possibility 'for enterprisers to obtain command of sufficient resources to put their projects into execution . . . on terms which they deem attractive [which depends] almost entirely on the behaviour of the banking and monetary system',[2] and not on the public's liquidity preference desires as to whether to store wealth in titles to capital goods or in money.

If, for example, in any period wage-earning households decide to hold all their savings in the form of money, while the banking system is willing to finance and fund an amount of net investment done by firms equal to workers' savings, then the profits net of borrowing costs and the use of this increment in the capital stock legally belong to the original share holders who need not abstain.[3] The workers have no claims at all on the ownership or use of the equipment; they have not increased their holdings of titles to the capital, and the increase in quantity of money is 'the means by which the public hold that part of their [increase in] wealth which is looked after by the banking system'.[4] An obvious consequence is that, as Joan Robinson notes, 'the outstanding stock of bonds at any one moment does not bear any particular necessary relationship to the value of the stock of goods in existence . . . nor is the issue of new bonds [to the public] over any one year closely related to the excess-investment [over the savings of firms] of that year'.[5]

[1] Keynes, *Treatise on Money*, I 315–16. See also II 126.

[2] ibid. II 149.

[3] If government is permitted to operate business firms, then, depending on whether government finances expansion via revenues, selling bonds to the public, selling bonds to the banking system, or taxation, the concomitant savings and 'ownership' of the government's capital stock will develop in different patterns.

[4] R. F. Kahn, 'Some Notes on Liquidity Preference', *Manchester School* (1954) p. 238.

[5] J. Robinson, *The Accumulation of Capital*, p. 230. If the monetary authority absorbs directly (via dealing in debts of all maturities) or indirectly (via rediscounting on open market operations) the private debt created to finance the net investment equal to the increased bear holdings

In the Pasinetti model, output is divided into three parts: (i) consumption by capitalists, (ii) consumption by workers and (iii) investment. The sum of (i) and (ii) is equal to available output, while (iii) is related to non-available output. Pasinetti defines investment in his model as that amount 'which has to be undertaken in order to keep full employment over time. This amount of investments, as a proportion of total income, is uniquely determined from outside the economic system, by technology and population growth'.[1] In essence, therefore, what Pasinetti is trying to explain is, given the propensities to save out of wages and profits, what distribution of income will generate a savings ratio that is compatible with the natural rate of growth at full employment, that is, what distribution of aggregate income is required for a Golden Age.

Since Pasinetti assumes that at any point of time both the full employment level of output and investment are 'uniquely and exogenously determined',[2] it follows that the quantity of available output (consumption goods) is a residual which is also exogenously determined. Consequently, the market-clearing (or demand) price which will divide up available output between worker and capitalist households will depend, if the flow of output and its composition is exogenously determined, solely on the relative money incomes of wage earners and profit recipients and their respective propensities to consume. It is only by utilising assumption (3) that Pasinetti is able to go from a conclusion about the distribution of the flow of available output without remainder between worker and capitalist households which, by hypothesis, *must* depend on both s_c and s_w to a statement that s_w does not affect the distribution between wages and profits.[3] If assumption (3) is not applicable to a monetary economy, then Pasinetti's conclusion is invalid.

---

of the public, then interest payments on this debt will leak from the system. If, however, all the interest payments go only to commercial banks within the system, then these become part of the gross profits of the banking industry, and will be divided between bank running expenses and profits. These secondary complications are dealt with in some detail by J. Robinson, ibid. p. 228.

[1] Pasinetti, 'The Rate of Profit and Income Distribution', p. 276.

[2] ibid. p. 276, n. 1.

[3] For a mathematical proof, see Appendix to this chapter.

In the Pasinetti analysis, even if s_w is higher, since investment and total output are exogenous, aggregate consumption output and therefore aggregate savings must, at each point of time, be exogenously determined. Nevertheless, under assumption (3) the proportion of titles in the increment of real wealth going to workers and therefore, under assumption (4), the amount of profits going to wage-earner households must *pari passu* be higher. Since, according to Pasinetti, workers consume more out of this profit sum than the capitalists would have had they received it, and since total available output is in each period given, the excess consumption by wage-earners out of these profits must just offset the assumed increase in s_w so that (a) total savings are unchanged, (b) workers obtain a greater share of the available output as the personal distribution of income shifts towards workers' households, but (c) the distribution between wages and profits is unchanged in order to match the unchanged (by hypothesis) distribution of output between consumption and investment goods.

If, however, workers' savings are not stored entirely in titles to *newly produced* capital goods (new issues) because money and spot securities markets dealing in second-hand securities provide alternative outlets, then Pasinetti's conclusion that s_w does not affect the profit-wage distribution is no longer generally applicable. In a money economy where the stock of money and financial assets are (superior) alternatives to the holding of resource embodying reproducible goods as a store of wealth, then if $s_w > 0$, the level of aggregate income and of gross profits (and therefore the distribution of income) will depend on s_w and s_c, as determined via equations (1) and (4) of Chapter 5.

If, for example, s_w is higher and this increase in the savings rate is stored in the form of money (or second-hand securities) rather than used to purchase titles to additional newly produced capital goods and net investment is not increased to offset the reduction in workers' consumption, then realised sales revenue will not be, in the aggregate, sufficient to cover all contractual wage, material, and interest costs *plus* normal profits. (To the extent that working capital costs are financed by bank loans, entrepreneurs may not be able to fully repay all short-term working capital loans.) Consequently, effective demand will have been found to be deficient relative to short-run entrepreneurial expectations and we are back in a Keynes world where the propensities to spend of all groups can affect gross profits and the level of income and employment. Thus, for example, when firms have financed their weekly payrolls via borrowing short-term credit from banks, and are anticipating repaying these working capital loans out of sales proceeds, then the higher saving propensity by wage-earners and their holding these savings in an asset which has a negligible elasticity of productivity will cause financial difficulties for entrepreneurs even if, in a neo-keynesian world, firms let their profit margins fall relative to the money-costs of production in order to clear the consumer goods markets. These financial problems will force firms to curtail production and employment.

If the full employment assumption is to be maintained when a comparison of two economies is to be made, where in the first economy $s_w > 0$ and workers store some of their savings in the form of money and/or second-hand titles, while in the second economy $s_w = 0$, and s_c is the same in both economies, then the share of investment in the full employment level of output must be greater in the former with the banking system buying the titles to the additional wealth and thereby increasing the money supply sufficiently to satisfy the bear hoards of the wage-earners.[1] Accordingly, the full employment assumption in a system where money or other assets with a zero elasticity of productivity can be used as a store of value is incompatible with Pasinetti's assertion that 'investment [defined as the amount of investments which has to be undertaken in order to keep full employment over time] . . . is uniquely determined from outside the economic system by technology and population growth'.[2]

Thus, even in a Pasinetti world as long as there exists money as a store of value which has elasticities of productivity and substitution of (near) zero, and as long as there are offer contracts denominated in money for hire and forward delivery, that is, as long as we are discussing a money wage and profits economy, then even a pricing mechanism in which profit

---

[1] Alternatively, dis-savings by other (capitalist) households may offset the higher s_w. See the discussion of Kaldor's Neo-Pasinetti Theorem below.

[2] Pasinetti, 'The Rate of Profit and Income Distribution', p. 276.

margins are flexible relative to money wages cannot assure, despite Kaldor's insistence, that the warranted rate will 'adjust itself to the "natural rate"'.[1] Moreover, there is nothing 'natural' about the natural rate of growth for it will depend solely on technology and population growth only if the necessary consumption (and therefore savings) behaviour of each income receiving unit is given and fixed.

If one interprets Pasinetti's model as an analysis of the income distribution requirements which will automatically generate a Golden Age growth path rather than as a behavioural theory of what actually happens,[2] then his unfortunate assumption (3) has (a) concealed the vital role money and finance markets must play if a Golden Age is to be attained, and (b) obscured the financial difficulties involved in achieving the natural rate of growth even if the required income distribution could be effectuated. As Richard Kahn has noted, in the neo-keynesian Golden Age growth analysis the state of finance has been implicitly built into the equilibrium system in such a manner as to accommodate a rate of growth equal to population growth plus technical progress.[3]

In the ensuing controversy that arose from Pasinetti's unfortunate and unwarranted conclusion regarding the irrelevance of s_w for the distribution of wages and profits, Samuelson and Modigliani were able to demonstrate that if $s_w > s_c$, and if Pasinetti's assumption (3) held, then the share of the capital stock held by workers would grow over time until effectively all capital was owned by workers and therefore all profit income accrued to workers.[4] This proof which the authors called the 'Duality Theorem' but which Kaldor labelled the 'Anti-Pasinetti Theorem' appeared severely to restrict the generality of the Cambridge England growth models. Consequently, Kaldor found it necessary to offer a rebuttal, a 'neo-Pasinetti

[1] Kaldor, 'Some Fallacies', p. 6.

[2] Pasinetti, 'The Rate of Profit and Income Distribution', p. 279.

[3] R. F. Kahn, 'Exercises in the Analysis of Growth', *Oxford Econ. Papers* (1959) p. 153.

[4] P. A. Samuelson & F. Modigliani, 'The Pasinetti Paradox in Neoclassical and More General Models', *Rev. of Econ. Stud.* 1966, pp. 269–302. Actually, the whole controversy over the relevance of s_w was, as we have demonstrated, barren and merely served to divert attention from the more important aspects of Pasinetti's model.

Theorem',[1] which presents some seminal ideas about the importance of financial markets and the demand for securities in the context of economic growth.

KALDOR'S NEO-PASINETTI THEOREM

In his 'neo-Pasinetti Theorem' Kaldor has attempted to associate the net acquisition of securities by the household sector with net personal savings, a relationship in which Kaldor explicitly assumes that the marginal propensity to buy placements out of personal savings (m) equals unity. If m equals unity, all personal savings become funds which are available for business investment, a view that was implicit in Pasinetti's assumption (3). In Kaldor's words:

> Net savings out of income sets up a demand for securities, [and] net dis-savings out of income (= net consumption out of capital or capital gains) sets up a supply of securities. There is also a net supply of new securities issued by the corporate sector. Since, in the securities' market, prices will tend to a level at which the total (non-speculative) supply and demand for securities are equal, there must be some mechanism to ensure that the [consumption] spending out of capital (or capital gains) just balances the savings out of income *less* any new securities issued by corporations.[2]

Since Kaldor is attempting to elucidate the necessary savings *and* financial conditions for an economy in a Golden Age under the assumption of given savings propensities and a given propensity to consume out of capital gains, the mechanism which he alludes to cannot be changed in the level of effective demand, which is (by hypothesis) exogenously growing at the 'natural rate'. Instead, it is the (spot) price of placements which not only equilibriates the demand and supply of securities available to the general public, but must, in Kaldor's view,

[1] N. Kaldor, 'Marginal Productivity and Macroeconomic Theories of Distribution', *Rev. Econ. Stud.* (1966) pp. 316–19.

[2] ibid. p. 316. There is, as Chapter 11 noted, no *a priori* reason why m should equal unity and in fact Keynes argued $0 < m < 1$. If m equaled unity there would never be any idle balances, an equilibrium condition which, Keynes points out, is compatible with the absence of uncertainty and the Quantity Theory of Money. See Keynes, *The General Theory*, pp. 208–9.

also equilibriate the net personal savings of households plus corporate retained profits with the full employment level of investment. The essence of Kaldor's position is given in the statement that:

> The net savings of the personal sector (available for investment by the business sector) will depend, not only on the savings propensities of individuals, but on the policies of the corporations towards new issues. In the absence of new issues the level of security prices will be established at the point at which the purchases of securities by the savers will be just balanced by the sale of securities by the dis-savers, making the net savings of the personal sector zero.[1]

If accepted at face value, Kaldor's statement is truly a surprising volte-face for Keynesian theory, especially since it is a neo-keynesian of Kaldor's stature who appears to be implying that given the distribution of income, given the level of net investment, and given the corporate new issue policy, the level of security prices (i.e. the rate of interest) will cause aggregate personal consumption just to fill the gap between the full employment level of output and investment spending. After all these years of verbal duels, acrimony, and clarification, Kaldor's analysis suggests that the rate of interest is the mechanism which ensures that effective demand is always maintained at the full employment level.[2]

In his attempt to defend Pasinetti's neo-keynesian analysis from the American neoclassical assault, it would appear, at first blush, that Kaldor has unwittingly reinstated the *deux ex machina* of the neoclassical system – the rate of interest – as the balancing mechanism not only for maintaining equilibrium in the spot market for securities (which it does) but also for creating 'forced spending' if necessary, to maintain full employment.

Fortunately for Keynes's economics, Kaldor's own analysis does not require this neoclassical mechanism once it is recalled

[1] N. Kaldor, 'Marginal Productivity and Macroeconomic Theories of Distribution', *Rev. Econ. Stud.* (1966), p. 318.

[2] Samuelson has, in a more jocular moment, referred to Jean Baptiste Kaldor. While I think this is scarcely appropriate, in the light of Kaldor's constant emphasis on full employment policy, there would be some point to the indictment if Kaldor really believed that the rate of interest induces consumption to fill the deflationary gap.

that Keynes recognised – insisted really – that the household savings or time preference decision is independent of the household portfolio balance or liquidity preference decision so that the m need not equal unity,[1] or, in fact, m need not even be stable over time. Once it is recognised that $0 < m < 1$, then Kaldor's neo-Pasinetti Theorem discussion of the demand and supply of securities in a growing economy can be a useful starting point for analysing the possible *financial* causes of why a monetary economy need not attain a Golden Age. As such Kaldor's approach is a perceptive elaboration on Keynes's basic monetary analysis and it permits us to illustrate readily how the traditional Keynes adjustment mechanism moves the economy towards paths which may or may not be full employment equilibrium ones.

THE BASIC RELATIONS

The public's demand for securities can be conceptualised (as in Chapter 10) as a stock demand for a store of value, and can, for present purposes, be simply written as

$$D_p = f_2 (p_p, \overline{R}, \lambda, \beta, \alpha, T_s, e, V) \qquad (2)$$

Where D_p is the quantity of placements demanded by the public, p_p is the market price of placements, R is the income claim per period ownership of a placement entitles one to, λ is a set of expectations about the rate of change of future security prices, β and α are indices of the public's aversion to income and capital risk respectively, T_s is the costs of moving between securities and money, e represents the number of wealth-owners and the distribution of wealth among them; and V stands for the magnitude of the public's total store of value at any point of time. This demand for placements, D_p, includes the Wicksteedian reservation demand for securities by the 'bulls'. Given λ, β, α, e, T_s, and V, a stock demand curve for placements can be drawn as downward sloping $D_1 D_1'$ in Fig. 12.1, i.e. $f_{1p_p}' < 0$, since as the price declines, the expected capital gain from purchasing a security increases, while the (income) opportunity cost of holding money balances as a store of value increases.

[1] Keynes, in fact, argued that $0 < m < 1$. See Keynes, 'The Ex-Ante Theory', p. 668.

Hence the public will want to substitute placements for money holdings as the price of securities declines. Furthermore, in each period, realised personal savings out of current income imply an increment in V and consequently an outward shift – or flow demand – of the D_1D_1' curve (i.e. $f_{1V}' > 0$) in Fig. 12.1. In line with his argument of over a quarter-century ago, Kaldor refers to this flow-demand for placements due to household savings as the non-speculative demand for securities;[1] it is directly due to an increase in household wealth and not due to a change in expectations about future spot security prices. In the terminology of Keynes's *Treatise*, on the other hand, this shift in the demand curve for securities would be an increase in bullishness, while in *The General Theory* if $m < 1$, there would be simultaneously an increase in 'liquidity preference proper' *and* an increase in the demand for securities, i.e. the flow-demand for securities and the flow-demand for money as vehicles for transferring purchasing power over time are complementary and vary directly with, *ceteris paribus*, household wealth.

At any point in time, a given stock of outstanding securities exists as inherited from the past. Accordingly, the stock supply schedule of placements facing the public (S_p) is perfectly inelastic (in Fig. 12.1 and 12.2) that is

$$S_p = a \qquad (3)$$

where a is a predetermined constant. If there are no new securities issued by corporations, then an equilibrium price of p_1 will be established.

Increases in the quantity of placements supplied will functionally depend on the entrepreneurial demand for investment goods *and* their demand for external funding to underwrite the investment. The flow schedule of placements can therefore be specified (as in Chapter 10) as

$$s_p = \frac{(1 - \bar{h})(\bar{g})[p_k(s_k - d_k)]}{p_p} \qquad (4)$$

where g is the fraction of investment which is externally funded, h is the fraction of long-term finance provided by the banking system, p_k is the flow-supply price of newly produced capital

[1] N. Kaldor, 'Speculation and Economic Stability', *Rev. Econ. Studies*, 1939, reprinted in *Essays on Economic Stability and Growth*, pp. 42, 48.

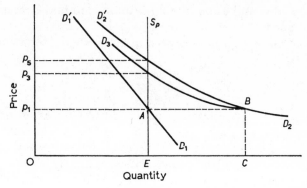

Fig. 12.1

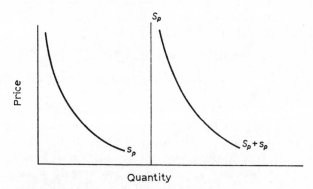

Fig. 12.2

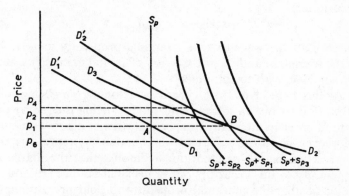

Fig. 12.3

goods, and s_k and d_k are the flow-supply and flow-demand for capital goods.

Equation (4) can be rewritten in line with Kaldor's symbols as

$$s_p = \frac{i g_n K}{p_v} \tag{5}$$

Where i reveals the fraction of the firms' current investment (denoted by $g_n K$, where K = capital stock, g_n = growth rate) which corporations decide to externally finance via the issue of new securities to the public. Given i, g_n, and K, the flow-supply schedule (s_p) with respect to the placement price, p_v, in any time period constitutes a rectangular hyperbola (see Fig. 12.2). The market supply schedule of placements in any period can be obtained by summating the inherited stock supply schedule (S_p) with the flow-supply schedule s_p as

$$S_p + s_p = \alpha + (i g_n K / p_v) \tag{6}$$

and is given in Fig. 12.2. (This apparatus has been developed in Chapter 10.)

Returning to Kaldor's argument, maintenance of equilibrium in the securities market requires that any increase in the demand for placements must equal the quantity of new issues supplied by corporations plus the liquidation of securities by shareholders wanting to obtain active money balances to finance consumption out of capital gains. Thus Kaldor writes the equilibrium condition or the excess flow-demand for securities as

$$s_w W = c G + i g_n K \tag{7}$$

where s_w is the wage-earners' marginal propensity to save, W is the wage bill, and c is the fraction of capital gains (G) which stockholders wish to consume.

At this stage, Kaldor is effectively assuming no savings out of profit distribution so that all capitalist saving is done by the firm in order to internally finance a portion of net investment.[1] Moreover, since the $s_w W$ term in equation (7) represents the increased demand for securities, it implies that the marginal propensity to buy securities out of personal savings (m) equals unity, so that the marginal propensity to hold precautionary

[1] Kaldor, 'Marginal Productivity', pp. 310, 318 n.1.

and speculative balances as wealth increases is zero.[1]

When no new securities are issued. Given the level of investment, the distribution of income between wages and profits, and the household savings propensities assumed by Kaldor in his neo-Pasinetti theorem, then if $m = 1$, the demand curve for placements will shift from point A to point B at the initial price of p_1 in Fig. 12.1. This shift from A to B is indicative of an increase in demand which is just sufficient to absorb (at a price of p_1 per unit) a value of additional placements equal to the personal savings out of wages; that is in Fig. 12.1, $ABCE$ must equal $s_w W$, if $m = 1$.

Since m is assumed equal to unity, the area of the rectangle obtained by taking the horizontal difference between the initial $D_1 D_1'$ and the new $D_2 D_2'$ curve and multiplying it by the ordinate height of the price level, *for any price*, will always equal total savings out of wages. (More generally, the area of the rectangle will equal m times savings out of *household* income or $m s_w W$ in this case.) Thus, the $D_2 D_2'$ curve will have a hyperbolic relationship with respect to $D_1 D_1'$; if consumption out of capital gains are precluded (that is, if $c = 0$ in equation (7)). If no new securities are issued, so that $i = 0$ in equation (5), then the price of placements would rise until p_5 in Fig. 12.1. This higher price level would induce the public to hold the same quantity of securities in their portfolio as initially even though the state of bullishness had risen (i.e. the demand for placements has increased) because of savings out of wages or flow-demand (or in Kaldor's terminology because of an increase in non-speculative demand).[2]

[1] This is the same assumption Kaldor applied over a quarter of a century ago. See, 'Speculation . . .', *Essays in Economic Stability*, p. 45 n. 1. In essence, therefore, the strict version of the neo-Pasinetti theorem assumes there is never any increment in the quantity of money held as a store of value, i.e. all increases in the supply of money are active balances in the neo-keynesian analysis. If $m \neq 1$, however, we are back in a Keynesian world of liquidity preference, money and uncertainty.

Although Kaldor's analysis makes no specific mention of the money supply, it is implicitly assumed that the quantity of money increases by an amount equal to $s_w W$.

[2] The higher placement price level has yielded an increase in the public wealth equal to $(p_5 - p_1)(OE)$, while the increase in the stock of real wealth for the economy is equal to $p_k(s_k - d_k)$. There is no necessary reason to expect $(p_5 - p_1)(OE)$ will equal net investment.

The magnitude of the increase in the price of securities will depend, *ceteris paribus*, on the value of m. If, for example, $m = 0$, then despite the existence of household savings, there would be no flow-demand for securities, and if firms financed investment entirely from retentions and/or increased obligations to the commercial banks, the valuation ratio, i.e. the ratio of the market value of securities held by the public to the value of stock of capital goods, would fall. In other words, as we have already noticed, there is no necessary relation between the spot market value of outstanding placements, and the depreciated cost of the stock of capital held by the firm. Depending on the slope of the speculative demand for securities, the resulting valuation ratio will depend on what portion of household savings is converted into securities and how much external funding is done by firms.

In addition, however, Kaldor has assumed that $c > 0$ and therefore, some shareholders are eager to sell some of their securities in order to finance consumption spending out of capital gains by an amount equal to cG.[1] Thus, at any price above the initial p_1 price, the 'reservation' demand for securities is contracted somewhat which, in turn means that there is a marginal propensity to demand placements (k), whenever there is a change in the price of placements, which is negative[2]

---

[1] See Kaldor, 'Marginal Productivity and Macroeconomic Theories of Distribution', p. 317. Keynes, on the other hand, believed that capital gains (or losses) due to changes in security prices did not directly affect the sale (or purchase) of securities; rather, it lowered (raised) the savings propensity of households. In other words, in Keynes's view, capital gains (or losses) would directly increase (decrease) s_w or s_c in Kaldor's neo-Pasinetti Model. (See Keynes, *Treatise on Money*, II 197 and *The General Theory*, p. 319.) For any given value of m, the net impact on the securities market will be the same whether it is assumed, as Keynes did, that G affects household savings propensities or, as Kaldor does, the net purchase of securities. Nevertheless, Keynes's approach has the virtue that it is logically symmetrical, i.e. a capital loss can raise savings propensities, while it may discourage the purchase of additional securities; Kaldor's approach implies that a capital loss will, if $c > 0$, induce households to purchase additional securities – a rather strange result.

[2] At prices below p_1, on the other hand, it is unlikely that savers will want to increase their purchases of securities to offset capital losses. Thus, we must assume that $k = 0$ for capital losses, an assumption implicit in Kaldor's association of changes in capitalists' consumption with capital

(i.e. $k < 0$). Accordingly, the portion of the D_2D_2' curve above p_1 does not correctly convey the magnitude of the aggregate demand for placements since the reduction in reservation demand will mean that the quantity demanded at any price will fall short of that shown on the D_2D_2' curve (for the latter is drawn on the hypothesis that $k = 0$).

The point is that curve D_2BD_3 depicts the stock demand for placements at any point of time when there is some positive consumption out of capital gains financed, in Kaldor's view, by the sale of securities to the public. Hence, when $m = 1$, and $k < 0$, the increase in placement prices will only mount to p_3 as the net increase in bullishness of the public is somewhat repressed compared to when $m = 1$ and $k = 0$.

If we initially posited a less than full employment equilibrium situation, then this additional consumption (out of capital gains) or 'forced spending' will lead, of course, to an uplift in economic activity and a multiple increase in output (as embodied in the traditional multiplier analysis). A new equilibrium output level will be established where the sum total of personal savings out of wages will be enlarged as employment and the wage bill expands, while capitalists spend in excess of their dividend income (as assumed by Kaldor) and thereby in effect, reduce savings out of gross profits. Money income, real output, and employment will be augmented.

If, on the other hand, we start with the neo-keynesian assumption of an initial given full employment equilibrium, then the increase in security prices when $c > 0$ induces an increase in aggregate consumption and consequently an increase in aggregate demand. The upshot is the familiar concept of an 'inflationary gap' (or an 'inflationary barrier' in Mrs Robinson's terminology).[1] This involves an initial disequilibrium

---

gains rather than losses. (The reader should note that the marginal propensity to demand placement when securities price change (k) of this chapter, differs somewhat from the marginal propensity to demand placements (j) of Chapter 11.) Thus for reasons of clarity as well as for reasons discussed in the previous footnote, Kaldor's neo-Pasinetti Theorem could have been simpler and more realistic if he had assumed that capital gains or losses due to changes in security prices affected personal savings propensities directly, and therefore $k = 0$.

[1] J. Robinson, *The Accumulation of Capital*, p. 13.

between investment expenditures and desired savings (an essential element in the fundamental equations of Keynes's *Treatise*) and with a free market, the Pasinetti model would require the market price to increase relative to money wages which would redistribute income from wages to profits via increased profit margins, a result which is identical to the formation of (windfall) profits in the *Treatise*.[1] Under the inflationary gap view of the post-1936 Keynesian revolution, on the other hand, the adjusting mechanism in a free market requires money wage rates and therefore supply prices to rise, forcing fixed income groups (*particularly bond-holding savers*) to cut their real consumption demand because of a reduction in real income. The consequent 'forced savings' of rentiers will restore equilibrium in the commodity market by squeezing net capitalist *personal* spending while expanding corporate profits and firms' savings so that, on net, savings out of gross profits rise to a level equal to investment spending minus savings out of wages.

In this view of the Kaldor–Pasinetti mechanism, of course, the forced savings of rentiers will be augmented by the forced savings of workers as the real wage declines when the mark-up over wage cost increases, i.e. gross margins rise proportionately more than money-wage rates. Thus, rentiers, and in the neo-keynesian world of Kaldor and Pasinetti, workers as well are forced, in the aggregate, to save as some shareholders attempt to increase their consumption of the available output. Nevertheless, even in this neo-keynesian world, once money and second-hand securities are explicitly recognised as substitutes for titles to newly produced capital goods as a store of value, then it is the price level of goods and/or changes in the level of production which is the mechanism through which aggregate consumption is redistributed among the various members of the public, forcing relatively fixed income groups to save.[2]

Thus, the level of output will be the instrument (at less than

---

[1] In fact, Pasinetti's stability analysis involves a differential equation which analyses the same factor (i.e. $I - S$), which leads to dynamic changes in the fundamental equations of Keynes's *Treatise*. Cf. Pasinetti, 'The Rate of Profit and Income Distribution', *Rev. of Econ. Cond.* p. 275 with Keynes, *Treatise on Money*, I 135–7.

[2] Cf. Keynes, *Treatise on Money*, I 316; II 124–7.

full employment) for equating net personal plus corporate savings with net investment, while the wage-price mechanism, the existence of fixed money income contracts, and sticky money wages relative to gross margins will ensure that the equating of savings and investment at full employment.[1]

With this analysis it is apparent that even in a neo-keynesian world the price of placements need not affect the total of personal savings directly (except for Kaldor's assumed real-placement-balance effect); rather the spot price of securities assures that the public holds all the placements made available to it. With $m = 1$ and $k = 0$ and no new issues forthcoming then there will be no actual change in the portfolio holdings of the public; the price of securities will rise to p_5 in order to induce households to hold the same quantity of securities as their bullishness increases. Alternatively with $k < 0$, when $m = 1$, then the price of securities need rise only to p_3 to reflect the smaller increase in bullishness on the part of the public as they continue to hold the same quantity of securities; while if $m = Q$, there will be no change in the price of securities even though the stock of capital goods and households' store of wealth increase.

Of course, it might be argued that instead of assuming an initial equilibrium level of employment, the comparable case for the neo-Pasinetti theorem should begin by positing that corporate savings plus wage-earner household savings exceed, at the initial employment level, the exogenously determined level of investment.[2] In this latter case, especially if $c = 0$, the

---

[1] For a more complete discussion of forced savings of rentiers at full employment and its implications for employment and money wages see P. Davidson and E. Smolensky, *Aggregate Supply and Demand Analysis*, ch. 11 or P. Davidson and E. Smolensky, 'Modigliani on the Interaction of the Real and Monetary Phenomena', *Rev. of Econ. Statistics* (1964) pp. 429–31 and S. Weintraub's seminal volume, *An Approach to the Theory of Income Distribution*, esp. ch. 6.

[2] This is most likely to be the case since it is usually assumed that internal finance of investment spending comes from corporate savings out of business income. Consequently, if household savings exceeds the firms' needs for external funds, aggregate savings (i.e. corporate plus household savings) must exceed aggregate (business) investment spending at the given employment level. If, however, assumptions such as firms' obtain long-term financing directly from the banks (or alternatively government spending is financed by the banking system) by an amount equal to household savings is explicitly added, then no new issues will be available to the public, while,

demand price for goods will be less than the supply price. This will result in windfall losses (i.e. less than normal profits) in Keynes's *Treatise* or lower profit margins in the Kaldor–Pasinetti model, or involuntary inventory accumulations in *The General Theory*, which should, via creating financial difficulties for firms expecting to use sales proceeds to repay working capital loans, induce entrepreneurs to contract output, and thereby lower the total wage bill until savings and investment are equal. Of course, if, following Kaldor, it is assumed that $c > 0$ and $m = 1$, and if a sufficiently large capital gain is produced by the excess flow-demand for securities so that capitalists are induced to significantly dis-save in the aggregate, then the magnitude of the contraction necessary to bring about equilibrium in the goods market may be much less. Kaldor, of course, assumes that capitalists' dis-savings will be sufficient to completely offset any increase in household savings out of wages so that full employment will be maintained, but there is no *a priori* reason to believe that the increment in spot prices of securities to p_3 (or even p_5) in Fig. 12.1, will be sufficient to 'force' such a level of dis-savings.[1]

Without protracting this analysis further by handling the other possible case where corporate plus wage earners' savings are initially less than exogenous investment *and* no new issues are forthcoming, it can be readily stated that it does not really matter whether equilibrium in the goods market is initially assumed or not, for it is the level of output and/or the wage-price mechanism and the existence of fixed money contracts and sticky money wages and not the spot price of securities which are the *primary* mechanisms for bringing aggregate supply and demand (i.e. savings and investment) into equilibrium in modern market-oriented, monetary economies.

---

at the initial level of employment, aggregate savings will equal aggregate autonomous spending. In the next chapter, the analysis of these additional assumptions will be specifically eliminated and the analysis of the financial adjustments required will be developed.

[1] Given the high concentration of securities among a very small segment of the population – even in developed countries such as the United States and the United Kingdom – it is difficult to envision consumption out of capital gains as having an aggregate effect sufficient to offset even a small increment in the propensity to save by wage earners.

External finance via new public issues. If corporations issue new securities to the public to finance some portion of net investment (I), then, using the method developed in Chapter 11, the analysis can be developed, via Fig. 12.3, by combining the stock-flow placement supply schedule of Fig. 12.2, with the demand behaviour of Fig. 12.1. For simplicity, we can follow Kaldor's assumption of a given propensity to save out of wages, while all dividend distributions to profit recipients are spent. If $m = 1$, then, as has already been demonstrated, the demand curve shifts from D_1D_1' to D_2D_2' if $k = 0$ (or to D_2BD_3 if $k < 0$ at prices above p_1) in Fig. 12.3.

If, when $m = 1$, in any period where the amount of external funding required equals total savings out of wages, so that the excess flow-demand for securities is zero at the p_1 price level, that is if $iI = ms_wW$, then demand for placements *at the initial price of p_1* (diagrammatically, a shift from A to B in Fig. 12.3) will be just sufficient to absorb all the newly issued securities. Accordingly, the market supply schedule of securities, $S_p + s_{p1}$, will be a rectangular hyperbola which passes through point B and the increase in the quantity of securities supplied at p_1 will just counterbalance and neutralise the increase in bullishness as households add to the quantity of securities they possess in their portfolios.

If external funding requirements is less than the savings out of wages which is desired to be held as securities, i.e. if $iI < ms_wW$, then the rectangular hyperbola market supply curve, $S_p + s_{p2}$, will locate to the left of point B. Accordingly, if $k < 0$, then the equilibrium price will rise to p_2 (or p_4 if $k = 0$) as the augmentation in household bullishness is not blocked by a large enough increase in the offering of new issues (plus any reduction in reservation demand to finance consumption out of capital gains) to maintain the initial price of p_1. The market price rises only enough to entice the more bullish (wage-earning) households to increase the portfolio holdings of securities by an amount equal to the quantity of new issues.[1]

If the amount of external finance required by firms exceeded savings out of wages which are to find a home in the form of

---

[1] Of course, as footnote 2, p. 309, indicates, unless there is some other source of autonomous spending, the condition that $iI < ms_wW$ is symptomatic of a lack of effective demand.

securities, i.e. $iI > ms_w W$, then the market supply schedule of placements, $S_p + s_{p3}$, would be a rectangular hyperbola lying to the right of point B. This means that firms attempt to float new issues in excess of the increase in bullishness at the initial p_1 price level. Accordingly, if $k = 0$ below p_1 then the placement price level declines to p_6 in order to stimulate households to add to their holdings of securities.

There is, of course, no reason to expect that the quantity of external funding desired by entrepreneurs will just equal the desired increment in personal holdings of securities at the p_1 price level in any period; that is, it will be fortuitous if $iI = ms_w W$. If the new issue houses or security underwriters had correctly foreseen the demand and supply conditions in the security markets when $iI > ms_w W$, they may have been reluctant to act as brokers to float, in the aggregate, a volume of new issues which will depress the market price. For, as Chapter 11 suggested, new issue houses desire to maintain their reputation for success and the goodwill of their customers of previous issues who will be unhappy if security prices decline. In such circumstances these financial institutions may restrict the investment plans of firms by refusing to provide credit facilities even if some investment projects have a present value far in excess of their current costs at the current (or even higher) rate of discount. Accordingly, if financial intermediaries are aware that $iI > ms_w W$, then in the absence of offsetting monetary policy, these financial middlemen may restrict capital accumulation by rationing credit even for profitable investment projects.

Even in the absence of credit rationing, if $iI > ms_w W$, the decline in security prices would involve higher rates of discount which would reduce the attractiveness of some capital projects. if, therefore, $iI > ms_w W$ at full employment, Golden Age growth may be impossible to maintain either because firms cannot obtain sufficient external funding for the full employment level of investment at costs they deem satisfactory, or because of credit rationing by financial institutions. (Of course, this abstracts from monetary policy specifically designed to reduce interest rates if full employment is not maintained.) These questions will be discussed in detail in the next chapter.

INCOME DISTRIBUTION, SAVINGS, INTEREST,
AND GROWTH

The analysis of this chapter has shown that given the savings propensities associated with wages and gross profits and given $0 < m \leqslant 1$, then, *ceteris paribus*, the spot price of securities will alter until the household sector absorbs into its portfolio all securities offered to it. The change in securities prices (and therefore in the rate of interest) does not in itself affect the total of personal savings or the distribution of available output between wage-earners and capitalists at a given level of employment. Given different degrees of bearishness between workers and capitalist households, the price of placements will of course alter the distribution of securities between them. It is only Kaldor's assumption of a real balance effect for placements when the price of securities rise (that is, a posited $c > 0$) which causes a change in the net savings behaviour of capitalists' households.

Nevertheless, it is either induced changes in savings due to changes in income (at less than full employment) and/or inflationary changes in money wages and prices (primarily at or near full employment) which cause 'forced savings' of groups on relatively fixed contractual incomes, which constitute the prime channels for working the appropriate changes in the level of personal savings to bring it into equilibrium with the exogenously determined level of investment. The flexibility of the spot market price of placements merely permits each household unit to hold as many placements as it desires, and to shift its portfolio holdings around as often as desired, while in the aggregate, the personal sector holds exactly the quantity of securities which is allocated to it. The rate of growth, on the other hand, is determined in a modern economy by the investment decisions (of business firms) which can be actually financed and carried out within both the monetary and resource constraints of the economy. It is only the seemingly innocent assumption that all personal savings are held in the form of titles to current increments in real wealth $(m = 1)$ which has led the Neo-keynesians to over-emphasise the savings propensities relative to the financial requirements for accumulating capital.[1]

[1] Finally, if the assumption of a real placement effect is to be made explicitly part of the neo-keynesian model, then it would be analytically

APPENDIX

Pasinetti reformulates Kaldor's model by dividing profits (P) into those occurring to capitalists (P_c) and that accruing to workers (P_w). Similarly the value of capital (K) is divided into that quantity owned by capitalists (K_c) and that part owned by wage earners (K_w). By algebraic manipulation of the savings-investment equality condition, where $I \equiv S_w W + s_c P$, and the income distribution condition $Y = W + P$, Pasinetti shows that

$$\frac{P}{K} = \frac{1}{s_c - s_w} \frac{I}{K} - \frac{s_w}{s_c - s_w} \frac{Y}{K} + \frac{rK_w}{K} \tag{1}$$

$$\frac{P}{Y} = \frac{1}{s_c - s_w} \frac{I}{Y} - \frac{s_w}{s_c - s_w} + \frac{rK_w}{K} \tag{2}$$

Where Y is the full employment level of output, I is the exogenously determined level of investment as defined above, s_w and s_c are the average (and marginal) propensities to save of workers and capitalists respectively, and r is the rate of interest paid on finance.

Assumption (3) permits Pasinetti to state that

$$\frac{K_w}{K} = \frac{S_w}{S} \tag{3}$$

while assumption (4) implies that

$$r = \frac{P}{K} \tag{4}$$

Using equations (3) and (4), with the proviso that

$$I - s_w Y \neq 0$$

Pasinetti reduces equations (1) and (2) to

---

clearer to associate such an effect with a change in savings propensities out of household income rather than associating only with portfolio adjustments via the securities markets. These changes in savings propensities would immediately suggest the Keynesian multiplier at less than full employment and forced savings via the wage-fixed-income-profit margin nexus at full employment as the primary mechanisms of change.

$$\frac{P}{K} = \frac{1}{s_c} \frac{I}{K} \tag{5}$$

and

$$\frac{P}{Y} = \frac{1}{s_c} \frac{I}{Y} \tag{6}$$

It is equations (5) and (6) which permit Pasinetti to state that s_w does not affect the rate of profits or the distribution of income shares.

CHAPTER 13

Financial Intermediaries and the needs of the Financial and Industrial Circulations

> Credit is the pavement along which production travels; and the bankers if they knew their duty, would provide the transport facilities to just the extent that is required in order that the productive powers of the community can be employed to their full capacity.[1]

IN a modern, non-commodity money economy, financial intermediaries and the banking system play an involved and unique role which can permit the installation of productive capacity and the expansion of output at a rate which would be virtually impossible in a commodity money world. These financial institutions permit and can even encourage firms to mobilise the value (in excess of the firms' revenues) of services of resources which otherwise might either produce consumer goods or even lie idle. The creation of bank money either may permit entrepreneurial investors to outrace (or outbid) some income recipients in accepting offer contracts and thereby force the latter to refrain from consumption (particularly at or near full employment) or it may permit investors to obtain immediate command over resources even when savers do not wish to give up such potential command (liquidity) for store of value purposes. Accordingly, the presence of a banking system and the associated financial institutions provide the potential to contribute significantly to economic growth. If a society is fortunate to have both Enterprise and such financial institutions, then at time of confidence it may be doubly-blessed, while in

[1] Keynes, *Treatise on Money*, II 220.

uncertain times it may be doubly-cursed. Through the operation of financial intermediaries and their preferential relationship to the banking system, Enterprise may often be encouraged to accumulate real wealth at a rate which otherwise
might be incompatible with normal savings (time preference)
and portfolio (liquidity preference) desires by households; while
at times of general insecurity, these institutions may magnify
the rush to liquidity and thereby accentuate slumps.[1] Hence
it is essential to account explicitly for how these institutions
link the industrial and financial circulation; even though
society may desire to save out of full employment income a
proportion which is compatible with the natural rate of growth,
a Golden Age may not be attainable unless voluntary actions
are taken by these financial intermediaries and accommodated
by the Monetary Authority.

In a free-market monetary economy, there is, as Harrod
has argued, no mechanism – not even a price mechanism which
redistributes income via flexible profit margins relative to the
money-wage rate – which automatically assures the confluence
of the actual, warranted, and natural rate of growth. In an
uncertain world, errors of foresight are inevitable; hence the
equality of the actual and warranted rate is never certain.
Nevertheless, an analysis of the operation of the financial
institutions which link the real and monetary sectors will
provide insights into the difficulties of achieving equality
between the warranted and natural rates, and thereby perhaps
suggest policies which can minimise these difficulties.

In a monetary economy, 'money matters' i.e. monetary and
financial institutions, are an integral part of the real economy.
The mechanism through which this influence was exerted
and its limitations were clearly sketched out by Keynes in his
Treatise on Money. Unfortunately, in *The General Theory*, the
'technical monetary detail falls into the background'.[2] Consequently many post-General Theory economists who took up
the cudgels for 'Keynesian' full employment policies, did so
without delving into the intricate earlier monetary analysis

---

[1] This is not to imply that in the absence of such institutions slumps
could not occur. Even in a commodity money world, as long as money
has the essential properties discussed in Chapter 9, slumps are possible.

[2] Keynes, *The General Theory*, p. vii.

of Keynes which underlay what factors he decided to treat as parameters and what as variables in the simplification he presented in his monumental 1936 volume. These post-keynesians (or Bastard Keynesians) were satisfied that a logically complete 'Simple Mathematics of Income Determination'[1] was the 'Keynesian' key to all macroeconomic analysis and they were, therefore, vulnerable to the barbed gibes of the 'Monetarists' school from Chicago. Because of this well-publicised and energetic schism between Keynesians v. Monetarists in the recent literature, one of the major objectives of this manuscript has been to expose the foolish nature of the controversy and to expand Keynes's more familiar model of effective demand to encompass many of the monetary aspects which Keynes developed in his *Treatise* but which he purposely repressed in his *General Theory* in his desire to focus on the overwhelming unemployment problem of the thirties. Hopefully, this current endeavour will turn professional discussions into more fruitful avenues of investigation.

Keynes recognised that in an uncertain world there would always be some durable asset which possessed the essential properties to make it money.[2] The existence of uncertainty is, of course, the ultimate cause of the major economic faults of a modern economy, namely 'the failure to provide full employment and . . . [the] arbitrary and inequitable distribution of wealth and income'.[3] Money, financial assets, and contracts are the major instruments which, though necessary for production in an uncertain world, bring about these economic defects. Moreover these economic flaws are often exacerbated by the fact that bankers and other financial middlemen pursued objectives which are (a) incompatible with the public interest and/or (b) unattainable under the existing political and economic rules of the game. Moreover, Keynes complained, these practical men could not be blamed for acting as they did since they were recipients of 'half-baked' monetary theories which

---

[1] P. A. Samuelson, 'The Simple Mathematics of Income Determination' in *Income, Employment and Public Policy: Essays in Honor of Alvin Hansen*, ed. L. A. Metzler *et al.* (New York: Norton, 1948).

[2] Keynes, *The General Theory*, p. 294. If no such asset existed, man would create one.

[3] ibid. p. 372.

were not of much value in practice.[1] It was, therefore, with his *Treatise on Money* that Keynes hoped to take the 'critical leap forward which will bring it [monetary theory] into effective contact with the real world'.[2] It is therefore particularly apropos in view of the rebirth of interest in 'Monetarism' that Keynes's views on 'monetary detail' be developed in a modern setting.

In this chapter, Keynes's ideas on the peculiar and strategic position of financial middlemen in determining the rate of accumulation, while in the next chapter the relationship between money and inflation, income distribution, and expansion, will be discussed.

FINANCIAL MARKETS AND LIQUIDITY

The business of the daily exchanging of existing titles to wealth absorbs a tremendous volume of resources and human energy and attention, yet the role of organised security market institutions as the link between the desire to accumulate capital goods by firms and the desire to store wealth by households is only vaguely perceived in standard economic texts. The existence of a continuous well-organised spot market in titles to real wealth makes the investment decision even more independent of the decision to save than it might be otherwise, for in the absence of spot securities markets

> Decisions to invest in private business were . . . largely irrevocable, not only for the community as a whole, but also for the individual. With the separation between ownership and management which prevails today . . . a new factor of great importance has entered in, which sometimes facilitates investment but sometimes adds greatly to the instability of the system . . . the daily revaluations of the Stock Exchange, though they are primarily.made to facilitate transfers of old investments between one individual and another, inevitably exert a decisive influence on the rate of current investment.[3]

[1] For example, see Keynes, *Treatise on Money*, I 204, 254, 273–4, II 336, 351, 368, 402, 406.
[2] ibid. II 406.
[3] Keynes, *The General Theory*, pp. 150–1.

In a world of perfect foreknowledge, of course, there would be no need for spot securities markets, while in a world of perfect certainty (in the sense that the sum of the probabilities of all possible expected events equals unity) insurance markets could provide the broker's function between savers and investors.

Nevertheless, organised security exchanges are not insurance markets – nor do middlemen between savers and investors operate on actuarial principles. Instead, some of these financial intermediaries have developed semi-privileged arrangements with the banking system which have provided a degree of liquidity to the possession of securities which cannot be associated with, in an uncertain world, the holding of real capital goods – thereby creating a potentially discordant schism between ownership and control of real assets. Moreover, the existence of these liquidity-creating arrangements between placement market intermediaries and the Monetary Authority either directly or indirectly (via commercial banks) has meant that, *under certain conditions*, the money supply will respond endogenously to changes in the needs of trade or even changes in the needs of the financial circulation. Accordingly, we now turn our attention to the factors gearing the money supply to real factors, and possible behavioural decisions that can cause slippage.

EXTERNAL FINANCE AND THE DEMAND FOR SECURITIES OUT OF HOUSEHOLD SAVINGS

In a stationary economy where sales expectations are being met, it is true that each firms' need to replace fixed and working capital per period could be financed from sales receipts over time. Of course, even in a stationary economy, as long as production takes time, firms may be required to make payments to resource owners before sales revenues are received. The financing of these factor payments could be accomplished via short-term loans from banks. When, at the end of the production period, sales expectations are met, then sales revenues will be sufficient to repay the firms' short-term obligations to the banks and to yield a 'normal' profit. Under these conditions, the volume of available short-term credit facilities is a 'revolving fund' of a more or less constant amount available to finance the working capital expenditures of the next period.[1] In equilibrium in a stationary economy, there will be neither a flow-supply of securities (new issues) nor a flow-demand for securities by the public out of household savings, since net savings and net investment are zero.

In a growing economy, on the other hand, there may be a flow-supply of securities if firms choose to externally fund a portion of net investment,[2] and a flow-demand for securities if households wish to purchase securities out of savings. Thus, while the flow-supply of securities is primarily associated with new issues (and the s_p function of Chapter 12), the flow-demand will be, for purpose of exposition in this chapter, associated solely with the shift in the D_p function of Chapter 12 induced by the marginal propensity to buy placements out of household savings (m), or, in Kaldor's terminology, by increases in 'non-speculative demand' for securities. Hence, unless otherwise noted, the following analysis ignores (a) the fact that open-market operations by the banking system can affect the net flow-supply of securities available to the public, and (b) factors causing changes in liquidity preference (changes in the precautionary and speculative demand for securities) can alter the net flow-demand for securities by households. Moreover, for purposes of analytically separating 'independent' economic factors, the following analysis emphasises household decisions about current increments in wealth and corporate decisions on increments of indebtedness as the major forces determining the excess-flow demand for securities, even though these current increments per period are only a trifling proportion of the existing blocks of wealth and indebtedness, and in reality are only a minor element in the matter.

[1] Amortisation of the outstanding long-term debt can also operate as a 'revolving fund' for the replacement of fixed capital. Cf. Keynes, 'Alternative Theories', *Econ. Jour.* (1937) **47** 247. Also see Keynes, 'The Ex-Ante Theory', p. 666.

[2] In a growth context, the ability to obtain external finance is related not only to the 'cost of borrowing' but to the proportion of the total value of the firm which has been internally financed, that is to the Retention Ratio. Accordingly internal and external finance may be complements rather than substitutes, and therefore corporate net investment spending will probably exceed corporate needs for external finance.

If there are continuous spot markets for securities, then, households will be continuously re-evaluating their entire wealth-holdings and the problem of matching the flow-supply of new issues with the flow-demand out of current household savings is complicated by possible simultaneous changes in the excess stock-demand for securities. By focusing the analysis on decisions involving the trifling increments in household wealth and firm 'indebtedness' however, it is easier to illustrate the impossibility of setting out of any simple quantitative rule for expanding the money supply which may not act as a brake on growth under certain conditions – even if there are no complications arising from changes in the speculative demand for the pre-existing stock of securities (the excess stock-demand for securities). In essence, therefore, it is assumed that if there is no change in either the public's expectations of the future spot price of securities, or their risk preferences, or their confidence in their expectations, or the pre-existing stock of securities *available* to the public, then the price of placements will increase (be constant, fall), if the excess flow-demand for securities at the current price is positive (zero, negative).

In a growing economy, entrepreneurs will be desiring to increase production and capacity in each successive period. consequently, capital expenditures will increase over time and the pool of short-term bank credit at the end of period t_1 will not be sufficient to finance all the demand for increased orders in t_2. Whether firms hope partly to finance the investment internally or hope to finance all these additional capital expenditures externally by issuing long-term securities (e.g. mortgages) in order to 'mobilise' the savings which are being generated over the period as the capital goods are being paid for and installed, the investing firms will require, at the beginning of the period, additional transactions balances – the finance motive of Chapter 7 – to meet the contractually agreed upon payments to suppliers which must be made at appropriate stages during the gestation period.[1]

It is therefore necessary for many investing firms to engage an investment banker (or promoter) before placing orders for

---

[1] It is these contractual agreements to hire *and* pay resource owners and suppliers of raw materials which are fundamental to a money wage-production-specialisation, and exchange economy.

additional fixed capital goods. After convincing themselves of the reasonableness of the firms' long-term expectations, these financial middlemen will be willing to underwrite the issue of long-term securities at the end of the period at some agreed price. Then, either the underwriters will borrow short-term from a commercial bank and make these facilities available to the firm, or the firm, armed with the underwriter's commitment, may borrow directly from the banks. As a consequence the money supply may be expanded during the period.

The investing firms, assured of short-term credit at the bank and long-term funding from the underwriter, can enter into contractual agreements for the delivery of plant and equipment from the capital goods producers. During the gestation period of the capital goods production, interim partial payments by the buyers from their short-term bank loans plus working capital finance which is at least partly obtained by short-term borrowing from the banks by the capital goods producers are used by these producing firms to meet their interim wage and raw material bills. If external funding is involved, the final payments by the 'investing' firm which is normally made when the fixed capital goods have been satisfactorily installed and most of the variable costs of production have been paid, is paid out of receipts from the floating of a long-term new issue. The revenues from the flotation are used, therefore, to complete payments to suppliers, to pay off the interim short-term bank credit obtained either directly or indirectly by the underwriter, and to pay for the value added of the resources used to market the issue. A portion of the final payment received by the suppliers is used to repay their working capital bank loans, and the rest is used for final payments of payrolls and raw materials, with any remainder becoming the gross profits of the capital goods producer. Thus these repayments of short-term credit out of the proceeds of long-term funding become a revolving pool of finance which can be used to maintain a similar level of investment expenditures in the next period.

The flotation of new issue – the flow-supply of placements – is normally carried out via financial intermediaries such as investment bankers, underwriting syndicates, or new issue houses. These financial intermediaries have either direct or indirect (via other financial intermediaries) access to savers who wish to purchase securities – access which would not easily be available to the investing firms directly. Each of these financial institutions can also normally expect preferential treatment from the banking system and even from the Monetary Authority if the stream of savings searching for placements outlets unexpectedly dries up. This recognised pre-emptive access to the institutions that create money, are the ultimate basis for liquidity in the financial markets.

In the last chapter, Kaldor's neo-Pasinetti theorem was used as the focal point for analysing the problem of bringing the volume of household savings looking for securities into equality with the firms' desires for external finance, i.e. the balancing of the flow-demand and flow-supply of securities. If, at the initial placement price, excess flow-demand for securities fortuitously happens to be zero, so that

$$iI = ms_h \Upsilon_h \qquad (1)$$

where i is the fraction of investment expenditures (I) which entrepreneurs, in the aggregate, wish to finance externally, m is the marginal propensity to purchase securities out of aggregate household savings, and s_h is the public's planned savings ratio out of household income (Υ_h), then the aggregate planned net 'debtor' position of firms is growing *pari passu* with the aggregate planned net creditor position of households.

If the funds used to internally finance investment spending is equal to corporate savings out of profits (s_cP), i.e. if $s_cP = (1-i)I$, and if entrepreneurial expectations of sales proceeds from current production are being realised, then aggregate savings out of household income must be equal to the fraction of spending which is being externally financed, that is $s_h\Upsilon_h = iI$. This implies, therefore, that if the warranted or equilibrium growth path is to be maintained while excess flow-demand for securities is zero, then m must equal unity. This is, of course, the basic message of Kaldor's neo-Pasinetti theorem.

Of course, as has already been noted in footnote number 2, p. 305 of Chapter 12, even if $m = 1$ so that households do not wish to hold additional idle balances as their wealth-holdings increase with growth, the demand by firms for increased money balances to finance higher payrolls, etc. will require the Monetary Authority to provide for the increasing needs of trade in advance of actual expansion.[1] Nevertheless, if the banking system is responsive to the needs for expanding short-term credit as they receive requests from underwriters, promoters, and even firms themselves requesting increases in working capital finance, and if $iI = ms_h Y_h$ when $m = 1$, then when entrepreneurs correctly foresee expected short-term sales proceeds, financial considerations will not be a constraint on the economy, as economic units do not desire to hold any increments in personal wealth in the form of money.

In a monetary economy, however, there is no reason to expect m to equal unity. In fact it is more reasonable to assume that as household wealth increases a portion will go to the accumulation of idle balances. Accordingly even if sales expectations are being met, so that $s_o P + s_h Y_h = (1 - i)I + iI$, excess flow-demand for securities is likely to be negative.[2]

GROWTH WHEN EXCESS FLOW-DEMAND FOR SECURITIES IS NEGATIVE

If the firms' demand for external funding exceed households' desire to purchase additional securities out of savings *at the current placements price*, that is if $iI > ms_h Y_h$, then even if entrepreneurial short-period expectations at the given level of employment could be met (so that the planned savings ratio equals entrepreneurial desires for non-available output as a proportion of total production) financial conditions will cause the economy to slow down – even if the banking system is responding to the needs of industry for working capital. When $iI > ms_h Y_h$, then *ceteris paribus*, the excess flow-demand for securities is negative[3] at the current placement·price, i.e. the

---

[1] Also see the analysis of the finance motive, ch. 7 above.

[2] If a portion of internal finance was obtained by drawing down idle balances so that $s_o p < (1 - i)I$, and if that portion equalled the excess of household savings over externally financed investment, then it would be possible for excess flow-demand for securities to be zero with $m < 1$ and entrepreneurial sales expectations were realised. In this lucky circumstance, the reduced bearishness of firms is just offsetting the increased liquidity desires of households at the current placement price level.

[3] Of course, as we have already noted, this assumes that the normal factors affecting liquidity preference, e.g. expectations about future spot

flow-supply of securities available to the public exceeds the 'non-speculative' or flow-demand for securities. Consequently, there will be downward pressure on placement prices as the 'needs' of the financial circulation are not being entirely met by the banking system. In an uncertain world, the underwriters will become aware of this negative excess flow-demand only as they observe a stochastic decline in the spot securities market and/or a resistance to buy by their normal customers. These financial intermediaries will attempt to protect their 'goodwill' with their normal customers (who have bought previous new issues) by reducing the pressure on security prices. These financial middlemen will therefore either (1) discourage some firms who currently desire to float new issues (thereby forcing these firms to reduce their planned investment spending) and/or (2) increase their indebtedness to the banking system in order to finance an 'undesired' increase in dealer inventories. By these methods, the underwriters hope to support the market against this unforeseen slump[1] *and* to maintain a continuous market for placements. To the extent that the financial intermediaries adopt the latter method and to the extent the banking system accommodates the financial requirements of the dealers via an expansion of the money supply, then the banking system is looking after that portion of the real wealth of the community which, for the moment, at the current rate of interest, the public does not wish to own.[2]

In sum, even if the real forces in the economy are such that the planned savings ratio at a given level of income is equal to the proportion of aggregate product which entrepreneurs want

---

prices of securities, risk aversion, etc. are unaltered, so only the minor increments in wealth affect the market price of securities.

[1] Cf. J. R. Hicks, *Critical Essays in Monetary Theory*, p. 48.

[2] Of course, if the underwriters were to draw down their precautionary balances to finance the 'undesired' increment in inventory (perhaps because they think the downward pressure is only temporary) the immediate impact is for these financial intermediaries to offset the 'excessive bear holdings' of the general public. Of course, these financial intermediaries could not continually add to their inventories by drawing down their precautionary balances, so sooner or later they must resort to either discouraging further flotations or borrowing from the banks. Cf. R. F. Kahn, 'Some Notes on Liquidity Preference', *Manchester School* (1954) pp. 237–8.

in the form of non-available output, *if* excess demand for securities is negative, i.e. $iI > ms_h Y_h$, then financial conditions in the securities market can, by themselves, induce a slow-down. This slackness can initially be avoided if investment underwriters finance their excessive security inventories via increased borrowing from the banks, and the banking system in turn, endogenously responds to these needs of the financial circulation (in excess of the needs of trade) by increasing the money supply.[1]

If, however, the Monetary Authority does not permit the banks to expand the money supply while the financial inter-mediaries have preferential access to the revolving fund of bank credit, then as security dealers borrow to finance their swollen inventories, the banks will have to ration the remaining credit among the borrowers from the industrial circulation. (This may take the form of raising the cost of bank loans in general and/or discriminating against small firms such as house builders, etc. who require working capital.) This ration-ing of credit to the industrial sector will obviously reduce growth and may even induce a slump, even if financial inter-mediaries took no voluntary actions of their own to staunch the forthcoming flow of new issues.

Even if, initially, the banking system were to permit expan-sion of credit to aid financial middlemen to hold their 'un-desired' inventories, these financial intermediaries will be un-willing continuously to increase their excessive holdings if the excess-flow demand for securities remains negative for any length of time. Instead, these financial institutions will feel encumbered by their increasing indebtedness and must ulti-mately severely limit their willingness to float new issues in the future until they can disgorge their swollen inventories without adversely affecting the spot price of securities. Hence, even if the banking system endogenously increases the money supply to help financial intermediaries finance excess inventories of

---

[1] Kaldor's neo-Pasinetti theorem avoids this result by assumingt hat the negative excess flow-demand for securities results in a capital loss which induces capitalist households to increase savings (since $c > 0$, and in this case $G < 0$) and to use these to buy additional securities, thereby bringing about equilibrium in the securities market but creating disequilibrium in the consumer goods market if originally savings equalled investment.

securities resulting from a negative excess flow-demand for securities, expenditures on the output flow of the capital goods industries will ultimately be reduced by such Procrustean devices as rationing access to long-term funding, and/or offering to float new issues at prices which are low compared to the current spot price of securities, and/or permitting a slow, continuous decline in security prices. These actions by the financial intermediaries will reduce the ability of entrepreneurs to obtain external finance and therefore prevent firms from entering into as many contracts for the delivery of capital goods per period as they would otherwise desire.[1]

The financial circulation can therefore restrict expenditures on new capital goods, even if the public propose to be sufficiently thrifty out of a given level of income just to maintain the warranted rate of growth. Even if the planned savings ratio is compatible with growth at full employment, a Golden Age may be interrupted or prevented solely by a negative excess flow-demand for securities. In such circumstances the Monetary Authority can redress the financial constraints on growth, by undertaking a monetary policy which will increase the excess flow-demand to zero – that is, by relieving the dealers of their unwanted inventories via open market operations and thereby supplying sufficient cash to meet all the bearishness desires of households *and* dealers. Thus as Keynes declared:

> The banks hold the key in the transition from a lower to a higher scale of activity. . . . The investment market can become congested through a shortage of cash. It can never become congested through a shortage of savings. This is the most fundamental of my conclusions in this field.[2]

Moreover, since expectations of future spot prices of securities can greatly affect the current security market conditions,[3] it may be necessary and desirable for monetary policy to operate *before* adverse expectations are generated in the securities market. In other words, it would be desirable for the Monetary Authority to purchase securities on the open market

[1] Cf. R. F. Hawtrey, *The Art of Central Banking*, p. 382.
[2] Keynes, 'The Ex-Ante Theory', pp. 668–9.
[3] A complication which we have previously avoided, by assumption, in this chapter.

prior to the negative excess flow-demand for securities appearing in the market. By removing securities from either the public or the dealers just before the excess bearishness appears, the Monetary Authority can create financial conditions such that the entire new issue can be voluntarily taken up by the public and/or the dealers.

In general, a growth-oriented monetary policy would necessitate providing increases in the money supply in *anticipation* of all the needs of trade *and* finance as long as the point of effective demand does not exceed full employment. Of course, to diagnose these needs in advance and to achieve an exact balance is not possible via any simple quantitative rule for expanding the money supply. Nor it is possible, in an uncertain world, to forecast excess flow-demands for capital goods *and* securities precisely using an econometric analysis of past events. Instead, if the Monetary Authority is to promote a financial atmosphere which is compatible with a Golden Age, then its decisions will have to be guided by a fragile mixture of the 'best' scientific forecasts of growth of the industrial circulation and the 'best' judgement forecasts of the trend of forces in the financial markets. As long as the world is uncertain and a continuous spot market for securities exists, the current spot market price will depend primarily on the precautionary and speculative demand for securities, that is, on expectations, and the Monetary Authority will need flexibility and discretion if they are to anticipate, or at least not frustrate, the 'needs' for the financial 'paving stones' which will permit the real factors to achieve the warranted rate of growth.

If, on the other hand, a simple quantitative rule based on the expected rate of growth of the industrial circulation is used as the basis for expanding the money supply, then unless both the excess flow-demand and the excess stock-demand for securities are both equal to zero at the current placement price, a steady rate of growth cannot be maintained. If excess flow-demand is negative while excess stock-demand is zero, then financial constraints will hamper growth. A positive excess flow-demand (while excess stock demand is zero), on the other hand, is symptomatic of a shortage of effective demand and unless the real factors can be increased, the real forces in the economy will induce a slowdown.

A POSITIVE 'NON-SPECULATIVE' EXCESS FLOW-DEMAND FOR SECURITIES MEANS CONTRACTION

When the 'non-speculative' excess flow-demand for securities is positive at the current placement price, i.e. when $iI < ms_h Y_h$, then in a two-sector model, although there is a tendency for the spot price of securities to increase, economic activity will either decrease or expand at a much slower rate than the warranted one. This seemingly paradoxical result of a recessionary economy in the presence of a rising or bullish security market is, however, easily explainable. Since internally financed investment expenditures are equal to total corporate savings (retentions) out of profit income, therefore, if household savings exceed the demand for external funding for investment by firms, then household savings plus corporate savings must exceed aggregate investment at the given level of income.[1] It therefore follows that since $m < 1$, when $iI < ms_h Y_h$, entrepreneurial short-period sales expectations associated with the given level of employment must be disappointed. Accordingly, if this level of employment is undertaken, some firms will be saddled with losses, or at least, they will have a smaller cash flow than expected and will be earning less than normal profits.

Entrepreneurs, faced with disappointing cash flows and possessing existing capacity which is deemed excessive for current realised sales, are unlikely to have visions of additional investment opportunities which can become profitable solely because of a decline in the rate of discount. Of course, with rising security prices, investment underwriters will find it easy and profitable to float new issues and they therefore may 'beat the bushes' in order to flush out additional investment projects from entrepreneurs,[2] particularly from those who might, under other circumstances, be part of the unsatisfied fringe of borrowers. If these financial intermediaries are successful they may be able to increase real investment and the demand for external finances sufficiently so that a slowdown is avoided.

If, on the other hand, the investment underwriters are not

---

[1] Since corporate savings $(S_c) = (1 - i)I$, if $iI < s_h Y_h$ then

$$S_c + s_h Y_h > (1 - i)I + iI, \text{ and therefore } S > I.$$

[2] Cf. Keynes, *Treatise on Money*, II 368–9, *The General Theory*, p. 151, n.1. Compare footnote 2, p. 309 in Chapter 12 above.

successful in encouraging additional investment spending, then the bullish behaviour of the public in the securities market will induce security dealers – especially stock specialists and stock jobbers whose function it is to maintain a continuous spot market in second-hand securities – to sell off inventories and to build up their cash position.[1] In essence, these financial intermediaries are draining cash (via savings out of household incomes) from the industrial circulation – they are absorbing cash in Hawtrey's terminology.[2]

The stock specialist is the residual buyer and seller in the second-hand market. He is not required to hold off a rise or a decline in security prices; his function is merely to maintain continuity. The major source of specialist profits is on intraday trading and on normal days his purchases and sales are almost in balance.[3] If, however, the stock jobber stochastically finds that his inventory of securities is declining and his cash position is rising, at some stage he will perceive this is a permanent change in excess demand, and he will use some of the profit revenues from the sale of securities to reduce his indebtedness to the banking system. Thus the public's excess-flow demand for securities permits the draining of cash from the industrial circulation initially to financial intermediaries; and then to the banks. Unless these funds can be recirculated into the industrial circulation by finding borrowers who wish to finance additional capital expenditures, an economic slow-down is inevitable.

In sum, as long as financial intermediaries act as residual buyers and sellers in a well-organised securities market, securities will be very good substitutes for money as a store of value; and if the public's (households plus firms) planned saving ratio out of current income exceeds that which is necessary to maintain effective demand at the current level of employment, it does

---

[1] The investment underwriter may also run down his normal inventories in order to prevent the spot price from rising too rapidly. Too rapid an increase in security prices would provoke the enmity of firms who have recently issued new securities via the underwriter. These firms might feel that the underwriter induced them to sell their securities at too low a price.

[2] See Hawtrey, *The Art of Central Banking*, p. 361.

[3] See *Report of Special Study of Securities Market of the Securities Exchange Commission*, Part II (Washington : U.S. Government Printing Office, 1963) p. 85.

not matter whether households desire money or securities as a vehicle for transferring purchasing power to the future, entrepreneurial sales expectations must be disappointed. Realised profits and cash flows will be lower than expected and entrepreneurs will be encouraged to retrench.[1]

Accordingly, Pasinetti's startling conclusion that the savings propensity of wage-earners is irrelevant for profits and growth, even if workers plan to use their savings to buy securities, is not true for the real world, i.e. for a monetary economy, where entrepreneurs may not be expanding fast enough to offset workers' savings and future investment plans can be affected by current disappointments about sales proceeds and profit realisations. Pasinetti merely assumes that the planned savings ratio out of wages (in essence, out of household income) can not exceed the proportion of resources currently being utilised in the production of capital goods; otherwise there would be a lack of effective demand and unemployment.[2] In a two-sector model of the real world, however, if the planned savings ratio out of wages plus profit distributions is greater than the proportion of investment spending which firms wish to externally finance, there will be an insufficiency of effective demand in the goods markets and entrepreneurial short-period sales expectations will be disappointed. Hence, even in this case, the savings propensities of both workers and capitalist households are relevant in determining realised profits and growth.

Kaldor, recognising the fact that 'no Keynesian macroeconomic distribution theory could survive for an instant let alone in Golden Age equilibrium'[3] if aggregate household savings out of wages plus profit distribution exceeds entrepreneurial desires for external funding (and therefore admitting that the savings behaviour of all households out of all types of

---

[1] To the extent firms are making out-of-pocket losses, they may partly finance these by additional borrowings from the banks (who, however, are unlikely to be willing to make such loans even if they have excess reserves). Cf. Keynes, *Treatise on Money*, 1 145. Even if firms finance losses by borrowing, they will be under financial pressure to cut costs and therefore production and hiring in the future.

[2] L. L. Pasinetti, 'New Results in an Old Framework', *Rev. of Econ. Stud.*, **33** (1966) p. 304.

[3] N. Kaldor, 'Marginal Productivity and the Macroeconomic Theories of Distribution', p. 311.

incomes can affect the neo-keynesian growth analysis), invented a 'real-placement' effect. This effect, which operates via the valuation ratio 'has exactly the same effect as a reduction of s_w, since it causes a reduction of the net savings of persons that is available to finance business investment'.[1] In other words, Kaldor concocts a mechanism which assures that aggregate household consumption spending will be sufficient to maintain a Golden Age when entrepreneurs are accumulating at the natural rate set by labour force growth and technical progress.

Both Pasinetti's assumption that $s_w < I/Y$ and Kaldor's real-placement effect are merely convenient inventions to assure that real spending behaviour will be compatible with a Golden Age. In a world of uncertainty, however, where money and securities are excellent substitutes as stores of value (and therefore there must be residual buyers and sellers in well-organised financial markets), while they have negligible elasticities of productivity and substitution with reproducible goods, neither Pasinetti's assumptions nor Kaldor's consumption due to capital gains mechanism can assure automatic growth at full employment (or any other growth rate) unless financial conditions permit it.

An adequate money supply to meet the needs of industry and finance at full employment is a necessary, but not a sufficient condition for a Golden Age. A negative excess flow-demand for securities not offset by the purchase of securities via open-market operations will prevent growth at full employment even if the *ex ante* real consumption and investment spending propensities are compatible with a Golden Age. On the other hand, if the real factors are not sufficient to bring about a Golden Age, then easier financial conditions can not *per se* induce the economy to expand at its natural rate of growth.

Harrod has succinctly summarised this central theme of the operation of a monetary economy:

> It was Keynes's contention, which was both a novelty and source of endless confusion among commentators that a tendency for savings to exceed investment had nothing whatever to do with people putting money into a stocking or even with their leaving it idle in a banking account. Savings

might exceed investment even if all savers immediately invested their money in industrial securities, and investment might exceed saving even if a great many savers were putting their money into stockings.[1]

In the absence of financial institutions which operate as residual buyers and sellers in spot placement markets, money alone would possess those elasticity attributes which assure that Say's Law is inoperative. The existence of such financial intermediaries, however, provides significantly greater liquidity to securities than to the real capital goods underlying these placements. The access these financial institutions have to the banking system, who is ultimately the lender of last resort supporting the placement market, is the institutional *coup de grâce* to both the neoclassical view that, in the long run, underemployment equilibrium is impossible, and the Kaldor–Pasinetti view that, in the long run, income distribution and the rate of interest will always adjust real consumption spending to assure full employment growth.

The financial arrangements between firms, investment underwriters, stock specialists and commercial banks provide a mechanism both for communicating the monetary needs of industry and finance, and a way for the Monetary Authority to respond to the current and anticipated monetary needs of the community. Unfortunately, the various financial institutions operating on this two-way street are often guided in their actions by principles of conventional wisdom which are oriented towards goals that often are, in an uncertain world, antithetical to the commonweal. Accordingly, it is not surprising that these human creations have not only at times constrained the rate of accumulation while resources were idle, but have also permitted a decision-making procedure to develop in which the services of the productive resources of society are utilised in ways which are adverse to the social interests.[2]

---

[1] R. F. Harrod, *The Life of John Maynard Keynes*, pp. 404–5. Also see p. 372, n. 1.

[2] It is the separation of ownership from control which is due to the growth of organised continuous security markets and not the lack of perfect competition in the traditional microeconomic sense which leads to Galbraith's scathing indictment of the misallocation of resources in a growing economy. See J. K. Galbraith, *The New Industrial State*.

SUMMARY

In sum, if the excess flow-demand for securities is positive then the planned savings ratio must, unless other spending factors can be introduced, exceed the proportion of total production which entrepreneurs are allocating to non-available output and a slowdown in employment and output is inevitable. If the planned savings ratio equals the proportion of total output going to non-available output, and if the money supply expands at the beginning of each period at the same rate as the growth in expected output, then if excess flow-demand for securities is zero, i.e. $iI = ms_h Y_h$ and $m = 1$, financial considerations will not upset the equilibrium growth of the economy. If, however, the excess flow-demand for securities is negative $(iI > ms_h Y_h)$, then even though the planned savings ratio each period is compatible with the warranted rate of growth, if the banking system only increases the money supply at the same rate as the expected growth in production, *then* financial market conditions will retard accumulation and growth.[1] If the warranted rate of growth is to be maintaintd when $iI > ms_h Y_h$, then the money supply must increase *more* rapidly than the growth in output in order to anticipate the needs of the financial circulation as well.

There is an asymmetry about money matters. If excess flow-demand for securities is negative, then more rapid expansion of the money supply can maintain growth while the banking system looks after the portion of the real wealth of society that the public does not wish to currently own; while if excess flow-demand (out of household savings) is positive, monetary policy may be powerless to encourage an expansion. This is the analysis which ultimately lies beyond the old monetary theory adage 'You can't push on a string'.

RULES AND MONETARY POLICY

Since for wealth-holding households the portfolio balance decision as to what proportion of their store of value to hold in

[1] Uncompensated increases in the financial circulation will limit investment spending in two ways (a) raising the rate of discount, and/or (b) reducing the availability of credit to entrepreneurs. Cf. Keynes, *Treatise on Money*, II 254.

the form of uncertain deferred claims (securities) and what proportion to hold as immediate claims (money) relate to their whole block of wealth at each moment,[1] and not to their current increment, the guidelines for monetary policy involving iI and $ms_h Y_h$ as developed in the previous sections, are much too simple. These rules were developed merely as convenient analytical ways of separating out the diverse financial forces creating complications for the smooth operation of monetary economy.

In the real world, new issues and household savings are trifling elements in the securities market. It is changes in the excess stock-demand for securities (the speculative and precautionary demand) which are induced by changes in public confidence and opinion about future spot securities prices which dominate the needs of the financial circulation and the spot price of placements. Any discrepancy between iI and $ms_h Y_h$ is likely to be swamped by the eddies of speculative movements by the whole body of wealth-holders who are constantly sifting and shifting their portfolio composition. Consequently, in an uncertain world, where financial market expectations are especially volatile and unpredictable, the relationship between increases in the quantity of money and the needs of the financial circulation are too complex and capricious to be handled by any simple rule, even if growth in the real factors underlying the needs of the industrial circulation could be accurately forecast. The solution lies:

> in letting Finance and Industry have all the money they want, but at a rate of interest which in its effect on the rate of new [externally financed] investment . . . exactly balances the effect of bullish sentiment. To diagnose the position precisely at every stage and to achieve this exact balance may sometimes be, however, beyond the wits of man.[2]

Any rule for expanding the money supply at the same rate as the growth in output will only fortuitously promote a steady rate of accumulation since the demand for securities out of households' savings and/or the public's liquidity preference proper may be changing at a different rate than the supply of securities.

[1] As long as there are continuous well-organised spot-markets for deferred claims.   [2] Keynes, *Treatise on Money*, I 254-5.

If the Monetary Authority as the ultimate creator of the medium of exchange gears its policy to maintaining the purchasing power of its creation in periods of rising flow-supply prices of reproducible goods (inflation), the growth of the money supply will be severely restricted. Consequently, it will be impossible to expand the revolving fund of finance even to meet the needs of a growing industrial circulation, and accumulation will be retarded even though households and entrepreneurs propose to behave in a manner consistent with maintaining a steady rate of growth. Moreover, if there are strong social and political forces causing spontaneous rises in flow-supply prices of reproducible goods, 'then the control of the price-level may pass beyond the power of the banking system'[1] even if the Monetary Authority holds the rate of growth of the money supply far below the growth in potential output. Accordingly, a monetary policy which is compatible with a socially desirable stable rate of growth and a relatively stable price level, must be co-ordinated with a fiscal policy which assures the proper balance of the real forces underlying aggregate demand, *and* a government policy on incomes oriented towards stablising the flow-supply price of reproducible goods over time –

If we have complete control of the Earnings (or Wages) System and of the Currency System, so that we can alter the rate of earnings by *fiat* . . . and can control the rate of investment, then we can . . . stabilise – the purchasing power of money, . . . its labour power, or anything else – without running the risk of setting up social and economic frictions or causing waste. . . .

But if . . . we have at least a partial control of the Currency System but not of the Earnings System, . . . (then) we have some power to decide what the equilibrium price level and rate of earnings is to be, but no power of bringing about this equilibrium except by setting into operating the mechanism of induced changes [in real spending behaviour].[2]

In the next chapter, the analysis of money, inflation, employment, and government policy will be analysed in detail.

[1] ibid. II 351.   [2] ibid. I 169.

CHAPTER 14

Inflation

IT is neither rising spot prices of non-reproducible goods such as rare paintings or sculptures, nor the prices of securities listed on the New York Stock Exchange, which are the main focus of public concern in discussions of inflation. Inflation becomes a major cause of public interest *only* when it is the market prices of *producible goods and services* that bulk significantly large in consumers' budgets that are continuously increasing. Keeping this pragmatic view of the public concern over inflation in mind, the problem can readily be analysed by concentrating on the linchpin of a monetary-production-specialisation-exchange economy, the short-run offer or flow-supply price of output.

In any money economy, the production of goods and services can be conceptualised as being sold via a forward market, since contractual commitments for hire and forward delivery are always undertaken by someone before production begins. In an economy where production is occurring, the spot price (or price for pre-existing durables-adjusted for remaining life) can exceed the forward (or flow-supply) price of any producible good by an amount limited only by the unwillingness of the buyer to pay the higher spot price than wait for forward delivery at the flow-supply price.[1] This situation is called 'backwardation'. As long as production is going on, the price that buyers are willing to pay for forward delivery can never exceed, and will normally equal, the short-run flow-supply price since the latter is defined as the money-price required to call forth the exertion necessary to produce any given amount of the commodity for any given delivery date.[2]

For commodities that are redundant, on the other hand, the

[1] See Keynes, *Treatise on Money*, II 143.
[2] See A. Marshall, *Principles of Economics*, 8th ed., p. 142.

spot price will fall below the short-run flow-supply price – a contango – by an amount sufficient to compensate the buyer for the carrying costs of the commodity until it is no longer expected to be redundant – at which time it will again be produced (by definition) at the flow-supply price.[1] Accordingly, the short-run flow-supply price *is* the pivot around which the spot price swings as the spot market is either in backwardation or contango. While the spot price can be very responsive to changes in demand, nevertheless, it is the components of the short-run flow-supply price which ultimately determine the prices at which current production will be offered to buyers.

Changes in spot prices relative to the flow-supply prices Keynes labelled *Commodity and Capital Inflation (or Deflation)*;[2] changes in these prices would be associated with commodities that had been previously produced, it would provide windfall capital gains or losses for holders of such real assets who decided to sell them in the current spot market. In other words, *Commodity and Capital Inflation,* primarily affects capital values of pre-existing durables rather than the flow of money income.

Changes in flow-supply prices or forward prices of goods being produced, on the other hand, are associated with an *Income Inflation (or Deflation)* by Keynes, since these changes in the costs of production are, if productivity per worker is unchanged, the conjugate of changes in money income payments to resource owners.[3] Since, in a money-wage production economy, the flow of output always requires some contractual commitment in advance via hiring and/or offer contracts, the relevant price level index for the flow of current production must be one based on short-run flow-supply prices of producible goods and services. Moreover, as long as households hold money as a temporary abode of purchasing power, the relevant price level index for converting money balances into a measure of the real value of command over production is an index of short-run flow-supply prices. In an uncertain world, it is this

---

[1] Keynes, *Treatise on Money*, II 144.   [2] ibid. I 155–6.

[3] ibid. I 156. In fact, Keynes separates a Profit Inflation which raises the gross margin over normal profits plus wage costs (realised by market-clearing prices) from an incomes inflation which involves wage costs and 'normal' profits. For present purposes, any increase in margins can be referred to as a profits inflation.

index which indicates the purchasing power of money in the
near future in terms of the output that can be bought in the
future either by currently accepting an offer for forward delivery
or by using the forward price as the *best* available market estimate of the spot price in the next period[1] when the individual
may suddenly want to buy goods 'spot' for money. Thus the
flow-supply price index is the one individuals use in calculating the 'real' balances they wish to hold.

This emphasis on flow-supply prices should not be interpreted as supporting the myopic view that demand factors
cannot affect the price of output; rather changes in demand will
immediately affect actual (or notional) spot prices and then
the demand will spill over into the forward market.[2] Nevertheless, if the flow-supply price for any good is not expected to
alter, then no matter how far the current spot price may be
momentarily displaced from the offer price for forward delivery,
as the stock of durables is augmented, the future spot price will
return to the current flow-supply price. Hence, if individuals
expect the current short-run money flow-supply price of output
to be sticky over time, then they can be confident in their use
of money as a vehicle for transferring power.[3]

THE THREE KINDS OF INFLATION[4]

The decisions on offer prices by suppliers depend on (1) the
factors which motivate entrepreneurial behaviour and offers
in an uncertain world, (2) the input prices and productivity
phenomena, and (3) the organisation of the markets in which

[1] H. Working, 'New Concepts Concerning Future Markets and Prices',
American Econ. Rev. **52** (1966) pp. 446–7.

[2] Cf. Keynes, *Treatise on Money*, I 156.

[3] Even if the retail market is conceived as a spot market, in the sense that
purchasers do not order for forward delivery, the retail price will not fall
below the flow-supply price, if the retailer operates as a going concern,
for he will have to replace shelf inventory with new output. (The obvious
exception is at the end of a model year – a clearance sale – when the
market is in a contango.) For consumer goods that have short gestation
periods, the retail 'spot' price is not likely to rise much above the flow-
supply price because any shortages that develop can be quickly alleviated.

[4] This section is derived from S. Weintraub, *An Approach to the Theory
of Income Distribution*, pp. 162–4.

the suppliers operate. Whether entrepreneurs behaved in a neoclassical short-run profit maximising mode or in a Marshallian-neo-keynesian target return on standard volume manner, depends, at least partly, on the degree of uncertainty about market demand and the availability of contractual arrangements. Given entrepreneurial behaviour patterns, input prices, and productivity phenomena, short-run flow-supply price schedules can be determined which will be the basis of offer contracts for the production of output.

In general, short-run flow-supply prices can increase for three main reasons (1) diminishing returns, (2) increasing profit margins, and (3) increasing money wages (relative to productivity increments).[1] Observed increases in the price level of current output will often be due to some combination of these three distinct inflationary processes. If, therefore, public policy is to minimise price increases while simultaneously limiting undesirable side effects, then it may be necessary to design different policies to control each type of inflation.

For more than a century, economists have taught that every expansion of the flow of output and employment will normally involve increasing costs and increasing supply prices because of the law of diminishing returns. Diminishing returns, it is held, are inevitable – even if all labour and capital inputs in the production process were equally efficient – because of the scarcity of some input such as raw materials or managerial talent. Actually, however, economic expansion will lead to increasing costs (and flow-supply prices) not only because of the classical law of diminishing returns but also because labour and capital inputs are really not equally efficient. Expansion of the flow of production in our economy often involves the hiring of less-skilled workers, and the utilisation of older, less-efficient standby equipment and therefore adds to diminishing returns. This phenomenon, which may be labelled *hiring path diminishing returns*, was emphasised by Keynes as a main reason 'for rising supply prices before full employment'.[2]

The severity of diminishing returns inflation will vary with the level of unemployment. When the rate of unemployment

---

[1] If imports are an important component of the output of reproducible goods, then rising import prices can affect the flow-supply price.

[2] Keynes, *The General Theory*, pp. 42–3 including footnotes, 299–300.

is high (say about 5 per cent), idle capacity will exist in most firms, so that diminishing returns are likely to be relatively unimportant. As full employment is approached, however, an increasing number of firms will experience increasing costs, and diminishing returns inflation will become more important. Although in the short-run diminishing returns inflation of either the traditional or the hiring path variety is ultimately an inevitable consequence of expansion in employment, it represents a once-over real cost to society for the increased flow of output. It cannot, in the short-run, be avoided and no policy need be devised to avoid the singular price increase it entails.[1] In the long-run, improvements in technology, Government-sponsored training and educational programmes, and increases in capital equipment per worker can offset this price rise.

The second type of inflation will occur when businessmen (particularly in our more concentrated industries) come to believe that the market demand for their product has changed sufficiently so that it is possible and even perhaps necessary for them to increase the mark-up of prices relative to costs. If managers in many industries increase their profit margins, we will experience a profits inflation as the supply or offer prices rises. From a strictly theoretical point of view, there is no reason to suspect that changes in profit margins are necessarily uniquely related to changes in effective demand. Harrod has, for example, hypothesised a law of diminishing price elasticity of demand[2] which implies the possibility of rising profit margins with growth; while others have suggested a greater collusion among firms in a slump; thereby suggesting an inverse relation between profit margins and the level of employment.

The modern Cambridge views of Robinson, Kaldor, and Pasinetti, on the other hand, tend to associate higher profit margins (on a given standard volume) with economic systems that possess higher rates of accumulation. These modern Neo-keynesians are reflecting and, in essence, updating Keynes's

---

[1] Unless the economic rents which accrue to enterprises are deemed to be socially undesirable. In that case, a tax may have to be levied on such rents.

[2] R. F. Harrod, *The Trade Cycle* (Oxford: Clarendon Press, 1936) pp. 21–22.

Treatise belief of the importance of a Profits Inflation in providing the wherewithal for more rapid accumulation.[1] In the *Treatise*, Keynes permitted, as Kaldor and Pasinetti do in their modern models, profit margins at full employment to vary relative to money wages in response to changes in demand. In this view, increased profits relative to wages not only free resources and make them available for more rapid accumulation[2] and the long-run enrichment of human life,[3] but they also provide internal finance which, in an uncertain world, is a prerequisite to the firms' ability to borrow externally.

In the third type of inflation, every increase in money-wage rates, which is not offset by productivity increases will increase costs, and if profit margins are maintained, increase flow-supply prices. Consequently, we can expect that increases in money wages induce price increases. This phenomenon is often referred to as wage-price inflation. Since as unemployment levels decline it is easier for workers to obtain (collectively and individually) more liberal wage increases, we may expect wage inflation to become more pronounced as employment rises as the Phillips curve suggests; wage inflation, however, can occur even without expansion, if labour is able to secure increases which exceed productivity increments.

As Keynes noted, 'since each group of workers will gain, *cet. par.*, by a rise in its own wages, there is naturally for all groups a pressure in this direction, which entrepreneurs will be more ready to meet when they are doing better business'.[4] In modern economies, where near full employment policies have been actively pursued by governments, the truculence of

[1] Keynes, *Treatise on Money*, II 162–3, especially:
Thus, if we consider a long period of time, the working class may benefit far more in the long run from the forced abstinence which a *Profit Inflation* imposes on them than they lose in the first instance in the shape of diminished consumption . . . *so long as wealth and its fruits are not consumed by the nominal owner but are accumulated*, the evils of an unjust distribution may not be so great as they appear.

[2] This 'forced savings' assumes the propensity to save out of profits is greater than the propensity to save out of wages.

[3] Keynes, only half-jokingly suggested that as a result of the profits inflation in Elizabethan England, 'We were just in a financial position to afford Shakespeare at the moment when he presented himself!' Keynes, *Treatise on Money*, II 154.

[4] Keynes, *The General Theory*, p. 301.

wage-earners (both collectively and individually) and the acquiesence of managers operating in rapidly growing markets has exacerbated the problem of wage inflation. Moreover, to the extent that workers view their well-being as relative to the income of others, the struggle about money wages becomes a struggle for those on the bottom of the wage ladder to reduce wage differentials, and for those on the top to maintain or increase them.[1] Thus, the growth of economic and political power by groups of workers plus the increasingly readily available information on the earnings of others in economies where near full employment is taken for granted, has created pressures which makes wage-price inflation the most dangerous of current economic problems.

In sum, historically, rises in the price level of output as a whole have been due to some combination of three inflationary forces due to either (a) changes in money-wages (relative to productivity), (b) changes in profit margins, or (c) diminishing returns.

Every significant expansion in economic activity will induce some price increases because of diminishing returns. With rising prices, workers will, at a minimum, seek cost-of-living wage increases. Moreover, as pools of unemployment dry up, workers will be more impenitent in their total wage demands. Managers will be more willing to grant wage increases in a rising market, for they are more certain that they will be able to pass the higher labour costs on in higher prices. Also, management will find that as they hire more workers to meet the rising demands for their products, the cost of searching out and training the remaining unemployed will increase; consequently, they will often attempt to bid away workers from other employers rather than to recruit from the remaining unemployed. In addition, if management believes that the growth in demand is sufficiently strong they will increase profit margins and increase the inflationary tendency. Finally, legislators may find that the legal minimum wage becomes sub-standard as inflation occurs, and therefore, in a humanitarian spirit, they may raise the legal minimum. All these factors feed back on each

[1] Keynes, *The General Theory*, p. 14. For an analysis of the labour market and the determination of 'the money wage rate' see P. Davidson and E. Smolensky, *Aggregate Supply and Demand Analysis*, ch. 11.

other to create mounting wage-price pressures for as long as the economic expansion is permitted to continue.

Since the rate of diminishing returns, the rate of increase in money-wage rates, and increases in profit margins may be related to *either* low unemployment levels *or* rapidly decreasing employment levels or both, 'traditional' anti-inflation policies are oriented to maintain a sufficiently high unemployment rate to control the impact of changes in these factors on price levels. Any monetary and/or fiscal policy aimed at preventing *all* price increases before full employment is reached can be successful only if they perpetuate sufficient unemployment, and even this may not be sufficient, for as Keynes warned over forty years ago, 'if there are strong social or political forces causing spontaneous changes in the money-rates of efficiency-wages, the control of the price-level may pass beyond the power of the banking system'.[1]

It should be obvious that any increase in aggregate demand would induce changes in the flow-supply price of producible goods, if there is no change in the money-wage rate (relative to productivity) or gross profit margins, *only to the extent that diminishing returns are present*. Moreover, this diminishing returns associated price rise would be a once-and-for-all rise associated with increasing real costs of expansion due to lower productivity. If, on the other hand, there is an increase in money wages in excess of productivity, *whether demand is unchanged or not*, the resulting supply price will be higher except if gross profit margins decreased proportionately. Similarly, increases in gross profit margins can induce price increases. Consequently, in the real world of changing levels of aggregate demand (usually at less than full employment) *an incomes policy* which controls both the money-wage and profit margins will provide more stability in the purchasing power of money than a policy which permits 'free' collective bargaining and unrestricted corporate pricing practices.

MONETARY AND FISCAL POLICY AND INFLATION

The money-wage rate, productivity, profit margins (or the average degree of monopoly in a neoclassical pricing structure),

[1] Keynes, *Treatise on Money*, II 351.

and the expected level of effective demand (or standard volume) are the basic determinants of the short-period flow-supply price of output as a whole. Monetary and fiscal policy can effect this price level only by altering one or more of these strategic determinants.

It is difficult to see any direct relationship, in the short-run, between a monetary or fiscal policy which is politically feasible, and the money-wage rate, profit margins, or productivity. Of course, a monetary and/or fiscal policy which gives incentives for technological improvements and more rapid accumulation is likely to improve the rate of increase in productivity. Nevertheless, the fruits of progress is a long-run rather than a short-run gain, and unless money-wages and/or profit margins are prevented from rising it is possible that increments in the latter factors may swallow up any possible gain in productivity.

Monetary and fiscal policies aimed at preventing all price increases before full employment can be successful only if they perpetuate a sufficient level of involuntary unemployment.[1] Such a policy which sacrifices employment for price stability has often been recommended and accepted. The reason for the social acceptance of such a policy derives from the effects of inflation on the distribution of income. Only the unemployed and the impersonal corporation (and perhaps the entrepreneur of the small unincorporated enterprise) stand to reap unmitigated benefits in real income from a simultaneous increase in employment and prices. Those who are already employed and who have some seniority or tenure and those who receive fixed money incomes have little to gain but much to lose.

As long as there is involuntary unemployment, expansion can occur with rising flow-supply prices due to diminishing returns while money wages are unchanged and the real wage

---

[1] In 1971, the United States Government, recognising that its plan to curb inflation by increasing unemployment had failed and stirred by the proximity of the 1972 Presidential election, opted for an expansionary programme to curb inflation, hoping that expansion would bring increasing returns and therefore decreasing costs. This policy could be successful only if the rate of increasing returns approached the rate of increase in money-efficiency wages, a very dubious possibility. In August 1971, the folly of this approach became evident, and President Nixon ordered a 90-day wage-price freeze. Any such temporary expedient is ultimately useless.

declines. Once full employment is reached, however, any further increase in effective demand will bring forth additional workers into the labour force only if the real wage rate rises.[1] At this stage an *Incomes Inflation* can be an allocative mechanism (albeit an inequitable one) which permits the real wage rate to rise as money-wages and flow-supply prices increase sufficiently so as to 'force savings', i.e. the real consumption of rentiers and workers on quasi-fixed incomes fall by more than any increase in real consumption of workers in general and profit recipients.[2] In this case, profit margins and/or labour costs in the consumer goods industries must rise more slowly than the average money-wage rate, either because the productivity of labour in the wage-goods industry rises as the number of workers in this industry declines, and/or the relative slackness in the consumer goods markets vis-à-vis fixed capital goods markets does not encourage consumer-goods producers to raise profit margins or money-wages as rapidly as the money-wage rate in general is rising due to tightness in the overall labour market. With increases in effective demand pressing on the capital goods and labour markets, however, inflation is likely to be very severe and/or prolonged.

INFLATION AND INCOME DISTRIBUTION

The distribution of income is both a cause and a consequence of inflationary processes. In the first place, all changes in the flow-supply price of current output will affect each individual's real income differently, since in an uncertain world, there are many kinds of money-contracts, money-customs, and money understandings fixed over relatively long periods of time which affect the relative distribution of future money income and

---

[1] Assuming no change in leisure-income preferences.

[2] This may force individuals from the rentier class into joining the labour force or induce normally non-working members of wage-earning households to take jobs.

Keynes identified 'forced savings' with inflation at full employment and approvingly quotes Bentham as indicating that the additional investment undertaken is at the 'expense of national comfort and national justice'. (See Keynes, *The General Theory*, p. 80.) Kaldor and Pasinetti view inflation at full employment as an automatic adjusting mechanism which assures that the warranted rate will equal the natural rate of growth.

commitments among households. This does *not* mean that some households suffer from greater or less degree of 'money illusion', it merely means that households at different stages in their life cycle or economic circumstances will have already entered into all sorts of long term contractual relationships in order (1) to order their customary 'life cycle' consumption pattern to their uncertain, but expected life-cycle income pattern and (2) to share the burdens of decision-making under uncertainty via socially determined institutional ways. Consequently, inflation will always have differential impacts on different households. Only if all contractual obligations were abolished for all times, could the effect of inflation on income distribution be avoided – but a production-specialisation exchange economy without any money contracts is a contradiction in terms.[1] Hence, in the real world, some income redistribution between households, and between some households and business firms is inevitable. The fact that inflation does not affect all persons and all transactions equally is what makes inflation significant.

Simultaneously inflation may be the result of some economic groups attempting to increase their share in the total real income of the economy. The aim of these groups may be to obtain a larger share of the current claims on resources in order to enhance their consumption *or* to increase their control over the means of production. Profits inflation which involves entrepreneurs increasing profit margins relative to wage costs may be due to firms trying to obtain control of a source of internal finance in order to increase the rate of accumulation out of a given level of income,[2] or it may reflect the desire of capitalists to increase their consumption of the available output. In other words, given the level of employment at each point of

---

[1] In the uncertain real world, continuous recontracting is incompatible with a production-specialisation-monetary economy.

[2] In an uncertain world, firms must guard against illiquidity while creditors fear the inability of firms to meet long-term obligations. Thus, both entrepreneurs and lenders are anxious to see that some portion of net investment is funded internally. In an uncertain world, therefore, internal and external finance are compliments rather than substitutes and a firm's access to the new issue market will normally be limited by institutional rules about Gearing Ratios, that is, on the ratio external funding to the value of the total capital stock.

time, greater profits can be associated with either a more rapid rate of accumulation or increased consumption of capitalists or both. This is the message of the Cambridge neo-keynesian models which emphasise growth rates and capitalists' savings propensities as the determinants of profit rates and profit shares.

Attempts by labour to raise the aggregate money-wage share at the expense of profits margins, will lead to inflation, if profit margins are not completely accommodating, and there is no reason to suspect that profit margins are readily squeezable. In the real world, wage-earners in particular industries recognise the relative inflexibility of profit margins in their own industry. In fact, the workers in each industry hope that the market for their output will be able continually to generate high profits for their industry, so that the employers will continue to be agreeable to increased wage demands in the future. The struggle for higher money-wages by individuals and groups of workers is, therefore, basically a struggle over the absolute and relative income differentials that make up the wage-earners' pecking order. First and foremost, firm- and industry-wide collective bargaining about money-wages is aimed at protecting and increasing, if possible, the relative wage of the group vis-à-vis all other workers.[1] Since, at any point of time, the aggregate wage share is determined by output per worker, the level of employment, the average money-wage rate, and the average mark-up or profit margin which goes into the flow-supply price of output as a whole, demands for increased money-wages by any small segment of the work force will not significantly alter these determinants of the wage share, while if they are successful, the workers will improve their relative position. If, however, each group of workers adopt such a strategy, this will merely exacerbate inflationary pressures.

In the United States, society has apparently decided that any attempt on the part of entrepreneurs to increase profit margins relative to wage costs is socially undesirable – even if the avowed purpose of such action is to permit financing a more rapid rate of accumulation. Antitrust laws specifically prohibit any collusively planned profits inflation, under the assumption that there is no such thing as 'beneficent monopoly'. On the other hand, society has, by and large, accepted attempts by

[1] Cf. Keynes, *The General Theory*, pp. 13–14.

labour in general as well as individuals and groups of workers to raise their share under the aegis of 'free' individual and collective bargaining and the right to strike or withhold their labour from the market. In other words, except for periods of dire national emergencies, there is no explicit social stricture against any group of workers attempting to increase their wages at the expense of others by exercising their economic muscle.

Any demand for increased money wages by workers in an industry can be acquiesced to by entrepreneurs as they concomitantly increase profit margins, as long as managers believe their offers prices are not out of line with similar increases in flow-supply prices in the economy as a whole *and* as long as they believe that the government and the Monetary Authority will be obligated to underwrite the current level of real effective demand.[1] Only if the entrepreneurs fear that their higher price-offer contracts induced by meeting higher wage demands will not be as readily accepted as before by buyers who no longer have sufficient command of purchasing power because of a deliberate policy not to permit the money supply to increase with the 'needs of trade' to finance the same level of transactions at higher offer prices, will entrepreneurs be willing to bear the present and future harvest of animosity from their employees which will be generated by resisting their workers' demands. Management recognises that such wage confrontations can only make it more difficult, in an economy that has low unemployment, to obtain labour's co-operation on the shop floor after the settlement has been reached. Hence it is ultimately in the economic and political interest of management and *their* unions to insist that governments actively and continuously pursue full-employment policies, while simultaneously rejecting the notion that government may have to interfere with 'free' wage and price decisions.

[1] In some import-competing and export industries where foreign competition is severe, entrepreneurs may also require government protection or subsidies. Nevertheless even under a fixed exchange rate system, foreign competition cannot be relied on to keep wage demands in check, for if workers throughout the world are truculent, then each nation need not be sobered by foreign competition. Rather each nation 'in accordance with a perfect standard of manners . . . [can] enjoy just that degree of tipsiness (or sick-headache) as characterises the company as a whole'. Keynes, *Treatise on Money*, 11 222. With flexible exchange rates, foreign competition can never keep money wage demands in check.

Ironically, the upshot of permitting unrestricted wage pressures is that as long as employment policy is underwritten by the government, profits and wages of those industries and workers with the greatest economic power base rise relatively to those on either fixed incomes (rentiers) and/or workers and entrepreneurs whose ability to survive in a free market is the weakest. Thus, a permissive society which sanctions free collective bargaining is providing a licence for the euthanasia of the economically weak and powerless.[1] Moreover, since the basis of a viable monetary system, which in a world of uncertainty is essential for a production-specialisation economy, is a belief in the relative stability of the money-wage rate; therefore from both the viewpoint of income equity and from the desire to have an efficient monetary system,[2] a deliberate policy to control money-wage rates and profit margins has much to recommend it. Under such a policy socially desirable redistribution of income between functional shares and between households can be determined on the merits of the case and in the absence of threats of economic blackmail. Moreover, if changes in the existing distribution are thought to be desirable, then a programme to phase in such alterations slowly within a context of a growing economy can be developed so as to minimise intergroup antagonisms. A policy which specifically spells out what a desirable distribution is to be, which permits rational adjudication of relative income disputes, and which permits implementation of the idealised income goals in stages without unduly upsetting the existing money contracts and social order would appear to be more desirable than the current Darwinian view of permitting relatively fixed income recipients to bear the brunt of inflation at the early stages of inflation, and the marginally employed workers and contractually committed corporations to suffer at the later stages when the Monetary Authority decides to take restrictive action in an attempt to constrain increases in flow-supply prices so as to stabilise the purchasing power of money.

It is often said that inflation is undesirable because its effects on income distribution is capricious. Nothing is further from

[1] Cf. Keynes, *Treatise on Money*, I 271. Also see Keynes, *The General Theory*, p. 268.

[2] Keynes, *The General Theory*, pp. 236–9, 268–71.

the truth. Inflation of the flow-supply price of output as a whole tends to redistribute income away from fixed income groups including those widows and orphans and workers whose economic power is weak, and towards those workers with significant bargaining ability, large and powerful corporations, and, given the progressive income tax, governments. If there are objections to inflation, it is precisely because the effects of redistribution are predictable and the outcome is judged socially undesirable from an equity point of view.

INCOMES POLICY AND RESOURCE ALLOCATION

Many economists have attacked any incomes policy which attempts to stabilise money-wage rates and profit margins as undesirable because they believe that such a policy would not permit markets to optimally allocate resources. Such a view is mistaken in that (a) it conceives all markets operating as if they were *spot* markets where the current price is responsive to fluctuations in demand and then (b) it assumes that production decisions are responsive to changes in *spot* prices.

For all producible durables, however, production is responsive to the premium of the (notional) spot price over forward or flow-supply price; the rate of production response, however, is directly related to the elasticity of supply in the appropriate goods producing industry. For non-durable goods, on the other hand, where no spot market can exist, production can only be responsive to the quantity demanded at the current offer or flow-supply price. Under any rational incomes policy, therefore, it is essential to control the components of flow-supply price in order to avoid inflation in the prices of current and future production.[1] If flow-supply price components are sticky, then output composition will change in response to differential rates of growth in demand for products over time *and* to differences in the real costs of production for different goods. Those industries whose product demand grows most rapidly will find,

[1] Fairness and the need to minimise social tensions will require control over the spot price of producible durables in order to prevent some producers or buyers from making capital gains by 'black marketeering', i.e. by purchasing goods on the forward market and reselling them on the spot market.

ceteris paribus, the quantity demanded at the flow-supply price growing most rapidly, while those industries whose real costs decline most rapidly (or rise least) will, *ceteris paribus*, find the quantity demanded increasing and will therefore expand most rapidly. Since, under this policy, expected changes in the future offer prices of output will depend primarily on expected improvements in technology, those individuals who do not wish to consume current claims on resources can utilise a non-resource embodying money as a vehicle for transferring purchasing power with considerable confidence, thus freeing resources for investment projects where the expected desirability need reflect only expected real future demands and not a mixture of expected increases in the demand for output plus expected inflation of the future supply price of the output and/or the capital project itself.

If it can be agreed that stickiness in money wages and prices is a desired social objective in that it protects income recipients who are in weak bargaining positions, then the only alternative to a social contract between all the groups in the economy which permits permanent, direct, over-all controls of money wages and profit margins in an economy where individuals are otherwise free to make offers, is to constrain the money supply in order indirectly to restrict demand (or via fiscal policy to restrict demand directly) to the extent necessary that actual losses and/or the threats of losses will force entrepreneurs into resisting wage demands and laying off a sufficient number of workers so that the threat of joining the reserve army of the unemployed limits wage demands.[1] But even this policy may not be very effective since a politically-acceptable rate of unemployment does not secure an all-round reduction in wage or profit pressure; rather its effects are concentrated on those in the weakest bargaining position and those firms who have made long-term contractual commitments on the expectations of continued growth in the economy. Thus those who are pushing inflationary wage and profit demands may be relatively unscathed by an economic slow-down.

The remedy for an inflationary period is not a period of sufficient stringency so that the economy should become so impoverished that it cannot be held up for economic blackmail

[1] Cf. Keynes, *Treatise on Money*, I 210.

by powerful subgroups in the economy who take action to improve their own well-being at costs to others in society. The remedy for an enlightened society lies in the adoption of a social contract among all groups in the community; where the contract recognises that the current income distribution is a result of the historical path of the system, and that gross inequities in the existing arrangements can be more readily worked out by processes of adjudication among reasonable men, in a context of sustained economic growth, rather than in a series of confrontations among avaricious groups who can only be kept 'in their place' by deprivation and threats to their survival. 'No one has a legitimate vested interest in being able to buy at prices which are only low because output is low'.[1]

But, the neoclassical economist may argue, the purpose of price changes is to allocate resources via the input markets between the various goods-producing industries. Accordingly, the neoclassical welfare economist would state, any incomes policy which caused the money-wage rate to be sticky would prevent labour markets from being efficient allocators. This view implicitly assumes that present labour markets with their arbitrary and unequal bargaining power and supply restrictions are efficient allocators. The response to such a myopic faith in the operation of markets in an uncertain world can, and must be, on at least five different levels.

(1) There is considerable empirical evidence that suggests existing labour markets with existing 'free' collective bargaining arrangements and institutional rules to limit growth in supply, are not very good allocators.[2]

(2) Even if labour markets could efficiently allocate, all that would be required would be changes in relative prices and not in the general wage and price level. Different variants of incomes policy have been suggested which would permit these relative wage changes while restricting a general wage and price level change.[3]

[1] Keynes, *The General Theory*, p. 328.

[2] S. Weintraub, *Some Aspects of Wage Theory and Policy* (Philadelphia: Chilton, 1963) ch. 5.

[3] ibid. ch. 6, also see A. P. Lerner, 'Employment Theory and Employment Policy', *American Econ. Rev. Pap. Proc.* (May 1967) **57,** pp. 1–18.

(3) Any possible loss in social welfare due to possible labour misallocation in the economy must be weighted against the welfare loss resulting from traditional restrictive monetary and fiscal policies which reduce the rate of accumulation. As long as there are several million unemployed in the United States who are willing and able to work but who are kept unemployed in order to temper wage demands, then an economy which continuously utilises these resources is less wasteful than one which requires them to be perpetually 'on the dole'. (The latter system also ultimately fosters social antagonism.)

(4) Any efficiency which may be obtained, even via a policy which permits relative wage changes while maintaining a sticky average money-wage level, must be weighed against the distributive justice (or injustice) such relative wage and price movements imply.

(5) In an uncertain world, stickiness in the money-wage rate is necessary for the efficient operation of the monetary system. Accordingly one must weigh the desirability of providing an efficient mechanism of permitting individuals to defer decisions about commitments against an efficient mechanism of allocating labour commitments for lack of an efficient vehicle for deferring decisions, when future events can prove the current decisions were unfortunate.[1]

An incomes policy obviously requires that the public interest be taken into account at the wage bargaining table and when management is making its pricing decisions. This policy must be considered a necessary supplement to monetary and fiscal policies which would *guarantee* continuous full employment. In return for this guarantee of full employment and high production levels, labour would be required to restrict its wage demands to, at most, rises in average productivity, while business must hold profit mark-ups constant.

---

[1] A final 'more practical' argument is that any wage and incomes policy will create incentives for people to cheat either by upgrading jobs, downgrading quality, etc. This argument is, of course, true for any policy which alters the *status quo*, it always creates a new margin where the rational economic man may improve his relative position, e.g. increased taxes encourage cheating on tax reports. Ultimately, the policy designer must rely on the belief that most citizens are 'law-abiding' and will operate within the rules of the game.

If, in fact, we could go even further and keep both money wages and gross margins constant, then with technological progress, price levels would decline. This would allow consumers, including rentiers, to share in the gains of technology. This ideal variant of an income policy (which is less likely to be politically acceptable) would provide the greatest degree of fairness; for as long as some groups in society have their income fixed in money terms, then equity should require that all remuneration be somewhat fixed in money terms.[1]

The desirability of instituting a full employment policy in co-ordination with a permanent incomes policy is clear. The problem is to find a political leader who will advocate these policies which will be, at least initially, unpopular. (Many people might find themselves liking the results of such a policy, once they got over the shock of it.)

If the government was to adopt policies oriented towards stability in money-wage rates and growth in effective demand in line with the natural rate of growth in the economy, then the remaining major economic problems would be (i) to minimise the effects of unavoidable errors of foresight and (ii) to decide on whether expansion should be oriented towards more rapid accumulation of capital goods or towards the provision of more current consumption. Development policies to alleviate these remaining economic problems must be based on practical rather than theoretical judgements.

Stickiness in wages and the ability to avoid 'stop-go' economic policy to prevent inflation should in itself reduce the uncertainty about the future events in which entrepreneurs have to operate. Nevertheless, to err is human, and government must be prepared to aid the innocent victims of the inevitable mistakes made by a prudent management in an uncertain world. Best that we should know the outcome of all decisions before we make them, but in the absence of such perfect certainty it would be unfair of a wealthy society to leave each individual's income to be entirely determined by demand quantities and flow-supply prices in an uncertain market. In an humanitarian approach, government must develop 'insurance' programmes for uninsurable economic uncertainties to make sure that no group suffers grievously because of outcomes

[1] Cf. Keynes, *The General Theory*, p. 268.

which were not predictable (acts of God?) when rational decisions and production commitments were undertaken. Accordingly, practical and political judgements will determine the best means of providing adequate family income for unemployed workers, compensation for relocation costs, financial aids to producers who enter into reasonable contracts in good faith but who through *no fault of their own* find that the passage of events has caused past production decisions to be in error.

The decision on whether to increase the growth in consumption at the expense of accumulation as well as the decision as to the type of capital projects which are socially (as opposed to commercially) desirable could be resolved on a theoretical plane only if it was assumed that all interpersonal and intergeneration welfare comparisons could be made with complete certainty and with complete knowledge of the most desirable distribution of income at each point of time. Since such information will never be available in the real world, economists must leave it to responsible politicians to make these significant allocative decisions. Economists should neither be the apologists nor the critics for any ideology *per se*. They should, of course, point out the irrationalities in the 'economic' arguments presented by one side or another. In a world of uncertainty, however, their most useful contribution to the policy-makers will be to trace out as best they can the ramifications associated with the alternative paths of development implicit in each allocative decision without making implicit value judgements as to the relative desirability of the various alternatives. If economists would undertake these tasks, then as Keynes noted: 'economists could manage to get themselves thought of as humble, competent people, on a level with dentists, [and] that would be splendid!'[1]

[1] J. M. Keynes, *Essays in Persuasion* (New York: Norton, 1963) p. 373.

CHAPTER 15

A Final Summing-up

ANY economic model which has as its objective the proposing of methods for improving the quality of human life must explicitly recognise that any such recommendations will require the substitution of more conscious social or political control (or modification) of existing human institutions relative to the manner in which these human creations currently operate. When the focus of an economic model is the betterment of the public weal via accumulation and growth, it is essential to recognise that monetary rules and institutions are an ultimate and integral part of the real economy. Accordingly, any growth theory which assumes that the monetary sector always passively accommodates to the real facts underlying growth and/or any growth model which ignores the peculiar role of money which exists only because of uncertainty is simply a myth. Such models may be logically impeccable within their own assumptions; they may even withstand pragmatic, Philistine econometric 'tests'; nevertheless they will be hopelessly misleading if they are used to provide insights into the improvement of economic life via growth.

It is, of course, not surprising that right-of-centre economists of the modern neoclassical schools (who have been described as being desirous of obtaining respectability and approval from the existing economic power structure[1]) should adopt such mythical models in order to obfuscate the need for fundamental changes in modern economic institutions, since such changes may threaten the existing distribution of income and economic power. What is somewhat more surprising is that the left-of-centre Neo-keynesian school, in a strategy oriented to overthrowing the neoclassical hold on the economics pro-

[1] J. K. Galbraith, *The American Left and British Comparisons* (Fabian Society pamphlet 104, London, 1971).

fession, has also adopted a mythical (Golden Age) model which subjugates monetary institutions to real factors and thereby discourages investigations into the possible need to alter the operation of existing financial institutions. As a result, neo-keynesian Golden Age models (perhaps inadvertently, considering this school's political orientation) implicitly suggest the desirability of distributing income towards the rich (the powerful corporation) whose 'propensity to save' is the highest and whose motive appears to be, as a first approximation, the purest – the desire to accumulate in order to increase capacity and productivity.

Keynes, on the other hand was a pragmatic agnostic. He realised that the major faults of modern capitalism – unemployment and an arbitrary and inequitable distribution of income – was due to the existence of uncertainty and the resulting operations of monetary institutions. Keynes constructed his analytical models under the assumption that suggestions for improving the existing situation are more likely to provide real progress if they are carried out with a clear understanding of the *actual* nature and tendencies of the system which they are proposed to modify or displace. Thus, Keynes did not attempt to dislodge the pervasive and credulous neoclassical fantasy by proving it logically fallacious (for there are an infinite number of various alternative unrealistic assumptions which can be introduced logically to support the neoclassical fable); rather he attempted to supersede the conventional analysis by providing an alternative portrait of the real world 'warts and all'; so that the neoclassical canard could be recognised for what it was.

Unfortunately, Keynes, practical as he was in economics, was a visionary in political economy. He thought that 'the power of vested interests is vastly exaggerated compared with the gradual encroachment of ideas'.[1] What he failed to realise is that most practical men, and even madmen in authority, have achieved their position by recognising and using the power of ideas. These men are not inadvertent 'slaves of some defunct economist',[2] rather many academic scribblers are obsequious servants of the men in power and/or their probable successors. Consequently, the historical path of the

[1] Keynes, *The General Theory*, p. 383.   [2] Cf. ibid. p. 383.

development of economic fashion and thought is a helix with so many twisting gyrations that it is often difficult for contemporaries to differentiate regression from advancement. Hence, every quarter of a century or so, it has been necessary to stand back, to return to 'square one', and restate the essential principles of the real world so that further progress can be made.

Many will suggest that there is little that is fundamentally new in this book. Admittedly so, for it was not written in an attempt to demonstrate virtuosity, novelty, sophistry, or even to provide intellectual entertainment for others. It is an attempt to set out clearly, and in a modern context, the distinctive characteristics of a decentralised monetary economy, and to show how these characteristics operate within the institutional structure to produce the recurrent problems which are associated with growth and the distribution of income in a modern capitalist society.

The two essential characteristics of such an economy where *'money buys goods and goods buy money, but goods do not buy goods'*[1] are

(2) *the existence of uncertainty* in the Knight–Keynes sense so that decision-makers recognise that the future is unpredictable, and therefore, expectations can be, and often are, disappointed, and

(2) *the existence of irreversible time* and the fact that production takes time and therefore it requires that commitments be undertaken by decision-makers before the outcome can be predicted.

The existence of uncertainty and man's recognition that the economy is moving from an irrevocable past to an uncertain future has led man to devleop certain institutions and rules of the game, such as (i) money, (ii) money-contracts and a legal system of enforcement, (iii) sticky money-wage rates, and (iv) spot and forward markets.

Whenever there is a contractual commitment requiring performance and payment at some future date, some form of forward market transaction is involved; hence, all transactions involving the current *flow* of production in the economy are, in essence, handled via forward markets. Spot markets are for

[1] R. W. Clower, 'A Reconsideration of the Microfoundations of Monetary Theory', in *Monetary Theory*, pp. 207–8.

transactions in pre-existing durables; these latter markets may be either 'notional' or real. If a spot market exists, and if it is well-organised and continuous, it can provide 'liquidity' for those individuals seeking 'safely' to defer commitments of current resources till some unspecified future date. Continuity in a spot market requires, in an uncertain world, the existence of institutions which 'make' the market by acting as residual buyers and sellers. If these financial institutions have (or are believed to have) preferential access to the banking system or to the Monetary Authority, they will endow the durables traded in the spot markets 'made' by these intermediaries with a degree of liquidity which approaches that of money.

The progenitor of this view of the essential characteristics and institutions of a real-world monetary economy was Keynes's rich analysis of the *Treatise* and *The General Theory*. The major conclusions which result from looking at the real world in this way – Keynes's view – are:

(1) An understanding of the process of growth requires an analysis which is applicable not only to equilibrium growth paths but also one which is relevant to conditions of surprise, disappointment, fear, and disequilibrium.

(2) Accumulation depends on the existence of a premium of the spot over the flow-supply or forward price. If this discrepancy exists at any point of time, buyers of durables will place orders with producers to augment the existing stock. The rate of accumulation per period will depend on the elasticity of supply response of the producers.

(3) Any change in demand will have an immediate impact on spot prices thereby altering the difference between the spot and forward prices and, via the mechanism indicated in (2) above, affect the rate of production and accumulation.

(4) Traditionally, by the 'purchasing power of money' is meant the exchange between a unit of money and the current (or future) *flow* of produced goods and services. The real value of national income or the aggregate *flow* of output per period (GNP) is, therefore, obtained by deflating the money value by an index of flow-supply prices.[1]

[1] See Keynes, *Treatise on Money*, 1, chs. 4 and 5 for a discussion of the meaning of different price levels.

(5) In an uncertain world, money is the primary vehicle for deferring 'real' decisions and transferring purchasing power over time. As such money has certain peculiar properties which make it distinctly different from readily producible durables such as peanuts. These properties are zero (or negligible) elasticities of productivity and substitution.

(6) Other durables may also possess similar properties. Any asset which is so endowed and for which there is a well-organised continuous spot market will have a high degree of liquidity. Only those durables whose spot markets are most continuous, and whose transactions *and* carrying costs are the least will be perfectly liquid. Such 'chosen' assets are money; hence which assets are the money of a given economic system, and which are 'near monies', will depend on the elasticities possessed by the assets *and* the institutional spot market structure for these assets in the particular economy.

(7) A monetary policy which is geared to providing for the needs of trade *and* finance is a necessary but not sufficient condition for either maintaining or stimulating rapid economic growth. If the desire for capital goods is weak because of poor long-term expectations and/or a lack of confidence in the future, then easily obtainable finance will not, by itself, do the trick. If, on the other hand, the desire for investment is strong, the banking system and financial intermediaries can play an essential role in providing funds on terms which investors deem attractive. Even if the real forces are compatible with a rapid rate of sustained growth, however, the liquidity preference of savers and the operations of financial institutions may constrain expansion unless the Monetary Authority is prepared to provide sufficient liquidity *at the proper time*.

(8) A stable, viable monetary system requires a general belief in the relative stickiness of the factors underlying flow-supply prices, namely the money-wage rate, productivity, and profit margins. The problem of inflation can therefore be solved most directly and efficiently by direct control of the elements of the flow-supply price of goods, that is by a direct *and* permanent incomes policy.

(9) The high propensity to save that is associated with profits and the consequent implied desirability of securing a large portion of aggregated income for the rich profit recipients if

rapid growth is to be fostered is based on two implicit (and inapplicable) assumptions: (a) full employment is readily attainable and easily maintainable in a decentralised modern economy and (b) households in general (and those of the poor in particular) are instant gratification machines which are unwilling voluntarily to forego exercising their current earned claims on resources. In modern capitalist economies, however, the existence of gigantic institutions (e.g. life insurance companies, mutual funds, finance companies, Christmas clubs, etc.) which arrange for the contractual commitment of savings from most households' income (and particularly the poor) plus the financial prudence (and tax advantages) of rapid amortisation of capital in excess of actual wear-and-tear and technical obsolescence suggests that the pre-Keynes view of the potential shortage of savings in the private sector out of full employment income is unrealistic. 'In contemporary conditions the growth of wealth so far from being dependent on the abstinence of the rich, as is commonly supposed, is more likely to be impeded by it'.[1] As long as the desire for accumulation of real wealth is related to the provision of capacity for future mass consumption, growth is more likely to be stimulated by redistributing income toward those who would consume more, rather than to those who would consume less or to those who would use current claims on resources to. order additional armaments, rockets to the moon, and other items of non-available output which do little to improve the commonweal. Only if we are convinced that the public wishes to *consume too much* out of full employment income need we encourage savings via income redistribution towards the rich and thrifty; and only if we are convinced that the public *will never consume enough* out of full employment income, need we direct income to those who would order more rockets to the moon.

Finance and financial institutions play a vital and unique

---

[1] Keynes, *The General Theory*, p. 373. It is only the fact that most governments, since the 1930s, live far beyond their means that has prevented repetitions of the Great Depression. It is obvious, even today, that as soon as a government merely cuts down the size of its annual planned deficit (i.e. saves more), the growth is retarded. Also see R. F. Harrod, 'Replacements, Net Investment, Amortisation Funds', *Economic Journal* (March 1970).

role in a growing economy. It is the task of monetary theory to provide an understanding of how the evolution and development of these institutions can promote the betterment of human life via accumulation. Keynes believed:

> It is not the ownership of the instruments of production which it is important for the State to assume. If the State is able to determine the aggregate amount of resources devoted to augmenting the instruments and the basic rate of reward to those who own them, it will have accomplished all that is necessary.[1]

In conclusion, it must be noted that the left-of-centre Socialist–Radical school have raised the question of 'accumulation to what end?', that is, which instruments and what activities should be favoured by growth. These are questions of great social significance and are ones which political economists should not fear to take a stand. But these are questions of a different nature and beyond the domain of monetary theory, *per se*.

[1] Keynes, *The General Theory*, p. 378.

CHAPTER 16

Why Money Matters: A Postscript

NEOCLASSICAL CONFESSIONS AND NOBEL PRIZES

The terms in which contracts are made matter. In particular, if money is the good in terms of which contracts are made, then the prices of goods in terms of money are of special significance. This is not the case if we consider an economy without a past and without a future. Keynes wrote that 'the importance of money essentially flows from it being a link between the present and the future' to which we add that it is important also because it is a link between the past and the present. *If a serious monetary theory comes to be written, the fact that contracts are indeed made in terms of money will be of considerable importance.*[1]

These perceptive words encapsulate one essential skein of the theoretical fabric developed in *Money and the Real World*. Yet they do not appear earlier in this volume because they were written by Professors Arrow and Hahn, pre-eminent leaders of the Neoclassical School, at approximately the same time that I delivered the first draft of the first edition of this volume to the publisher. Arrow and Hahn have concluded that in 'a world with a past as well as a future in which contracts are made in terms of money, no [general] equilibrium may exist'.[2]

Thus, two of the most distinguished neoclassical scholars (one a Nobel Prize winner) have discovered that the present state of general equilibrium (or axiomatic value) analysis does not permit the construction of a 'serious monetary theory'. Moreover, Arrow and Hahn have cast serious doubts as to whether any 'general competitive analysis' can even seriously

[1] K. J. Arrow and F. H. Hahn, *General Competitive Analysis* (San Francisco: Holden-Day, 1971) p. 357. Italics added.
[2] ibid., p. 361.

model a real world economic system which exists in historical time and which utilises money contracts since, as Chapter 6 above stressed, time, money and money contracts are 'intimately and inevitably related'.

Another Nobel Prize winner, Sir John Hicks, has recently written a powerful recantation regarding the use of general equilibrium and the IS-LM framework as a conceptual device for analysing a real world monetary economy.

Hicks declares that, unlike general equilibrium concepts which 'signal that time, in some respects at least, has been put on one side', Keynes's monetary framework was an 'in [calendar] time' approach which recognised 'the irreversibility of time . . . that past and future are different' and that an uncertain future (and not a probabilistic one) shaped economic behaviour.[1] The lack of recognition of the concept of 'in [calendar] time' by neoclassical 'Keynesians' meant, according to Hicks, that

> The 'Keynesian revolution' went off at half-cock. The [general] equilibrists did not know that they were beaten . . . they thought that what Keynes had said could be absorbed into their equilibrium system; all that was needed was the scope of their equilibrium system should be extended. As we know, there has been a lot of extension, a vast amount of extension; what I am saying is that it has never quite got to the point . . . to look over my own work, since 1935, and to show how some aspects of the struggle, and the muddle, are reflected in it . . . I have found myself facing the issue, and (very often) being baffled by it.
> I begin (as I am sure you will want to begin) with the old ISLM (or SILL) diagram . . . I must say that diagram is now much less popular with me than I think it still is with many other people. It reduces the *General Theory* to equilibrium economics; it is not really *in* time.[2]

In a preface to a new book, *Economic Perspectives*, Hicks provides an even more vigorous condemnation of the false

---

[1] J. R. Hicks, 'Some Questions of Time in Economics', in *Evolution, Welfare and Time in Economics* ed. A. M. Tang, F. M. Westerfield and J. S. Worley (Lexington: Lexington Books, 1976) pp. 135–6.

[2] ibid., pp. 140–1.

trails that general equilibrium theory has provided for modern neoclassical economists. Hicks indicated that he had 'mixed feelings' about accepting the Nobel Prize in 1972 (which he shared with Arrow) for his work on general equilibrium and welfare economics. Hicks states:

> This is work which has become part of the standard literature of what is called in modern controversy 'neo-classical economics'. But it was done a long time ago, and it was with mixed feeling that I found myself honoured for that work, which I myself felt myself to have outgrown . . .
>
> In spite of all that happened to that particular piece of theory—the further elaborations at the hands of Samuelson, of Debreu and of so many others, not to speak of the econometric applications that have been found for it—the time came when I felt that I had done with it. But what I really regretted was that it had played so large a part as it did in the other part, the so-called 'dynamic' part of *Value and Capital*. . . . The concentration on what happens in a particular period ('my week'). . . as embedded in a historical process, so that it has *past* and *future*; the effects of past decisions now become immutable, upon the form of the capital stock . . . the effect of expectations of the future in determining the present form of capital investment; all this right, and all this I would still maintain. Where I now feel that I went wrong was in my attempt to represent the markets of that week as being in equilibrium, even in 'general equilibrium' in the sense of my static theory. . . .
>
> It was this device, this indefensible trick, which ruined the 'dynamic' theory of *Value and Capital*. It was this that led it back in a static, and so in a neoclassical direction.[1]

When such pre-eminent neoclassical scholars as Arrow, Hahn and Hicks have indicated the impossibility of modelling via traditional neoclassical concepts a real world economy where time, uncertainty,[2] contracts, finance and market institutions are essential factors and that any serious monetary

---

[1] J. R. Hicks *Economic Perspectives* (Oxford University Press, 1977).

[2] Hicks notes that 'one must assume that the people in one's models do not know what is going to happen, and know that they do not know just what is going to happen. As in history.' (ibid.)

analyst must explicitly account for these factors, then it is time for many other fair-minded neoclassical economists to recognise there is at least a paradigm's worth of difference between the economics of Keynes and general equilibrium economics. It is only in the Keynes's framework that real world monetary characteristics are prominently and explicitly developed so that 'money matters'.[1]

With the dramatic confessions and recantations of winners of the 1972 Nobel Prize for the development of general equilibrium theory, the path is now cleared for the majority of macroeconomists to turn their attention from the precise but simple-minded and wrong-headed neo-Walrasian analytics to the further development of Keynes's seminal work which was unfurled in my first edition of this book. With this in mind, I have tried in this chapter to clear up some difficulties and pursue some developments of the model developed in earlier chapters of this book. In this chapter I will deal with the following topics:

(1) the modelling of expectations in neoclassical macro models and in Keynes's framework
(2) price stability, inflation and indexing
(3) Monetarists versus Keynesians versus Keynes on the crowding out effect
(4) money and time related markets
(5) financing asset holding

EXPECTATIONS AND MACRO MODELS

In a generally unfavourable review of the first edition of *Money and the Real World*, David Laidler, a leading expositor of the Monetarist School of Economics, grudgingly admitted that

> the central analytic contribution of Keynes's General Theory was the recognition that it is of the essence of a

[1] Since the 1972 Nobel Prize winners have apparently comprehended this message, can it be much longer before the 1976 Nobel Prize winner recognises the inevitable logical inconsistency between his motto and his neoclassical theoretical framework? Clearly Professor Friedman had not yet even perceived the problem in his 'Debate' with me. See *Milton Friedman's Monetary Framework: A Debate with His Critics*, ed. R. J. Gordon (Chicago: University of Chicago Press, 1974) pp. 148–57, especially pp. 150–1 and footnote 13.

monetary economy that economic decisions are taken about the future in conditions of uncertainty and that once taken many of their consequences are irrevocable. Professor Davidson understood that at a time when many of his professional colleagues did not, and deserves credit for that as he does for recognizing the role of Professor George Shackle in carrying this analytical tradition.[1]

Of course, as even the Monetarists have come to realise in recent years, expectations play the key causal role in the economic process. For Monetarists in recent years the expected rate of inflation has been the crucial variable in their discussion of the 'natural rate of unemployment'. As Laidler has recently stated,

> We have argued that any rate of inflation is consistent with a state of zero excess demand in the economy provided it is *fully expected*. If to this we add the proposition that there is a unique level of unemployment in the economy associated with a situation of zero overall excess demand then we have it by implication that *this so-called 'natural' unemployment rate is consistent with any fully anticipated rate of inflation*.[2]

Expectations in Neoclassical Macro Models

Two models of expectations formation have been advanced by both Monetarists and neoclassical Keynesians to buttress their positions: (1) the adaptive expectations (error learning) model and/or (2) the rational expectations model.

In the adaptive expectations approach, erroneous expectations are revised (adapted) in proportion to which realised events deviate from what is expected. The realised events are assumed to be determined by the stable (over time) structural parameters of the economic system; consequently any errors in expectations are assumed to be reduced over time as economic agents' anticipations 'zero-in' on the long run equilibrium path of the economy. Thus, the adaptive expectations model surreptitiously permits the use of the perfect certainty economy with known parameters in each period as

[1] D. Laidler, 'In the Beginning', *Financial Times*, 4 Jan 1973.
[2] D. Laidler, 'Expectations and the Phillips Trade Off: A Commentary', *Scottish Journal of Political Economy*, **23** (1976) p. 59.

the generator of a time path towards which the real economy has a propensity to approach. This model simply ignores the fact that the corollary of erroneous expectations is ubiquitous false trading in every period where such errors occur and hence whatever equilibrium the economy converges to, *if it converges at all*, must be different from the equilibrium which would have occurred if there were no errors of expectations.

In the rational expectations model it is assumed that economic agents behave as if they had complete knowledge of the economic structure (i.e. the parameters of the real world) so that their expectations depend 'in a proper way' on the same things that neoclassical theory says actually determine each real world variable.[1] In other words, economic agents have complete and perfect information about how the economy will behave now and in the future.

Of course, once the foundations of either of these expectational formation models are made explicit, even Professor Laidler recognises that these approaches are found to be either 'naive' and 'arbitrary' or 'inconsistent'.[2] 'The simplest lesson to be learned from consideration of the rational expectations hypothesis,' Laidler concedes, 'is that there is likely to be far more to the formation of expectations than the blind application of some mechanical formula to a body of data. . . . [Moreover] we must face the implication that heterogeneity of expectations at any moment is more likely to be the rule than homogeneity.'[3]

Of course, heterogeneity of expectations guarantees that tomorrow's events will prove most of today's expectations wrong so that mistakes, false trades and changing parameters are unavoidable in the real world. Yet the fundamental Monetarist concept of a 'natural rate of unemployment' upon which elaborate Monetarist policies for fighting inflation are developed, requires, as even Monetarists admit, a 'fully anticipated' future—a future which 'can only be perfectly anticipated in any actual economy if *all* people hold the same expectations since otherwise some expectations are bound to be wrong.'[4]

[1] ibid., p. 63.
[2] ibid., pp. 62–3 including footnote 14.
[3] ibid., p. 69.
[4] D. Laidler and M. J. Parkin, 'Inflation: A Survey', *Econ. Jour.* **85** (1975) p. 743.

In a moment of extreme candour, Laidler recognises that

> ... with the passage of time, any change in the behavior of the economy may be met not just by changing expectations but also by changing the manner in which expectations are formed ... [and] an agent committed to act in a particular way as the result of entry into a long-term contract acts 'as if' his expectations are just as they were at the moment of entering into the contract for as long as the contract in question persists.[1]

Having reached such 'depressingly unspecific and negative' conclusions[2] regarding the usefulness of neoclassical modelling of expectations for macroeconomic analysis, and having come close to espousing Keynes's own approach for the handling of expectations for periods of contractual commitment, Laidler would normally be expected to express a willingness to give up the neoclassical format for a more Keynesian approach. Despite the grudging recognition of the logical incompatibility of neoclassical concepts and real world phenomena, however, a Panglossian optimism continues to permeate neoclassical economic writings in general, and Laidler's in particular. For example, in their 1975 survey articles on inflation, Laidler and Parkin state:

> Thus we have an important unsolved problem. The analysis of anticipated inflation needs to be so conducted that it covers all the varying extents to which inflation may be anticipated, including unequal expectations and lack of certainty about them. We do not pretend to know how such integration is to be achieved, but a much clearer idea than we have at present of the way in which economic agents form expectations, and of the way in which they change their behaviour in the light of changed expectations, will be required before we can expect to get very far with this problem. It is notable that, in the context of the analysis of

[1] D. Laidler, 'Expectations and the Phillips Trade Off: A Commentary' pp. 69–70. Cf. Keynes's definition of the daily output of the firms as determined by its short-term expectations. '*Daily* here stands for the shortest interval after which the firm is free to revise its decision as to how much employment to offer.' Keynes, *The General Theory*, p. 47, n. 1.

[2] Laidler, op. cit., p. 70.

inflation, expectations—even if erroneous—are usually treated as if held with certainty, or it is assumed that any variance in expectations does not influence behaviour. There exists a well-developed analysis, based on probability theory, of individual behaviour in the face of risk elsewhere in our subject and there surely are gains to be had from applying this analysis to aspects of the problem of inflation. This at least would be our view, but there are many economists, notably Davidson (1972) and Shackle (1955), who presumably regard the application of such analysis as misconceived (though possibly better than assuming all expectations to be held with certainty). They would stress that *uncertainty* in the Knightian sense as opposed to risk lay at the root of the problem. Certainly an analysis of behaviour of this kind would provide an interesting alternative to the approach based on probability. There can be no guarantee *ex ante* as to which line of work will prove more fruitful, as a means of replacing the widespread assumption (often unstated) that people's actions are the same as if their expectations were held with certainty.[1]

Surely the existing evidence is that neoclassical theory, despite the millions of economists' man-hours spent on refining it in the decades since *The General Theory*, has been virtually vacuous relative to the advances provided by Keynes's original structure. Consequently a return to Keynes's paradigm is bound to prove more productive.

Keynes on Expectations[2]
With the publication of volumes XIII and XIV of *The Collected Writings of John Maynard Keynes* (which include early drafts of *The General Theory*), it is possible more adequately to document and develop Keynes's approach to the use of expectational phenomena in his macromodel.

In 1936, upon reading the *General Theory*, Gerald Shove wrote to Keynes:

[1] Laidler and Parkin, op. cit., p. 795.

[2] The following is based on P. Davidson and J. A. Kregel, 'Keynes's Paradigm: A Theoretical Framework for Monetary Analysis' (mimeo, 1975); see also J. A. Kregel, 'Economic Methodology in the Face of Uncertainty', *Econ. Jour.*, **86** (1976).

I thought you were too kind to the 'classical' analysis
... unless very artificial assumptions (e.g. perfect and
instantaneous fluidity of resources) are made, it seems to me
either wrong or completely jejeune. I have been groping all
these years after a restatement of it on lines similar in some
respects to your solution for the system as a whole, stressing
in particular 'expectations' and the influence of current and
immediately past experience upon them. But I can't make it
precise.[1]

Thus Shove expressed the same need for 'precision' as do many
modern day neoclassical scholars.[2] Keynes's response is an
important lesson for economists who prefer precision to reality,
i.e. who prefer to be precisely wrong rather than roughly right.
Keynes wrote,

... you ought not to feel inhibited by a difficulty in making
the solution precise. It may be that a part of the error in
the classical analysis is due to that attempt. As soon as one
is dealing with the influence of expectations and of transitory
experience, one is, in the nature of things, outside the realm
of the formally exact.[3]

Keynes took for granted that the economic system to be
studied was a monetary-production economy in which the
future is uncertain and in which there can be no market

[1] *The Collected Writings of J. M. Keynes*, vol. XIV (London: Macmillan,
1973), p. 1; hereafter referred to as *CWK*.
[2] Recently, when I wrote to Nobel Prize winner Kenneth J. Arrow that
Keynes's theory was at variance with general equilibrium theory, he
responded, 'I am not yet convinced that the distinction between uncertainty and risk is really vital. ... The problem in all this is to create something which is genuine theory, that is, a well articulated framework with
implications. It is interesting that the parts of Keynesian theory that became
popular were, as you suggest, a retrogression from Keynes' deeper insights;
but this is no accident. One part of the theory was in fact capable of development even though it was an impoverished version of the whole;
the other part, deeper though it was, could not in fact be developed.'
I would hope that even prize-winning theorists will realise that economists
need not accept retrogression as development.
[3] *CWK*, XIV, p. 2.

institutions that would permit the effective pre-reconciliation of all trading and production plans for all economic agents.[1]

Within the context of a production economy with an uncertain future, Keynes sought to shift the emphasis from actual to expected values of the economic variables.[2] In essence Keynes was insisting that the economic paradigm should be composed of thoughts about thoughts.[3] Thus, Keynes made the general state of expectations an explicit independent variable of all the functional relationships in the system.[4]

In order to elaborate what Keynes felt to be his most fundamental contribution—the theory of effective demand—he chose to elaborate, in *The General Theory*, on a model where it was assumed that once the state of expectations is given, it would continue for a sufficient length of time for the effect on employment to have worked itself out. This static Keynes model permitted the specifications of simple, stable functional relationships that a dynamic or shifting expectational model would have rendered impossible.[5] The use of this simple

---

[1] In *Value and Capital* (Oxford University Press, 1939), J. R. Hicks recognised that there is a device whereby coordination of expectations can occur in a private enterprise system, namely forward contracting. A complete 'Futures Economy' where all goods were always and only bought and sold forward should eliminate inconsistency in expectations, but the possibility of errors due 'to *unexpected* changes in wants or resources would *not* be removed' [p. 136, italics added]. Hence even in such an economy, markets cannot pre-reconcile all trading plans and eliminate unwanted occurrences.

[2] *CWK*, xiii, p. 434.

[3] Cf. G. L. S. Shackle, *Epistemics and Economics* (Cambridge University Press, 1972) p. 71.

[4] *CWK*, xiii, pp. 441–2.

[5] Keynes, of course, was aware of how precarious it was to balance his static model on the parameter of long-term expectations. He hoped that his analysis of spending propensities would 'not in any way be precluded from regarding the propensity itself as subject to change' (*CWK*, xiii, p. 440). In an early draft, Keynes explicitly included in his propensity equations a variable, E, which represented the 'state of long term expectations' (*CWK*, xiii, pp. 441–2). Hence if there is either an autonomous change in expectations or if current realisations differ from previous expectations and thereby induce a change in expectations about the future (i.e. if *ex ante* does not equal *ex post* this causes a shift in the state of expectations), then there will be shifts in the functional relations of the system and Keynes's simple static model is inapplicable.

static model was a pedagogical device to separate the effect of a given set of expectations in determining the equilibrium level of employment (which could be less than full employment) from the effect of disappointment and changes in expectations on shifting the level of employment; for it had already been understood that changing entrepreneurial errors of optimism and pessimism could result in a trade cycle. While recognising the importance of expectations, Keynes thought that these parts of the economic nexus could be initially relegated to the background in order to give full scope to the role played by effective demand in producing an equilibrium level of employment which could be less than full employment.[1]

In his chapter on expectations in *The General Theory*, Keynes introduces two possible models of macroeconomic analysis—a static model and a dynamic model. In the static approach the state of entrepreneurial expectations is unchanged so that expected propensities can be uniquely specified, and actually realised results have (by assumption) no effect on long term expectations. In this model, even if small mistakes occur, such discrepancies may be eliminated by trial and error changes while entrepreneurs are 'not confused or interrupted by any further change in expectations'.[2] The 'steady level of employment thus attained may be called long-period employment',[3] while 'long period equilibrium' is defined by Keynes as 'a state of expectations which is both definite and constant and has lasted long enough for there to be no hangover from a previous state of expectation'.[4] In essence the Keynes static analysis has two possible submodels: Static Model 1A, where expectations are always and instantaneously met (not due to any market mechanism—just coincidentally), and Static Model 1B, where

---

[1] 'Having, however, made clear the part played by *expectation* in the economic nexus and the reaction of realised results on future expectation, it will be safe for us in what follows often to disregard express reference to expectation. It is important to make the logical point clear and to define the terminology precisely so that it will apply without ambiguity in all cases. But when once this has been done, considerations of practical convenience may legitimately take charge . . .' (*CWK*, XIV, p. 397).

[2] Keynes, *General Theory*, p. 49.

[3] ibid., p. 48.

[4] *CWK*, XIV, p. 105.

individual entrepreneurs may experience disappointment but there is no change in expectations.[1]

Keynes's second approach is a dynamic model where expectational propensities change over time, whether expectations are being fulfilled at any moment or not. This dynamic approach has two possible submodels: Dynamic Model 1A, where there are autonomous changes in expectations occurring whether current expectations are met or not, and Dynamic Model 1B, where there are no autonomous changes in expectations but discrepancies between expectations and realisations induce changes in expectations about the future vis-à-vis *previous expectations* about the same future dates.[2] Thus the dynamic approach is applicable whenever there is either an autonomous or an induced change in expectations.

For Keynes, the difference between a dynamic and a static model involved 'not the economy under observation which is moving in the one case and stationary in the other, but our expectations of the future environment which are shifting in the one case and stationary in other.'[3]

These two approaches to economic analysis are given differing weights in Keynes's writing and especially when Keynes is discussing policy. Often it is not always crystal-clear whether his prescriptions are based on the fully developed static model of *The General Theory*, where expectations are unchanged and so as a logical exercise (*and not as a projection in time*) the position of equilibrium can be determined; or whether the prescription is based on his less explicit, dynamic approach where expectations are changing while the economy is moving through time.

The usual interpretation is that Keynes held the state of

[1] Thus Model 1A is the equivalent of Joan Robinson's tranquillity world—but the economic agents still recognise they do not know the future (even in an actuarial sense) and their expectations can be wrong; while Model 1B assumes that the elasticity of expectations (see below) is zero.

[2] Dynamic model 1B assumes the elasticity of expectations is not zero. Although this model assumes that errors in expectations alter views about the future, it is not similar to the neoclassical adaptive expectations approach, for the latter assumes that errors induce learning regarding the 'true' parameters of the system, while the former merely implies that errors induce changes in views about the uncertain and unknown future.

[3] *CWK*, xiv, p. 511. This differs from Hick's definitions, where statics is 'where we do not trouble about dating', while dynamics is where 'every quantity must be dated', Hicks, *Value and Capital*, p. 115.

expectations constant while discussing functional relationships, hoping that with 'the introduction of the concepts of user costs, and of the marginal efficiency of capital' to give a role to expectations and bring static theory 'back to reality, whilst reducing to a minimum the necessary degree of adaptation'.[1] On occasion however, Keynes did appear to introduce the effects of diappointment into the static discussion of the stable spending propensities,[2] thereby tending to weaken the link between disappointment and shifts in expectations.

After he completed *The General Theory*, Keynes recognised that his indiscriminate treatment of the relationship between disappointment and a given state of expectations could confuse the reader about the theory of effective demand. In his 1937 lectures, Keynes stated:

> . . . If I were writing the book again I should begin by setting forth my theory on the assumption that short period expectations were always fulfilled; and then have a subsequent chapter showing what differences it makes when short-period expectations are disappointed.
>
> For other economists, I find lay the whole emphasis, and find the whole explanation in the *differences* between effective demand and income; and they are so convinced that this is the right course that they do not notice that in my treatment this is *not* so. . . . The main point is to distinguish the forces determining the position of equilibrium from the technique of trial and error by means of which the entrepreneur discovers where the position is . . . *Ex ante* savings and *ex ante* investment *not* equal. . . . *Ex ante* decisions in their influence on effective demand relate solely to *entrepreneurs'* decisions . . . the disappointment of expectations influence the next *ex ante* decisions.
>
> . . . [but even if we] suppose the identity of *ex post* and *ex ante*, my theory remains. . . . I should have distinguished more sharply between a theory based on *ex ante* effective demand, however arrived at, and a psychological chapter indicating *how* the business world reaches its *ex ante* decisions.[3]

[1] Keynes, *General Theory*, p. 146.
[2] ibid., p. 51.
[3] *CWK*, xiv, pp. 181–3. In his mention of 'other economists', Keynes is referring primarily to D. H. Robertson's model where income is determined

Thus Keynes gives an insight into the intermingling of approaches that he used. On the one hand, there is the stark static model where, given expectations, the theory of effective demand is the prime determinant of the level of employment. In this model, where either autonomous or disappointment-induced shifts of expectations are removed, Keynes demonstrates that unemployment was not necessarily a short-run disequilibrium phenomena; that booms and slumps need not be the result of faulty entrepreneurial expectations, but that a monetary system could settle, as a theoretical matter, in equilibrium at almost any level of employment.

To this stark model complicating factors of disappointment were added to some points, but not before the static model is completely laid out. Wholesale shifts in expectations were forcibly removed from the initial picture in order to permit the derivation of the stable functional relationships necessary for the elucidation of the theory of effective demand. When such large changes in expectations are discussed they are held separate from the static model, thus leading Friedman to catalogue these discussions of Keynes as 'many correct, interesting, and valuable ideas, although some wrong ones, and many shrewd observations on empirical matters . . . but all . . . are strictly peripheral to the main contribution of *The General Theory*.'[1]

in a previous period while effective demand is determined in the current period and hence they may differ. Recently it has again become voguish among neoclassical Keynesians to make differences between effective demand and income the basis for macroeconomic models (e.g. see J. Tobin 'Keynesian Models of Recession and Depression', *American Econ. Rev. Pap. Proc.* (1975)). Nevertheless Keynes insisted that 'the theory of effective demand is substantially the same if we assume that short-period expectations are always fulfilled . . . subsequent discussion has shown that this seems to differentiate my treatment much more than I realised at [the] time, from those of other contemporary economists who have been thinking more or less about the same problem' (*CWK*, xiv, p. 181). Keynes believed that this approach would permit greater emphasis on why 'the economic system may find itself in stable equilibrium with N at a level below full employment, namely at the level given by the intersection of the aggregate demand function with the aggregate supply function' (*General Theory*, p. 30).

[1] M. Friedman *et al*, *Milton Friedman's Monetary Framework: A Debate With His Critics* (University of Chicago Press, 1974), pp. 148–9.

In his 1937 lecture notes, Keynes has suggested that he might have better convinced his audience if he had more clearly separated the principle of effective demand under a given set of expectations from the effect of disappointment on effective demand changes.

Keynes and Hicks on Expectations and Economic Analysis
Hicks's analysis of expectations in *Value and Capital* can be fruitfully used to clarify the distinctions between Keynes's static and dynamic approaches. Hicks suggests that there are three influences which affect expectations. The first two are due to either 'non-economic' or economic factors generated by forces other than those under discussion. These, Hicks suggests, cause autonomous changes in expectations, and although 'we must never forget that . . . expectations are liable to be influenced by autonomous causes, . . . we must leave it at that'.[1] Hicks's third influence occurs when today's realised values differ from previous expectations about today's realised values, thereby inducing a change in expectations about future values of the relevant variables. Hicks's elasticity of expectations (E_e) measures the magnitude of this induced change in expectations. E_e is defined as the ratio of the proportionate change in the expected future values of x to the proportionate change in the current realised value of x vis-à-vis the previous expected value of the current x.[2]

Hence if there are no autonomous changes in expectations during the period of observation and if $E_e = 0$, then even though all variables are dated (Hicks's definition of dynamics), the analysis involves Keynes's static method.[3] If, on the other

[1] Hicks, *Value and Capital*, p. 205.

[2] Elasticity concepts are taxonomic and permit a classificatory methodology to be applied to economics. Shackle has called this approach *Keynesian Kaleidics* and argued that economic 'theory ought explicitly to be a classificatory one, putting situations in this box or that according to what *can happen* as a sequel to it. Theories which tell us what *will* happen are claiming too much . . .' (Cf. Shackle, op. cit., pp. 72–3).

[3] Even in Hicks's dynamic model if $E_e = 0$, static conditions apply. (See Hicks, *Value and Capital*, p. 250.)

In his Inaugural Lecture, Hahn, recognising the irrelevance of traditional general equilibrium methodology, has redefined the concept of equilibrium so that 'an economy is an equilibrium when it generates messages which do not cause agents to change theories which they hold or policies they pursue'.

hand, either $E_e \neq 0$ and/or there are autonomous changes in expectations, then Keynes's dynamic analysis is applicable.

In sum Keynes's static model (where $E_e = 0$) permits stable aggregate demand and supply functions to be derived, and a point of effective demand to be developed which need not be full employment. The static analysis need not have a constant equilibrium level of employment as long as existing expectations should been foreseen sufficiently far ahead so that employment changes have been anticipated; nevertheless, by hypothesis, realisations cannot alter current expectations about the future. That this process was not one that Keynes expected to actually occur over time in the real world is emphasised by his calling the resulting equilibrium employment level a 'long-period' position and his direct method of severing the extent to which anything can alter existing expectations about the future.

Keynes's Dynamic Model 1B can provide models of shifting but stable equilibrium if $E_e \neq 0$ but it is not greater than unity,[1] when, as Keynes assumed was the normal human condition, *ex ante* and *ex post* are unequal. Nevertheless, in a dynamic economy there is no necessary constant relationship between realisations, E_e, and autonomous changes in expectations; nor need E_e even be constant over time. Only in the unlikely event that $E_e = 0$, will realisations of errors not alter the state of

This equilibrium concept, Hahn claims, is 'not at all clear', it is an 'ill-specified hypothesis' but it does permit application to 'rare instances' where realisations differ from expectations so long as these 'rare' occasions do not induce agents to change their plans. (See F. H. Hahn, *On the Notion of Equilibrium in Economics* (Cambridge University Press, 1973) pp. 25–7.) Contrary to Hahn's claim, however, this is the well-defined Keynes static approach where $E_e = 0$. Thus after millions of man-hours of economic research and progress in general equilibrium theory, the latest development is to work with a model which might be labelled as a 'no learning by doing' system. For Keynes to start with such a pedagogical device 40 years ago in order to clarify the principle of effective demand to his 'fellow economists' (*General Theory*, p. v) is, at least, understandable. For modern *savants* to present this ancient tool as the culmination of decades of research is lamentable.

[1] A system where $E_e > 1$ 'is definitely unstable' (Hicks, *Value and Capital*, p. 255). Keynes recognised there was nothing in the logic of the analysis that required $E_e < 1$, nevertheless the real world was not violently unstable. Hence Keynes was continuously searching for conditions which are capable of causing the $E_e < 1$ (Cf. *General Theory*, p. 250).

expectations. 'The actual course of events is more complicated
. . . for the state of expectations is liable to constant change'[1]
thereby shifting the independent behavioural propensities.
Thus, Keynes's Dynamic Model 1B of shifting equilibrium will
describe an actual path of an economy over time chasing an
ever-changing equilibrium—it need not ever catch it.

This latter approach of shifting equilibrium due to changing
expectations is, however, conceptually distinct from the
neoclassical approach which was the adaptive and/or rational
expectations model. In Keynes's full view of the system it is
the conjectural and often figmental state of human expectations
which are the prime movers of a free enterprise economic
system. Thus, in the Keynes paradigm, supply and demand
functions exist at any point in time but they need not be stable
over any length of historical time. As Shackle argues, this is
just as much a part of Keynes's message as the static exposition
of effective demand, for 'stable curves and functions are
allergic to the real human economic scheme of things.'[2] It is in
the shifting equilibrium analysis that the crucial role of historical
time as well as the difficult methodological problems are most
clearly seen.

Keynes believed that the time duration between the enacting
of decisions based on *ex ante* expectations and the resulting *ex
post* outcome was 'incapable of being made precise' so that
there could be no specification of a 'definite relationship
between aggregate effective demand [as expected by entre-
preneurs] at one time and aggregate income [realisations] at
some later time'.[3] Thus, Keynes explicitly gave up on the
ex ante–ex post approach to handling time.[4]

[1] Keynes, *General Theory*, p. 50.

[2] G. L. S. Shackle, 'Keynes and Today's Establishment in Economic
Theory', *Jour. Econ. Lit.*, **11** (1973) p. 517.

[3] *CWK* xiv, pp. 179–80.

[4] As Keynes stressed in a letter to Harrod, *ex ante* is what entrepreneurs
plan to do, not what they *ought* to do to assure the equality of *ex ante* and *ex post*
(*CWK* xiv, pp. 322–7). In a dynamic (realistic) model of the real world,
therefore, when entrepreneurs carry out plans which lead to a realised
effective demand (actual rate of growth) which differs from that level of
effective demand where plans are reconciled (warranted rate of growth),
the result may be for economic agents to change their state of expectations
(shifts in behavioural propensities) which may lead to a further divergence
between actual and warranted paths.

I used to speak of the period between expectations and results as 'funnels of process' but the fact that the funnels are all of different lengths and overlap one another meant that at any given time there was no aggregate realised result capable of being compared with some aggregate expectation at some earlier date.[1]

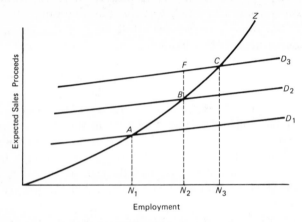

Fig. 16.1

Instead of a Robertson period analysis or a Swedish *ex ante–ex post* approach, Keynes initially presented his static model which allowed, in a very arbitrary but exact way, the tracing through of the influence of a given state of expectations to the 'long period level of employment' associated with it. Keynes chose to associate 'short run' with 'the shortest interval after which a firm is free to revise its decisions as to how much employment to offer. It is, so to speak, the minimum effective unit of time.'[2] Simultaneously he chose to blur the distinction between realised and expected sales proceeds by referring to a large overlap between them so that the static model could be used to highlight the importance of entrepreneurial expectations in determining the actual level of employment.

[1] *CWK*, xiv, p. 185.
[2] Keynes, *General Theory*, p. 47 n. 1. Thus short-run decisions are not independent of contractual obligations.

Thus, for example, if in Fig. 16.1 the aggregate supply curve (Z) is derived on the basis of expected production techniques and factor prices, and a family of expected demand curves $(D_1, D_2,$ etc.) each one representing a different state of expectations of possible sales in the minds of entrepreneurs.[1] Thus in Fig. 16.1 there is a long period level of employment associated with each possible expected point of effective demand, N_1 with point A, N_2 with B, etc.

Given a specific state of entrepreneurial expectations regarding the sales proceeds which can be expected to be spent by buyers for alternative levels of employment—as represented by D_2 in Fig. 16.1 for example—entrepreneurs expect effective demand to be at point B. (Assume further, merely for expositional simplicity, that this point of effective demand is expected to prevail for a number of future production periods.) Acting on such expectations entrepreneurs hire N_2 workers in the current period. If D_2 is the realisable aggregate demand curve, as Static Model 1A assumes, then expectations will be fulfilled and N_2 will remain the equilibrium level of employment until there is a change in the state of expectations.

What if, however, the realisable demand function in the current period turned out to be D_3? Logically, the Keynes Static Model 1B suggests that as long as entrepreneurs expect D_2 to prevail, i.e. as long as $E_e=0$, employment will remain at N_2 even if realisations differ from expectations. The actual realised result, however, will only be relevant to employment insofar as they cause a modification of subsequent expectations, i.e., only if $E_e>0$. That, however, would require Dynamic Model 1B rather than Static Model 1B. Keynes's static approach can apply to this situation only by employing a verbal sleight of hand which Keynes was not above using in order to convince his fellow economists. If the actual aggregate demand curve is, say, D_3 when they expected D_2, then entrepreneurs should be surprised by subsequent events when they

---

[1] The aggregate supply curve is derived essentially in the same conceptual manner as the Marshallian micro-supply curve. Thus, for example, in the case of profit-maximising 'price-taker' firms, the micro-supply curve is obtained from the points of intersection between a family of alternative 'expected' demand curves and the 'expected' marginal cost curve. (Cf. P. A. Samuelson, *Economics*, 9th ed. (New York: McGraw Hill, 1973), p. 454.)

find either an unexpected increase in spot market prices, and/or an unintended run-down of inventories, and/or an increased queue of buyers (as the realisable aggregate demand price associated with the actual hiring of N_2 workers is given by points F). The discrepancy between the expected and realisable aggregate demand functions (D_2 and D_3) should, it would seem, alter entrepreneurial expectations so long as $E_e \neq 0$. Keynes however blurred the difference between the state of entrepreneurial expectations underlying the initially expected aggregate demand curve (D_2 in Fig. 16.1) and the expectations that would have brought forth the realisable demand curve (D_3) in the minds of entrepreneurs in order to maintain his static model assumptions by assuming

> ... in practice the process of revision of short-term expectation is a gradual and continuous one, carried on largely in the light of realised results; so that expected realised results run into and overlap one another in their influence. . . . Thus in practice there is a large overlap between the effects on employment of the realised sales-proceeds of recent output and those of the sales-proceeds expected from current input.[1]

In other words, despite the surprise that the point of realisable effective demand is C not B, one way of simplifying the situation so it can be handled within a static framework is to assume that entrepreneurs can switch from the expectations underlying D_2 to those underlying D_3 *without a change in the state of expectations* occurring. Thus entrepreneurs will increase their hiring towards N_3. This verbal legerdemain was necessary if the simplest static Keynesian model was to have an impact on the 'fellow economists' to which *The General Theory* was addressed.

In a similar context, R. F. Kahn has noted Keynes often represented economic phenomena via well defined and fairly stable functional relationships 'despite his institutional horror of undue formalism, but his treatment can be justified by the need at the time for a forceful and clear-cut exposition if it were to carry any weight at all'.[2]

[1] Keynes, *General Theory*, p. 51.

[2] R. F. Kahn, 'Some Notes on Liquidity Preference', *The Manchester School* (1954), p. 250. But see pp. 124–5 above to see how this situation has led to differences between Keynes's followers.

Of course Keynes realised that 'the actual course of events is more complicated' than his static analysis, since expectations 'are liable to sudden revision' before any state of expectation 'has fully worked itself out',[1] i.e., the aggregate supply and/or demand curve could shift before point C (in Fig. 16.1) is reached. Thus, Keynes envisioned his real world model as one of shifting equilibrium, a world in continuous movement without the necessity for the plans of the economic agents ever to be reconciled.

DYNAMICS, TIME AND STABILITY

If we are to utilise the dynamic Keynesian theory, where the state of expectations can and does change as the system moves irreversibly along the calendar time axis, it becomes essential to recognise that there is nothing in the logic of the dynamic theory which rules out violent instability. Nevertheless, Keynes noted the 'outstanding characteristic of the economic system in which we live, whilst it is subject to severe fluctuations . . . it is not violently unstable.'[2] Hence there must be certain conditions in the economic environment which promote relative stability in a dynamic world so that inevitable disappointment and surprise do not lead to violent alterations in the state of expectations, so that the $E_e < 1$.

As long as the future is uncertain the state of expectations may be liable to rapid unpredictable changes and hence the economic system is potentially very unstable. Recognising the mercurial possibility of the economic system, man has, over time, devised certain institutions and rules of the game, which, as long as they are operational, avoid such catastrophes by providing a foundation for a conventionality of belief in the stability of the system and hence in the quasi-stability of the state of expectations. It is the existence of spot *and* forward markets, money, and concurrent seratim time–length money (forward) contracts and their enforceability, as well as the expectations that these institutions will continue to operate with continuity or 'orderliness' for the foreseeable future, which limits the magnitude of E_e and keeps real world economic

---

[1] Keynes, *General Theory*, pp. 50–1.
[2] ibid., p. 249.

fluctuations in bounds.[1] If these institutions break down, as they did for example in Germany between 1921–3, a modern monetary economy may exhibit violent instability. For most developed interdependent production economies, however, where production requires considerable calendar time and therefore contractual commitments for the hiring of resources must occur a long time before everyone can possibly know how valuable the outcome will be, such instability will mean the breakdown of production flows. This occurrence is so costly to society that most members of the economy will cling to the hope that even a crippled monetary system can be resuscitated. This hope maintains some stability in states of expectations, i.e., $E_e < 1$, but if the situation deteriorates so that almost everyone is completely uncertain as to the meaning of contractual commitments then a catastrophic breach in the continuity of the system is inevitable.

Stability of Economic Functions

The well defined, *stable* functions of Walrasian (or even Marshallian) microeconomics do not exist over calendar time, and are of little use for economic forecasting in the real world for they can be defined only for a given state of expectations. What Keynes insisted on was not stable demand and supply functions—they could shift every time the unpredictable state of expectations changed—but they must exist momentarily. This means we cannot predict what will happen over a period of calendar time, only what can happen for given state of expectations.

Keynes spent considerable time discussing the formation of expectations in his *Treatise* and his *General Theory* but he remained adamant that there was no uniform relationship between a set of observable events and the subsequent state of expectations. In Keynes's paradigm, the '*indefinite* character of actual expectations' is the free autonomous variables which govern everything else, rather than being governed by everything else.[2] In the real world expectations may only be tenuously

---

[1] Cf. Hicks, *Value and Capital*, pp. 264–7, 270–1, 297–8. In an economy where all contracts were made simultaneously for instantaneous payments only, there would be no liquidity and no money, i.e. it would be a general equilibrium non-monetary system.

[2] *CWK*, xiv, pp. 106–7.

related to past economic facts as politics, acts of God, thoughts and life-styles are also determinants—thus Keynes's and the post-(neo-)Keynesians's emphasis on 'animal spirits'.

Keynes's independent psychological propensities—consumption, investment, and liquidity preference—would be stable *but not independent* in any system where time and uncertainty are absent. Keynes's assumption of a given state of expectations about an uncertain future and the belief of economic agents that all production, consumption, investment and liquidity decisions do not have to be made simultaneously and for all time at the initial date (or at any other point of time) permitted Keynes to deal with these propensities as formally independent stable relations within his static framework. This static Keynes model, although unrealistic because of its undue formalistic approach, did form the core of the Keynesian revolution. It liberated 'men's thoughts from the concept of general equilibrium . . . [and] made possible the construction of effective theories of a *varying* level of output and employment'.[1]

Keynes's dynamic model is more applicable to a real world economic system which lurches from one historical position to another without even necessarily being in equilibrium. Unfortunately the dynamic model makes predictions about the future a very tricky and unsafe business. Unlike a general equilibrium system which is closed once tastes and endowments are given, Keynes's dynamic model is open, with constantly changing and unpredictable expectations driving the system onward through calendar time. Economists, unlike astronomers (but like weathermen?), are stuck with an open system. As Laidler has recently recognised, economists cannot use the mechanistic approach to expectation formation; with the passage of time not only can expectations change, but the manner in which they are formed can change. Accordingly economists should provide a classificatory theory of economics using, when relevant, the E_e concept which puts situations into one box or another according to what can happen as a sequel under a given set of circumstances, not what will happen. This philosophy about the nature of economic models was summed up by Keynes in a letter to Harrod, in which he said:

[1] G. L. S. Shackle, *Expectations, Investment and Income*, 2nd ed. (Oxford University Press, 1968) p. xxi.

... economics is a branch of logic; a way of thinking. ...
Progress in economics consists almost entirely in a progressive
improvement in the choice of models. ... But it is of the
essence of a model that one does not fill in real values for the
variable functions. ... The object of statistical study is not so
much to fill in missing variables with a view to prediction as
to test the relevance and validity of the model.

Economics is a science of thinking in terms of models
joined to the art of choosing models which are relevant to the
contemporary world. It is compelled to be this, because
unlike the typical natural science, the material to which it
is applied is, in too many respects, not homogenous through
time. ... Economics is essentially a moral science and not a
natural one. That is to say, it employs introspection and judgements of value.[1]

REAL WORLD STABILITY AND
THE CURRENT INFLATION

Keynes's dynamic analysis threatens the logical possibility of
violent instability. Yet, except for rare historical episodes,
capitalism has been relatively durable and homeostatic. Hence
it is important in these days of worldwide inflation and continuing prophecies of the coming of an economic cataclysm
to delineate those characteristics of the economic agents in
modern economies and their institutions which have provided
a homeostatic mechanism in an uncertain world. Any stabil-
ising mechanism must involve institutions which normally not
only tend to limit the elasticity of expectations to less than
unity but also make large autonomous changes in expectations
unlikely. Our search is for those human institutions which
normally assure 'sticky' expectational behaviour in a world of
uncertainty.

Contracts and Price Stability

Forward contracting is the most important human institution
yet devised for controlling the uncertain future. Since production takes time, entrepreneurs are always entering into
forward contracts to assure the future costs of inputs and, in a
non-integrated production chain, into sales contracts to assure

[1] *CWK* xiv, p. 296.

prices and revenues in the future. In fact, one may look upon the private institution of contracts as the way free enterprise markets attempt to assure wage and price controls. Businessmen abhor what general equilibrium theorists desire, namely recontracting.

Since the money wage contract is the most ubiquitous forward contract in modern economies and since the duration of money wage contracts normally exceeds the gestation period for the production of most goods, it is the human institution of forward labour contracting which provides a basis for the conventionality of belief in the stickiness or stability in the price of something over time. Such a convention is necessary if entrepreneurs are going to take long-term positions in productive facilities and goods-in-process (working capital) inventories.

In a market-oriented private enterprise economy some people are willing to employ labour via forward contracts expecting to earn money quasi-rents at future dates from the sale of the output of that labour. During the interim between input hiring and output sales these people will have taken a 'position' in intermediate and final products. Simultaneously other people in the economy desire to save, i.e. not to exercise all of their currently-earned money claims on new goods produced by labour. Savers must hold money or resaleable assets that can last through time with a minimum of carrying costs and therefore serve as a store of value, unless they know what specific thing they will want to possess at a specific future date, for then they can buy a forward contract for the production of the item wanted and its delivery at the desired future date. But Keynes stressed, 'an act of individual savings means ... *not* ... to consume any specified thing at any specified date'.[1] Hence any savings out of current income which do not have a specific expenditure goal at a specific future date require the possession of stores of value that are durable and liquid. Liquidity of anything but money requires resaleability!

Durables possess liquidity only if there is a well-organised spot market in which they can be readily resold at any future date for a money claim on resources available at that date. (As long as labour-hire contracts are made in terms of money

[1] Keynes, *General Theory*, p. 210.

wages, then money will be the primary claim on newly produced goods.) The current (spot) money value of any resaleable durable can increase or decrease *without limit* if expectations of future spot prices change. If, however, the durable has relatively high elasticities of production and substitution, a counterbalancing factor due to new production (or, in the case of decrease in value, carrying costs and physical deterioration) comes into play, as over time the costs of production and the availability of new supplies limit the increase in future spot prices expected at future dates and hence constrain today's spot prices.

On the other hand, for those assets which have negligible elasticities of production and substitution and are sold in well-organised spot markets (e.g. financial assets, collector's items, etc.), their conditions of supply (resource-using reproducibility and hence costs of production) do not, indeed cannot, act as a counterweight limiting expectations of future spot prices and hence constraining present (spot) market values. Thus standardised non-reproducible durables which are actively traded in well-organised spot markets are inherently potential objects of speculation *par excellence*. The current value of such assets depends solely on what people today think tomorrow's spot price will be, while the actual spot price tomorrow will depend (as everyone knows) on what people tomorrow will expect the spot price to be on the day after tomorrow, etc. Consequently, the spot price of financial securities, old masters, philatelic material, etc. are all inherently restless, for some traders in such markets desire price movements for the opportunities of capital gain which only such price movements over time can provide, while other traders are either obliged (e.g. market makers) or desirous (traders and brokers looking for the first signs of any price trends) to be vigilantly responsive to such movements even if they initially do not desire them.[1] Constancy over calendar time in spot bond prices (for example)

---

[1] Shackle, *Epistemics and Economics*, pp. 200–1. At any point of time, the spot prices of speculative assets depend not only on the balancing of the bull and bear expectations but also on the balancing of the market maker's expectations of bull and bear sentiment vis-à-vis his commitment to maintain an orderly market. Spot prices in such assets are therefore inherently restless while not overly pliant in their movements over time.

is contrary to the differing expectations of both the bulls and the bears who determine the spot price at each point in time. Nevertheless, 'orderly' movements are normally maintained in such spot markets via institutional market arrangements.

For producible goods, however, since (1) the current spot price of all readily resaleable durables ultimately depends on their expected future spot price, (2) the forward price of all durables reflects the current expectations of the spot price at the future delivery date, and (3) in backwardation, the forward price of reproducible durables is equal to the Marshallian flow-supply (cost of production) price, then it logically follows that the only thing which will provide an anchor of stability for the money price level of producible goods over time is the belief in the stability or stickiness of money costs of production (including profit margins) over time.[1] Hence, as long as forward labour contracts are set in monetary terms for a period of calendar time which exceeds the gestation period of production (and profit margins are sticky), economic agents can expect stickiness in the costs of production and thus in the price level of new goods and services. It is the money wage contract and the resulting stickiness of money wages (and the explicit assumption of an *unchanging* degree of competition[2]) which permitted Keynes to discuss the real world in terms of a stable but potentially shifting equilibrium model. As Hicks emphasised, Keynes's less than full employment equilibrium analysis

> assumes a unity elasticity of expectations only for [spot] prices expected to rule in the near future; for prices expected in the further future [where new production can come to market], he [Keynes] assumes that they move with money wages. . . . Consequently the instability of the system is . . . in abeyance so long as money wages are kept constant (for then more distant prices have a zero elasticity of expectations and this acts as a stabiliser).[3]

[1] For producible but non-resaleable goods (e.g. haircuts, surgery), the purchase price will reflect the costs of production including the profit mark-up. If the good is durable but not resaleable then its purchase is, like marriage, 'indissoluble except for death and other grave causes' (Keynes, *General Theory*, p. 160) and the durable is illiquid.

[2] Keynes, *General Theory*, p. 245.

[3] Hicks, *Value and Capital*, p. 256.

Keynes did not have to, nor did he, assume constant money wage rates; he merely presumed 'sticky' ones, so that E_e need not equal zero: E_e will be very inelastic as long as there are long term forward contracts for money wages.

The stability of the level of money prices over time, therefore, depends on habit and/or convention which makes the money price of something relatively sticky over time so that people can 'expect' price stability. In the real world, in normal times, the efficiency money wage, i.e. money wages relative to productivity, is nearly constant enough to provide some basis for the convention of price stability to be incorporated into entrepreneurial expectations and, therefore, encourage them to undertake productive commitments.[1] The necessity of some conventionality of price stability is 'a fundamental assumption essential to *any* dynamic economics'.[2]

Indexing and Instability
The staunchest defenders of the 'free enterprise system', on the other hand, advocate freely flexible money wages to relieve capitalist economies of the problems of unemployment and inflation. Sticky or controlled money wages (whether by private contract or social contract), in their view, inhibit a free enterprise economy from achieving a stable, full employment growth path over time—a state of bliss. Perfect flexibility of money wages could be possible if the labour market was a 'bourse'. Hence, if there was a well-organised spot market for slaves then wages could be perfectly flexible and continuous full employment of slaves could be attained. Rightly or wrongly,

[1] Keynes explained the historical relative stability of price level in terms of the balance between money wages ('wage-unit') increases and the increase in the efficiency of labour. Keynes predicted that 'the long run stability or instability in prices will depend on the strength of the upward trend of the wage unit (or more precisely of the cost unit) compared with the rate of increase in the efficiency of the productive system' (*General Theory*, pp. 308–9). In these days of rising raw material costs, the cost unit may be more relevant.

[2] H. Townshend, 'Liquidity Premium and the Theory of Value', *Econ. Jour.*, **47** (1937) p. 163. Hicks reminds us that if 'all prices were equally flexible and all price expectations equally flexible', any change will lead to a 'complete breakdown' of capitalism, and the only thing that prevents this instability is 'price-rigidities' and 'beyond price rigidity, . . . people's sense of normal [i.e. sticky] prices' (Hicks, *Value and Capital*, pp. 297–8).

modern economies have made such slave markets illegal, and in orderly capitalist countries almost all labour is hired on a forward contract basis with the duration of the contract equalling or exceeding the production period.

Friedman, however, has publicly advocated reducing the duration of the labour contract to a time period less than the production period in order to fight inflation. Friedman's recommendation is to 'index' all labour contracts and most other contracts to a current price index.

Widespread indexing of labour contracts would create wage flexibility and simultaneously destroy the conventionality of price stickiness which is necessary for capitalist entrepreneurs to undertake production commitments.

In his classic study *The Economics of Inflation*, Bresciani-Turroni showed that although Germany had suffered from double digit inflation since almost the beginning of World War I, the inflation really began to accelerate at the end of 1922.[1] The period from the end of 1922 to the end of 1923 was different in that it 'was characterized by an enormous rise in nominal wage-rates . . . due, in great part, to the influence of the trade unions . . . the system of fixing [indexing] wages became general'[2] throughout Germany. The cost of living index which had been calculated monthly before 1922, was calculated twice a month in 1922, and weekly in 1923 as more wages were geared to the index. But even that was found to be insufficient as each increase in money wages pushed up domestic prices. By mid-1923 a daily index was substituted by most industries as wages were paid daily. But that only accelerated price increases, so that by the end of 1923 a daily index of forecasted prices was being used. The result was an accelerating inflation rate of over 400 per cent per month.

In this historical period indexing failed either to limit inflation or to stabilise and maintain the real wages of workers. In 1920 and 1921, before widespread indexing, Bresciani indicates that the real income of workers increased, while it decreased during 1922 and 1923. Moreover, real wages fluctuated wildly from month to month during the period of

[1] C. Bresciani-Turroni, *The Economics of Inflation* (London: Allen and Unwin, 1968), p. 442.
[2] ibid., pp. 308–10.

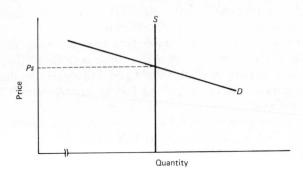

Fig. 16.2(a)

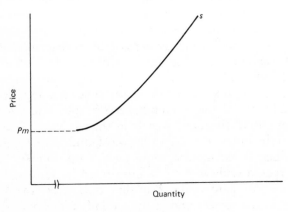

Fig. 16.2(b)

indexed labour contracts. For example, the real wages of coal miners varied from highs (in January and May 1922, March and October 1923) which were approximately 80 per cent of 1913 real wages to lows that were about half of the pre-war real wage (in October and November 1922, January, July and November 1923).[3]

This historical episode of widespread indexing can be viewed as simply a form of incomes policy. Unfortunately it is the

[3] ibid., pp. 312–13, 450.

worst form of an anti-inflationary incomes policy since it will keep wages and prices stable only if they are already stable and there is nothing which alters expectations of their remaining stable.[1] Anything which touches off expectations of inflation can, under the indexing scheme of Friedman's, lead to unending inflation and wildly fluctuating real incomes. In other words, under indexing, thinking that inflation will occur in the future can make it so!

This bootstrap theory of inflation under indexing can be readily analysed via a Marshallian analysis of the interaction of the market period (spot) prices and short-run flow supply (forward) prices analysis that has been developed in Chapter 4. In Fig. 16.2(a), D represents the initial Marshallian demand schedule (including Wicksteedian reservation demand) for a durable good,[2] while the vertical line S represents the stock of the good inherited from the past. If this good is not reproducible then the resulting spot price p_s would allocate the stock without remainder among demanders. If the good is reproducible, the stock can be augmented by a flow of output if buyers are willing to promise to pay the flow-supply price and wait the gestation period for delivery. The curve s (Fig. 16.2(b)) represents the industry's Marshallian flow-supply schedule, i.e. it shows the alternative production offerings at alternative flow-supply prices. If producers are short-run profit maximisers, then p_m is the lowest point on the average variable cost schedule and represents the minimum flow-supply price.

The total market situation for a good is obtained by laterally summing the stock-and-flow-supply schedules to obtain $S+s$ in Fig. 16.3. Superimposing the demand schedule D onto this figure indicates that the spot price, p_s, exceeds the forward or

---

[1] A stable indexed economy would require that all contracts are ideally indexed and are compatible with a fixed equilibrium real wage or, given the future rate of change of labour productivity, the indexing scheme may incorporate this equilibrium rate of change in real wages. Hence indexing as an incomes policy is balanced on a Harrodian knife-edge, for if any event changes the equilibrium real wage there is no price mechanism available to establish this new value.

[2] For expositional and diagrammatic simplicity in the following analysis we will assume that the flow demand due to depreciation is negligible and hence it can be omitted from the diagram.

flow-supply price, p_f, as some buyers are willing to pay a premium for immediate delivery rather than wait the gestation period for a new unit to be produced.[1] This situation (where $p_s > p_f$) is known as *backwardation* and production of $Q_2 - Q_1$ units will be forthcoming at the delivery date.

Assume *all* money-wage contracts are geared to a price index which includes the spot price of many durables (e.g. housing, used cars, standardised commodities, tanker rates, etc.). Since the height of the *s* curve (Fig. 16.2(b)) depends on the money wage rate (or wage unit) at any point in time, the higher the price index, *ceteris paribus*, the higher the wage unit and the higher s.[2]

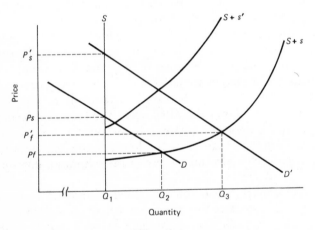

Fig. 16.3

[1] If the good in question is not durable, then the stock supply schedule is coincidental with the ordinate axis and only a forward flow-supply market exists. If the good is not reproducible (i.e. its elasticity of production is zero), then only a spot market exists, or if forward markets are developed, the forward prices will, in a world of uncertainty, represent speculation as to future spot prices for goods where flow-supply considerations cannot affect the outcome.

[2] If some basic raw material such as petroleum is also linked to the same index then we could adopt Keynes's 'cost unit' as underlying the position of the short-run flow supply curve, s, in Fig. 2(b).

Assume that at some initial date the economy is in equilibrium so that there will be a given real wage rate and hence a level of investment and aggregate output which is compatible with it. At this equilibrium employment level, *any* attempt to change the rate of investment, the distribution of income, etc., will automatically upset the price index and induce shifts in the flow-supply curve as the indexing clause in wage contracts becomes operative.

Let us analyse an extreme situation where the initiating force for change is an autonomous change in the state of expectations so that (given current production costs) buyers suddenly expect prices of all goods to rise more rapidly in the future than they did when the demand curve, D, was derived. This expectation of inflation will raise the marginal efficiency of all durables thereby shifting D outward to D' in Fig. 16.3, immediately increasing all spot prices[1] (to p'_s) relative to existing flow-supply prices and thereby encouraging some buyers to order more goods for future delivery.

Forward prices would rise, *as long as money wage rates (and user costs)* are unchanged, from p_f to p'_f, only if the elasticity of supply was not perfectly elastic. Moreover, even if the forward price rose because the short-run flow-supply elasticity was less than ∞, if money wages were *not* indexed, the resulting increase in production flow would increase the existing stock over time (shifting S rightward) and ultimately return the flow-supply price and the spot price to the initial p_f and p_s levels (assuming no further change in expectations). If, however, money wages are indexed, the immediate rise in spot prices (and those forward prices of goods whose flow-supply elasticity is less than perfect) will increase money wage rates and therefore shift up the flow-supply function and the market supply function (in Fig. 16.3) to $S+s'$, thereby raising forward prices even more. This indexing-induced increase in forward prices could produce an additional increase in Marshallian demand curves as (1) workers realise that their money wage income is increasing and (2) the indexing-induced rise in forward prices raises the marginal efficiency of durables even further as buyers recognise that indexing will assure that $E_e = 1$; *indeed it will institutionalise this belief*. Hence D' would shift out again

[1] Keynes, *General Theory*, p. 142.

(in Fig. 16.3) and this will lead to money wage increases shifting up the supply curve $S+s'$ once again. Thus indexing, by establishing a unitary E_e, will cause an initial disturbance to spot prices (a commodity inflation)[1] due to any cause, ephemeral or not, to spill over into an *incomes inflation* which can feed back into a further spot price inflation, etc.

This institutionalisation of an $E_e=1$ via indexing must create an unstable economy, for as Hicks has noted 'if all elasticities of expectations are unity, the stability of the system can only be maintained by the existence of rigid wage-rates; but if all elasticities of expectation are unity why should [money] wage rates be rigid?'[2] Hicks's response to this rhetorical question was that money wages could remain fairly rigid if wage earners 'have fairly *inelastic* price-expectations'—the exact opposite of indexation. In fact, Hicks pointed out that once workers' E_e approached unity, negotiators will have recourse to indexing and 'the rigidity of money wages ceases altogether'. Stability requires, Hicks concludes, 'A tendency to rigidity of certain prices, particularly wage-rates, but there must also be a tendency to rigidity of certain price expectations as well'.[3] One must add that these tendencies are to be found in the modern institutions of forward contracting in general and money-wage forward contracts for labour in particular.

Although in Fig. 16.3, the destabilising process was set off by a hypothetical autonomous change in expectations creating an increase in demand in spot markets, the process could have been initiated by a reduction in supply as well. Thus an Act of God or Man, such as either a drought which prevents re-

---

[1] See p. 339 above.

[2] Hicks, *Value and Capital*, p. 270.

[3] ibid., p. 171. Of course, even if money wages are not indexed, the initial rise in spot prices may be perceived as a permanent increase in the cost of living by workers whose wage contracts come up for renewal in the near future. Consequently, these workers will demand higher wages than otherwise to try to recoup this unexpected lost real income level, i.e. workers' $E_e=1$. As other wage contracts come up for renewal other workers may join this higher wage-demand bandwagon or even attempt to leapfrog $(E_e>1)$ over earlier wage settlements. Thus stickiness in spot prices (via a buffer stock scheme) may be a necessary adjunct to obtain workers' agreement to an incomes policy which attempts to maintain stickiness of production costs and forward prices of goods.

placements to the stock supply as a commodity is consumed, or an international cartel which deliberately holds supplies off the market will cause a rise in spot commodity prices and thereby, via indexing, start the process of a domestic incomes inflation which can only exacerbate the initial price increase problem.

Hence the unnerving conclusion that in a dynamic Keynesian model, where equilibrium need never have time to establish itself, nor even if it is established need it long endure, it is only the stickiness *and* long duration of forward labour contracts which provide the conventionality of price stability required to avoid violent instability. In the absence of the institution of seratim forward contracting in money terms expectations of future price increases and/or spot market supply shortages could impinge on Marshallian supply and demand curves, shifting them up almost without limit as *long as entrepreneurs can obtain working capital funds to finance their constantly escalating production commitments.*

In sum, if the conventionality of price stickiness is broken down by destroying the duration of private labour contracts fixed in money terms, then, since production takes time, a free enterprise system can become violently unstable. Furthermore, widespread indexing could destroy the liquidity of the existing monetary system for no product produced in the system would have a sticky flow-supply schedule to limit its possible future spot price. In the absence of sticky flow-supply schedules the expected prices of all future goods are determined by the same volatile expectations of the future prices of non-producible durable goods.

In any perfectly indexed economy, any increase in the price index would start a process of continually shifting the flow supply curves of all goods upwards, causing people to fly from currency (i.e. there is a dramatic fall in the liquidity of money) as people will prefer to hold liquid goods (whose future spot price is expected to be inflation-proof). Thus without the 'expectations of a relative stickiness of wages in terms of money' one does not have the corollary: the 'excess of liquidity premium over carrying cost being greater for money than for any other asset' and hence the way is open for a system to become a 'non-monetary economy' where 'there is no asset for which liquidity premium is always in excess of the carrying costs'.[1] In such a world, time-consuming production processes will grind to a halt for no one will accept the required long-term production commitments of taking a position in fixed and working capital goods. Hence a dynamic capitalist economy with widespread indexing would be precariously perched on a knife edge. Anything which set off spot price changes or even expectations of spot price changes will cause such an indexed economic system to oscillate violently with prices racing to infinity (or to zero if indexed in both directions).[2]

Under this conceptualisation of the real world, the indexing of wage contracts is almost certain to bring about the destruction of any capitalist monetary system, especially if the index contains some spot price components whose basis is not anchored to the stickiness of production-flow prices. An upward movement (ephemeral or otherwise) in spot prices of producible goods will immediately set off a process of legalised upward wage and price automatic recontracting agreements which can continue as long as buyers' agents can meet (finance) their contractual commitments. Even if the money supply was not to endogenously increase as entrepreneurs required more working capital funds, expectations may encourage a flight from money sufficient to finance the ever-increasing cost of production *and* inventory speculation for a long time.

Monetary stringency, if and when it become binding, will occur when the debt structure of entrepreneurs becomes so precarious that they are unable to borrow additional sums to meet their forward contract production commitments. The inevitable chain of bankruptcies that will follow along the non-integrated production system will ultimately mean the end of the system as all contracts become meaningless. Such a catastrophe, by wiping out all existing contracts simultaneously, provides a foundation for developing a new monetary unit of account which is not indexed and which therefore can be utilised in denominating new input price contractual commit-

[1] Keynes, *General Theory*, pp. 237–8. Keynes noted that in a flight from currency, e_w, the proportional change in money wages compared to the proportional change in effective demand becomes 'large', i.e. wages are no longer sticky (ibid., p. 306).

[2] Cf. ibid., pp. 269–70.

ments with a reasonable expectation of these prices being sticky. Thus the system will attempt to restore flexibility of real wages at the same time as it stabilises money wages in terms of the new monetary unit. Without this property, the economy could not adapt to inevitable unpredictable changes over time with any degree of stability.

Hence economic society, in the unconscious recesses of its being, knew what it was all about when men developed long-term forward contracts for labour and abolished spot markets for slaves. In so doing society provided institutions which ensured that an uncertain future does not mean an unstable future for any dynamic monetary economy where expectations govern decisions that drive the system through its environment of shifting equilibria.

This view was summed up by Townshend, one of the first to recognise the implications of Keynes's dynamic model.

> There can be no such thing as long period dynamic economic theory failing the . . . discovery of a plausible long-term convention of price stability. It is perhaps now being generally realised that such long-term dynamic theories as there are conceal unplausible ones. It is not unnatural that those who forecast the future in algebra or geometry should be chastened by hard fact more slowly than those who have to forecast it in arithmetic. Nor is the conclusion that the search for laws to enable us to predict economic events far ahead, like eclipses, must be given up, so surprising—not to say nihilistic—as it may seem (to some economists) at first sight.[1]

SOME FURTHER TIDYING UP

Since the completion of the final draft of the original edition of *Money and the Real World* in May 1970, several mainstream concepts are being developed in economic literature; these new ideas, however, are closely related to Keynes's well-developed views on the money and good markets. Two such neoclassical notions are: (1) the crowding out effect and the effect of financing government deficit spending and (2) Okun's auction versus customer markets analysis of inflation. The first has already led to needless confusion and controversy

[1] Townshend, op. cit., p. 166.

and the second is likely to be equally diverting to the neo-classical schools of economic thought. In order to provide a consistent framework for notions such as these, I will demonstrate in this section how these neoclassical ideas can be brought into conformity with Keynes's analysis as developed in *Money and the Real World*.

Monetarists versus Keynesians versus Keynes on the Crowding Out Effect

During the Ford Presidency in the United States, Secretary of the Treasury Simon and the Ford Council of Economic Advisors adopted an argument developed by Monetarists that if the U.S. Government attempted to borrow to stimulate the economy during the 1974-75 recession (the severest since the Great Depression) the effect would be to 'crowd out' private borrowers from credit markets thereby further depressing private sector spending.[1]

Since those who do not study history (of economic thought) tend to repeat the errors of the past, American Keynesian scholars such as Tobin, Heller, Solow, Okun and Schultze dismissed the 'crowding out' theory as a lack of understanding of the basic Keynesian principle that before full employment there can never be a shortage of savings 'to finance' any level of investment (or government) spending. Of course, it was the American Keynesians and not the Monetarists and Ford Economic Advisors who did not understand Keynes. As Chapter 7 above explains Keynes's finance motive demonstrates that any increase in planned expenditures will create 'congestion' (to use Keynes's word) in the money markets and

> ... inhibit the improvement, no matter how thrifty the public purpose to be out of their future income. . . . If there is no change in the liquidity position, the public can save *ex ante* and *ex post* and ex anything else until they are blue in the face, without alleviating the problem in the least. . . . The investment market can become congested through a shortage of cash. It can never become congested through a

---

[1] R. W. Spencer and W. P. Yohe, 'The "Crowding Out" of Private Expenditures by Fiscal Policy Actions', *Fed. Res. Bank of St Louis Rev.* (Oct. 1970).

shortage of saving. This *is* the most fundamental of my conclusions within the field.[1]

Thus, forty years ago, Keynes recognised the 'congestion' or
the crowding out effect as the most fundamental conclusion of
his monetary analysis. In terms of the IS-LM model used by
both Monetarists and neoclassical Keynesians, this involves
the recognition that the parameters of the planned expenditure
function are also parameters of the demand for money function,
i.e. the IS and LM functions are interdependent.

To paraphrase Harry Johnson's gibe (see p. 162 above), the
ability of neoclassical Keynesians (but not Keynes) to insist
that changes in planned spending can affect money markets
only after realised output changes is a credit to their ability to
prevaricate rather than to their scientifically inquiring minds.
Even Professor Friedman has discovered that the difference
between Neoclassical Monetarists and Neoclassical Keynesians
'clearly is not and never has been whether the LM curve is
vertical or has a positive slope';[2] rather when money matters
it does so because of the interdependence of the real and
monetary sectors.

Friedman, in an analysis that is similar in some respects to
Keynes's fundamental conclusion regarding the finance motive,
has at least recognised that under certain circumstances when
the IS curve shifts because of an increase in planned spending
the LM curve will shift concomitantly. Unfortunately Friedman has not correctly perceived all the ramifications of the
interrelationships of the IS and LM curves but at least he
appreciates the possibility of the principle of interdependence
of the monetary and real sectors' functions—a principle which
is basic to Keynes's approach but which has, so far, escaped
the perception of the leading proponents of the Neoclassical
Keynesian School.

Friedman, accepting the 'crowding out' effect (without
realising its origin in Keynes's finance motive analysis), argues
that, given a permanent once-for-all shift in the IS function due
to a deficit financed increase in government spending from G_0
to G_1, the deficit will be financed by a concomitant increase

[1] J. M. Keynes, 'The Ex-Ante Theory of the Rate of Interest', *Econ. Jour.*, **47** (1937) pp. 668–9.
[2] Friedman, *Debate with His Critics*, p. 142.

in the money supply (to avoid 'congestion') not only in the first period when income increases from Y_0 to Y_1, but in each future period so long as the deficit continues even though government expenditure and income remain unchanged. Thus the LM curve continues to shift rightward in each future period so that its movement 'must swamp the effect of the once-for-all shift of the IS curve'.[1]

Of course, Friedman has not recognised that when the IS curve shifts outward, the finance motive will cause the LM curve to shift inward and therefore an increase in the money supply in the initial period to finance the initial increase in government spending will offset the inward LM shift. Whether Friedman is correct in arguing that the LM curve must continue to shift outward in each future period after the once-for-all shift of IS function, however, depends on the flow demand for securities in future periods. The flow demand for securities, as we have demonstrated,[2] depends on the magnitude of m, the marginal propensity to purchase securities out of each period's savings. Since once the higher level of income Y_1 is established from the once-for-all shift in IS, the additional savings in each future period (compared with savings which would be forthcoming if Y remained at Y_0) will just equal $(G_1 - G_0)$. If $m = 1$, then this additional savings sum will *all* be spent on securities, so that the additional new issue of government debt in each future period, *ceteris paribus*, can just be absorbed by the private sector net flow demand for securities out of savings and no additional money need be forthcoming to float the additional government debt. Thus if $m = 1$, the LM curve will not shift in future periods in response to the once-for-all shift in IS. In other words both functions will shift about in the initial period only.

If, on the other hand, $m = 0$, then there will be no additional flow demand for securities by the private sector in each future period, and hence government bonds (at the current rate of interest) can only be sold to the banking system so that Friedman's scenario of the money supply increasing *pari passu* with the $G_1 - G_0$ deficit in each future period is applicable.

As we noted in Chapter 7, however, Keynes believed that

[1] ibid., p. 141.
[2] See pp. 272, 277–80, 304–12, 324–35 above.

$0 < m < 1$, and hence some part of the new issue of government debt used to finance the $(G_1 - G_0)$ spending in each future period will be absorbed by the private sector and part will have to be financed by an increase in the money supply. Thus, whether the continuous shifting of the LM curve 'swamps' the once-for-all shift of IS depends on the magnitude of m. Money clearly matters, but so does the liquidity preference (and hence the asset holding desires) of the private sector.

Money and Time Related Markets

In a perceptive article which attempts to lay bare 'The Anatomy of Monetary Theory' Clower recognised that the 'literature of monetary economics—again from Aristotle on—is replete with instances in which writers have inadvertently used the world "money" as if it were synonymous with the phrase "organized markets".'[1] Of course, the message of *Money and the Real World* is that any model of real world monetary economies *must* necessarily and explicitly specify seven basic characteristics including 'the different degrees of organization of spot and future markets';[2] that is, a monetary economy must be modelled within a framework of time-related organised markets.

Since 1975, mainstream economists at the Brookings Institution have apparently discovered that any analysis of real world inflation requires an analysis of contracts *and* two different types of markets: ' "auction" markets . . . with instantaneous market clearing and "customer" markets in which economic incentives induce long-term contractual arrangements'.[3] Although there are obvious similarities between the Okun–Gordon–Poole auction and customer market

[1] R. W. Clower, 'The Anatomy of Monetary Theory', *Amer. Econ. Rev. Pap. Proc.*, **67** (1977) p. 209.
[2] See p. 146 above.
[3] R. J. Gordon, 'The Theory of Domestic Inflation', *Amer. Econ. Rev. Pap. Proc.*, **67** (1977) p. 130. See also A. Okun, 'Inflation: Its Mechanics and Welfare Costs', *Brookings Papers*, **6** (1975) and W. Poole, 'Rational Expectations in the Macro Model', *Brookings Papers*, **7** (1976) p. 466.
   The fact that I was a Brookings Economics Panel member in 1974 and tried, both in my Brookings sponsored paper and in the general discussion of the work of others (e.g. 'Oil: Its Time Allocation and Project Independence', *Brookings Papers*, **5** (1974) pp. 411–26; also p. 115), to get my Brookings colleagues to analyse economic problems via time-related spot and forward markets, perhaps had a subliminal impact on their thinking.

concepts and the spot and forward market analysis of *Money and the Real World*, nevertheless, my former Brookings colleagues still have not drawn quite the correct distinction between these two types of market. For the Brookings people the difference appears to turn on the existence of an auction (and the implicit absence of contracts) in the one and the existence of contracts (and the absence of an auction) in the other. Contracts, however, are the essence of both 'auction' and 'customer' markets. It is the time duration of the contractual commitment in each type of market, and not whether the market is orgnised on an auction basis or not, which is the important fact. (It is possible to have well-organised auction markets for forward contracts—even though each contract involves long-time contractual arrangements.)

The existence of time related market and contracts for performance and money payments is the essence of a money economy!

FINANCING ASSET HOLDING AND CASH FLOWS:
WHY MONEY MATTERS

Marshall warned in the preface of the first edition of his *Principles* that the 'element of Time is the centre of the chief difficulty of almost every economic problem'[1] and hence it should not be surprising that economic man has developed different markets for dealing with the transactions for immediate 'spot' delivery and payments and for forward delivery and payment at a specified future date. Spot markets are equivalent to Hick's flexprice markets (because the stock supply is, by definition, perfectly inelastic) and hence any change in the public's demand will be immediately and completely reflected in a change in the spot price[2] while forward markets are (because of the fixed terms of the contracts) equivalent to Hicks's fixprice markets in a calendar

---

[1] A. Marshall, *Principles of Economics*, 1st ed. (London: Macmillan, 1890), p. viii.

[2] To the extent that the public demand change is not offset by a change in reservation demand of the market makers of these spot markets. Even in spot (auction) markets the degree of price flexibility depends on this reservation demand of market makers, i.e. their reactions and interpretation of sudden changes in the public's market behaviour and the institutional rules governing how market makers are supposed to maintain 'orderliness' in spot prices over calendar time.

time setting. As the last section noted, Brookings economists have recently discovered that flexprice and fixprice markets coexist in the real world, despite the logical impossibility of this occurring in the general equilibrium microfoundations used by these macrotheorists.

In a neoclassical world such as described by Debreu, all prices (for either factors of production or products) are paid simultaneously *at the initial instant of time*. Accordingly, no economic agent need worry about his ability to meet future contractual payments when they fall due since *all* payments and receipts are instantaneously done and recorded in each agent's balance sheet.[1] Since this initial instant accounting process occurs in the (assumed) absence of false trades, there can be no future payment obligations and consequently rational agents would not worry about solvency; hence inhabitants of a neoclassical world would not demand liquidity. By defining prices as those which are paid in the initial instant for all transactions over time, *neoclassical theory has removed the flow of payments from the time dimension!*

This neoclassical treatment of payments is the same even in a world of uncertainty where the latter is defined as 'uncertainty of the environment . . . [which] originates in the choice that nature makes among a finite number of alternatives.'[2] In an 'uncertain' neoclassical world 'a contract for the transfer of a commodity now specifies, in addition to its physical properties, its location and its date, an event on the occurrence of which the transfer is conditional.'[3] The payment for the commodity however is instantaneous and non-conditional since the price of any commodity is 'the amount paid . . . . *initially* by . . . . the agent who commits himself to accept . . . . delivery of one unit of that commodity. *Payment is irrevocably made although delivery does not take place if specific events do not obtain.*'[4]

Thus the basic concept of prices in neo-Walrasian analysis requires the removal of both money and money income receipts

[1] G. Debreu, *Theory of Value* (New Haven: Yale University Press, 1959) p. 28.

[2] ibid., p. 98. From a Knight-Keynes view, this is risk, not uncertainty!

[3] ibid., p. 98.

[4] ibid., p. 100. Italics added.

and outpayments from any historical time setting; instead the flow of all payments is in real goods and, more importantly, all payments are firmly and 'irrevocably' in a timeless 'initial instant'. In the real world, on the other hand, payments and receipts are primarily in the form of money and occur in a sequential time setting as buyers and sellers make contracts in both spot and forward markets. In such a world the threat of insolvency leads to a demand for liquidity. It is only in this world that the institutions of money and money contracts have an essential role to play.[1] It is only in this world that cash flows over time are essential to asset holding positions.

Real capital assets are either working capital goods which have a useful life of one production period, or fixed capital goods which have a life span of two or more production periods. Financial assets, on the other hand, have temporal lives which are normally specifically spelled out in the contractual base of the asset. To take a 'position' in an asset is to purchase and hold stock of the asset over time. The purchase price of the stock must be financed. The position is held until the 'date of realisation' when the asset is converted back into money; at the realisation date, the position is liquidated.

Types of Assets

There are three types of assets[2] in which positions can be taken:

(a) *Illiquid Assets* which are durables whose spot market is poorly organised, thin or even notional. Illiquid assets are

---

[1] It should be noted that the neoclassical concept of commodity prices in a timeless dimension of a neoclassical world will not permit any logically consistent analysis of either inflation or the indexing of contracts despite some airy policy suggestions by both Monetarists and mainstream Keynesians on the causes of inflation and the desirability or undesirability of indexing. Inflation (which is a rise in commodity prices over a period of calendar time) and indexing (which involves increasing cash inflows over time in response to unanticipated inflation) are logically impossible in a neoclassical world where all commodity prices and their concomitant cash flows occur simultaneously at the initial instant of time. Inflation and indexing are phenomena which can be analysed only in a world where the passage of time is recognised by economic agents who utilise forward contracts to require delivery *and* payments in the future.

[2] Cf. J. R. Hicks, *Critical Essays in Monetary Theory* (Oxford University Press, 1967) p. 36.

held by firms primarily for their expected money income stream, i.e. for the expected 'dated' cash flows or yields over their useful life. Fixed capital, consumer durables and most working capital goods can be considered in this category. (Consumers hold illiquid assets for the expected stream of dated services.) If an asset is illiquid, then realisation (liquidation) occurs only on dates of expected net cash sales inflow (i.e. dates when the final output made using the capital goods are sold). Working capital goods normally have a single realisation date, while fixed capital goods are liquidated in small segments over many future realisation dates.

(b) *Liquid Assets* are durables which are traded in well-organised and orderly spot markets. They are held for the dated stream of cash inflows the asset is expected to yield (net of carrying costs) including any sales revenue from liquidating the asset in a spot market at the expected realisation date prior to the end of its useful economic life. If an asset is re-saleable, it has some degree of liquidity.

(c) *Fully Liquid Assets* include money or any other asset which can immediately be converted into money in a spot market where the market maker 'guarantees' a fixed and unchanging net spot price. Thus, fully liquid assets represent directly or indirectly the availability of a specific quantity of undated cash which can be used for the discharge of contracts at any time.

Obviously, the boundaries between these classes of assets are not absolutely distinct, hard and fast, or unchanging over time. The degree of liquidity depends on the degree of organisation and orderliness of the relevant spot market. Depending on social practices and institutions, the degree of liquidity of any asset can change from time to time as the spot market for various assets changes. The smaller the transaction costs and the greater the stickiness of the money spot price of the asset over time, the greater the degree of liquidity of any asset. These factors depend, in large part, on the functioning of a market maker who maintains orderliness. Money is fully liquid because the spot price of money in terms of itself is certain and unchanging (no capital gain or loss in nominal terms). As long as money has this store of value characteristic plus the fact that it is commonly used in the discharge of contracts (medium of exchange) for the purchase of things that most members of the economy want, then money will be the basic fully liquid asset in a monetary economy.

Financing Asset-Holding[1]

The holding of any asset must be paid for or 'financed' by the holder; that is, the holder must pay a purchase price at the time of initially obtaining possession of the asset. This payment may be either *equity financed* or *debt financed*. In the case of equity finance the buyer has at the purchase date in historical time already amassed sufficient purchasing power via money savings out of previous income, and/or the sale of other assets (including new issues of equities), to pay the entire money purchase price upon delivery. In the case of debt financing, the buyer must borrow all (or some[2]) of the purchase price via a *debt contract* (i.e. a contract for forward delivery of interest payments and the return of principal) in order to meet the delivery payment obligation.

(a) *Equity Financing.* If equity financing is used, the asset holder is operating as an Equity Fund (hereafter EF) which, in essence, is a body to which a certain amount of funds has been entrusted without any specific contractual obligation for the return of these funds, and only a hope that the return on these funds will be made as large as possible. The EF works solely on the asset side of its balance sheet—in a manner of speaking, 'its liabilities are asleep'.[3]

Mainstream monetary theory with its preoccupation on a portfolio balance is implicitly assuming all asset holders behave as if they are EFs (albeit in a timeless world). Hence modern monetary theory ignores completely the question of debt financing of positions and its implications for economic activity.

(b) *Debt Financing.* In the case of debt financing, the asset holder's liabilities are not asleep. Most businessmen use debt

[1] This section attempts to synthesise the ideas of Hicks, *Critical Essays*, Chs. 2 and 3, and H. P. Minsky, *John Maynard Keynes* (New York: Columbia University Press, 1975) and 'The Financial Instability Hypothesis', *Nebraska Jour. of Econ. and Bus.*, **16** (1977), with Keynes's *Treatise* and *General Theory* analysis.

[2] The remainder of the purchase price is equity financed.

[3] Hicks, *Critical Essays*, p. 47.

financing to hold some, if not all, of their illiquid assets. Working capital goods are usually financed by short-term bank loans (the duration of which is normally related to the gestation period of production) while fixed capital assets are often financed via long-term debts. Hence the production flow of goods and services which make up the GNP of any economy depend in large part on the ability of entrepreneurs to initially debt finance their production commitments and then to maintain sufficient liquidity to meet the resulting debt liabilities as they fall due while utilising the resulting illiquid real assets to produce the goods which make up the standard of living of the economy. Keynes's monetary theory of production recognised the importance of this debt financing process, while modern neoclassical theory, by assumption, denies its existence.

The debt financing of positions can be divided into two basic situations, sinking fund finance and floating fund finance.

Sinking Fund Finance (hereafter SFF) occurs when the debt contractual obligations are written in money terms in a time sequence so that the expected money quasi-rents earned by the asset and/or other unencumbered cash inflows expected by the holder exceeds the contractually due interest and any amortisation of principal in each period by a sufficient amount to at least provide for the redemption of the remaining debt principal at the maturity date. Thus, when a firm finances a position via SFF, the expected present value of the asset will normally exceed its supply price at any given rate of time discount.

Positions in almost all working capital goods, consumer durables, and many fixed capital goods are normally financed via SFF, since SFF is the basic tenet of 'sound' and 'prudent' financing. As long as expectations of future cash inflows are not disappointed, future contractual payment obligations are assured and neither the holder nor the lender need fear insolvency. Of course, if expectations regarding future cash inflows are disappointed by events, solvency can be jeopardised. Hence, most SFF contracts are written so that expected cash inflows *exceed* obligations in each period and even then, as a precautionary measure, the holder may desire (or be required by the lender) to hold additional liquid assets.

Floating Fund Finance (hereafter FFF) occurs when the debt contractual payment obligations are written so that the expected quasi-rents and other unencumbered cash inflow are *not* sufficient to meet the contractually due interest and amortisation payments in each period and provide for the redemption of the remaining principal at the maturity date. FFF can occur even though the present value of the asset (for its economic life) exceeds its present cost, particularly if the asset is long-lived and its earning power is concentrated in the later part of its life, while the life of the debt contract is limited to a shorter life either by institutional rules or lenders' tastes. Thus FFF always involves the problem of solvency, for even if expectations are not disappointed, quasi-rent inflows will not be sufficient to meet obligations and hence, asset-holders must watch their liquidity position.

Holders of FFF assets must manage their liabilities very carefully even if events never disappoint their expectations. FFF positions will be undertaken only if the asset holder believes he can either re-finance the asset at later dates as needed until such time as it can be re-financed on a SFF basis, *or* it can be sold at a later date in a well-organised spot market at a money price which can be used to pay off the remaining debt. (Hence the asset holder using FFF is often someone who believes that the current market's assessment of the future is wrong, and thus he will make a capital gain, when the market corrects its faulty view and permits capital appreciation in nominal terms at a future date in the spot market.)

Of course, if the FFF asset holder's expectations are disappointed, then his solvency problems will be exacerbated. Hence, those who use FFF to maintain a position must also maintain greater precautionary cash balances and other liquid assets than those financiers who operate under SFF principles. FFF contracts will be written when both the borrower and the lender expect the debtor to be able to refinance his position (and/or the borrower has enough precautionary liquid assets to meet any unforeseen contingency). FFF is used (a) in the margin purchases of securities; (b) by bankers in obtaining deposits; and (c) in the purchase of speculative real assets (e.g. oil and other mineral properties and other speculative real estate properties). FFF is also used by many governments to finance either capital or operating deficits where no specific asset of the government is pledged against the debt.

Minsky has introduced a subclassification of FFF which he terms Ponzi Financing but which may more descriptively be called Rising (or Pyramid) Fund Financing (RFF). In RFF the contractual cash outflows in one or more near future periods exceeds the expected cash inflow of the debtor, hence, the debtor must increase his indebtedness merely to meet his initial debt obligations. RFF can occur when (1) as in the Ponzi case, the debtor misleads the lenders with false or even fraudulent information regarding the future cash inflow power of his asset holdings or (2) as a result of honest but faulty expectations about future cash inflows which can cause an initial SFF position to become an FFF position or even an RFF position (e.g. the 1975 financial situation of New York City).

Debt Finance, Indexing, Liquidity and Solvency

(a) *SFF Correct Expectations and Changing Money Market Conditions.* As long as the initial expectations about future cash inflows are met, asset holders will not have any solvency problems because of their SFF obligations. Nor will changes in interest rates or money market conditions affect the position in assets held via SFF. All debt obligations can be met out of anticipated cash inflows as long as the debt is denominated in the same (nominal) terms as the expected cash inflow. Thus any production that is already under way which uses working capital and/or fixed capital goods already financed via SFF will not be interrupted by changes in current money market conditions as long as sales expectations are met.

(b) *SFF Correct Expectations and Indexing.* If, however, SFF contracts financing fixed and working capital assets were to be indexed, then, even if initial expectations of cash inflows are met, these obligations could become FFF debts (or even RFF) if the price index to which the debt payments are linked rises more rapidly than the prices underlying the expected cash inflows from sales by the asset holder. Thus indexing of all debt contracts can create greater liquidity and solvency problems especially for firms who produce goods with long gestation periods and who use debt finance for some or all of their working capital and fixed capital requirements. More-over, as will be described below, all FFF asset holding positions become vulnerable to changing money market conditions. Thus, in a period of inflation, if debt contracts are indexed, producers (even if they use SFF) will experience liquidity difficulties which will be exacerbated if the Monetary Authority, at the same time, undertakes tight money policies to fight ongoing inflation.

Only if *all* prices move at an identical rate simultaneously for each day in the future, so that the prices underlying the expected cash inflows of real capital asset holders (producers) do not get out of line with those used to index debt obligations, will the widespread indexing of debt contracts not create disruptive insolvency and liquidity problems for producers. Since these conditions can never be met in the real world where the future is uncertain, those who advocate the wide-spread use of indexing are recommending a policy which contains the seeds for debilitating or even destroying modern monetary market-oriented production economies. Indexing of 'sound' SFF can, in a period of inflation, in and of itself, upset and impede production plans because of the financial and liquidity problems it creates! Indexing will be inculpable in a monetary economy where production requires the financing of fixed and working capital goods only if the rate of inflation is insignificant, and then indexing is inept.

(c) *SFF and Disappointed Expectations*. If expectations regarding future cash flows are not met, then asset holders may find that they have difficulties meeting their debt obligations and their SFF may thereby be transformed into a FFF situation and, in severe cases, even into an RFF status. Consequently, any disappointment in expected sales revenues will not only affect producers' current expectations about the future, hence reducing the marginal efficiency of investment and their expectations of future sales and therefore also reducing future planned production; but disappointing sales revenues will also directly create liquidity problems for producers. These liquidity problems hinder current production if current working capital positions cannot be maintained. In severe situations producers using prudent SFF for working capital goods could find themselves forced to liquidate their working capital positions via bankruptcy or similar proceedings and thereby cause current production schedules to be halted or at least curtailed.

(d) *FFF and Changing Money Market Conditions.* When FFF is used to finance a position, the asset holder is vulnerable not only to disappointed expectations regarding future cash inflows, but, in contradistinction to an SFF position, even if expectations of cash inflows are correct, the FFF asset holder can be adversely affected at the re-finance date by higher interest rate charges and money market conditions which can increase the carrying cost of the position or create insolvency and even bankruptcy. A sufficient increase in interest rates at a re-finance time can reduce the present value of the existing stock of assets being held below the value of the remaining outstanding debt principle thereby making re-financing undesirable and encouraging the asset holder to abandon the (physically productive) assets especially if they are long-lived (e.g. residential housing).

Hence, if FFF is widely used, then if money market conditions become tighter at a period of time when re-financing of positions in real capital goods becomes necessary, the result can be widespread abandonment of assets and bankruptcies. The resulting reduction in aggregate demand can cause remaining SFF positions to become FFF situations as asset holders find their cash inflow expectations disappointed. Thus, a deliberate policy of tight money can create liquidity problems which will disrupt current production which utilises existing assets if it happens to coincide with a period of re-financing widespread FFF positions.

(e) *Finance, Disappointments, and Liquidity Crises.* SFF and FFF are both vulnerable to unexpected declines in aggregate demand and its attendant reduction in cash flows whether due to a change in aggregate private spending or deliberate government policies. Whenever aggregate demand does not meet entrepreneurial expectations, 'prudent' sinking fund financiers as well as daring FFF asset holders face a growing threat of insolvency. It therefore follows, as Minsky has continually argued, that economic growth (which requires additional financing as the stock of real capital increases) inevitably creates a system of 'financial fragility' where any disappointment in the actual growth of aggregate demand can create a liquidity crisis or crunch which can bring down one asset holder after another like a house of cards.

(f) *Are the Principles of Sound Finance Expedient?* To those with a conservative turn of mind, principles of sound finance suggest that all asset holding financed by debts uses the SFF approach. As long as the SFF asset holder has sufficient foresight, financial collapse does not seem possible. Although this view is appropriate for the individual, it does not necessarily hold in the aggregate. In other words, the principles of 'sound' and 'prudent' finance are subject to the fallacy of composition. As Keynes noted,

> [S]inking funds, etc. are apt to withdraw spending power from the consumer long before the demand for expenditure on replacements . . . comes into play, i.e., they diminish current effective demand and only increase it in the year in which the replacement is actually made. If the effect of this is aggravated by 'financial prudence' i.e. by its being thought advisable to 'write off' the initial cost *more* rapidly than the equipment actually wears out, the cumulative result may be very serious indeed.[1]

Moreover, it is not only in the private sector where the belief in sound finance is prevalent. Governments—in particular state and local—are often admonished if they do not provide sinking funds for the discharge of public debt, especially if the debt is due to investments made by local authorities or public boards. But this can be disastrous for the economy if over a period of time such actions involve 'a change-over from a policy of government borrowing to the opposite policy of providing sinking funds (or *vice versa*) [which] is capable of causing a severe contraction (or market expansion) of effective demand'.[2]

In the consumer sector, sound finance also suggests that households who purchase houses, automobiles, refrigerators, etc. via debt finance should pay off the debt out of ordinary future income more rapidly that the asset actually wears out. (Home mortgages and most consumer debts are SFF obligations.) Thus if some of the debt financing of long-lived real

[1] Keynes, *General Theory*, p. 100.
[2] ibid., pp. 95, 101.

capital assets held by businessmen, governments and consumers is financed on a sinking fund basis, any bunching of such expenditures at a given point of time will, *ceteris paribus*, result in a lower level of aggregate demand due to the sinking fund 'oversavings' in a following period. This 'oversavings' in turn could cause expectations of cash inflows (which encouraged the initial period's purchases of assets via SFF) to be disappointed, thereby creating insolvency problems for the asset holders in the second period. In sum, if too many economic agents engage in SFF for the purchase of long-lived durables in a given period, this can create a tendency to lower aggregate demand (with deficient cash flows), so that sinking fund obligations become FFF or even RFF in the future.

If instead, in the initial period, most economic agents used FFF to pay for their newly ordered long-lived real assets, then aggregate demand in future periods would not, *ceteris paribus*, be as low as if asset holders used SFF to purchase the same quantity of assets. Compare two economies, Alpha and Beta, with the same expectations, labour force, technology, aggregate consumption function, and gross investment spending over a period of time. If the Alpha economy used SFF for its real investment purchases while the Beta economy used FFF, then the Alpha economy will, in the future, have a greater tendency towards recession and disappointed cash flow expectations than the Beta economy. Consequently, the sinking fund obligations in Alpha are likely to become floating fund obligations over time while the Alpha economy will be continually under threat of widespread insolvency and bankruptcy. In the more expansive Beta economy, however, expectations of cash flows may prove to be too conservative and hence there will be a tendency for debts that were expected to have to be re-financed in future periods to be redeemable (as if they were sinking fund obligations) as windfall (unexpected) cash inflows and tax revenues yield surpluses sufficient to retire some or all of the debts that were expected to have to be re-financed. Thus, under certain circumstances, Beta's floating fund debts can easily be retired (sunk) while Alpha's sinking fund obligations may have to be refloated.

This result appears to conflict with Minsky's ingenious analysis of 'financial fragility' in which he suggests that the greater the weight of speculative finance (FFF) in the total financial structure, the greater the fragility. Thus, according to Minsky, as an economy moves from SFF to FFF, the financial structure moves from a robust to a fragile system. Despite the apparent conflict, there is nothing incompatible between Minsky's analysis and the above comparison of the Alpha and Beta economies. Minsky is implicitly assuming under the *ceteris paribus* clause that the level of sales and cash flows in each future period is unchanged no matter whether SFF or FFF is utilised. Once it is recognised that 'sound' SFF can, if pervasive enough, lead to lower aggregate demands and reduced cash flows (as Keynes noted in *The General Theory*) while FFF can increase demand and cash flows and therefore reduce solvency problems, then it is no longer clear which method of finance is robust and which is fragile. In the real world, of course, there is a continual mix of these two forms of finance; what a proper balance between these two forms of finance should be is too difficult to specify in advance.

It was a basic tenet of Keynes's counter-cyclical policy that government deficits to offset private 'oversavings' need not be a sufficient policy to maintain full employment over time, if the government financed investment projects via SFF. The result might be that 'even if private individuals were ready to spend the whole of their incomes it would be a severe task to restore full employment in the face of this heavy volume of statutory provision by public and semi-public authorities, entirely disassociated from any corresponding new investment'.[1]

For example, the conventional wisdom of sound finance, which insists that home mortgages and auto loans be paid off before the durable financed by this debt contract wears out, forces consumers to save more than otherwise, thereby placing a drag on the economy.[2] This hobbling of demand will be especially pernicious if a period of tight money brought about by deliberate monetary policy follows a period of a building boom. Tight money will have an immediate impact on the

[1] ibid., p. 101.
[2] For example, it is my understanding that in Sweden mortgage contracts are amortised over a period of 50 years or more rather than the 20 to 25 years that is normal in the U.S. Thus, consumption, *ceteris paribus*, would be higher in the former economy compared to the latter.

production and sales of new houses, but it is expansion in this sector (or others) which will be required to offset the drag of the sinking funds involved in the home mortgages created during the boom.

In sum, the way asset holders use debt to finance their position in new real capital goods and consumer durables can affect the real output of the economy *independent* of the marginal efficiency of investment and the consumption function. In an economy characterised by private holdings of all sorts of real capital assets—as well as financial assets—financial arrangements for maintaining 'positions' can have important impacts on the real economy. Ours is not just a real barter economy of the neoclassical type upon which money plays no essential part. Neoclassical microanalysis can provide no theoretical underpinnings for the macro-behaviour of ongoing real world economies.

Equity Financing of Positions

So far, only debt financing of real capital goods has been analysed in detail. The omission of equity financing has been primarily for expositional ease and the reader should not be led into thinking that if firms were financed solely via EF, all solvency problems of business firms would be avoided. Two real world complications prevent a world of solely equity financing from occurring. These are:

(1) The very nature of modern banking systems involves FFF. Commercial banks are always borrowing short to lend long, hence bankers hold portfolios financed primarily via FFF. If banks were to finance their portfolios via EF, depositors would become owners rather than creditors, and depositors would be unable to make withdrawals except when dividends (interest payments) were declared by the bank. Since modern banking systems are always based on FFF, the monetary systems of most modern economies are particularly vulnerable to liquidity crisis and only the existence of a lender of last resort who agrees *always* to be available either (a) to re-finance a banker's portfolio positions by making a spot market in bankers' IOUs, or (b) to permit ready liquidation of a banker's asset-holding by making a spot market in the assets that normally

are held by bankers, has prevented the episodes of financial panic which plagued earlier economies.

(2) The flotation of new equity issues of business firms by investment bankers as well as the holding of second-hand equities securities by the public for liquidity purposes require FFF either because of margin purchases or the need to maintain inventories of securities by new issue houses and stock specialists who make the spot markets which bestow liquidity properties on equities.[1] Thus, many business firms are able to use EF for their holdings of real capital assets used in the production process only because the buyers of the equity securities (and the market makers of these securities if need be) are willing at least partially to finance their positions by borrowing directly or indirectly from commercial banks. In essence, therefore, even if all business firms decide to use EF to carry out their investment projects, 'the pace at which the entrepreneurs will be able to carry their projects into execution ... depends on the degree of compliance of those responsible for the banking system',[2] and therefore ultimately on the existence of FFF.

Thus it is the operation of the banking system and its arrangement for debt finance in combination with the asset holding desires of the private sector which determines what proportion of the stock of real wealth is owned directly by the public and what proportion is owned and looked after by the banking system. To the extent that FFF is used by stock specialists, investment bankers and private investors (via margin purchases) to hold some of the equity securities of business firms who have used EF for real capital goods, then the spot markets for corporate equities are vulnerable to interest rate fluctuations and money market conditions whenever large segments of these asset holders need to refinance their position. Furthermore, to the extent that FFF of positions in such securities was undertaken in the expectation of realising capital appreciation or gains (i.e. the spot price at a future date is expected to be higher than the spot price at the purchase date) by liquidating the position in the future, then unless such expectations are ultimately justified by events the spot market in securities will collapse of its own accord. For example a period

[1] See Chapter 13.
[2] Keynes, *Treatise on Money*, II, p. 97.

of stable securities prices following a bull market in which FFF
is used to purchase securities can result in a stock market crash
when holders of securities find their expectations of further
capital appreciation disappointed. The low margin requirements which permitted substantial FFF of securities in the
1920s and the exuberant expectations of higher spot prices of
stock which led to the Stock Market Crash of 1929 is a well-
documented historical episode.

Mainstream economic theory has never been able to find a
place for an economic relationship between the FFF of positions
in securities and the resulting shattering impact on the real
economy (the Great Depression). The monetary analysis
developed in these pages and by others, on the other hand,
provides a framework for integrating such financial arrangements with an analysis of employment and production fluctuations. Of course, much analytical work remains to be done.
It is my hope that readers of these pages will recognise not only
the unfinished state of this analysis, but will also perceive the
advances in our understanding of the economy in which we
live which can be made by pursuing further development via
this Keynes monetary-finance approach. The few of us who
have been working in this area clearly need and welcome all
the help we can get from our colleagues.

CONCLUSION

Progress in economics is indeed a slow process. In this chapter
I have tried (1) to suggest the slow but perceptible proper
change in direction that has occurred in the current of mainstream economics since the publication of the first edition of
Money and the Real World, and (2) to encourage further movement in this direction. True progress in science is made by
standing on the shoulders of geniuses who went before. Unfortunately too many of our most eminent mainstream
economists have tried to build edifices while standing on the
hunchback of a French bell-ringer rather than on the strong
shoulders of the Bursar of Kings Chapel. Nevertheless I am
convinced that time and the pressure of events are on the side
of the latter. Ultimately the passage of history will separate
the true and relevant framework from the false and irrelevant.

Index

DISCHARGED

DISCHARGED

DISCHARGED

DEC 14 1991
DISCHARGED

DISCHARGED

DEC 0 1 1991